REPRESENTATIONS

REPRESENTATIONS

Doing Asian American Rhetoric

edited by
LUMING MAO AND MORRIS YOUNG

UTAH STATE UNIVERSITY PRESS
Logan, Utah
2008

Utah State University Press
Logan, Utah 84322–7800

Manufactured in the United States of America
Cover design by Barbara Yale-Read
Cover art, "All American Girl I" by Susan Sponsler. Used by permission.

ISBN: 978-0-87421-724-7 (paper)
ISBN: 978-0-87421-725-4 (e-book)

Library of Congress Cataloging-in-Publication Data

Representations : doing Asian American rhetoric / edited by LuMing Mao and Morris Young.
p. cm.
ISBN 978-0-87421-724-7 (pbk. : alk. paper) – ISBN 978-0-87421-725-4 (e-book)
1. English language–Rhetoric–Study and teaching–Foreign speakers. 2. Asian Americans–Education–Language arts. 3. Asian Americans–Cultural assimilation. 4. Asian Americans–Intellectual life. 5. Intercultural communication–United States. I. Mao, LuMing, II. Young, Morris
PE1405.U6R47 2008
808'.0428–dc22

2008036160

CONTENTS

FOREWORD

Min-Zhan Lu and Bruce Horner

We applaud this project for its effort to address two related questions: how to best study Asian American rhetoric, and why. Using as cases in point a whole range of symbolic practices by Asian Americans across time, social sites, and purposes, the contributors make a convincing case for the viability of defining Asian American rhetoric as a knowledge-making process and for the need, when analyzing the rhetorical strategies of individual discursive acts, to pay attention to the history of specific symbolic systems and individual symbols being deployed, the material conditions—different relations of asymmetry—informing the specific rhetorical situation (and their formal features such as purpose, audience, contexts), and the material and symbolic consequences of these.

We especially appreciate the various ways in which the editors and contributors foreground the processes of translation and transformation involved in any rhetorical acts that resist official dis-positioning of the purposes and logics of peoples other than, othered by, the dominant, and in particular, our need to treat the Others of transcultural communication as agents of knowledge making rather than the objects of "study" and domination. The emphasis on transformation depicts transcultural communication as a dialectical rather than a unilateral, top-down movement. And the emphasis on translation calls attention to the ethical responsibility of both the listener-reader and the speaker-writer to their role in processes of geopolitical, social, economic, and cultural mediation. To perform Asian American rhetoric "into" the American imaginary is also always to rebuild the official, the dominant. In that sense, we might argue that to stay alive, American rhetoric as well as the American imaginary depend as much on the rhetorical work of Asian Americans as the other way around.

In the process of analyzing the rhetorical strategies of various Asian Americans working in response to diverse and specific social, political, cultural conditions and with symbolic resources as varied as verbal, visual, or bodily discourses, the fourteen chapters also posit a rich array of alternative reading methods for transcultural communications—rhetorical strategies for making sense of and characterizing discursive practices delegitimized by official notions of "correct," "good" uses of both the western rhetorical tradition and the English language. From that perspective, we see this volume as potentially making two extra contributions to English studies, including courses in literature, creative writing, or rhetoric and composition that do not specifically focus on the study of Asian American rhetoric.

To begin with, teachers and students might explore the ways in which these chapters enact ways of reading that can be used to problematize not only the dichotomy of the "true" vs. the "other," "hyphenated" Americans but also the dichotomy of "authorized" vs. "student" writers along with the dichotomy of "standard" vs. "nonstandard" users of English, given the historical interlocking of issues of ethnic discrimination with issues of class injustice and educational elitism. For instance, the methods used by the contributors to make sense of and evaluate the works of Asian American (published) writers and public figures such as Kingston or Cho point to a manner of "listening" (Royster 1996) to the words of student writers, including the work of students whose prose might make them appear as if they do not know how to think or speak proper English. This might in turn help teachers in English studies develop pedagogical strategies aimed at helping students to respond "responsively and respectfully" to the rhetorical moves of not only "minority" writers but also their peers. The pedagogical moves we have in mind are those that highlight the need (1) to be reflexive and to problematize habits of reading—"systems of hearing" (Royster 1996)—we've been "educated" to impose on the words and deeds of Othered persons and peoples; (2) to be responsive to and respectful of the logic of the historically silenced and to the specific ways in which these writers bend the rules of standardized English—style, grammar, syntax, vocabulary—to make it carry the weight of conditions and relations that are vital to their day-to-day existence but systematically delegitimized by standardized uses; (3) to be attentive to one's own needs and rights to tinker with English and academic discourse in the process of using them to make sense of and write about relations and experiences central to one's past, present, and future life but consistently undervalued in college classrooms.

Second, teachers and students of English might explore ways of using the methods of reading enacted by the contributors in this volume to combat not only the dichotomy of the West vs. the rest but also that of the "native" vs. "second-language" or "foreign" users of English. Given the global spread of a "free" market economy, peoples the world over are living under the pressure to abide by English-only rulings—the rules of a version of English that represents the geopolitical, economic, and cultural interests of the dominant groups of (technologically over-) developed countries such as the United States. How to make sense of the living-English work of users across the world is becoming an increasingly urgent task for those of us granted by the academy the status of fluency in "native"-sounding English, Standard Written English, or Edited American English. This is in part because our disposition toward "idiomatic" English often (inadvertently) functions to sponsor English-only rulings, effectively silencing the work and efforts of users across the world interested in making English carry the weight of experiences—relations and conditions of life—that so-called native-sounding English has been geared to dismiss: for example, uses of English such as China English that sound jarring to the hearing system to which years of education have habituated us. As the editors quote Frank Chin's argument in the introduction, "The universality of the belief that correct English is the only language of American truth has made language an instrument of cultural imperialism" (Chin et al. 1991, 23). In this first decade of the twenty-first century, the "American truth"—the Truth of the (technologically) Developed World—is being used by international organizations such as the World Bank to constrain life in "developing" and "underdeveloped" worlds. For those of us teachers and students endowed with fluency in "native"-sounding English who are interested in a better world for all, learning to use the methods of "listening" this volume puts forward in its study of Asian American rhetoric can help us resist our official designation as sponsors of Edited American English-only rulings.

More specifically, it can help us shift our energy from the English-only Q&A to a living-English perspective. English-only Q&A asks, "What can Edited American English do *for* nonnative users?" and answers, "It can help them gain access to educational and job opportunities—economic, cultural, symbolic capital." But a living-English perspective asks, "What can Edited American English *not* do for nonnative users?" and it answers, "It cannot help them limn experiences—relations and conditions of life—delegitimized by the 'development' scheme." A living-English perspective asks, "How have others tinkered with dominant uses of English to keep English and themselves alive?" and, "Given the realities of my life and the lives of those near and dear to me, how might I learn from such living-English work in my own discursive practices?"

The rhetorical movements of the Asian Americans whose works are featured in this volume and of the contributors in their analyses of this body of work can help teachers and students endowed with fluency in "native"-sounding English to listen to and learn from the logic of non-idiomatic uses of English by users across the world. More specifically, it can help them explore the question of how U.S. composition teachers and students might best go about (1) examining the political-economic-cultural specificity of our so-called native, idiomatic, and correct English usages; (2) developing vigilance toward our often inadvertent sponsoring of English-only rulings; and (3) actively participating in what Lu has called Living-English work (2006).

Let us begin with a disclaimer. In suggesting that we dive into these lines of inquiry, we are not dismissing the need for U.S. composition teachers to be responsive to students' need and desire to use English in ways that will help them succeed in their career pursuits. What we are suggesting, however, is that we acknowledge both the variety of other reasons and occasions for which they might also want to use English and that we treat those reasons and occasions as critical resources for, rather than impediments to, their effective use of English (see Lu 2004). That is, we need to present a different image of the relations between English and its individual learners and users from the image perpetuated by English-only projections.

We might use three quotations to picture the scene of living-English work. The first quotation is from the African writer Chinua Achebe, who argues, "The price a world language must be prepared to pay is submission to many different kinds of use" (2000, 432). We read Achebe as maintaining that for English to stay alive as a world English, the language would need to adjust its formation to suit the multiple reasons peoples across the world have for using it and the multiple contexts shaping their language practices. Our second quotation comes from an article in a 2003 issue of *English Today* by a Chinese scholar, Jiang Yajun, who observes that "[China] English is no doubt becoming an important component of world Englishes as China gets more and more involved in the process of economic and cultural globalization" (7). In a 2005 issue of *English Today,* another Chinese scholar, Hu Xiaoqiong, uses data collected from questionnaires completed by 589 teachers of English working in five universities in the province of Hubei to illustrate the recognition among teachers of English in China that learners should "no longer be tied to [learning] one alien variety of the language," such as Edited American English. Instead, they should be taught to also work on a variety of English characterized by Chinese language and culture (32).

The emergence of a variety of English termed China English, distinct from Chinese English or Chinglish, illustrates Chinese English users' sense of their need and right to make English "carry the burden" of "China-specific things"—language, culture, lived experience, and viewpoints often rendered "peculiar" by so-called idiomatic uses of English (see Achebe 2000, Baldwin 1993; Chuangui Ge in Jiang 2003, 6). China English is, we believe, one kind of the "many different" uses to which Achebe argues English "must be prepared to" submit if it hopes to become a "world language." To put it another way, real living-English work is being done on the ground, by learners and users of English in China as in other nations across the world. The question then arises: For those of us who are uneasy about our designation as sponsors of English-only rules, what can we do in our day-to-day work in the United States to participate in living-English work?

We see the work in this volume posing three possible directions for developing a pedagogy of living-English work. First, it provides methods of reading that might help us to peculiarize the standardized usages of Edited American English. For instance, instead of presenting rules such as using an "s" to indicate plural and third-person singular as the "native" and logical way and thus, *the* way, it can invoke the voices we often encounter in writing centers from speakers of other languages such as Chinese, such as "Isn't it redundant to put an 's' after 'apple' when the word is preceded by 'three'?" Or "an 's' after 'speak' when it is preceded by 'Mary' or 'John'?"

Second, it provides methods of reading that might help us to listen to the logic of seemingly "alien" usages of English. Media reports and Web site discussions are full of examples of "incorrect" English translations that "native"-English-speaking tourists and expatriates have found irritating, amusing, or charming and that local government officials and educators deem signs of "national disgrace" and vow to eradicate ("Beijing"). One often-cited instance is the literal English translation of a Chinese sign to warn park visitors to keep off the lawn: "Little Grass Has Life." Listening to the logic leading a Chinese user of English to choose "Little Grass Has Life" over "idiomatic" expressions such as

"Keep Off the Grass" or "No Trespassing" might involve discussions of different notions of why people shouldn't tread on the grass lawn: out of respect for property laws—public or private—or also out of respect for all living things—big or small, human or nonhuman. It would involve approaching that difference in terms of the different legal, economic, political, cultural, historical trajectories and relations across them in countries such as the United States and China.

A third possible direction this volume might help us to probe is to call attention to the material costs shouldered by peoples the world over as a result of the global push of U.S. linguistic and "lifestyle" standards. For instance, in light of the "privilege" to "host" the 2008 Olympics in Beijing, all road or shop signs in the city had to include an English translation. Lack of access often compels small business owners to rely on translation software to meet these government mandates, hence the repeatedly cited English store sign for a fast-food restaurant owned by the Wangs that read "No Translation or Server Error." On the one hand, it can be interpreted as a hilarious example of the owners' "ignorance" of the English language. On the other hand, this instance can be used to talk about the intricate work of transcultural communication. To begin with, it can be used to jump-start critiques of software's false promise that Americans can now enjoy global access without having to sweat over the learning of another language. Furthermore, it can be used to consider the material cost to peoples the world over to survive and thrive in a globalizing neoliberal free market. What material burden do small business owners bear to come up with money to produce a "correct" translation of the restaurant's name and a sign bearing the "correct" translation?

Competition to host the Olympics also led the government to take other measures so that Beijing would meet first-world standards. These included efforts to "green" the city according to the standards of the developed world. What might be the material effect that such "development" brought on city residents, such as people being uprooted from neighborhoods? In a country where vast regions of northern China have had to yield their water access to the city of Beijing even during severe drought, how has the thriving of green landscaping in Beijing to meet western standards come into competition with the survival of billions of people in surrounding provinces? These are questions that a volume such as this one prompts teachers and students of English to probe in response to media representations of new trends in "developing" and "undeveloped" worlds. The link between English-only language policies and the geopolitical-economic ambitions of neoliberal market fundamentalism is something U.S. teachers and students must examine if we are to consider the ethical implications of the internationalization of U.S. education and Standard Written English.

In highlighting the rhetorical work Asian Americans have done to keep English alive, this volume can serve as both a critical resource and a timely impetus for investigating the questions of the kinds of retooling U.S. teachers, scholars, and administrators need to do if we are interested in disrupting our commission to sponsor English-only rulings intra- and internationally, and if we are also interested in joining English users across the world to sponsor living-English work.

REFERENCES

Achebe, Chinua. 2000. African Writers and English. In *The Routledge Language and Cultural Theory Reader*, edited by Lucky Burke, Tony Crowley, and Alan Girvin. New York: Routledge.

Baldwin, James. 1993. If Black English Isn't a Language, Then Tell Me, What Is? In *In Depth: Essayists for Our Time*, 2nd ed., edited by Carl Klaus, Chris Anderson, and Rebecca Faery. New York: Harcourt.

"Beijing Launches Campaign against Bad English-Language Signs." Associated Press Archive 7 Dec 2002. *Access World News*. NewsBank. University o Louisville Libraries. <http://infoweb.newsbank.com.echo.louisville.edu> (accessed 10 July 2008).

http://www.cbsnews.com/stories/2002/12/09/nationa/main532348.

Chin, Frank, Jeffrey Chan, Lawson Inada, and Shawn Wong, eds. 1991. *AIIIEEEEE! An Anthology of Asian American Writers*. New York: Mentor. (Orig. pub. 1974.)

Hu, Xiaoqiong. 2005. China English, at Home and in the World. *English Today* (July): 25–35.

Jiang, Yajun. 2003. English as a Chinese Language. *English Today* (April): 3–8.

Lu, Min-Zhan. 2004. An Essay on the Work of Composition. *College Composition and Communication* 56:16–50.

———. 2006. Living-English Work. *College English* 68:605–618.

Royster, Jacqueline Jones. 1996. When the First Voice You Hear Is Not Your Own. *College Composition and Communication* 16:29–40.

ACKNOWLEDGMENTS

Completing a project like this one indeed depends on a collective effort, one that involves many conversations, countless e-mail exchanges, and the support and generosity of colleagues and friends. We have many people to thank for helping us bring this project to fruition.

First, our thanks must go to each and every one of colleagues featured in this volume. Their contributions have both inspired us and made our own work so easy and so enjoyable to carry out. We have learned much from their work and from their commitment to doing Asian American rhetoric. And we have so much more to learn.

We are also very grateful to members of the Asian/Asian American Caucus of the Conference on College Composition and Communication who have shared in these conversations about Asian American rhetoric for several years. Additionally, friends and colleagues in the field of rhetoric and composition have been supportive in helping us think about this work. For their encouragement, we thank Deborah Brandt, Anne Ruggles Gere, Keith Gilyard, Susan Jarratt, Shirley Wilson Logan, Renee Moreno, Gail Okawa, Malea Powell, Jacqueline Jones Royster, C. Jan Swearingen, and Victor Villanueva.

Our colleagues and friends in the Department of English at Miami University have continued to support our work. We have benefited from their words of encouragement and wisdom. We thank Mary Jean Corbett, Cynthia Lewiecki-Wilson, Tim Melley, Susan Morgan, Kerry Powell (chair of the department), and Kate Ronald. Keith Tuma, former chair of the Department of English and now associate dean of the College of Arts and Science at Miami, has always supported our work and has helped create an environment where we feel energized and motivated to work.

We also thank Michael Spooner, director at Utah State University Press, who shared our vision for this project from the get-go and who has never wavered. We owe him a lasting debt of gratitude. And we are equally grateful to two anonymous reviewers for the press, as their thoughtful comments and suggestions have helped improve our work immensely. We are solely responsible, however, for whatever errors and infelicities might still remain in this work.

Finally, we dedicate this work to all Asians and Asian Americans whose work we are honoring and celebrating here. Limited as it might be, this volume, we hope, continues their tradition as it attempts to represent it.

INTRODUCTION
Performing Asian American Rhetoric into the American Imaginary

LuMing Mao and Morris Young

In the fall of 2001, Morris Young was preparing a grant proposal for the National Endowment of the Humanities Summer Stipend competition. The project, "'A Ready Tongue Is an Evil': The Possibility and Predicament of Asian American Rhetoric," looked to examine how Asian Americans use language as a resource to address their conditions in America, to understand why a "ready tongue" (a Chinese expression appropriated by Maxine Hong Kingston) becomes a necessity as they seek a way to respond to American culture. After the proposal was submitted for review at the university level and selected as the "junior faculty" nomination, Morris was provided with the reviewers' comments. Aside from the expected questions asking for clarification about specific concepts and details of the argument, one reviewer expressed a clear skepticism about the value of examining *rhetoric* and about why rhetoric *mattered* to Asian Americans. And there was even some confusion about whether this was a project more suited to funding in the social sciences or education if the focus was on language *usage* by Asians.

In the summer of 2004, LuMing Mao, together with two other colleagues at Miami University, took a group of students, both graduate and undergraduate, to China. For three weeks they visited four universities in four different cities and had numerous conversations with students and faculty. During one conversation with a group of English majors at Beijing Jiaotong University about life in the United States, one of the students asked LuMing, "How do you negotiate speaking English and Chinese both in the U.S. and in China? Which of the two languages do you feel more comfortable speaking? Do you feel conflicted at all—linguistically and/or emotionally—when you speak one or the other language?" What ensued was one of the liveliest, most contested, discussions, conducted in both English and Chinese, on language and identity that LuMing had participated in for a long while.

While the reviewer's skepticism and the student's pointed questions might not be particularly expected on these two specific occasions, neither of us are strangers to them. Not only because they—the skepticism and the questions—directly draw attention to the dynamic, complex relationship between language use and identity formation, but also because they speak to some of the very issues we have been trying to address both professionally and in our everyday lives—issues that have also led us to undertake this project and to investigate specifically how Asian Americans use language and other forms of symbolic action to bring about necessary changes and to advance and complicate our understanding of the self, the other, and the world.

In the past decade we have seen tremendous growth in scholarship about Asian Americans and their cultural work, especially with regard to literary productions, visual arts, popular and mass culture, community and activist work, to name a few categories of examination. These and many other forms of discursive expression have significantly contributed to writing Asian Americans into the national American narrative. On the other hand, we have seen little work that focuses directly on how Asian Americans use the symbolic resources of language in social, cultural, and political arenas to disrupt and transform the dominant European American discourse and its representations of Asians and Asian Americans, thus re-presenting and reclaiming their identity and agency. Nor have we seen work that directly draws attention to, and thus draws out, those ambivalent and contradictory moments where Asian Americans *both* experience the performative or constitutive power attending each and every utterance *and* participate in reinforcing or reinscribing what Judith Butler calls "the historicity of force." That is, commenting on the conditions or limits of developing a new and affirmative set of meanings for the word "queer," Butler points out that discourse—of which words such as "queer" are an integral part—"has a history that not only precedes but conditions its contemporary usages, and that this history effectively decenters the presentist view of the subject as the exclusive origin or owner of what is said" (1993, 227). Therefore, any recuperative efforts, be they directed at "queer" or at any other demeaning term, may be constrained and compromised because of discourse's power to decenter or implicate its user. It is these moments of constraint and complicity in Asian American discursive experiences that we seek to confront and examine in the following pages.

It must be noted that work by writers and scholars such as Maxine Hong Kingston, Lisa Lowe, Kent Ono, and John Sloop has certainly drawn our attention to the importance of language use within the Asian American context and to the need to invent a "new American language" to represent Asian Americans and to create the literature of a new culture. For Kingston, this new American language "not only grants her characters full linguistic freedom to attempt a higher level of linguistic, racial and cultural assimilation into which Chinese immigrants' distinctive language forms and cultural traditions are incorporated, but also begins an ideological debate on the linguistic rights and status of Chinese Americans" (Li 2004, 274). This new American language can also assist Asian Americans in their efforts to challenge Standard American English as the only language of knowledge and truth and to repudiate a cultural politics that "relies on the construction of sameness and the exclusion of differences" (Lowe 1991, 28). For Ono and Sloop (2002), this new American language can be located in both civic and vernacular discourses, both of which challenge existing social paradigms and hold promise for substantive social transformations. On the other hand, we have seen few systematic studies that focus on how Asian Americans use language to perform discursive acts and on how they develop persuasive and other rhetorical strategies to create knowledge and to effect social, political, and cultural transformations. Nor have we seen any concentrated efforts directed toward illuminating those conflicting, ambivalent moments that are central to Asian American discursive experiences. In short, there is not much work done on the making of Asian American rhetoric.

We define Asian American rhetoric as the systematic, effective use and development by Asian Americans of symbolic resources, including this new American language, in social, cultural, and political contexts. Because these contexts are regularly imbued with highly asymmetrical relations of power, such rhetoric creates a space for Asian Americans where they can resist social and economic injustice and reassert their discursive agency and authority in the dominant culture. In this sense, Asian American rhetoric is intimately tied to, and indeed constituted by, particularizing speech settings, specific communicative purposes, and situated discursive acts. Its uptake and its performative force bring about material and symbolic consequences that in turn destabilize the balance of power and privilege that exists between the majority and minority cultures.

We credit the emergence of Asian American rhetoric to a number of factors that have been converging in the recent past. First, Asian American rhetoric has both been mobilized by, and directly participates in, an ongoing dialogue that aims to reexamine and reconceptualize rhetoric's purposes and functions beyond the paradigm of western rhetoric. Such a dialogue not only problematizes the Rhetorical Tradition and its canonical ways of representation, but also makes it possible for Asian American rhetoric, or any other ethnic rhetoric, for that matter, to find its voice and to secure its uptake. As a minority discourse that has long been ignored, marginalized, and/or excluded, Asian American rhetoric becomes an integral, but no less distinctive, part of this complicated and dynamic American narrative.

Second, with the publication of such works as Robert Oliver's *Communication and Culture in Ancient India and China* (1971) and Geneva Smitherman's *Talkin and Testifyin: The Language of Black America* (1977), we came to realize that rhetoric—the systematic and effective use of symbolic resources—was not an Anglo-American phenomenon only, and that the use and study of rhetoric existed in other communities and in other regions around the world. We also began to experience and consciously perform discursive acts whose rhetorical features and significances had hitherto gone unnoticed or unnamed. The emergence of Asian American rhetoric speaks to this desire to give voice to the voiceless and to accord long-overdue legitimacy to those ways of speaking that have long been the stuff that Asian Americans are made of. It further challenges the binary discourse that regularly views all other non-western rhetorics as the very antitheses to western rhetoric and as the "unruly borderlands" in want of exploration, cultivation, and conversion.

Third, thanks to the interpretative turn that the field of rhetoric and composition has now embraced, rhetoric is seen as more than just the art of discovering the available means of persuasion. Rather, it is part of the knowledge-making process that is situated in every specific occasion of language use and that is always socially and politically constructed. Such an understanding of rhetoric draws our much-needed attention to the temporal-spatial nature of language use and to its material and symbolic consequences. Asian American rhetoric serves as a compelling example of how Asian Americans have been using language to bring about changes that affect the attitudes, beliefs, and actions of their intended audience as well as their very own. It also presents students, teachers, and scholars with new ways to approach rhetoric and to engage specific rhetorical situations and their formal features such as purpose, audience, and context.

While we very much want to claim that Asian American rhetoric commands a sense of unity or collective identity for its users, we want to note that such rhetoric cannot help but embody internal differences, ambivalences, and even contradictions as each and every specific communicative situation—where Asian American rhetoric is invoked, deployed, or developed—is informed and inflected by diverse contexts, by different relations of asymmetry, and by, most simply put, heterogeneous voices. As a minority discourse, Asian American rhetoric reflects and responds to existing social and cultural conditions and practices while gathering and disseminating the illocutionary force of past practices. Or in the words of James Paul Gee, "Words have *histories*. They have been in other people's mouths and on other people's pens. They have circulated other Discourses and within other institutions. They have been part of specific historical events and episodes. Words bring with them as *potential situated meanings* all the situated meanings they have picked up in history and in other settings and Discourses" (2005, 54; emphasis in the original).

However, as a performative, Asian American rhetoric also actively engages and impacts such conditions and practices. That is to say, as it reflects and responds to these conditions and practices, Asian American rhetoric creates its own illocutionary force, thus challenging or turning against "this constitutive historicity of force" (Butler 1993, 227). To the extent it does, Asian American rhetoric becomes a rhetoric of becoming: it is a rhetoric that participates in this generative process, yielding an identity that is Asian American and producing a transformative effect that is always occasioned by use.

As a rhetoric of becoming, Asian American rhetoric is also an example of hybridity. Operating in a space that is "crisscrossed with a variety of languages, experiences, and voices" and that "intermingles with the weight of particular histories that will not fit into the master narrative of a monolithic culture" (Giroux 1992, 209), Asian American rhetoric draws upon discursive practices *both* from the European American tradition *and* from Asian, as well as other ethnic and worldly, traditions. Its emergence and its identity are therefore very much tied to our present-day social-cultural, transnational tendencies marked in part by various forms of cultural and linguistic intertextuality. In addition, since Asian American rhetoric is being produced within the histories of highly asymmetrical relations of power, its discursive fate can be quite indeterminate, if not perilous. Like Pratt's autoethnographic texts, it could experience miscomprehension, incomprehension, and/or simply a multitude of meanings (1991, 37). And it could be quickly appropriated or even stereotyped by the dominant tradition, thus losing its otherwise creative, invigorating energy. On the other hand, it is this state of becoming or indeterminacy that makes it possible for Asian Americans to be transformative, carving out new spaces for critical and productive engagement.

For Asian Americans, as with others often placed on the margins of culture, language provides the possibility to realize the rhetorical construction of identity and write oneself literally into the pages of history and culture. In fact, such discursive practices can create and indeed become topoi in the larger narrative of America. Rhetoric is also employed by Asian Americans to address specific occasions, whether responding to acts of racism, expressing culture, or forming community. These specific spaces that Asian Americans inhabit, where identities are constructed and negotiated and responses to particular conditions are generated, can be conceptualized as Asian American rhetorical space. In particular, spatial metaphors are especially important for Asian Americans as rhetorical devices to address travel and mobility, containment and community, and imagined or real geographies.

In her essay "Of Gender and Rhetorical Space," Roxanne Mountford examines the function of space in rhetorical situations, focusing on the role of the pulpit as both a rhetorical and gendered space that has cultural and material consequences for both speaker and audience. Mountford defines "rhetorical space" as "the geography of a communicative event" that, like all landscapes, "may include both the cultural and material arrangement, whether intended or fortuitous, of space"; such spaces "carry the residue of history upon them, but perhaps, something else: a physical representation of relationships and ideas" (2001, 42). Her definition is particularly useful in considering the use of rhetoric by Asian Americans.

In the case of Asian Americans, the residue of history includes a legacy of U.S. racial ideology that has often placed Asians and Asian Americans in particular spaces, whether metaphorical or material. As Kandice Chuh argues: "Embedded in such terms as 'immigrant' and 'exile' and in the difference between 'native' or 'birthright' and 'naturalized' citizenship is this spatial logic. Theoretically, according to U.S. nationalism, departure from *there* and arrival *here* is a narrative whose closure may be found in being made like one was native-born through naturalization. Positing the naturalness of the relationship between the native-born and the nation, such an ideology depends upon territoriality for coherence and, more specifically, upon a spatialized logic that holds as discretely and naturally distinct 'here' and 'there'" (2003, 86–87).

Thus, functioning in contradictory ways, rhetorical space for Asian Americans is often constructed as both foreign and domestic, as a site of both containment and community. For example, while the early twentieth-century immigration detention center Angel Island acted to contain Chinese immigrants, keeping them from entering America, it also resulted in rhetorical action by these immigrants, who literally wrote their protests into the walls of their barracks (see Lai, Lim, and Yung 1991). Or, while the Japanese American internment camps of World War II held Japanese and Japanese Americans as threats to the nation without any other evidence than their race, these internees produced camp newspapers protesting their condition and composed *tanka* poetry expressing their frustration and resistance (see Mizuno 2001, 2003). What complicates Asian American rhetorical space is the apparent necessity, or imposition, of defining Asian America against the Nation rather than as constitutive of it. Thus, in conceptualizing Asian American rhetorical space there is a need to understand the ideological underpinnings that have imagined, and continue to imagine, Asians (whether in America or elsewhere) as Other, and as foreign against the domestic space of the United States.

While we were putting together this collection as our rhetorical response to this construction of Asian Americans as Other, we grew increasingly mindful of another response, which is to enact an Asian American cultural nationalism, a project of asserting a claim on America for those who imagine themselves fully as cultural if not national citizens of the United States. One example of such a claim that takes on an explicitly rhetorical dimension is the argument put forth by the editors of *AIIIEEEEE!* and *The Big AIIIEEEEE!*, two edited collections of Asian American writing that are often turned to as important early critical expressions about the cultural work of Asian American writing. In their introduction to *AIIIEEEEE!*, "Fifty Years of Our Whole Voice," Frank Chin, Jeffrey Chan, Lawson Inada, and Shawn Wong focus their critique on racist discourse by examining the requirements of language often placed on racially marked others. For them, the expectation of literacy in Standard English that has been often used to define "legitimacy" (whether in literary production or cultural/national citizenship) also operates to construct Asian Americans as a particular type of subject:

> The universality of the belief that correct English is the only language of American truth has made language an instrument of cultural imperialism. The minority experience does not yield itself to accurate or complete expression in white man's language. Yet, the minority writer, specifically the Asian American writer, is made to feel morally obligated to write in a language produced by an alien and hostile sensibility. His task, in terms of languagc alone, is to legitimize his, and by implication his people's orientation as white, to codify his experience in the form of prior symbols, clichés, linguistic mannerisms, and a sense of humor that appeals to whites because it celebrates Asian American self-contempt. (1991, 23)

For the *AIIIEEEEE!* editors, the emphasis on language privileges a certain type of experience that reinforces a binary of "minority" and "model minority" (or in later manifestations of this argument, "real" and "fake").[1] Additionally, the *AIIIEEEEE!* editors argue that this American rhetoric of orientalism also acts to feminize Asian American writing, to create foreign objects for domestic consumption that will maintain difference.

It must be noted that the *AIIIEEEEE!* editors also offer what might be considered an early definition of Asian American rhetoric: "to legitimize the language, style, and syntax of his people's experience, to codify the experiences common to his people into symbols, clichés, linguistic mannerisms, and a sense of humor that emerges from an organic familiarity with the experience" (1991, 23). The emphasis we place on the use of symbolic recourses to reclaim discursive agency and authority as part of our definition of Asian American rhetoric bears some resemblance to their characterization here. For the *AIIIEEEEE!* editors, then, the project of Asian American writing (or rhetoric for our purposes) becomes twofold. On the one hand, writing becomes an act of questioning what is "legitimate," to expand the boundaries of what are defined as American

1. In his essay in *The Big AIIIEEEEE!*, "Come All Ye Asian American Writers of the Real and the Fake," Frank Chin further develops the binary of "minority" and "model minority" by arguing that the "real" experiences and sensibilities of Asian Americans (i.e., experiences and sensibilities that reflect racism and discrimination as well as culture and community) are often displaced by the "fake," representations of experience and culture that feed an orientalist desire by dominant white culture (1991). Thus, a writer like Maxine Hong Kingston, often a focus of Chin's criticism, is accused of straying from "authentic" Chinese culture and tradition and reimagining Chinese and Chinese American experiences that feed, reinforce, or create stereotypes that uninformed readers easily consume and accept as real.

cultural texts and of who can write those texts. On the other, the larger project is to overcome systematic oppression, to dismantle those structures that act to maintain cultural control either through discourses of dominance (such as explicit legal restrictions against Asians and Asian Americans) or through the more subtle hegemonic acts of educational and cultural production that define what it means to be a citizen.

As the reader may have already noticed, we have chosen "Asian American *rhetoric*" as our term in preference to "Asian American *rhetorics*" or "Asian American *rhetoric(s)*."[2] The choice here, which embeds an apparent paradox, is a considered one. The use of the singular, rather than the plural noun "rhetoric" in "Asian American rhetoric" might appear to imply that Asian American rhetoric is monolithic, unified, or unaffected by shifting social and cultural forces. The appearance here, however, cannot be more deceiving. That is, Asian American rhetoric, like any other ethnic rhetoric, is infused with competing voices, internal contradictions, and shifting alliances at every given discursive moment, and it is necessarily *plural* in form and in meaning. Not to mention the fact that many separate national identities will inevitably inflect or intrude upon the making of Asian American rhetoric.

Why did we then decide to favor the singular at the risk of encoding something that defies reality? The answer is simple: We see our use of the singular "rhetoric" as an example of what Gayatri Spivak calls a "*strategic* use of positive essentialism" (1987, 205; emphasis in the original). Namely, we want to use "Asian American rhetoric" as a specific signifier to contest and complicate the dominance of European American rhetoric or even the broader definition of the Rhetorical Tradition. In so doing, we seek to articulate a distinctive rhetorical identity to celebrate differences and to challenge stereotypes—hence positive essentialism. At the same time, we are acutely aware of the internal complexities and multiplicities that inevitably attend the making of Asian American rhetoric or any other ethnic rhetoric, including, we might add, European American. As a matter of fact, our characterization of Asian American rhetoric as a performative occasioned by use and tied to each and every particularizing context speaks to this awareness, and the chapters that

---

2. Elaine B. Richardson and Ronald L. Jackson II use "African American rhetoric(s)" to describe "the study of culturally and discursively developed knowledge-forms, communicative practices and persuasive strategies rooted in freedom struggles by people of African ancestry in America" (2004, xiii). It is clear that by placing the plural form within parenthesis they want to acknowledge both the unity and diversity—a discursive move that has been practiced by many others.

follow amply demonstrate the rich and diverse nature of Asian American rhetoric. Our use of the singular in representing Asian American rhetoric is in part inspired by Lisa Lowe's characterization of "Asian American" as a specific signifier of ethnic identity that both disrupts the exclusionary discourse of the dominant culture and reveals their internal differences and even contradictions (1991, 40).

The paradox that accompanies the use of the singular also helps to give prominence to two major themes that run through this collection. First, the use of the singular highlights the tension or contradiction between the desire to claim a sense of unity or homogeneity for Asian Americans in America and elsewhere and the realization that our discursive practices are fraught with differences, defying any clear-cut, categorical characterization. Such a tension, we believe, permeates the rhetorical space for Asian Americans where identity, community, and memory are inflected with uneven historical relationships and vexing contemporary contradictions. Second and related, the use of the singular calls our attention to the ambivalence experienced by Asian Americans. That is, the making of Asian American rhetoric represents an example of members of a speech community inventing a mode of discourse to fulfill their discursive wants and dreams and to perform their claim on the American imaginary. At the same time, this desire to belong, to be part of America, is consistently tempered by a countervailing desire to cling to what sets them apart and what makes them *singularly* distinct. Such ambivalence becomes another important signifier for Asian Americans as they use their rhetoric to rewrite history, to reclaim their agency, and to reimagine the future for themselves and for *their* America.

To further foreground this tension or contradiction in our conceptualization of Asian American rhetoric, we appeal to the tropes of "translation" and "transformation." On the one hand, translation and transformation are employed in rhetorics of assimilation that assume the "foreignness" of Asian Americans and their language practices, confirming the critique of the *AIIIEEEEE!* editors, who see Standard English as the language of empire and an attempt to transform Asians and Asian Americans into all-American subjects. Eric Cheyfitz argues that translation is an act of western imperialism that operates to make the Other accessible to the empire and also to maintain difference: "From its beginnings the imperialist mission is, in short, one of translation: the translation of the 'other' into the terms of the empire, the prime term which is 'barbarian,' or one of its variations such as 'savage,' which, ironically, but not without a precise politics, also alienates the other from the empire" (1991, 112). On the other hand, translation and transformation become important tropes in the project of Asian Americans who play off the expectation and construction of Asians/Asian Americans as Other in order to perform their own transgressive acts of "translation." Asian Americans are no longer the objects of translation and transformation; rather, they become the agents of translation and transformation as they make *their* claim on America through their rhetorical acts.

We have assembled fourteen chapters in this collection and grouped them into two major sections: "Performing Asian American Rhetoric in Context" and "'Translating' and 'Transforming' Asian American Identities." By organizing the chapters in this collection this way, we are certainly not suggesting that there are no other valid ways in which they can be grouped. Rather, we want to use this kind of grouping to further foreground two major themes that have emerged from these chapters and that are so central to the understanding and development of Asian American rhetoric.

As we have suggested above, as a rhetoric of becoming, Asian American rhetoric engenders its own illocutionary or transformative meanings and effects at every discursive turn possible. In the process such a rhetoric challenges and extends what has been codified and privileged by the dominant rhetoric and culture. In other words, it is through participating in situated or contested occasions of use that Asian American rhetoric becomes constituted and that it effectively performs Asian American narratives into, and thus transforms, the larger American narrative in complex and dynamic ways.

The seven chapters in the first section of this book all center on the use of language and other symbolic recourses by Asian Americans in different speech communities and in different cultural sites and on how these discursive practices, involving both the present and the past, enrich and further complicate the making of Asian American rhetoric. In chapter 1, "Transnational Asian American Rhetoric as a Diasporic Practice," Rory Ong begins this collective undertaking of ours by addressing the dilemma facing resident Asians in the United States, Pacific Islanders, and multigenerational Asian Americans and by theorizing how we can best respond to such a dilemma. That is to say, to participate in the national American narrative Asian Americans must rationalize their disparate (dis)placements or (dis)positions; in the process they cannot help but become implicated in defining an

American discourse. Using Pierre Bourdieu's concept of *habitus* to highlight "the material interlacing of daily life and human agency," Ong argues that Asian Americans practice "transnational Asian American rhetoric" to face "a hybridized and heterogeneous transnational and transcultural way of life" and to unveil and critique competing and asymmetrical power relations within the Asian diaspora. Such a rhetoric not only poses a direct challenge to the dominant European American discourse, but also serves to illustrate these historical, cultural, and economic moments of entanglement and contradiction.

In chapter 2, "Reexamining the Between-Worlds Trope in Cross-Cultural Composition Studies," Tomo Hattori and Stuart Ching pick up and further explore this transnational and transcultural theme developed by Ong. Situating their argument between composition studies and Asian American studies, Hattori and Ching seek to develop a discourse that can transcend the "caught-between-worlds" metaphor that not only signifies the existence of Asian Americans, but also prescribes for them "a position of subjection and subjugation." They specifically argue that such a metaphor falsely confines bilingual and bidialectical speakers to two linguistic worlds, thus failing to reflect how ethnic identity and citizenship can and should be imagined and constituted both within and beyond a nation-state. By advancing this argument, they develop an Asian American rhetoric that disrupts literacy's equation with national citizenship and that replaces the concept of nation as narration with transnation as narration. For them, the between-worlds trope becomes a misnomer because new immigrants' transfiguring culture of global movement subverts and transforms institutions of national pedagogy and scholarship.

Doing Asian American rhetoric, as we have been suggesting, involves engaging with the past as well as with the present. It further calls for remembering and restoring—another form of performance—Asian American experiences in the American imaginary. It is the role of rhetorical memory in the making of Asian American rhetoric that Haivan V. Hoang addresses in her chapter, "Asian American Rhetorical Memory and a 'Memory That is Only Sometimes Our Own.'"

During the 2000 presidential campaigns Senator John McCain used the racial epithet "gooks" to refer to his North Vietnamese prison guards, and Asian American activists in California protested his use as being bigoted and offensive. While he later apologized, Senator McCain continued to justify this use by appealing to his prisoner of war memory as the objective basis for his representation of the past. However, the art of memory, argues Hoang, is necessarily rhetorical, because memory confers significance on signs, especially on those highly charged ones like "gook," "jap," or "chink," in relation to changing Asian American racial formation and to their historical participation in the United States. Therefore, to remember rhetorically, for Asian Americans, is to investigate histories that are formed through the transnational ties among Asia and the United States, and to trace and stitch together memories of seemingly disparate moments and cultural sites. Doing so enables Asian Americans to control cultural production of memories and thus to claim agency and identity in the mainstream construction of who they are.

Central to our interest in the making of Asian American rhetoric is how Asian Americans use language and other symbolic resources to perform their identity in their own communities. Therefore, we have included in this section four chapters that focus on one or more specific Asian American communities and on how such communities practice Asian American rhetoric. In her chapter, "Listening for Legacies; or, How I Began to Hear Dorothy Laigo Cordova, the Pinay behind the Podium Known as FANHS," Terese Guinsatao Monberg takes us to the Filipino American National Historical Society (FANHS) and to its founder and executive director Dorothy Laigo Cordova. Drawing upon work by such feminist historiographers as Jacqueline Jones Royster, Malea Powell, and Krista Ratcliffe, and using "listening" as a distinctive methodological approach of feminist historiography, Monberg seeks to "recover" the rhetorical legacy of Cordova, who has often been hidden from traditional scholarly references to FANHS, and thus to help us better understand the rhetorical activities and significances of FANHS.

What makes Monberg's work most exciting is how she uses "listening"—"rethinking interpretive frameworks, listening for patterns within an emerging tradition, and looking to other disciplines in a larger effort to understand the context in which words can mean"—to uncover the spatial metaphors and other pedagogical theories in Cordova's work and to challenge the binary between rhetorical theory and practice that is so problematic for the making of Asian American rhetoric. She argues that Cordova's vision of FANHS as a rhetorical space and what this space offers the Filipino American community would be largely invisible to a methodology that privileges the use of sight to navigate traditional maps and catalogs of knowledge. By uncovering a potentially lost legacy of

Cordova's work, Monberg demonstrates how Asian American feminist rhetoric depends on alternative forms of institutional or public memory, and how space, history, and memory intersect with one another to inform and constitute the articulation and performance of Asian American rhetoric.

We follow Monberg's study with Subhasree Chakravarty's "Learning Authenticity: Pedagogies of Hindu Nationalism in North America." Chakravarty studies how some diasporic Hindu communities in North America develop discursive strategies to nurture and foreground national sentiments and to create narratives of cultural and religious identity. Taking into account how discursive formations inscribe subjects in the material contexts of their experiences, Chakravarty specifically focuses on the Hindu Swayamsevak Sangha (Hindu Volunteer Corps) and its other three affiliated organizations. She examines their various forms of pedagogic practices, ranging from regularly organized educational camps to meetings and publications of instructional books and pamphlets. Through some careful analysis, she argues that these organizations use "an exclusivist rhetoric" to invoke a transnational, yet "authentic," Hindu identity and to promote a religious ideology (authentic Hinduism) that incites religious nationalism and awakens the diasporic Hindu Indian Americans. Her study once again illustrates how Asian American communities enact particular forms of rhetoric to revisit history, to challenge or subvert the constructions of Asian Americans by the dominant culture, and to represent them discursively by drawing upon ideologies domestic or transported over from far afield.

Next, in "Relocating Authority: Coauthor(iz)ing a Japanese American Ethos of Resistance under Mass Incarceration," Mira Chieko Shimabukuro takes us back to World War II, to one internment camp in Heart Mountain, Wyoming, examining how a group of Japanese American internees in this community collaboratively wrote, published, and distributed bulletins that explicitly refused the military draft as long as members of the community were still "interned" against their will. Drawing upon the work of camp historians and using the theoretical frameworks of "minority discourse" and literacy sponsorship, Shimabukuro argues that these internees, who organized themselves into a committee called the Heart Mountain Fair Play Committee (FPC), developed a resistant rhetoric that drew its discursive authority from sources both "friendly" and "hostile." Or to use her own terms, this resistant rhetoric was "coauthorized" by local and global agents of both collective "damage" and collective "sponsorship." For these local and global agents, she considers the role of the government-sponsored camp newspaper, the racist rhetoric of U.S. politicians and mainstream newspapers, Japanese cultural models of ideal behavior, the effects of pre–World War II Americanization initiatives, and the organizing efforts of camp Issei (first-generation immigrants). She further argues that the role of "historical location" matters in our conceptualization of resistant rhetoric, and she closes her chapter with a brief discussion of a contemporary Japanese American war resister and the lasting significance of the FPC's writing as a "coauthorizing" force of resistance for Asian Americans today.

We conclude this section with Robyn Tasaka's "Rhetoric of the Asian American Self: Influences of Region and Social Class on Autobiographical Writing." In this chapter Tasaka takes us to Hawai'i to investigate how Asian American students use language to write themselves into the larger American autobiographical narrative. According to Tasaka, much of the literature on the autobiographical writing of Asian Americans and other people of color seems to suggest that members of these groups write in certain ways—which include, for example, displaying double consciousness, making social statements, and providing guided tours of their cultures. However, by studying the autobiographical writing of three Asian American English majors at the University of Hawai'i, Tasaka demonstrates that these students write in ways that are markedly different from what has been attributed to them and to their community. Moreover and most noticeable, race is barely identifiable in their writing. She argues that this absence of race reflects the influences of region and social class on Asian American experience. That is, Asian Americans are a majority in Hawai'i and some groups—including the Chinese and Japanese—tend to occupy higher socioeconomic status. In addition, race is also discussed quite differently in Hawai'i than it is on the mainland. What her study illustrates is that we must consider factors like region and social class when discussing Asian American autobiographical writing and experiences and that the making of Asian American rhetoric must take into account, in our terms, where we are and where we have been.

If the first seven chapters are in one sense aimed at how Asian Americans invent, remember, and recover certain discursive practices to enact different forms of Asian American rhetoric, the next seven chapters direct their focus toward the issue of representation and resistance or, more specifically, toward how Asian Americans use rhetoric to combat misrepresentations and stereotypes and to develop representations for their very own that are directly based upon their own experiences as Other and upon their own struggles for political, racial, and linguistic justice.

Given the overdetermination of racial, ethnic, and cultural categories, we want to suggest that representation constitutes a primary consideration in Asian American rhetorical practices. Asians and Asian Americans have long been constructed discursively in the United States. We see these representations through official discourses such as legislation and governmental policies that addressed immigration, naturalization, property rights, or national security in times of war. Popular discourses in mass media have also contributed to these representations because such discourses raised fears of a "yellow peril" during the late nineteenth and early twentieth centuries, created "model minorities" in the 1970s and 1980s, or blamed economic hard times on Japanese carmakers and the rise of Asian technology industries. However, in recent years such representations constructed through dominant discourse have been challenged more vociferously and from a host of cultural sites and perspectives. In our second section, "'Translating' and 'Transforming' Asian American Identities," we have gathered chapters that specifically illustrate how representations of Asians and Asian Americans by dominant discourses have been challenged and how Asian Americans have used rhetoric to create their own representations of identity, community, and culture. We chose "translating" and "transforming" for part of the title of this section in order to accentuate the importance of these two tropes we discussed earlier in representing Asian American identities and in the making of Asian American rhetoric.

For example, in "'Artful Bigotry and Kitsch': A Study of Stereotype, Mimicry, and Satire in Asian American T-Shirt Rhetoric," Vincent N. Pham and Kent A. Ono examine a specific case of representation and counterrepresentation and ideological tensions that frame the production and reception of images. Focusing on a line of Asian-themed T-shirts produced and distributed by clothing retailer Abercrombie and Fitch (A&F) in 2002, Pham and Ono unpack the use of the stereotypical yellow peril imagery of Asians and Asian Americans that resulted in a contemporary "spectacle of racism." They also consider the response by the Asian American–owned clothing company Blacklava, which made its own T-shirt, employing satire to rework and refigure A&F's original racist imagery. Exploring Bourdieu's concept of symbolic domination and Bhabha's concepts of mimicry and mockery to document A&F's attempt at symbolic domination over Asian Americans, Pham and Ono argue that Blacklava's T-shirt—recirculated with A&F's images but substituting the words "Artful Bigotry & Kitsch" for "Abercrombie & Fitch"—is a counterrhetorical act that illustrates Asian American resistance to that domination. Further, Pham and Ono argue that wearers of the Blacklava T-shirt enact an embodied resistance that challenges A&F's symbolic violence, racism, and corporate mimicry and mockery. Their study, therefore, points to a new arena where Asian Americans engage in resistance work in creative and transformative ways.

Similarly, in "Beyond 'Asian American' and Back: Coalitional Rhetoric in Print and New Media," Jolivette Mecenas examines articulations of Asian American identities within the cultural contexts of two contemporary publications, the print and online versions of *Hyphen* and *Giant Robot*. Building on Judith Butler's theory of performativity, Mecanas examines the rhetorical force of identity claims in the public sphere through popular culture. By analyzing specific examples (including a blog dialogue in which participants clarify the differences between Hawaiian and Asian identities and a video podcast that parodies Asian stereotypes), Mecenas argues that descriptive rather than normative articulations of Asian American identities delimit what such an identity may mean, thereby engendering various possibilities for coalitional political agency across multiple identities of race, gender, sexuality, and nationality. Asian American identities and cultures thus are transformed when coalitions are created that focus not on articulating a shared identity as the end goal, but on making meaning through shared practices, such as engaging in pop culture, that may reshape the prevailing cultural ideology into one that nurtures coalitions of creative and nonracist people.

While Mecenas focuses on the production of Asian American texts that have a primarily Asian and Asian American audience, Mary Louise Buley-Meissner turns her attention to the reception of Asian American texts by largely white readers. In her chapter, "On the Road with P. T. Barnum's Traveling Chinese Museum: Rhetorics of Public Reception and Self-Resistance in the Emergence of Literature by Chinese American Women," Buley-Meissner investigates the rhetoric of public reception in popular reviews of three foundational Chinese American women writers: Sui Sin Far at the turn of the century, Jade Snow Wong in the 1950s, and Maxine Hong Kingston in the 1970s. As mainstream reviewers influence public perceptions of how an emerging body of work by "minority" writers contributes (or is marginal) to "majority" literary interests, they reinforce dominant beliefs about who belongs in this country and why. Buley-Meissner echoes the argument of the *AIIIEEEEE!* editors as she illustrates how reviewers consistently regard Chinese American women writers as Chinese rather than American, as if their foreignness is their most important qualification for being noticed. To counter these public receptions or these acts of public displacement, Buley-Meissner argues, these Chinese American women writers developed the rhetoric of self-resistance by articulating bicultural realities and by enacting the roles and responsibilities they were committed to fulfilling in their work. Across generations, these writers are not politically or historically innocent, but acutely aware of social conditions influencing response to their interpretations of identity, difference, and community.

These chapters together directly address issues of representation, responding to questions like: What are the representations of Asian Americans in dominant culture? What representations do Asian Americans create of themselves? At the same time, they also begin to suggest how Asian Americans develop strategies of resistance to construct their identities and culture. Chapters by Bo Wang, Jeffrey Carroll, Michaela Meyer, and Hyoejin Yoon examine how Asian Americans develop discourses of resistance and perform their identities and culture through different rhetorical acts, from journalistic and imaginative writing to stage comedy and musical virtuosity, from athletic feats to educational instruction.

While Burley-Meissner focuses on how Sui Sin Far, or Edith Eaton, together with the other two Chinese American women writers, has been received by popular discourses in the United States, Bo Wang, in "Rereading Sui Sin Far: A Rhetoric of Defiance," vividly illustrates how she developed rhetorical strategies to create spaces for Chinese and other ethnic minorities and to resist and challenge social and cultural norms. Drawing on Kenneth Burke's concept of rhetoric as identification and narrative criticism as major critical lenses, Wang argues that Sui's works—she is recognized by literary scholars as the first Chinese American immigrant writer to depict the Chinese in America with empathy—should be considered not merely as aesthetic undertakings, but rather as rhetorical texts. That is, these imaginative writings reveal her personal struggles as a biracial writer, her inventive rhetorical strategies, her breaking of the silences and invisibility of Chinese immigrants in North America, and her commitment to the change of that racist society. Wang also argues that Sui Sin Far explored rhetorical strategies such as the reshaping of literary genres, conventions, and character types that could facilitate efforts to challenge prejudice and racism. Marginalized writers, Wang suggests, can develop resistance to cultural norms when they have little access to political arenas. Through discursive practices they can create rhetorical spaces where marginalized social groups are able to challenge dominant ideologies, develop their own political and social beliefs, and have their voices heard.

In his chapter, "Margaret Cho, Jake Shimabukuro, and Rhetorics in a Minor Key," Jeffrey Carroll focuses on two entertainers, Margaret Cho and Jake Shimabukuro, who have managed, against industry odds or racial odds—or both—to create a particular sense of an Asian American rhetoric. This rhetoric and its position in relation to American culture are defined through an exploration of both entertainers' performances. More specifically, Carroll sees their performances as recuperating the classical rhetorical canon of delivery or "the language of the body." Further, such performances serve not to exclude what is surely a complex of relations that exist between Asian American performers and their material and audience, but to display a modality of that position that may, in fact, be a marker of what is possibly "Asian" about Asian American rhetoric. Carroll also argues that both performers move back and forth, and easily, from a rhetoric of collective or shared experience to the personal and sometimes startlingly rare art of encountering and recognizing a minor narrative of the personal, in which Asian identities are the explicit subject.

Michaela D. E. Meyer, in her chapter, "'Maybe I Could Play a Hooker in Something! Asian American Identity, Gender, and Comedy in the Rhetoric of Margaret Cho," also focuses on Margaret Cho but on different aspects of her performativity and its rhetorical effects. Meyer argues that Cho is rhetorically "playing" with her identity, representing herself as both an insider and an outsider in both Eastern and western contexts. For western audiences Margaret Cho is the "Other"– she looks Asian, but her knowledge and experience within American society coupled with fluency in a language familiar to western audiences simultaneously positions Cho as an "insider." The ambiguity of Cho's ethnic identity then lends itself to challenging the binary definition of race applied in American contexts. Thus, her Asian body, coupled with American social mores, becomes the rhetorical site of embodiment, opening a space for a unique "cultural rhetoric" in her everyday performances.

To close off this section, we have included K. Hyoejin Yoon's "Learning Asian American Affect." In this chapter Yoon examines the relationship between affect and the racialized and gendered body. Building on discussions of model minority discourse, affect, and gender, Yoon theorizes the various pedagogical functions that the Asian American female body serves, from the performance of an Asian American cheerleader injured in a fall to explorations of her own position as an Asian American teacher whose performance fulfills different ideological purposes for a variety of audiences. In particular, Yoon illustrates how these performances through the Asian American body are both rhetorical and pedagogical and that the Asian American (gendered) body often is read in particular ways by dominant culture to fulfill desire, but is also rhetorical and pedagogical in the interests of Asian Americans. Her study, together with Carroll's and Meyer's, shows how Asian Americans can mobilize language and body to empower themselves and to effect social and cultural changes.

It has been seven years since that reviewer questioned the value of rhetoric for Asian Americans. It has been four years since the student from Beijing Jiaotong University raised those pointed questions. We think often of these two encounters because they keep reminding us of the need to perform a narrative where Asian Americans, or any other ethnic minorities, for that matter, can use a language that, in the words of Gloria Anzaldúa, "they can connect their identity to, one capable of communicating the realities and values true to themselves" (1999, 77). We offer this collection as one such narrative, as our collective, but no less heterogeneously inflected, response to that reviewer's skepticism and to that Chinese student's questions. In short, we see this work as our effort to articulate and perform this language we call "Asian American rhetoric."

As we are about to close this introduction, we must emphasize that this collective response of ours does not imply any claim on our part to uniqueness or coherence for Asian American rhetoric, because, as will be made clear in the next fourteen chapters, nothing of this sort can really be had. Rather, we want to claim that doing Asian American rhetoric is an act always situated in a space of linguistic, cultural, and transnational multiplicity and fraught with histories and memories of asymmetrical relations of power and domination. Further, it is an act that not only resists and challenges the dominant representations that deny or subordinate our language and our rhetoric as the Other, but also openly engages the tension or contradiction that informs both the very naming of our discursive practices and the actual process of translating and transforming our experiences into the larger American imaginary.

As a rhetoric of becoming, Asian American rhetoric has also served us well. Not only has this rhetoric made it possible for us to complete this project, but it has also given rise to, and indeed served to constitute, a new space where we can engage in the work of performative transformation. To advance such work, we must further develop new theoretical models to systematically account for our discursive practices and their significances. While practices of resistance to dominant cultural and rhetorical norms by Asian Americans are aplenty, it is up to us to uncover and legitimate them. Moreover, it is no less imperative that we continue to discover and develop rhetorical strategies and genres that can help open up access to political and cultural arenas that have heretofore been denied to Asian Americans. Such efforts will lead us to focus more intently on specific, particularizing sites, on how Asian Americans in their respective communities use rhetoric to bring about positive changes and to shape new realities. Finally, as we have been arguing all along in this introduction, doing Asian American rhetoric entails conflict, contradiction, and ambivalence. Such an act becomes further entangled with the ever-present fluidity of culture, identity, and tradition, because we use Asian American rhetoric with a body that is already socially codified and thus predetermined, and because Asian American rhetoric can take on discursive features that are suggestive of other rhetorical traditions and/or are being appropriated by the dominant tradition. It is these moments of entanglement that call for further systematic investigations where boundaries of different cultures, traditions, and identities conflate, and where acts of conflict and interdependency abound.

REFERENCES

Anzaldúa, Gloria. 1999. *Borderlands/La Frontera: The New Mestiza.* 2nd ed. San Francisco: Aunt Lute.

Butler, Judith. 1993. Critically Queer. In *Bodies That Matter: On the Discursive Limits of "Sex."* New York: Routledge.

Chan, Jeffrey Paul, Frank Chin, Lawson Inada, and Shawn Wong, eds. 1991. *The Big AIIIEEEEE!: An Anthology of Chinese American and Japanese American Literature.* New York: Meridian.

Cheyfitz, Eric. 1991. *The Poetics of Imperialism: Translation and Colonization from "The Tempest" to "Tarzan."* New York: Oxford University Press.

Chin, Frank, Jeffrey Chan, Lawson Inada, and Shawn Wong, eds. 1991. *AIIIEEEEE! An Anthology of Asian American Writers.* New York: Mentor. (Orig. pub. 1974.)

Chuh, Kandice. 2003. *Imagine Otherwise: On Asian Americanist Critique.* Durham, NC: Duke University Press.

Gee, James Paul. 2005. *An Introduction to Discourse Analysis: Theory and Method.* 2nd ed. London: Routledge.

Giroux, Henry. 1992. Resisting Difference: Cultural Studies and the Discourse of Critical Pedagogy. In *Cultural Studies,* edited by Nelson C. Grossberg and P. Treichler. New York: Routledge.

Lai, Him Mark, Genny Lim, and Judy Yung, eds. 1991. *Island: Poetry and History of Chinese Immigrants on Angel Island, 1910–1940.* Seattle: University of Washington Press. (Orig. pub. 1980.)

Li, Juan. 2004. Pidgin and Code-Switching: Linguistic Identity and Multicultural Consciousness in Maxine Kong Kingston's *Tripmaster Monkey. Language and Literature* 13:267–287.

Lowe, Lisa. 1991. Heterogeneity, Hybridity, Multiplicity: Marking Asian American Differences. *Diaspora* 1:24–44.

Mizuno, Takeya. 2001. The Creation of the "Free" Press in Japanese-American Camps: The War Relocation Authority's Planning and Making of the Camp Newspaper Policy. *Journalism & Mass Communication Quarterly* 78 (3): 503–518.

———. 2003. Journalism Under Military Guards and Searchlights: Newspaper Censorship at Japanese American Assembly Camps during World War II. *Journalism History* 29 (3): 98–106.

Mountford, Roxanne. 2001. Of Gender and Rhetorical Space. *Rhetoric Society Quarterly* 30 (1): 41–71.

Oliver, Robert T. 1971. *Communication and Culture in Ancient India and China.* Syracuse: Syracuse University Press.

Ono, Kent A., and John M. Sloop. 2002. *Shifting Borders: Rhetoric, Immigration, and California's Proposition 187.* Philadelphia: Temple University Press.

Pratt, Mary Louise. 1991. Arts of the Contact Zone. In *Profession 91.* New York: MLA.

Richardson, Elaine B., and Ronald L. Jackson II, eds. 2004. *African American Rhetoric(s): Interdisciplinary Perspectives.* Carbondale: Southern Illinois University Press.

Smitherman, Geneva. 1977. *Talkin and Testifyin: The Language of Black America.* Detroit: Wayne State University Press.

Spivak, Chakravorty Gayatri. 1987. *In Other Worlds: Essays in Cultural Studies.* New York: Methuen.

PART ONE

Performing Asian American Rhetoric in Context

1

TRANSNATIONAL ASIAN AMERICAN RHETORIC AS A DIASPORIC PRACTICE

Rory Ong

Too often, the dilemma for resident Asians in the United States, Pacific Islanders, and multigenerational Asian Americans centers on explaining away their disparate (dis)placements or (dis)positions in the national American narrative. Transnationalism has fast become one rhetorical commonplace that attempts to resolve these discontinuities that have been historically engendered by geopolitical and economic border crossings, the impact of global trade, and a growing global economy. Some of the earliest discussions around transnationalism and Asia Pacific focused on the economic reforms occurring in newly industrialized countries like China, Hong Kong, Malaysia, the Philippines, Singapore, South Korea, Taiwan, and Thailand (Cummings 1998). The emphasis was on the consistency and like-mindedness of so-called miracle Asian economies and their citizen workforce, which adopted western values of trade, commerce, and consumption. However, alternative scholarship on the Asian diaspora (Chow 1993; Dirlik 1998; HuDehart 1999; Ang 2001; Grewal 2005) has begun to articulate a transnationalism that takes stock of disparate and uneven Asian transcontinental and transoceanic crossings in order to illumine the contradictions and inconsistencies in im/migrant Asian lives and identities.

One of the difficulties in articulating a rhetoric particular to the Asian diaspora in the United States has to do with its multivalency and the long history of an Asian *habitus* in the West.[1] An Asian habitus is produced from overlapping and embedded quotidian relations involving the sociohistorical, political, and economic structures that thread the material interlacing of daily life and human agency. This also accounts for the complicity of Asian diasporic subjects, whose various articulations of material life are sutured to quotidian systems and structures of

1. I draw from Pierre Bourdieu's notion of *habitus*. For more, see all of chapter 2 in *Outline of a Theory of Practice* (1989) but specifically pp. 78–85.

classification such as language, immigration legislation, and economic policies as well as to racial formations, sociopolitical arrangements, and distributions of power. An Asian habitus, therefore, involves the everyday practices, discourses, and cultural lore invented in conjunction with the material conditions of multigenerational and transnational Asian Americans whose lives, as Lisa Lowe points out, are "juridically legislated, territorially situated, and culturally embodied" (1996, 2). Lowe particularly refers to the ways in which the architecture of U.S. citizenship, the systemic exclusion and alienation of Asians in the United States, and the militarization and colonization of the Pacific have contributed to the national imagination of Asia, and Asians, in an American empire (4–5). Such a habitus is replete with diasporic identities and cultural practices that are in tense and uneven relation to a western hegemony that is delineated around U.S. conceptualizations of national affiliation, territory, and economic and military dominance across Asia and the Pacific. An Asian habitus accordingly produces a hybridized and heterogeneous transnational and transcultural way of life to negotiate the moral and ethical valuations that encode Asians in the West. A rhetoric that is in tandem with an Asian habitus would, therefore, have to contend with the multiple and incongruous Asian communities—those long-standing, those newly arrived, as well as mobile transnational communities—now inhabiting the geographical, sociopolitical, economic, and cultural axes in the States, in its territories, and perhaps across the Americas.

The heterogeneous identities and practices that an Asian habitus generates have resulted in some differing opinions regarding how to fully comprehend Asian American daily lives, let alone what might constitute their rhetorics. While some scholars have pointed to the maintenance of ethnic, kinship, and national ties, others point to the practice of family and political organizations to bring about community solidarity. Many, however, continue to look to the expansion of economic, transportation, and communication networks and to the growth of entrepreneurial elites in a global economy as factors that preserve an Asian cultural continuity (Anderson and Lee 2005, 8–10). In spite of these popular trends, a critical Asian diaspora scholarship has been developing that interrogates the nationalist and essentialist agendas that underlie the fact that "for Asian populations across the Americas, ethnic and diasporic identities and practices exist not simply in uneasy tension with each other, but are caught between nation-states and their national agendas"

(10). The complex material conditions and the transnational intersections that compile an Asian habitus and the production of diasporic lives and cultural practices are in many ways complicit with the national projects of western colonizing nation-states. Robbie Goh reminds us that such an understanding of cultural practice "is not only true of the formerly colonized nation, but also of migrants, immigrant societies, and global diasporic contexts . . . which can be found beyond the nation, among the ethnically diverse, transnationally oriented citizens of contemporary global zones" (2004, 6). Coming to terms with the historico-material conditions of an Asian habitus recasts the Asian diaspora amid the ongoing debates around nationalism, citizenship, white supremacy, immigration, globalization, and the war on terror in the United States. A rhetoric and rhetorical practice specific to that of an Asian diaspora in the United States must, therefore, account for the dialectical relationship of its habitus with western structures of domination.

ASIAN AMERICAN "AUTODOCUMENTARY" AS A TRANSNATIONAL RHETORIC

With the uneven movement of Asian communities across Asian and Pacific continents and oceans as part of a U.S. economic and cultural hegemony in circulation, transnational Asian American rhetorical practices have already begun to materialize. These have taken the form of cultural projects across a variety of disciplines and everyday cultural practices that engage in the reinvention, rearticulation, and rememory of transmigrations, particularly as they expose the Asian diaspora in relation to western expansion rather than mere cultural travel or sharing across national borders (see Chen 1998; Abbas and Erni 2005; Lim et al. 2006). Some of these undertakings might be considered rhetorical projects which, by their very telling, are closer to life narratives or testimonio. Testimonio, as Caren Kaplan writes, "is a form of 'resistance literature'; it expresses transitional material relations in neo- and postcolonial societies and disrupts mainstream literary conventions. . . . testimonio may refer to colonial values of nostalgia and exoticization, values that operate via a discourse of truth and authenticity" (1992, 122–123). The exposure of, and interruption in, cultural nostalgia and exoticization can both be understood as a product of the transnational work of life narratives as they cross the genres of ethnography and autobiography with colonial subjugation, something that Mary Louise Pratt (1991) has referred to as autoethnography.

Autoethnography, as Pratt theorizes, is a hybrid text that formerly colonized subjects created by merging metropolitan discourses with indigenous idioms. These hybrid discourses invent self-representations that challenge dominant metropolitan forms of understanding by providing an alternative framework for discursive practices to draw from colonial contexts and conditions that interrupt the colonial episteme. In order to do this, Pratt depends on the preserved indigeneity of a colonial subject's idioms to alter the subordination by, and thus the privilege of, the colonizers. By virtue of the remnant indigeneity of their idioms, Pratt's autoethnographers challenge their colonial imbrication. Their indigenous idiomatic infiltration into the hegemony creates a discord within the colonial process, and thus intervenes in the production of colonial discourses and power relations.

To the contrary, Asian American subjects wrestle with the concomitant production of their subjectivity and rhetorical practice (their idioms) in relation to colonial productions of discourse and power relations. Their very hybridity, produced by their multigenerational and transnational identities, complicates any notion of an indigenous cultural or idiomatic prerogative. In fact, Asian American subjectivity is in relation to the territorial expansion, the overwhelming military and economic power, and the legislative hegemony of an expanding American empire, all of which underwrites the rhetoric of an Asian diaspora in the United States. An Asian American diaspora and its discourses are entangled with the cultural flows across the Pacific, which have been fetishized as cultural commodities, conscripted as labor, or have served as proxies of western values through either a military or a global capitalist economy.

In the last decade, several projects have emerged in the form of life-narrative documentaries depicting an Asian American diaspora within these encumbered conditions. *Bontoc Eulogy* by Marlon Fuentes (1995), *Xich-lo* by M. Trinh Nguyen (1996), and *First Person Plural* by Deann Borshay Liem (2000) are examples of such projects. Though uneven, inconsistent, and certainly not incontrovertible, these life narratives parse out a critical practice that is produced from their representation of competing and contradictory subjects living within the bureaucratic apparatus of a colonial or imperial nation-state. They disclose the construction of Asian American subjects, their everyday lives and discourses, *in the midst* of a colonial and imperial scheme, and articulate discordant discourses that reflect the tension-filled spaces (the disorientation) of *trans*Asian, *trans*Pacific, and *trans*American identities. Moreover, rather than frame these life-narrative documentaries as autoethnographies that look to indigenous idioms as a means of resistance and critique, we might think of them as *Asian American autodocumentaries*—critical and self-reflexive visual representations that illustrate an Asian habitus through *diasporic idioms.* Unlike indigenous idioms, diasporic idioms are commonplaces constitutive of a U.S. colonial and imperial hegemony that cloak the scattered communities of Asians in America. Through their use of diasporic idioms, Asian American autodocumentaries reimagine and revalue commonplace markers with the tensions and contradictions of transnational border-crossing subjects, and in this way give shape to the counterhegemonic narrative of a diasporic rhetorical practice.[2] For example, they (1) reimagine and revalue the commonplace of *nation* by identifying it with western colonial and imperial involvement across the Asia Pacific region and with the scattering of Asian and Pacific communities; (2) reimagine and revalue the commonplace of *community* as constitutive, yet critically self-reflexive, of western colonial culture; and (3) reimagine and revalue the commonplace of *family* through the very tensions and contradictions that their heterogeneous Asian American location engenders.

First, Asian American autodocumentaries reimagine and revalue their relation to the commonplace of *nation.* They characterize the extent to which western colonization and empire building in the Asia Pacific region has played a significant role in the deployment of an Asian diaspora and Asians' transnational life stories. We can see this in Marlon Fuentes's *Bontoc Eulogy*, for example, as he imagines his Filipino grandfather as Markod, the legendary Bontoc warrior who disappeared after he came to the United States in the early 1900s (see Feng 2002, 25–33). Because very little is known about his grandfather outside of a fragmented family narrative, Fuentes combines old archival footage with contemporary reenactments to visualize what might have been his ancestor's narrative in the United States. As he pieces this story together, Fuentes wonders if Markod was among those Filipinos who were brought to the United States as part of the Philippine exhibit for the 1904 St. Louis World's Fair. He reminds us that the Philippines had

2. See Antonio Gramsci's use of hegemony in *Prison Notebooks,* especially as he notes: "Critical understanding of self takes place therefore through a struggle of political 'hegemonies' and of opposing directions, first in the ethical field and then in that of politics proper, in order to arrive at the working out at a higher level of one's own conception of reality" (1971, 333).

been colonized by Spain, becoming a U.S. territory only a year after the Spanish-American War, once the United States had silenced the remains of the Philippine revolution (see Bonus 2000). After its conquest by the United States, the Philippines became highly valued as a geopolitical spoil of war, but it also became valued as a new dependent nation of the "white man's burden"[3] and a spectacle of subjugation for the fair's attendants. While the Philippine exhibit provided the pretense of cultural difference and respect for "our brown brothers from across the Pacific"(Fuentes 1995), in reality it exoticized and commodified Fuentes's imagined patriarch and all those brought in from across the Philippine Galapagos. It is through the reimagination of his grandfather as Markod that we envision the imprint of colonial hegemony, which led to the dissociation and displacement of the Philippines as a nation as well as to the cultural fragmentation and configuration of a Filipino diaspora in the national space of the United States.

Similarly, M. Trinh Nguyen associates her national displacement and diasporic imagination with the French and U.S. occupation of Vietnam. In *Xich-lo* she records her return visit to relatives in Hanoi many years after relocating to the United States with her family. Like Fuentes, Nguyen recounts this mobile history by combining old film footage with more contemporary footage she shoots during her return. She emphasizes her transient consciousness by being filmed on the move, either on a *xich-lo* (bicycle taxi) or on a moving train, while she narrates. As she moves about the city and countryside, Nguyen recounts her family's national status when they were in Vietnam and reveals that they were of the educated and cultural elite. We learn, for example, that prior to coming to the United States, she and her siblings were schooled by French missionaries, and that her father worked as a military consultant for U.S. forces and was well paid for his services. She also remembers that her family was visited by high-ranking U.S. military officers, who brought expensive gifts for the children. Nguyen tries to remember something about her background that is not laced with a colonial presence, whether French or American. She finds, however, that her most prevalent memories of national belonging are in relation to her French education and Catholic religion, which are compounded by the violence in the landscape around her, and none more so than her father's involvement with U.S. military operations in Vietnam.

---

3. There is a nice historical overview with rhetorical implications in Foster, Magdoff, and McChesney 2004.

Deann Borshay Liem's autodocumentary *First Person Plural* also reimagines the commonplace of nation as she links her own adoption to the flow of adopted Korean children into the United States after the Korean War. A small portion of her narrative describes the adoption of orphaned and/or abandoned Korean children as part of a postwar relief effort that the United States provided through charitable adoption agencies and the institutionalization of orphanages in Korea. More specifically, as Tobias Hübinette explains, transnational adoptions in Korea were a combination of "American empire building and international relations, and Korean military authoritarianism and patriarchal modernity" (2006, 140). This complements the views of historians who argue that the Korean War had little to do with the Korean people themselves, but rather with the Pacific region and its potential ties to communist regimes. Their focus is on how the stalemate of the Korean War precipitated numerous discussions of nuclear first-strike strategies that became such a prevalent part of cold war discourse (Whitfield 1996, 6). Still other scholars extend the stigma of nuclear arms and communism around Asia Pacific to the conflation of its inhabitants as they became synonymous with a cold war rhetoric that not only militarized but helped to racially manage the region (Johnson 2004). In either case, the colonial relationship was clear: Korea became a client, or dependent, nation in need of a colonial (read: U.S.) bureaucracy. By tracing her transnational adoption back to postwar U.S. charity and the institutionalization of orphanages in South Korea, Borshay Liem demonstrates how the maintenance of orphanages was part of a lifeline that helped to establish a continued U.S. presence in Korea. The transnational adoption of orphaned or abandoned Korean children became a way for the United States, and the South Korean government, to continue to rebuild the nation by increasing the flow of currency needed to manage and modernize (read: westernize) the country socially, politically, and economically. The material conditions that led to Borshay Liem's national displacement from Korea also gave impetus for her national placement in the United States.

In addition to amending the commonplace of *nation*, these autodocumentaries also reimagine and revalue the commonplace marker of *community*. They do so by connecting their respective community narratives to the transnational cultural flows that are also engendered by colonial and imperial forces in the Asia Pacific region. Marlon Fuentes imagines, for example, that Markod and other villagers from the Philippines were brought to America by organizers of the 1904 World's Fair. Because the Philippine exhibit brought tribal communities from all over the Galapagos, Fuentes surmises that many of them probably had never seen each other before and in some cases might not have known of each other's existence. Reimagining the scale of this turn-of-the-century Filipino transpacific crossing, Fuentes underscores the ways in which the American colony conflated the archipelago of the Philippines into a mass of one tribe, one community. Reducing the heterogeneous inhabitants of the Philippines into America's little *brown brothers*, and making them new colonial subjects, resonates with Fuentes as he rethinks his own immigration to the United States and confesses that for more than two decades he has never desired to return. He uses this lament to eulogize the forced passage of his Filipino ancestors, and to explain the imbrication of his own narrative with the incongruity of his community's collective narrative.

Trinh Nguyen's autodocumentary takes a slightly different approach to *community* as she recognizes how the accumulation and weight of her memories compel her to simultaneously reject both Vietnamese and American communities. She proclaims, "I have no true family, no social gang; I do not quite fit into mainstream America, nor do I quite fit into Vietnamese America, and I don't remember fitting into mainstream Vietnam" (1996). Nguyen tells us she is on a quest for some insight into her community lineage, and in so doing she tries to imagine an alternate location for her identity. She contrasts this current search in Vietnam with past visits to her father's family when they have told her she is too American and that she has lost her roots. "But the only example of Vietnameseness they offer," she muses, "is the measurement of one's worth by how much material wealth one owns." Although Nguyen is critical of her paternal family's classism masquerading as ancestral lineage, she also recognizes her own familiarity with, and imbrication in, western capitalism as she considers paying a street vendor with her credit card. The incongruity of her ancestral line gets even murkier.

First Person Plural is no less murky, and is itself a primary example of the ways in which the displacement and dissociation of *community* exposes the highly politicized arrangements that supplement cultural agency and subjectivity. Borshay Liem's Pacific crossing, her transnational adoption as a consequence of U.S. military action, is an example of the colonial discourse that overdetermines the ideological interests and practices in the Pacific region and in its inhabitants.

Her autodocumentary unmasks the master narrative hovering over the Korean diasporic community as she comes to understand that transnational adoptions were caught up in the postwar fragmentation of Korean families and the many orphaned or abandoned Korean children, who represented the new national currency in exchange for rebuilding Korea as a nation in the image of its new colonial masters. And as a way of preventing further communist influence in the region, Korean children became one of the United States's and Korea's greatest political, economic, and moral commodities on the road to modernization. The transnational adoption of Korean children operated, in this way, as a two-pronged nationalist project that established a community of transplanted colonial subjects while also amending Korea's social and political relation to the United States.

A third revisionary tactic that these autodocumentaries deploy further aggravates the colonial dilemma by reimagining and revaluing the commonplace of *family*. Therefore, as Fuentes considers the dislocation and displacement that may have befallen his imagined family patriarch, he also wonders whether the role he and several generations of his community play is any less fragmented. To highlight this transgenerational diaspora, Fuentes juxtaposes contemporary footage he films of an actor's reenactment of Markod recording his voice on a gramophone with footage of Fuentes's own image listening to this recording on a gramophone. Combined with another striking image of his U.S.–born children taking photos of each other mimicking their father's behavior with the camera, what Fuentes leaves us with is a Filipino American identity as simulacra upon simulacra. The representation and reenactment of the family patriarch on film, and of recorded Filipino voices being listened to by a Filipino, or of Filipinos photographing other Filipinos, feign the anthropological objectivity of the family as it also mocks it.[4]

Nguyen's autodocumentary, on the other hand, supplements her notion of *family* with a reconfigured memory of her maternal relatives who remained in Vietnam. After the war, her mother's relatives decided to continue living near the Mekong Delta rather than flee to America as did her father and his kin. Nguyen reminisces about the stories told of her maternal grandmother having an old ancestral knowledge, a wisdom not respected by either capitalists or communists. Her grandmother, as the story is told, took in a biracial child left homeless after the

4. For a discussion of the style and structure of the film and its "mockumentary" status, see Petrova and Aufderheide.

war at a time when neither side was attending to the human lives left in the aftermath. Nguyen readily admits that this recollection comes by way of only a few stray photos and concedes it is made up of "mostly flashes of memory disjointed and after nearly two decades maybe imagined" (1996). The narrative opposition that she creates (in this case between paternal and maternal narratives) is common among transnational subjects who seek an alternative site for revaluing cultural memory. What is most interesting is the conscious selection to reclaim her reimagined maternal family memory (as fragmented as it is) over her lived experience with her paternal family. She embraces this as a reinvented and reconfigured history of maternal ancestral wisdom and places it in tension with patriarchal, militaristic, and capitalist western logic. In this way, Nguyen reconfigures the lore of her own history by complicating the boundaries of family and nation with the contradictions of empire and war, and alternatively embraces gender and hybridity as a way to supplement her family memory in the midst of fragmentation and loss.

Borshay Liem's autodocumentary echoes the narratives of Trinh Nguyen and Marlon Fuentes as she seeks to revise her family history from fragments of information and documentation. As in the earlier films, Borshay Liem also uses a variety of footage to piece together her entry into the United States. Borshay, both a transnational and transracial adoptee, documents the rediscovery of her biological family in Korea. She explains that in 1966, Arnold and Alveen Borshay adopted a Korean girl named Cha Jung Hee through the Foster Parents Plan, an American adoption program developed in response to the numbers of Korean children left orphaned by the Korean War. After looking through her adoption documents and contacting the orphanage in Korea, what Deann (a.k.a. Cha Jung Hee) eventually found was that her real name was Ok Jin Kang. It was Cha Jung Hee, another child in the same orphanage, who was in the process of being adopted by Arnold and Alveen Borshay. At the last minute, however, Cha Jung Hee's father decided that he wanted his daughter back and retrieved her from the orphanage. Since the adoption process was well under way with the Borshays, the officials at the orphanage simply replaced Cha Jung Hee with a different child (Ok Jin Kang) and gave her the identity of Cha Jung Hee to keep the adoption active (2000). Once reconnected with her biological family, Borshay dedicates a large portion of the film to the difficult and painful process of reunification. While Borshay Liem's Korean family, the Kangs, are very happy to be reunited with Ok Jin, now a woman in her forties, they realize that Deann/Cha Jung/Ok Jin is more American than Korean by culture, language, and national identity. Borshay Liem, and the audience, have to come to terms with the reality that her biological family is no longer her family—rather, her adoptive American family has become her family. Her familial identity is not based in nature or biology at all, but rather comprised of a web of historical, social, and political constructs.

Each of these autodocumentaries imitates a recovery project that assumes an a priori essentialism around the commonplaces of nation, community, and family. However, the contradictions they encounter proclaim the fissures in nationalist discourses and expose the ideological sutures around western interests in the Asia Pacific region and its inhabitants. They expose, in other words, the overdetermined subjectivities and the cultural paradoxes operating in the lives of transnational Asian Americans. The rather fascinating and complex outcome is that the dissonant resolve of each autodocumentary competes with our commonsense assumptions that look to the nostalgic recovery and harmony of identities. Instead, these Asian American autodocumentaries reimagine *nation*, *community*, and *family* as diasporic idioms that are revalued into critical and hybrid discursive supplements that are deployed in a transnational rhetoric.

THEORIZING A TRANSNATIONAL ASIAN AMERICAN RHETORIC

The entanglements with western colonialism and imperialism represented in these autodocumentaries reveal the difficulties for essentialist articulations of a universal "Asianness," or the difficulty in employing culturally indigenous Asian idioms, and make problematic nationalist notions of static cultural and geopolitical Asian identities, especially in the United States. In fact, the dilemma for transnational Asian Americans is their compound sociohistoric and cultural representation as contradictory subjects of an American empire who are antithetical to, yet at the same time a necessary part of, the flow of culture and capital across the Pacific. This configuration of Asia Pacific challenges the idea of unmitigated national and cultural spaces that, as Arif Dirlik points out, have seen crossings exponentially multiply since 1965. We've witnessed, not the development of an alternative transnational or transcultural identity signifying a new site of global critical agency, but rather the rearticulation of the discourse of a dominant cultural hegemony. Diaspora may inspire the possibilities of a postcolonial transnational community as an alternative to western hegemony, but we cannot seriously consider an alternative paradigm if we disregard existing structures of power and their relentless (re)production within diasporic spaces (1998, 42–43).

Asian American autodocumentaries give us a glimpse of how alternative articulations of Asian American rhetorical practices might account for the contradictory characteristics of diasporic cultures and identities that develop in tension with the conditions of power and privilege that riddle competing interests in the Pacific Rim. Rather than romanticize national or culturally based identity projects, or imagine an ahistoric transnational Asian community that contiguously spans the Pacific, Asian American autodocumentaries acknowledge a history of western militarization, colonization, and empire building as part of the common articulation of Asia Pacific, its diasporas, and its disparate discursive practices. It is this kind of colonial consciousness and reflexivity that may provide the possibility for an alternative imagination to reinvent common discursive markers into diasporic idioms that expose the variant and competing meanings that revolve around Asian im/migrations. A *transnational Asian American rhetoric as a diasporic practice,* then, unveils competing and contradictory discursive power relations within the Asian diaspora as they have become articulated in relation to an American empire. The spectrum of various loci and counterloci [5] that accompany the representation of Asia Pacific in the West is understood as inscribed with sociohistorical, political, and economic tension in relation to the swell of western imperialism across the Pacific. As a discursive practice, a transnational Asian American rhetoric rearticulates (i.e., it reimagines and gives diasporic value to) the colonial discourse that implicates an Asian diaspora within the United States.

A transnational Asian American rhetoric would in fact function in much the same way as Gayatri Spivak's notion of postcolonial *transnational literacy.* Transnational literacy, as Spivak explains it, stands in dialectical relation to "the mobilizing potential of unexamined culturalism," and builds a community consciousness from national and political organizations but not, she emphasizes, "with that other feeling of community whose structural model is the family." A transnational literacy exchanges natural or essentialist affiliations (like kith, kin, culture, and

5. E.g., exotic and sensual vs. spiritual; barbarous and morally corrupt vs. culturally rich; yellow peril, coolie, brown monkey, foreign, inassimilable vs. model minority; enemy-alien, spy, terrorist vs. citizen.

family) with a materialist episteme that details ideologically driven circuits of the nation-state (i.e., citizen, immigrant, il/legal or resident alien, border crosser, overseas contract worker, sweatshop laborer). This exchange is not politically neutral, nor would such an exchange arise miraculously from the quotidian spaces of the transnational agents themselves (e.g., indigenous idioms), because everyday spaces and their discourses are also politicized and replete with colonial rubrics of power and bureaucracy. Rather, Spivak emphasizes that the full transformation of a class (i.e., postcolonial, transnational im/migrants) "is not an ideological transformation of consciousness on the ground level, a desiring identity of the agents and their interest. . . . It is a contestatory replacement as well as an appropriation (a supplementation) of something that is 'artificial' to begin with." A transnational Asian American rhetoric as a practice of the Asian diaspora would, as exemplified in the above autodocumentaries, strategically engage in the epistemic upheaval of commonplaces such as "culture and nation" or "kith and kin" as *natural* sites of meaning production, and supplement them with "use value" by unmasking the already existing ideological lexicon of the American empire that envelopes its imagination of Asia (Spivak 1999, 261).

However, in order to begin the process of (re)inventing the trope(s) of Asia Pacific to that of "use value," we must advance the notion that transnational Asian American identities and practices are indeed already caught up in an ideological pretense associated with the material and discursive encumbrances fostered by western expansion. This shifts the axes of rhetorical production and meaning to the complexities of everyday life *within a western epistemology and discourse.* As we recognize that rhetorical production within the Asian diaspora is linked to material conditions and power dynamics transpiring around western influence, we can then begin to articulate the relationship between the material and the rhetorical. This is an important critical—as well as ideological—turn. Contemporary rhetorical theorists and cultural critics have long been examining the relationship between the production of meaning within the intersection of the material and the discursive (see Mckerrow 1989; Aune 1994; Wander 1999). Stuart Hall, for example, has recognized the burden of material conditions over our lived experience. He specifically acknowledges the significant role discursive practices play in the production of meaning surrounding material conditions. He explains that "events, relations, structures do have conditions of existence and real effects, outside the sphere of the discursive; but . . . it is only within the discursive, and subject to its specific conditions, limits and modalities, [that] . . . they have or can . . . be constructed with meaning" and that discourse, therefore, plays a formative and structural role in the shaping of material events (not merely an after-the-fact description) (1996, 443). Hall's premise revitalizes the ways in which we can begin to comprehend the production of Asian diasporic meaning as having use value stemming from transnational lived conditions constitutive *in the West*, rather than from an essential or innate value *outside or beyond the West*, or as merely the afterlife of domination as well. The Asian diaspora in the United States is comprised, therefore, of material and discursive sites fraught with sociohistoric value (military, economic, legislative, etc.) that give shape to the everyday lives and practices around the subjectivity, identity, and culture of Asian im/migrants *in the West*.

In spite of Hall's observations, there persists a common presumption that national identities remain homogeneous and autonomous. But as Partha Chatterjee explains, the continued desire for a national homogeneity can be traced to discourse production during industrialization (1986, 5). "Nationalism," he writes elsewhere, "sets out to assert its freedom from European domination. But in the very conception of its project, it remains a prisoner of the prevalent European intellectual fashions." The key, as Chatterjee describes it, is to understand how nationalist discourse is shaped around universal values and their enforcement by strictures of colonial power. Nationalist discourse stems from "a much more general problem, namely, the problem of the bourgeois-rationalist conception of knowledge, established in the post-epistemic foundation for a supposedly universal framework of thought which perpetuates, in a real and not merely a metaphorical sense, a colonial domination" (1996, 10). Thus, any postcolonial attempt at reimagining culture beyond colonization as "free" or "independent" must reckon with a dialectic of power that is concurrently framed within this same universal episteme, or postepisteme, developed around colonial power. Chatterjee's recognition that colonial power is sutured to postcolonial discourse is part of the self-reflexive critique that a transnational Asian American rhetoric, as a diasporic practice, may produce.

CONCLUSION

Reimagining Asian America through a diasporic rhetoric that is critically situated in colonial history initiates the process of (re)inventing the trope of Asia Pacific from a uniform and essentializing discourse to a more complex articulating category that elicits an alternative use value of Asian diaspora. Such a rhetoric would begin critical analysis with the diasporic dilemma—that is, the dilemma of a resident colonial imaginary and habitus that has been produced through the structured institutions of a western nation-state. In this way, a transnational Asian American rhetoric as a diasporic practice would not confirm new-world-order fantasies that, as Ien Ang points out, "[consist] of self-contained, self-identical nations—which is the ultimate dream of the principle of nationalist universalism," and "is a rather disturbing duplication of the divide-and rule politics deployed by the colonial powers to ascertain control and mastery over the subjected." In fact, because diasporas are transnational, "linking the local and the global, the here and the there, past and present, they have the potential to unsettle static, essentialist and totalitarian conceptions of 'national culture' or 'national identity" (2001, 34). Therefore, a transnational Asian American rhetoric that operates as a diasporic practice creates alternative discursive spaces that can potentially reveal and unravel the social, cultural, and economic sutures that administer the Asian diaspora in the United States. Such a rhetoric transpires from transnational border-crossing practices that redeploy commonplace markers like nation, community, and family as diasporic idioms that account for the incongruous lived experiences of Asian diasporic subjects. The greater hope is that a transnational Asian American rhetoric has the potential to provide a framework for reimagining and revaluing a more critically robust and radically democratic rhetoric and critically reflexive practice that exposes the colonial and imperial suture.

REFERENCES

Abbas, Ackbar, and John Nguyet Erni, eds. 2005. *Internationalizing Cultural Studies*. Malden, MA: Blackwell.

Anderson, Wanni W., and Robert G. Lee. 2005. *Displacements and Diasporas: Asians in the Americas*. New Brunswick, NJ: Rutgers University Press.

Ang, Ien. 2001. *On Not Speaking Chinese: Living between Asia and the West*. New York: Routledge.

Aune, James Arnt. 1994. *Rhetoric and Marxism*. Boulder, CO: Westview.

Bonus, Rick. 2000. Filipinos and Filipinas in America. In *Locating Filipino Americans: Ethnicity and the Cultural Politics of Space*. Philadelphia: University of Temple Press.

Borshay Liem, Deann, director. 2000. *First Person Plural* [documentary]. San Francisco: Center for Asian American Media.

Bourdieu, Pierre. 1989. *Outline of a Theory of Practice*. New York: Cambridge University Press.

Chatterjee, Partha. 1986. *Nationalist Thought and the Colonial World: A Derivative Discourse*. Minneapolis: University of Minneapolis Press.

———. 1996. *The Nation and Its Fragments: Colonial and Postcolonial Histories*. Princeton, NJ:

Princeton University Press.

Chen, Kuan-Hsing, ed. 1998. *Trajectories: Inter-Asian Cultural Studies.* New York: Routledge.

Chow, Rey. 1993. *Writing Diaspora.* Bloomington: Indiana University Press.

Cummings, Bruce. 1998. Rimspeak; or, The Discourse of the 'Pacific Rim.' In *What Is in a Rim: Critical Perspectives on the Pacific Region as an Idea,* edited by Arif Dirlik. Lanham, MD: Rowman and Littlefield.

Dirlik, Arif, ed. 1998. *What Is in a Rim: Critical Perspectives on the Pacific Region as an Idea.* Lanham, MD: Rowman and Littlefield.

Feng, Peter. 2002. *Identities in Motion: Asian American Film and Video.* Durham, NC: Duke University Press.

Foster, John Bellamy, Harry Magdoff, and Robert W. McChesney. 2004. Kipling, the "White Man's Burden," and U.S. Imperialism. In *Pox Americana: Exposing the American Empire,* edited by John Bellamy and Robert W. McChesney. New York: Monthly Review.

Fuentes, Marlon, director. 1995. *Bontoc Eulogy* [documentary]. San Francisco: Independent Television Service.

Goh, Robbie B.H. 2004. The Culture of Asian Diasporas: Integrating/Interrogating Immigration, Habitus, Textuality. In *Asian Diasporas: Cultures, Identities, Representations,* ed. Robbie B.H. Goh and Shawn Wong. Hong Kong: Hong Kong University Press.

Gramsci, Antonio. 1971. *Selections from the Prison Notebooks.* New York: International.

Grewal, Inderpal. 2005. *Transnational America: Feminisms, Diaspora, Neoliberalisms.* Durham, NC: Duke University Press.

Hall, Stuart. 1996. New Ethnicities. In *Stuart Hall: Critical Dialogues in Cultural Studies.* edited by David Morley and Kuan-Hsing Chen. New York: Routledge.

Hübinette, Tobias. 2006. From Orphan Trains to Baby Lifts: Colonial Trafficking, Empire Building, and Social Engineering. In *Outsiders Within: Writing on Transracial Adoption,* edited by Jane Jeong Trenka et al. Cambridge, MA: South End.

HuDehart, Evelyn, ed. 1999. *Across the Pacific: Asian Americans and Globalization.* Philadelphia: Temple University Press.

Johnson, Chalmers. 2004. *The Sorrows of Empire.* New York: Henry Holt.

Kaplan, Caren. 1992. Resisting Autobiography: Out-Law Genres and Transnational Feminist Subjects. In *De/Colonizing the Subject: The Politics of Gender in Women's Autobiography,* edited by Sidonie Smith and Julia Watson. Minneapolis: University of Minnesota Press.

Lim, Shirley Geok-lin, et al. 2006. *Transnational Asian American Literature: Sites and Transits.* Philadelphia: Temple University Press.

Lowe, Lisa. 1996. *Immigrant Acts: On Asian American Cultural Politics.* Durham, NC: Duke University Press.

Mckerrow, Raymie. 1989. Critical Rhetoric: Theory and Praxis. *Communication Monographs* 56 (June): 91–111.

Nguyen, M. Trinh, producer and director. 1996. *Xich-lo* [documentary]. San Francisco: Taro Root Films.

Petrova, Velina, and Patricia Aufderheide. Bontoc Eulogy. *Cinema Guild,* www.centerforsocialmedia.org/documents/bontoceulogy.pdf, (accessed September 24, 2007).

Pratt, Mary Louise. 1991. Arts of the Contact Zone. In *Profession 91.* New York: MLA.

Spivak, Gayatri Chakravorty. 1999. *Critique of Postcolonial Reason.* Cambridge, MA: Harvard University Press.

Wander, Philip. 1999. The Third Persona: An Ideological Turn in Rhetorical Theory. In *Contemporary Rhetorical Theory: A Reader,* edited by John Louis Lucaites et al. New York: Guilford.

Whitfield, Stephen. 1996. *The Culture of the Cold War.* Baltimore: Johns Hopkins University Press.

2

REEXAMINING THE BETWEEN-WORLDS TROPE IN CROSS-CULTURAL COMPOSITION STUDIES

Tomo Hattori and Stuart Ching

The between-worlds trope has significantly shaped and informed cross-cultural composition pedagogy and research. Two landmark works in cross-cultural composition studies exemplify this claim: in *Hunger of Memory*, Richard Rodriguez (1983) is neither bracero nor scholarship boy, neither of the home nor of school, a stranger in his own household. In *Bootstraps*, Victor Villanueva describes the cross-cultural minority adrift between continents upon a linguistic sea: the "minority lives in a netherworld. Not quite American. No home to return to" (1993, 28). Rodriguez's image evokes a sense of absolute confinement; Villanueva's—the individual linguistically and culturally adrift with no land in sight—suggests confinement through a metaphor of absolute space. Within the sphere of nationalism and its binary construction of race (i.e., black-white, color-white, alien-citizen), there is no home or homeland for the linguistic minority speaker, the mixed blood, the border character who must navigate opposing communities en route to achieving linguistic competence.

Attempting to create a more spacious discourse in cross-cultural composition studies, this chapter reexamines the "caught-between-worlds" trope through an analysis of Asian American rhetoric. By tracing the history of the between-worlds metaphor in two disciplinary narratives—cross-cultural composition studies and Asian American studies—and by placing these histories in dialogue, this chapter argues for the retirement of the between-worlds trope as both an institutional framework and a pedagogical principle in cross-cultural composition and rhetoric studies.

In advancing this argument and dialogue, this chapter disrupts and refigures two foundational concepts in cross-cultural composition studies: (1) literacy's equation with national citizenship; and (2) narration's equation with nationhood or the nation-state.[1] Challenging the first concept, this chapter acknowledges the relationship between literacy and citizenship and additionally complicates this relationship by illustrating how national citizenship initiates forms of illiteracy in the context of global awareness. Challenging the second concept, this chapter replaces the concept *nation as narration* with *transnation as narration.* While work in composition studies has appropriated postcolonial and cultural studies research that has already moved from national to transnational models, the seemingly unbreakable connection between literacy and national citizenship continues within the context of composition studies to locate our discussions predominantly within the national sphere. This location unintentionally reproduces the hegemonic narratives that compositionists who have used the between-worlds metaphor attempt to subvert. In other words, while the between-worlds trope has motivated composition research to define conflicts between home and school cultures and has informed pedagogical research that attempts to bridge or deconstruct such divides, the trope, cast upon a solely national geography, harms the very participants for whom cross-cultural research advocates. Within a national border, to exist between worlds signifies alienation and exclusion; in contrast, across a global geography, to imagine traveling among worlds becomes a space of possibility.

BETWEEN WORLDS IN COMPOSITION STUDIES

Composition research has both imagined and accommodated the between-worlds trope in varied forms over the past four decades. Significantly shaping composition's process pedagogy movement, Britton's and Vygotsky's models and concepts of language development imagine a gap, or middle space, separating a learner's existing and targeted levels of linguistic and cognitive development. In *Language and Learning,* Britton figuratively defines literacy acquisition as a map. This

---

1. The relationship between narrative and nationalism has been widely explored in the field of cultural studies. For example, in *Culture and Imperialism,* Edward Said argues that historically, "narrative" determined "who owned the land, who had the right to settle and work on it, who kept it going, who won it back, and who now plans its future." He continues: "As one critic has suggested, nations themselves *are* narrations. The power to narrate, or to block other narratives from forming and emerging, is very important to culture and imperialism, and constitutes one of the main connections between them" (1993, xii-xiii emphasis in the original). This area of inquiry also figures significantly in rhetoric and composition research concerned with the relationship among literacy, citizenship, and the nation.

map, which the individual articulates through language, composes the individual's worldview. New learning experiences (particularly in schooling) become comprehensible in proximity to the individual's existing worldview. In contrast, learning experiences far removed from this worldview remain incomprehensible since they exist within a kind of middle space between the individual's existing schema and her target level of development (1970, 11–33). Two of Vygotsky's concepts—the zone of proximal development and scaffolding—affirm this cognitive and linguistic middle space. The zone of proximal development describes the developmental stage between an individual's existing cognitive development and the systems and conventions of logic that she has not yet acquired. Scaffolding signifies curricular and pedagogical bridges that facilitate learning within the zone of proximal development (1978, 79–91).

Throughout the 1970s and 1980s, Britton's and Vygotsky's work highly influenced writing instruction. Pedagogical concepts and strategies such as the writing conference, peer-revision workshops, innovative writing and grammar minilessons, modeling, and numerous prereading and prewriting exercises provided educators with concrete instructional tools, or *scaffolding*, for working within the cognitive and linguistic middle spaces separating a learner's existing and targeted levels of development. By the 1990s, then, these representations of the between-worlds trope as a transitional stage between two levels of development or cognitive maturation were firmly rooted in both composition research and instruction.

Postprocess research and pedagogy have complicated Britton's and Vygotsky's models of the between-worlds trope, motivating volumes of valuable research that attend specifically to cross-cultural contexts in writing instruction. This emphasis has further entrenched the between-worlds trope in composition studies. For example, Heath (1983) has studied the ways in which children's home literacy practices affect literacy acquisition in school and has encouraged educators to bridge cultural divisions between home and school that may impede acquisition of academic literacies. In addition, countering myths and language policies that elevate Standard English and subordinate Black Vernacular English, Gilyard (1991) has called attention to the cultural and linguistic gaps that separate learners' linguistic experiences on the streets and their literacy acquisition in school. Challenging Rodriguez's binary either-or model of literacy, which insists that acquiring Standard English necessitates cultural loss (see *Hunger of Memory*), Gilyard argues that

Rodriguez's model binds bilingual and bidialectical speakers between two linguistic worlds. Like Heath and Gilyard, rather than define this bilingual and cross-cultural position as confinement, additional studies have reconstituted this site between linguistic and cultural worlds with critical power. For example, compositionists have used Pratt's concept of "safe houses" (1991, 40), or imagined places of solidarity amid conflicting cultural and political positions, to advocate spaces within the classroom where marginalized students may cultivate a critical collectivity that counters the dominant culture. Compositionists have additionally used Freire's (1970) ideas of liberatory pedagogy to populate marginalized positions with critical, enabling power.

Revisiting the themes of recent CCCC conventions (CCCC is the premier conference in composition studies) suggests that composition research still largely invests great energy into vesting the between-worlds metaphor with political and critical power: CCCC 2002, "Connecting the Text and the Street"; CCCC 2003, "Re-writing Theme for English B: Transforming Possibilities"; CCCC 2004, "Making Composition Matter: Students, Citizens, Institutions, Advocacy"; and CCCC 2005, "Opening the Golden Gates: Access, Affirmative Action, and Student Success." The "street"; the rhetor's position in Langston Hughes's famous poem; and the spaces of "advocacy," "access," and "affirmative action" all evoke cultural, institutional, and political middle spaces that composition studies seeks to transform from positions of oppression into positions of power.

Despite these efforts, the caught-between-worlds metaphor still remains a position of subjection and subjugation. For example, Fu has studied the conflicts between the home and institutional literacies of Asian students attending American schools. Fu describes her four student subjects caught between cultural and institutional worlds: "Standing far from center stage, Tran, Cham, Paw, and Sy, like any newcomers, are wondering, trying to figure out the contours of their new stage. It is so unfamiliar, so different from their old one. . . . They cannot, nor do they want to, discard their past, but they need to find a way to survive as the selves they choose to be in the new environment." As the title of chapter 2 of the volume suggests, they stand "at the edge of the new culture," between their pasts and the American Dream (1995, 33). Reminiscent of DuBois's image of the citizen who lives between two states of conflicting consciousness and Rodriguez's scholarship boy (separated from the home community by language and from the school community by skin color), they remain frozen in development, unable to mature. They are caught between worlds.

Hence, in the postprocess era, the between-worlds trope—initially a transitional stage between two places of cognitive development—becomes a transitional place between two stages of cultural, political, institutional, and economic development. Students like Tran, Cham, Paw, and Sy, who live on linguistic and cultural borderlands between home and school (or both figuratively and problematically in the popular imagination, between homeland and America or American Dream) remain developmentally frozen or caught in the middle between dichotomized images of the globe (East-West, third world–first world, bound-free, foreign-domestic, barbaric-civilized). Such dichotomies fail to reflect adaptive and mobile ways of imagining and constituting ethnic identity and global citizenship.

Three seminal literacy narratives—Gloria Anzaldúa's *Borderlands/La Frontera* (1999), Victor Villanueva Jr.'s *Bootstraps* (1993), and Morris Young's *Minor Re/Visions* (2004)—have pointed composition studies toward alternative routes beyond national borders. That is, although the discipline has interpreted and applied these works within national literacy debates and contexts, all three authors summon their political and critical power from imagined global locations. Our purpose here, then, is not to explicate the entirety of these rich texts, but to illustrate how three key word usages locate these narratives in transnational locations beyond the U.S. border: "borderland" (Anzaldúa 1999), "folkloristic" (Villanueva 1993, 135), and "deterritorialize" (Young 2004, 40, 72). Mah y Busch emphasizes that the title of Anzaldúa's book, "after all, is not 'borders' but 'borderlands'" (2005, 150). For Anzaldúa, borderlands constitute a fluid space within a transnational geography that is a paradoxical location on "both shores at once" (100). The borderland is never a fixed border; rather it is a continual crossing over and through. Hence, in *Borderlands/La Frontera*, Anzaldúa's story and argument originate within this space. As such, her text resists closure. Instead, it remains an open wound, "una herida abierta where Third World grates against the first and bleeds. And before a scab forms it hemorrhages again, the lifeblood of two worlds merging to form a third country—a border culture" (25). According to Mah y Busch, this liminal space, along with numerous metaphorical and mythical references, enables Anzaldúa to articulate a kind of "palimpsest, a conceptual layering" that, through articulations, colonial erasures, and rearticulations, locates the narrator within both the indigenous and the cosmic simultaneously (148).

In *Bootstraps,* while Villanueva positions his argument within a national border, it similarly achieves its generative power by reaching through and beyond national borders toward a more spacious transnational geography. Drawing from Gramsci, Villanueva challenges the "folkloristic," or the ideological that passes as neutral fact or condition rather than political consequence (1993, 95). To do this, he proposes introducing alternative folklores into the writing curriculum: "Those who comprise the various cultures in the classroom would be encouraged to discover their own folklores" (136). And in a later volume of *College English* entitled "Rhetorics of Color," Villanueva seeks these varied folklores in "memory," or *la memoria,* which is a "friend of ours" (2004). Such folklores, implicitly stated in Villanueva's argument, might encompass indigenous ethics and myths that originate beyond America's borders. As such, they reach through the national imaginary, excavating colonial global attachments and relationships and call attention to the ways in which such attachments reveal themselves within the oppressive realities of certain minority communities within the national border.

Like Villanueva, Young positions his argument within the national border. Additionally similar to Villanueva, Young advances his national argument by evoking a transnational geography. Here, we want to focus particularly on the term *deterritorialization,* which Young uses to illustrate Victor Villanueva's critique of the ideologies populating the dominant national discourse that enslaves minor narratives and their languages of origination (2004, 56, 72, 81). While Young applies "deterritorialization" primarily within a national context, the arc of his narrative forges a clear connection between internal colonization and global colonization among nations (both the Philippines and Hawai'i, major subjects in Young's study, were once U.S. territories). This spacious geography becomes even more clear in his discussions of Carlos Bulosan and America's colonial history with the Philippines, as well as Hawai'i's literature and its literacy policies that discriminate against speakers of Hawai'i Creole English. These subjects frame Young's discussion of national literacy policy within the colonial relationships that America has had and continues to have with the Philippines, Hawai'i, and other nations.

As we have asserted, all three studies discussed above, though currently applied by compositionists predominantly in contexts of national citizenship, articulate attachments to global communities. In this way, these authors resist binary representations of race and literacy. Eschewing the between-worlds trope, they instead opt for fluid and multiple articulations of culture, ethnic identity, and citizenship within the nation. Additionally, they attempt to narrate and reconstitute themselves and the larger cultural, intellectual, and institutional communities in which they participate. Because of their importance in composition studies, the three landmark literacy narratives cited above continue to influence the field of composition and rhetoric significantly. Anzaldúa's and Villanueva's works are among the most highly cited volumes in cross-cultural composition research within the last ten years. Young's book, which earned the prestigious 2006 CCCC Outstanding Book Award, promises the same in the future. As a discipline, we can learn much more from these narratives, for as Mah y Busch notes, in Anzaldúa's work, the "movement from la frontera to the New mestiza is not narrowly physical. The shift ultimately concerns awareness and its role in a person's ability to act" (2005, 148). Movement, therefore, is a function of the individual's capacity to imagine. Composition studies may fully realize the vision of these authors and extend these visions as well, if it reimagines literacy globally beyond the physical national border and travels the routes these authors have opened on a transnational geography.

Recent studies have taken promising turns in these directions: challenging college composition's singular (and uncritical) commitment to an " English-only" policy, Horner and Trimbur encourage pluralizing composition studies. In other words, they support an "internationalist perspective capable of understanding the study of teaching written English in relation to other languages and the dynamics of globalization" (2003, 624). Citing Chiang and Schmida (1999, 85), Horner and Trimbur emphasize the detrimental effects of tacit English-only policies, which force some bilingual college writers into locating themselves "between worlds" (610). Building on Horner and Trimbur's work, Canagarajah articulates one specific version of pluralizing composition studies, arguing that we should encourage students to produce texts that interweave diverse varieties of world Englishes. Such textual "meshing" would challenge the hegemonic functions of Standard English both nationally and globally (2006, 598).

The national border, however, is not easily reconstituted or dismantled in matters of literacy. Indeed, literacy and American citizenship have long been inextricably and problematically connected. In "The Politics of English Only in the United States: Historical, Social, and Legal

Aspects," Carol Schmid offers a concise overview of this troubled history. According to Schmid, increased immigration has historically produced two national responses: fear of foreigners and fervor for Americanization. Both responses remain inextricably interwoven with literacy policies that erase minority languages and that enforce English as the nation's official language. Drawing from a range of sources, Schmid chronicles language policies from 1917 to 1924 directed at the new immigrants from eastern and southern Europe. These policies included English-only instructional laws in Oregon; California legislation requiring foreign-language newspapers to publish English translations; and national legislation in the Espionage Act, which required English translations of all war articles written in German. This legislation resulted in ten German newspapers printing their news exclusively in English. Moreover, this legislation was further reinforced by psychological research purporting that bilingual children were handicapped in language development in comparison with monolingual children (2000, 62–66).

Schmid's summary of English-only U.S. national and local policies from the late twentieth century to the present further illustrates literacy's seemingly unbreakable bond with citizenship. Unlike the wave of southern and eastern European immigration at the turn of the century, which coincided with a rapidly expanding economy, recent Asian and Latin American migration has occurred at a time when the economy has grown much slower, fueling attempts to blame minority languages for the existence of social ills that have resulted from economic challenges. Current language policies are also intertwined with other heated political issues such as immigration law, educational policy, and increased patriotism stemming from economy uncertainties (Schmid 2000, 67–73). One thing remains consistent, however, across both ends of the century: within the complexity of political conflict and uncertainty, "the English language has taken its place beside the American flag as a symbol of what it means to be an American" (73).

In addition, citing exclusionary language policies in connection with contemporaneous anti-immigration policies, Schmid argues that national identity is always "articulated through concepts of race, language, country of origin, and religion" (2000, 66). Similarly, responding to English-only policies in the late twentieth century, Aparicio insists that because military aggression cannot be deployed against citizens within its borders, America has inflicted violence against minorities and has excluded these citizens from its political body through other means, such as language policy: "Language, then, has emerged as a discursive site through which the United States, as a nation, re-imagines itself as desirably homogeneous. Such a nation would necessitate one language to 'glue' its culturally disparate citizens" (2000, 249). As Schmid notes, "Counter symbols that challenge the melting pot theory, such as the legitimacy of speaking and perhaps even maintaining a language in addition to English, add to the current social conflict." Hence, the recent passing of California's Proposition 227, which states that English instruction may be done only in English, exemplifies the inextricable connection between language and national citizenship (Schmid 2000, 73). To be taught English in any other language fuels fears of balkanization and disunity within the nation's borders and the fracturing of the physical border itself.

BETWEEN WORLDS IN ASIAN AMERICAN STUDIES

Composition studies can learn from the ways in which Asian American studies has struggled with the between-worlds trope from its implantation within the discipline's original cultural nationalist discourse to its various recurrences within the discipline's efforts to accommodate more spacious and complex transnational flows. The between-worlds trope in Asian American studies is best understood within that discipline's history as a component of the American ethnic studies movement. Ethnic studies comes into existence during the highly charged decade in recent American history after the civil rights movement and during the national protests against the Vietnam War. It forms as an institutional response to the demands of American college and university students for a more culturally representative and diverse curriculum. The first ethnic studies programs in the country are established at San Francisco State University and UC Berkeley after student strikes in 1968. The Web site of the Department of Ethnic Studies at UC Berkeley documents a "Chronology of Ethnic Studies at Berkeley" that details the sit-ins, demonstrations, and protests that brought ethnic studies into existence.[2] Today, ethnic studies is a vocationally and intellectually integrated institution; the College of Ethnic Studies at San Francisco State University helps students to "teach Ethnic Studies subjects in elementary, secondary, community and college level institutions: or combine this with professional and vocational skills such as business, social welfare, law, and

2. See http://ethnicstudies.berkeley.edu.

medicine."[3] Berkeley's department of ethnic studies "encourages the comparative study of racialization in the Americas" and seeks to situate American ethnic groups "within national and transnational contexts, and to understand how racial and ethnic formation articulate with other axes of stratification such as class, gender, and sexuality."[4] Over the last four decades, ethnic studies has become a distinct if not entirely autonomous discipline like English or composition and a familiar feature of liberal education in American colleges and universities. But while ethnic studies seeks to erase vocational and intellectual marginalization, it does not seek to erase minority culture or identity. Ethnic studies supports vocational assimilation while insisting on racial and ethnic distinction and difference.

Ethnic studies can be understood as the cultural and academic arm of the civil rights movement, with its foundational interest in social equality and justice. Asian American studies begins with the ethnic studies movement as one of its founding constituent areas.[5] At the same time, however, another discourse of American belonging emerges to distinguish Asian Americans in particular from other American minority groups. This is the discourse of the model minority. The model minority idea first appears in American journalism in 1966. In January of that year, an article by sociologist William Petersen appears in the *New York Times Magazine* that declares Japanese Americans "better than any other group in our society, including native-born whites" (21). Later that year, the *U.S. News and World Report* announces: "At a time when it is being proposed that hundreds of billions be spent to uplift negroes and other minorities, the nation's 300,000 Chinese Americans are moving ahead on their own, with no help from anyone else" ("Success Story" 1966, 73–78).[6] The competitive vision of race relations inscribed in the model minority thesis exists in tension with the cooperative and egalitarian ethos of ethnic studies. The tension between the desire to be equal and the desire to win ripples through the conversations of Asian American culture.

3. See http://www.sfsu.edu/~ethnicst/.
4. See http://ethnicstudies.berkeley.edu.
5. The other conventional areas of ethnic studies are African American studies, Chicano/Latino studies, and Native American studies.
6. For a good introduction to the model minority discussion in Asian American studies, see the essays in "Part VIII: The Construction and Deconstruction of the 'Model Minority'" in Zhou and Gatewood 2000. Vijay Prasad (2006) offers an interesting review of model minority formation in relation to other recent discourses of American racial formation. See also the passage "Myth of the 'Model Minority'" in Takaki 1989

One of the notable early efforts by Asian Americans to find a unique cultural voice comes in 1974 in the form of the scream "*AIIIEEEEE!*" by the editorial collective of *AIIIEEEEE! An Anthology of Asian American Writers.* In this initial and founding cultural nationalist phase of what William Wei calls "The Asian American Movement" (1993), this group of Asian American writers explains its anthology's rationale and the title's meaning: "Our anthology is exclusively Asian American. This means Filipino, Chinese, and Japanese Americans, American born and raised, who got their China and Japan from the radio, off the silver screen, from television, out of comic books, from the pushers of white American culture that pictured the yellow man as something that—when wounded, sad, or angry, or swearing, or wondering—whined, shouted, or screamed '*aiiieeeee!*'" (Chin et al. 1991 [1974], xi-xii).

What this small scream represents to the editorial group is the racial wound of growing up Asian in a white male American media culture. In response, the editors of the anthology rearticulate and amplify this abject and pathetic scream into a bold scream of power and protest: "Asian America, so long ignored and forcibly excluded from creative participation in American culture, is wounded, sad, angry, swearing, and wondering, and this is his *AIIIEEEEE!!!*" The editors claim that this newly reimagined scream is "more than a whine, shout, or scream"—instead, it represents "fifty years of our whole voice" (Chin et al. 1991 [1974], xii).

An inquiry into the rhetorical agency of this scream exposes the editors' misrecognition of domination as equality. Apart from uppercase lettering and two additional exclamation points, the *AIIIEEEEE!* editors claim that the new scream has the backing of an entirely new discourse of Asian American cultural being. This is not the only time this editorial group will scream like this. Seventeen years later in 1991, this group releases *The Big AIIIEEEEE! An Anthology of Chinese American and Japanese American Literature* (Chan et al. 1991). The full consideration of this speech act thus presents to us three primal screams: the first lowercase "*aiiieeeee!*" noted in 1974 is the derogatory and racist representation of Asian men in white American culture; the second "*AIIIEEEEE!*", spelled in uppercase letters, is the antiracist retort of the Chinese and Japanese American male editorial group; and the third "*AIIIEEEEE!*", the "Big" one, is the 1991 supplement by that group to its first declarative enunciation in 1974. The redundancy of the third scream is the act that exposes and deflates the power of the whole rhetorical triad. To be sure, the second scream, the scream of the Asian American editors, is itself a dependent mimicry. It lacks the subversive irony of the colonial mimicry and "sly civility" that Homi Bhabha describes in *The Location of Culture* (1994); it lacks the multiform invention and mythological resonance of feminist theorist Helene Cixous's "Laugh of the Medusa" (1976). The only rhetorical invention of both "The Big *AIIIEEEEE!!!*" and the first Asian American "*AIIIEEEEE!*" to their respective immediate predecessors is, strictly speaking, size and volume. What escapes the *AIIIEEEEE!* editors is that their rhetoric of minority assertion thus subscribes to the same values that rationalize the domination of majorities over minorities. In appealing to the logic that bigger and louder is better and prouder, their very act of proclaiming autonomy and independence reveals a rhetorical and intellectual dependency on the logic of cultural domination. In appealing to the logic of domination to construct an alternative to it, the *AIIIEEEEE!* editors inadvertently alienate themselves through their own strategy of self-empowerment. In this sense, one can see their self-inflicted alienation as an unintended implantation of the between-worlds trope within the heart of contemporary Asian American selfhood.

The most literal application of the between-worlds trope in Asian American criticism might be Amy Ling's metaphor of the Asian subject in the West as a "bridge" in her 1990 book, *Between Worlds: Women Writers of Chinese Ancestry*. In this book Ling argues for a positive understanding of the role that women writers of Chinese ancestry have had in late nineteenth- and twentieth-century American and European culture as cultural diplomats who bridge the gap between Eastern and western civilization: "On the one hand, being between worlds can be interpreted to mean occupying the space or gulf between two banks; one is thus in a state of suspension, accepted by neither side and therefore truly belonging nowhere. . . . On the other hand, viewed from a different perspective, being between worlds may be considered as having footholds on both banks and therefore belonging to two worlds at once. One does not have less; one has more. When those who are entirely on one bank wish to cross the gulf, the person between worlds is in the indispensable position of being a bridge" (177).

Ling accepts as given an elemental distinction between East and West that is the defining feature of orientalist thought as elaborated by Edward Said in *Orientalism* (1978). The intriguing element of this otherwise obvious presentation of the bridge as metaphor for the between-worlds condition is the modification she makes to it as she excavates her underlying cultural desire.

What Ling wants to do in *Between Worlds* is to give value to the literary output of writers who have been neglected or debased in twentieth-century European and American culture for their membership in two social categories: Chinese ethnicity and female gender. After arguing for the positive function of Asian subjects as bridges, Ling concludes: "Thus, the factors—one's Chinese face and heritage, for example—that created a sense of alienation in one world are the very factors that enable one to perform the act of bridging; disadvantages turned into advantages by alchemy, dross transmutes into gold" (1990, 177). The argument that a person is valuable because she is in an "indispensable position" of being able to provide "a service not many are able to render" is an argument based on the utility of that person's social function. Ling's small but telling shift in her metaphor of the Asian subject from "bridge" to "gold" locates an important contradiction in competing principles of assessing the value of Asians in American society and life. The difference between the value of bridges and the value of gold is that the value of a bridge is based on function and utility whereas the value of gold is intrinsic. Unlike bridges and other constructed tools, gold has a role in human culture as the standard of value for other commodities. The value of gold in this role is not measured by function or utility as a physical bridge might be. However, in capitalist culture, the utility of a bridge can be measured and expressed as an equivalency to gold. Ling's idea of an "alchemical" transformation of Asian subjects in the West does not criticize the evaluation of Asian Americans for their utility to other cultures rather than for their intrinsic merit. Nonetheless, Ling is aware at least that some form of radical transformation is necessary. In that regard, Ling's between-worlds expression can be seen as an intermediate step in Asian American thought from the monologic cultural nationalism of the *AIIIEEEEE!* group to a preliminary dialogic conception of Asian American transnational subjectivity.

This dialogic conception of Asian American culture also preoccupies Asian American historian Gary Okihiro in *Margins and Mainstreams: Asians in American History and Culture* (1994). The title of this book's second chapter, "Is Yellow Black or White?", succinctly establishes the context of Okihiro's between-worlds discussion. Okihiro's idea of Asian Americans as occupying an intermediate state in national culture differs from Ling's in that Ling thinks about Chinese women writers between two national cultures, whereas Okihiro's context is the binary structure of the black/white American color line. Okihiro diverts the focus of his question away from the Asian American racial subject, the "yellow," to the conditions in American racial culture that make such a question material and relevant.

"Implicit within the question," Okihiro observes, "is a construct of American society that defines race relations as bipolar—between black and white—and that locates Asians (and American Indians and Latinos) somewhere along the divide between black and white." This construct is "not mere ideology but is a social practice that assigns to Asian Americans, and indeed to all minorities, places within the social formation" whose "relationships function to institute and perpetuate a repression that begets and maintains privilege." In the face of this repression, Okihiro sees the necessity of asserting that yellow is "neither white nor black; but insofar as Asians and Africans share a subordinate position to the master class, yellow is a shade of black, and black, a shade of yellow" (1994, 33–34). Thinking of yellow and black as comparable signifiers of racial disempowerment exemplifies the ethos of ethnic studies and its civil rights era commitment to the antiracist solidarity of oppressed races.

The model minority thesis, on the other hand, argues that yellow is a shade of white and that blacks and browns (Latinos) could improve their economic status if only they adopted some "yellow" (Asian) social characteristics. Okihiro's own answer prefers the affinities of yellow to black. "We are a kindred people, African and Asian Americans," he declares, as he notes the shared histories of migration, European colonization, American racial oppression, and American struggle for freedom and equality that convince him of this kinship. But despite a kinship "forged in the fire of white supremacy and struggle," Okihiro wonders, "[H]ow can we recall that kinship when our memories have been massaged by white hands" and "when our storytellers have been whispering amid the din of western civilization and Anglo-conformity?" (1994, 33–34). As historically perverse and dysfunctional as the kinships of white with black and white with yellow have been, historically dominant whiteness is the family name under which African Americans and Asian Americans discover their kinship: yellow is black because white is neither. Despite their different framings of the Asian subject relative to the boundary of American national culture, Ling's and Okihiro's between-worlds metaphors both privilege the marginal status of the Asian racial sign as the frame of reference for the political work of cultural belonging.

Lisa Lowe's *Immigrant Acts: On Asian American Cultural Politics* (1996) follows in this tradition by arguing that Asian American subjectivity and culture stand as "countersites" to American national culture. Echoing Ling, Lowe observes that "the Asian American, even as a citizen, continues to be located outside the cultural and racial boundaries of the nation." Lowe persistently challenges the European intellectual culture of universalism, which she sees as the founding logic of national culture and which she calls "the universality of the national political sphere." Rather than assimilating into this universality, Lowe believes that the Asian immigrant in the United States is "at odds with the cultural, racial, and linguistic forms of the nation" and that this "distance from the national culture constitutes Asian American culture as an alternative formation that produces cultural expressions materially and aesthetically at odds with the resolution of the citizen in the nation" (4, 6). Lowe concludes: "Rather than expressing a 'failed' integration of Asians into the American cultural sphere, this distance preserves Asian American culture as an alternative site where the palimpsest of lost memories is reinvented, histories are fractured, and the unlike varieties of silence emerge into articulacy" (6).

One can hear Ling, Okihiro, and the basic premise of difference that grounds the project of ethnic studies in this last sentence. What is different about Lowe is that she advocates a postnational cultural practice that, unlike Ling, does not situate the Asian subject between two fixed national cultures and that, unlike Okihiro, does not situate the Asian American subject between the American racial constructions of blackness and whiteness. Okihiro at least emphasizes that American race is a construction and not a natural or predestined state of being. Lowe challenges the structuring assumptions of European Enlightenment thought to situate Asian American subjectivity and culture in a location that, by virtue of exclusion by a historically Eurocentric national culture, is free from the boundaries and constraints of both nationalism and universalism.

Lowe elaborates upon a vision of postnational culture structured not on the unity of the same and the expulsion of the different but on a more varied and plural set of cultural operations that she calls "heterogeneity, hybridity, multiplicity."[7] Lowe stresses heterogeneity, hybridity, and multiplicity in Asian American culture "as part of a twofold argument about cultural politics, the ultimate aim of which is to disrupt the current hegemonic relationship between 'dominant' and 'minority' positions" (1996,

---

7. "Heterogeneity, Hybridity, Multiplicity: Asian American Differences," which appears as the third chapter of *Immigrant Acts,* was originally published in *Diaspora* 1, no. 1 (1991).

66–67). The dominant and minority positions that Lowe refers to are not the white and black of Okihiro's discourse. Lowe does not want to situate Asian Americans between dominant and minority culture. Rather, she wants to dissolve the rhetoric and the power of the system of difference represented by those two symbiotic terms. While Lowe's argument about the heterogeneity of Asian American culture "is part of a strategy to destabilize the dominant discursive construction and determination of Asian Americans as a homogeneous group," she also calls for "a dialogue within Asian American discourse, to point to the limitations inherent in a politics based on cultural, racial, or ethnic identity." Lowe's concern is that Asian American culture is just as invested in nationalism and its habit of definition by exclusion as the dominant national culture under which it exists: "I argue for the Asian American necessity to organize, resist, and theorize *as* Asian Americans, but at the same time, I inscribe this necessity within a discussion of the risks of a cultural politics that relies on the construction of sameness and the exclusion of differences" (68; emphasis in the original). Lowe's placement of the Asian American subject for once situates Asian Americans outside of a between-worlds model and instead places Asian Americans on the side of heterogeneity and difference against the overall culture of dominant and minority nationalism and universalism.

Not everyone in Asian American studies is happy to lose the coherence of national form. Sau-Ling Wong describes the trends inspired by Lowe's work as a "denationalization" that threatens both the cultural and political core of the discipline. Wong worries in "Denationalization Reconsidered" that new trends toward interdisciplinarity and diasporic perspectives will seduce Asian American scholars into an "unwitting subsumption into master narratives" and an uncritical depoliticization of a discipline whose origins are in student radicalism and the activism of minority communities. Wong's critique of the postnational turn in Asian American studies in the mid-1990s divides the phenomenon into three functions: the easing of cultural nationalist concerns, the growing permeability between "Asian" and "Asian American" studies, and the shift from a domestic to a diasporic perspective: "I have found myself raising questions about the consequences of an uncritical participation in denationalization, as if it represented a more advanced and theoretically more sophisticated (in short, superior, though proponents rarely say so directly) stage in Asian American studies" (1995, 12).

Wong's objections contain a distinct trace of professional envy when she describes the postnational or "denational" trend as appearing "to promise novelty, intellectual excitement, delivery from the institutional ghetto of ethnic studies, or even, perhaps, better funding" (1995, 2). Lament over the intrusion of economic interest into the culture of minority knowledge production, however, also marks the boundary between the national racial egalitarianism of ethnic studies and the postnational frontier of global capitalist difference. Wong claims to be arguing from a position of pragmatic political interest: "Not only are one's time and energy for action finite, but whatever claiming one does must be enacted from a political location—one referenced to a political structure, a nation" (19). Wong's essay appeared in *Amerasia Journal* in 1995. The terrorist attacks of September 11, 2001, serve as an accessible contemporary symbol for the obsolescence of Wong's conception of pragmatic locale.

THE POTENTIAL OF RHETORIC

In this chapter, we have explained the emergence and the persistence of the between-worlds trope in two disciplines. In composition studies, the between-worlds trope remains entrenched, first, because influential cognitive models (for example, Vygotsky and Britton) have privileged a middle space between two sites of cognitive development. Likewise, social-political models (for example, Rodriguez, Villanueva, and Gilyard) have privileged a middle space between conflicted sites of culture and oppositional sites of race. Collectively, these models have accommodated and have presumed the notion of an individual's spatial location between two cognitive stages, between two cultural universes, and between two racial worlds. Second, literacy's equation with national citizenship continues to position cross-cultural debates largely within the national border. This spatial location continues to accommodate and reify binary and dehumanizing models of race and national identity that imagine individuals in absolute categories: citizen, alien; self, other; privileged, marginalized. Those who do not fit into one or the other remain, as in the case of Rodriguez's *Hunger of Memory*, caught between worlds. Finally, as we have argued, while the works of Young, Villanueva, Anzaldúa, Canagarajah, and Horner and Trimbur have imagined literacy's place and potential beyond national boundaries, the discipline's history and literacy's shared identity with citizenship continue to resituate our discussions within the national border.

As we have illustrated, despite the move toward a postnational imaginary, the between-worlds trope also remains entrenched in Asian

American studies. Wong's anxiety over the denationalization of Asian American studies is the same root fear that anchors the "between-worlds" trope in current composition studies. Letting go of a stable world, one that depends on the presumption of unity, even if unity is only an illusion, is difficult in any era. The rhetorical and political problem of postnational criticism in the humanities is that it has not yet created an honest and accurate language to describe how humans will occupy and inhabit the space vacated by nationalism. The very phrase "postnational Asian American studies" or "postnational American studies" is contradictory or at least unclear about what the term *American* refers to in the absence of a national frame.

In place of nationalism, one could propose a "global citizenship." However, there is, in reality, no such entity as a global citizen in the same fashion as national citizens. No one state exists that covers the entire globe with a uniform administration of state and citizenship rights. Outside of metaphor, the only citizenship that currently exists on the globe is administered by national governments, none of which is extensive enough, even in federation, to administer the rights and privileges of civil society across the globe. To even the most casual political observer, other institutions easily exceed and surpass the nation in the speed and flexibility of their global reach: capitalism, fundamentalism, terrorism. Thus, with no fully articulated alternative to the discourse of nationalism, the between-worlds trope persists, as do the schisms that we posit between the rigidly defined national borders that we imagine.

In seeking an alternative discourse, we turn to the potential of rhetoric. As Berlin argues, social-epistemic rhetoric locates epistemology at the nexus of thought, linguistic utterance or composition, and social-political context (1987, 165–179). As forms of social-epistemic rhetoric, the works of Young, Anzaldúa, Villanueva, Horner and Trimbur, and Canagarajah are promising because they create new epistemological potential by situating linguistic utterance in conflicted spaces of national identity that, counter to common wisdom, reject presumptions of unity and homogeneity. Lowe's postnational thesis in Asian American studies is also largely rhetorical. Her conception of the cultural subject defies both dominant and minority nationalism. Rhetorically, she attempts to reconfigure the ways in which we imagine nation-states and global relations—to move us from an imagined finite existence to the precarious and provisional reality of hybrid nations and citizenries that are always becoming something other.

THE COMPOSITION AND RHETORIC TEACHER AS COUNTERTERRORIST

Translated into post-9/11 politics, Lowe's subject defies both the imperialist and the insurgent. In an ideal ethical struggle, a campaign like the War against Terror should have a warrior who fights against terror as a tactic rather than terror as simply the term for the actions of the enemy. Her battle is rhetorical. She knows that to a free mind and to a liberal education, the enemy is terror itself.

In composition pedagogy, scholars such as Anzaldúa, Young, Villanueva, Horner and Trimbur, and Canagarajah have pointed us in promising directions toward such liberation. Collectively, they remind us that, certainly, a literate composer writes deftly across many genres and purposes, but a deft composer is not truly literate—in fact, remains impoverished—until she has a full understanding of her medium—that is, the local and global contexts of empire that shape the English language and those who use it. Our dialogue between composition and one branch of ethnic studies is our attempt to add to the conversation that extends the literacy of national citizenship beyond the borders of the nation-state. Such an approach inquires into the ways in which imperialism reveals itself in local contexts of literacy, and how local attitudes toward literacy illuminate one's perception of global conflicts. Such an approach in a writing class would engage students in various tasks of composing while engaging students and teacher alike in a variety of critical inquiries into historical, local, national, and transnational sites where race, power, language, and empire intersect. The dialogue that our chapter has initiated between composition and Asian American studies serves as one potential domain of inquiry that might drive a writing classroom and that would invite, illuminate, and complicate the kinds of textual meshing that the scholars we have cited advocate both in their literacy narratives and in their formal research.

When a writing teacher sits in a class or office and does what liberal education calls teaching, the golden opportunity opens to retire the "between-worlds" trope that creates, formalizes, and freezes the disabling differences of the "different" student. Danling Fu's student newcomers, Tran, Cham, Paw, and Sy, "[s]tanding far from center stage," challenge the literacy of teachers as much as the literacy of teachers challenges them. The teacher's success at the former challenge is integral to the students' success at the latter. The world that is created when a teacher meets a student is not the result of one world's assimilation of the other. It is not even in our thinking an intermediate space or bridge between two worlds. Rather, we argue for seeing this encounter as an opening of possibility in which the oppositions and identities that choke the cultural world have yet to secure their stultifying closures. This instance of potential is where teaching happens and where meaningful composing begins. It is the moment that rhetoric can enter to refigure the discourse of human relations in ways that do not compress the intricacies of transnational flow into the static unities and intransigent oppositions of the between-worlds trope.

REFERENCES

Anzaldúa, Gloria. 1999. *Borderlands/La Frontera.* 2nd ed. San Francisco: Aunt Lute.

Aparicio, Frances R. 2000. Of Spanish Dispossessed. In *Language Ideologies: Critical Perspectives on the Official English Movement,* edited by Roseann Dueñas González and Ildiko Melis. Urbana, IL: National Council of Teachers of English.

Berlin, James. 1987. *Rhetoric and Reality: Writing Instruction in American Colleges, 1900–1985.* Carbondale: Southern Illinois University Press.

Bhabha, Homi. 1994. *The Location of Culture.* London: Routledge.

Britton, James. 1970. *Language and Learning.* Coral Gables: Florida: University of Miami Press.

Canagarajah, A. Suresh. 2006. The Place of World Englishes in Composition: Pluralization Continued. *College Composition and Communication* 57:586–619.

Chan, Jeffery Paul, Frank Chin, Lawson Inada, and Shawn Wong, eds. 1991. *The Big AIIIEEEEE! An Anthology of Chinese American and Japanese American Literature.* New York: Meridian.

Chiang, Yuet-Sim D., and Mary Schmida. 1999. Language Identity and Language Ownership: Linguistic Conflicts of First-Year University Writing Students. In *Generation 1.5 Meets College Composition: Issues in the Teaching of Writing to U.S.-Educated Learners of ESL,* edited by Linda Harklau, Kay M. Losey, and Meryl Siegal. Mahwah, NJ: Lawrence Erlbaum.

Chin, Frank, Jeffrey Chan, Lawson Inada, and Shawn Wong, eds. 1991. *AIIIEEEEE! An Anthology of Asian American Writers.* New York: Mentor. (Orig. pub. 1974).

Cixous, Helene. 1976. The Laugh of the Medusa. Translated by Keith Cohen and Paula Cohen. *Signs* 1 (4): 875–893.

Freire, Paolo. 1970. *Pedagogy of the Oppressed.* New York: Seabury.

Fu, Danling. 1995. *"My Trouble Is My English": Asian Students and the American Dream.* Portsmouth: Heinemann.

Gilyard, Keith. 1991. *Voices of the Self: A Study of Language Competence.* Detroit: Wayne State University Press.

Heath, Shirley Brice. 1983. *Ways with Worlds: Language, Life, and Work in Communities and Classrooms.* Cambridge: Cambridge University Press.

Horner, Bruce, and John Trimbur. 2003. English Only and U.S. College Composition. *College Composition and Communication* 53:594–630.

Ling, Amy. 1990. *Between Worlds: Women Writers of Chinese Ancestry.* New York: Pergamon.

Lowe, Lisa. 1996. *Immigrant Acts: On Asian American Cultural Politics.* Durham, NC: Duke University Press.

Mah y Busch, Juan. 2005. Gloria Evangelina Anzaldúa. In *Latino and Latina Writers,* edited by Alan West-Durán. New York: Charles Scribner's Sons.

Okihiro, Gary Y. 1994. *Margins and Mainstreams: Asians in American History and Culture.* Seattle and London: University of Washington Press.

Petersen, William. 1966. Success Story, Japanese-American Style. *New York Times Magazine,* January 9, 20–21, 33, 36, 38, 40–41, 43.

Prasad, Vijay. 2006. Ethnic Studies Inside Out. *Journal of Asian American Studies* (June): 157–176.

Pratt, Mary Louise. 1991. Arts of the Contact Zone. *Profession* 91:33–40.

Rodriguez, Richard. 1983. *Hunger of Memory.* New York: Bantam.

Said, Edward. 1978. *Orientalism.* New York: Vintage.

———. 1993. *Culture and Imperialism.* New York: Alfred A. Knopf.

Schmid, Carol. 2000. The Politics of English Only in the United States: Historical, Social, and Legal Aspects. In *Language Ideologies: Critical Perspectives on the Official English Movement,* edited by Roseann Dueñas González with Ildiko Melis. Urbana, IL: National Council of Teachers of English.

Success Story of One Minority in the U.S. 1966. *U.S. News and World Report,* December 26, 73–78.

Takaki, Ronald. 1989. Myth of the "Model Minority." In *Strangers from a Different Shore: A History of Asian Americans.* New York: Penguin.

Villanueva, Victor Jr. 1993. *Bootstraps: From an American Academic of Color.* Urbana, IL: National Council of Teachers of English.

———. 2004. Memoria Is a Friend of Ours: On the Discourse of Color. *College English* 67 (1): 9–19.

Vygotsky, L. M. 1978. *Mind in Society: The Development of Higher Psychological Processes.* Cambridge, MA: Harvard University Press.

Wei, William. 1993. *The Asian American Movement.* Philadelphia: Temple University Press.

Wong, Sau-Ling C. 1995. Denationalization Reconsidered: Asian American Cultural Criticism at a Theoretical Crossroads. *Amerasia Journal* 21 (1–2): 1–27.

Young, Morris. 2004. *Minor Re/Visions: Asian American Literacy Narratives as a Rhetoric of Citizenship.* Carbondale: Southern Illinois University Press.

Zhou, Min, and James V. Gatewood, eds. 2000. *Contemporary Asian America: A Multidisciplinary Reader.* New York and London: New York University Press.

3

ASIAN AMERICAN RHETORICAL MEMORY AND A "MEMORY THAT IS ONLY SOMETIMES OUR OWN"

Haivan V. Hoang

We have a memory of water. Ankle deep, back bent by the sun, verdant fields. Shallow basins, eyes sealed with tears, ornate cathedrals. Salt water shrouds, lips cracked, silent flotillas. We have a memory of water. A memory that is only sometimes our own.

Barbara Tran, Monique T. D. Truong, and Luu Truong Khoi, *Watermark: Vietnamese American Poetry and Prose*

Memory (the deliberate act of remembering) is a form of willed creation. It is not an effort to find out the way it really was—that is research. The point is to dwell on the way it appeared and why it appeared that way.

Toni Morrison, "Memory, Creation, and Writing"

The willful desire to claim a "memory that is only sometimes our own," the unremitting imperative to rearticulate cultural memory, is fundamental to Asian American rhetoric.

In early March 2000, a struggle over memory—who remembers, what gets remembered, and to what effect—pressed Asian American activists to protest against Senator John McCain's reference to "gooks." While campaigning for the Republican presidential nomination, McCain recalled his years as a Vietnam War prisoner of war and referred to North Vietnamese soldiers as "gooks." Criticism of his use of a racial slur ensued, and the news media that followed McCain's Straight Talk Express bus gave the story brief treatment. Was McCain repentant? No, he was entitled to his memory and speech. The *New York Times* quoted him on February 18: "I will continue to refer to them in language that might offend some people here, because of their beating and killing and torture of my friends. I hated the gooks and I will hate them for as long as I live." A few more days passed before he apologized, but the apology felt delayed, even reluctant. When the Straight Talk Express bus rolled into southern California's Little Saigon in March, an Asian American student activist organized a protest in order to counter McCain's racialization of the Vietnamese prison guards. What was at stake was a contest over cultural memory—a struggle between McCain's understanding of "gook" as a personal memory (and perhaps also a nationalist one), on the one hand, and the activists' recall of the word from cultural memories that have effectively racialized Asians and Asian Americans, on the other.

The Asian American need to *re*member the American imaginary with Asian American peoples is poetically declared by the Vietnamese American writers of *Watermark*: "We have a memory of water" (Tran, Truong, and Khoi 1998, 224). If we understand that the Vietnamese word for "water" (*nuóc*) also means "nation," the declaration becomes a claim to not only a Vietnamese American memory, but also a national memory. Quite simply, memory is central to Asian American rhetoric, a rejoinder to the persistent forgetfulness that displaces Asian Americans from commonplace understandings of what is American and also an opening up that fosters the "willed creation" of Asian American solidarity. Asian American rhetorical memory, then, has most often articulated *counter*memories that destabilize and then reconstitute the American subject.

And yet, even though it is clear that activist racial projects since the 1960s and '70s yellow power movement have been about recovering and claiming entitlement to cultural memories, important questions remain: What is the nature of a *rhetorical* memory in Asian American cultural production? What recollecting practices could Asian American speakers and writers use to shake up an objective notion of cultural memory and also appreciate the lived realities that make up Asian American history?

In this essay, I wish to throw light on the ways the protest and, more importantly, the protest organizer Duc's later recollection of the conflict register larger concerns surrounding rhetorical memory: the conditions that call up Asian American rhetoric, the struggles over entitlement to memory, and the strategic and layered recall of past Asian American experiences. Duc, then a local university student who belonged to a political student organization called the Vietnamese American Coalition

(VAC), told me about the protests in an interview during my 2002 ethnographic case study of VAC's activist rhetoric.[1]

As he wove together the "gook" utterance amid multiple cultural memories, the fabric of his memory work became important to making meaning of the utterance. Notably, what makes his performance of rhetorical memory possible is earlier advocacy for Asian Americans' right to participate in cultural memory work. In what follows, I begin with a discussion of the renewed interest in memory within Asian American studies and rhetorical studies since the 1960s and, drawing on this rhetorical heritage, I then read Duc's narrative closely. By studying his rhetoric as a performance of long-embattled claims to memory that have been building momentum in the last half century, we can glimpse the ways rhetorical memory shifts in relation to changing racial constructions of Asian Americans. These shifts are not simply about archaeological shifts to different memorial *objects* but, more so, the epistemological shifts that guide the *practice* of how to remember. In this post–civil rights movement moment, as Duc's recall so aptly illustrates, Asian American memory production involves threading together plural memories among plural *loci* and cultivating a related appreciation for *copia*. To be sure, such rhetorical production of Asian American memory is instructive to our understanding of memory as rhetorical art and social engagement.

RENEWED INTEREST IN THE RHETORICAL ART OF MEMORY

Memory is surely no stranger to rhetorical or related cultural studies. In fact, with the oft-cited "social turn" of the 1960s, memory saw renewed interest from rhetorical studies, ethnic studies, literary theory, philosophy, anthropology, history, and sociology.[2] The inquiry has grown, in part, as a result of concerted efforts to lend value to marginalized

1. The interview with Duc is part of a larger ethnographic case study conducted in the spring and summer of 2002; see Hoang (2004). (The study received IRB [Institutional Review Board] exemption approval, and all participants signed informed consent forms. While pseudonyms are used for the participants, the VAC students suggested that I use the actual name of the student organization.

2. For a discussion of the development of memory in classical Greek and Roman rhetoric, medieval monastic culture, and the mimetic memory of modern scientific inquiry, see the following: Yates 1966;. Havelock 1986; Carruthers 1990; Reynolds 1993; Crowley 1993; Francoz 1999. Moreover, memorial recovery has generated inquiry across the humanities and social sciences: in Asian American studies, Chan 1991; in African American literary studies, Fabre and O'Meally 1994; in anthropology, Climo and Catell 2002; in history, Nora 1989; Kammen 1997; Matsuda 1996; and in philosophy, Margalit 2002.

voices and to complicate dominant histories: What memories have been suppressed? Which memories are legitimated and why? For the Asian American movement in the 1960s and '70s, the conscious remembering of past Asian American realities played a large part in that historical moment's activism, and it is on the shoulders of these activist scholars that Asian Americans like Duc and I stand. As important as the movement's memory work has been to our understanding of Asian American racial formation, these early approaches to memory problematically tended less toward the rhetorical and more toward what Sharon Crowley describes as "methodical memory," or the modern preference for objective representation (1990). Such methodical memory ironically risked reifying racial categories while critiquing that same racialization. Still, these and related energetic efforts to "dwell" are important, as they have resulted in fruitful inquiry into the practice of rhetorical memory in the decades since the 1960s.

Early Activism for Asian American Engagement in Cultural Memory

Not surprisingly, calls for cultural memory were prominent in the Asian American movement, which was more broadly about claiming a politicized Asian American identity that challenged the juridical, pseudo-scientific, and cultural racialization of Asian American bodies—named Mongol, Oriental, Asiatic, and yellow peril—reiterated in the United States at least since the nineteenth century. The 1960s appropriation of the race-based identity "Asian American" marked an unprecedented coalition whose formation, in turn, led to a political rhetoric. For the movement's activists, the purpose of recollection was to attend to past Asian American realities as well as challenge the persistent forgetting of the historical processes that have made Asian Americans a racial Other. After all, as Jacqueline Jones Royster and Jean C. Williams argue in "Histories in the Spaces Left," exclusionary histories distort our "interpretive frameworks" (1999, 564); Asian Americans continue to be read as the "foreigner-within" (Lowe 1996); our contributions to America are made inconsequential; and racial injustices are obscured by constructions of Asian Americans as race-neutral ethnics.[3]

Early in the movement, Asian American memory work was about challenging distorted representations of history and recovering Asian

3. Michael Omi and Howard Winant (1994, chapter 1), for example, discuss the difficulties in attending to ethnicity in the United States without recognizing historical processes of racial formation.

American experiences. *Roots: An Asian American Reader*, published through UCLA in 1971, was one early effort at this kind of recovery (Tachiki, Wong, and Odo). A collection of sociological and historical academic essays as well as a "contemporary expression of the Asian American condition by the people themselves," *Roots* was meant to be read as "a documentary of our time" (vii). Editor Franklin Odo wrote that *Roots* signified the dual purpose of "going to the 'roots' of the issues facing Asians in America" and discussing how "our 'roots' go deep into the history of the United States . . . [to] explain who and what we are and how we became this way" (vii-viii). He continued, "Disregarding or misinterpreting the background of the particular group is one of the most important reasons for the failure to make meaningful changes in the ethnic community" (ix). The emphasis on uncovering "roots," recording a "documentary collection," and making accurate interpretations suggests that the editors would tell the *real* story. Similarly, over a decade later, Elaine H. Kim's 1982 *Asian American Literature: An Introduction to the Writings and Their Social Context* was another first—the first book-length entry into Asian American literary scholarship—that was to remove distortions from cultural memory. Asian American literature, she explained, must be understood within "sociohistorical and cultural contexts . . . because, when these contexts are unfamiliar, the literature is likely to be misunderstood and unappreciated" (xv). Such statements presuppose that there is a true understanding and appreciation of Asian American literature.

Memory in *Roots* and *Asian American Literature* was to serve as a corrective to the prevailing dismissal of Asian American culture, but in this way, both Odo and Kim risked adopting not a rhetorical but a modern understanding of memory. The problem with a modern social realism approach to Asian American culture is that such approaches may reify an authentic and unchanging Asian American identity and history and thus trouble the writers' critique of existing overdetermined constructions of Asian Americans. Sharon Crowley's *The Methodical Memory: Invention in Current-Traditional Rhetoric* (1990) is instructive in understanding the prevalence of modern memory. She explains that only in relatively recent history has memory become arhetorical, an objective representation of past reality. During modernism, rhetorical practices were heavily influenced by efforts to advance scientific inquiry and reason, and memory assumed a positivist epistemology. Memorizing began with sensory perception, recall entailed accurate investigations of reality, and language would accurately translate the memory. Perhaps because *Roots* and *Asian American Literature* were firsts, an appeal to modern representation could be attributed to the need to strategically legitimize such perspectives within academe, especially when Asian American studies was in its infancy. Or perhaps such texts only appeared to offer true representations because there were few to no related texts against which one might destabilize the category of Asian American. Regardless, these early subversions of cultural memory offered a crucial springboard for the growth of an Asian American *rhetorical* memory that would seek not simply to uncover, but moreover to articulate cultural memories and to interpret the ways such articulations mediate our understandings of memories.

Rhetorical Memory and an Appreciation for Copia

Indeed, as many scholars across disciplines have engaged in memory, it has become clearer that the concept of memory as a rhetorical art requires deeper understanding. Memory, according to anthropologists Jacob Climo and Maria Catell, is marked by "imprecision of concept" and "lack of theoretical development" (2002, 5). Moreover, rhetoricians John Frederick Reynolds and Kathleen Welch separately contend that the art of memory requires clarification in terms of its form, production, interpretation, and social life (Reynolds 1993a; Welch 1993). Long before the modern emphasis on scientific inquiry, classical rhetoricians had heralded memory as the custodian of all the canons of rhetoric. By juxtaposing the unlikely pairing of classical and medieval rhetoric, on the one hand, and Sucheng Chan's 1991 *Asian Americans: An Interpretive History* and David Palumbo-Liu's 1999 *Asian/American: Historical Crossings of a Racial Frontier*, on the other, I suggest that we might arrive at a working understanding of rhetorical memory in general and Asian American rhetorical memory in particular.

While most students of the western rhetorical tradition call to mind ancient mnemonic exercises when considering memory, it is important to understand that the art of memory was selective, crafted, and textured. Mary Carruthers's *The Book of Memory*, a study of medieval monastic memory and its classical rhetorical heritage, offers an impressive theoretical articulation of memory's social life. To begin, the practice of gathering memories started with introspective investigation, which Albertus Magnus called "the 'tracking down' (*investigatio*) of what has been 'set aside' (*obliti*) through and by means of memory" (Carruthers 1990, 20). Such recollection calls up not the real-world referent but the memorial symbols, thus relying on a complex system of signification. "Because it recalls signs," Carruthers writes, "reminiscence is an act of interpretation, inference, investigation, and reconstruction, an act like reading" (25). And an act like writing.

But this only began the process that made memory public. Gathering memories was a composition process, refined through copia and suitability to the occasion. Copia, in particular, was the measure of good memory, referring to the abundant layering of memories. The point was not, as in modernism, to retrieve a single accurate memory. Rather, copious recollection meant weaving together memories in order to produce a plural and textured composition. Finally, "[p]ublic memory," elaborates Carruthers, "is a needed ethical resource for its contents to complete the edifice of each individual's memory" (1990, 185). Just as the public would complete the individual, individuals had the civic and moral responsibility to share their memorial compositions in public realms. This meant that, in composing, rhetors should tailor memorial compositions for their intended audience and speaking occasion. The social nature of memory was basic to medieval rhetoric, for "[a]n author who does not share his work and launch it, as it were, into the stream of literature is thought to be guilty of a sin against community" (208). Memory, then, was essential to the creating and sustaining of cultural heritage and community identity. In sum, the art of memory was traditionally about thoughtfully investigating memorial signs, interweaving memories, and thereby engaging the public to which one belonged.

For scholars like Sucheng Chan and David Palumbo-Liu, Asian American recollection has proceeded with an investigation of memorial traces across not only mental loci but the cultural sites tied up with Asian American history. The term "cultural memory," for Winifred Horner, refers to the institutions that house memory (e.g., libraries, schools, popular media) (Reynolds 1993a, 11). But given our histories, Asian American scholars have grown increasingly interested in the national and transnational sites that become sites of cultural memory. Chan's *Asian Americans: An Interpretive History*, for instance, illustrates the ways Asian American rhetorical memory is mapped onto the cultural sites of migration. Rather than begin the Asian American history with the commonplace of immigration experiences in the United States, she recenters the history on the emigration-immigration hyphen and cautions that her narrative is "an interim effort" and "interpretive"; the history thereby creates an opening for additional memorial work (1991, xiii-xiv).

Palumbo-Liu's *Asian/American: Historical Crossings of a Racial Frontier* more emphatically focuses on memorial practices that migrate among national and transnational cultural sites. He writes, "[T]he role of memory becomes increasingly significant, as individuals and groups trace their relation to place, even as those traces may be covered over or erased, overlaid with different memories or claims to possession, as well as with memories and histories from different lands that have been brought over as part of the psychic makeup of dispossessed peoples and which constitute an irredactable perceptual grid through which the diasporic landscape is read" (1999, 218).

The attention to multiple places with historical layers invigorates the production of *plural* memories, and this "irredactable" performance of copia gives texture, dispelling the authority of any single memory. In fact, Palumbo-Liu suggests that it is this preference for copia that makes architect Maya Lin's design of the Vietnam War Memorial so powerful; that is, "the abstract memorial rejects the literalizing and therefore stabilizing and codifying function of the realistic memorial" (1999, 252).

Together, the memorial work practiced among these Asian American scholars indicates a shared interest in rememorializing Asian American racial formation in the United States and, at the same time, provides a glimpse into the complexity of memory work. The memorial imperative among "yellow power" activists led to authentic representations of Asian American experience that could offset a naturalized conception of Asian Americans as foreigners. But as Morrison emphasizes, memory is a deliberate act—not only recovery but also production, *copious* production. For Asian Americans, whose histories are formed through the transnational ties among Asia and the United States, an investigation into memory entails journeying through the cultural sites of memory (whether those sites are institutions, specific locales, or nations) and knitting together these memorial traces; this memory work weaves together Asian American heritage. Moreover, Asian American rhetorical memory, the *copious* (even if contradictory) investigation across cultural sites, demands tailoring to particular social conditions and moments. It is this rhetorical art that we see among the Asian American activists in the "American Gook" protest.

RECOLLECTING "GOOK" THROUGH ASIAN AMERICAN MEMORIES

Recollecting "gook" critically requires an investigation into how past uses of the sign could impact its present (and future) meaning, and the Asian American activist leading the protest was armed with both an Asian American studies background and rhetorical agility. Duc was an undergraduate student at a southern California university when, in 2000, newspapers were reporting that Senator John McCain, a contender for the Republican presidential nomination and a former Vietnam War POW, was initially unapologetic about calling former North Vietnamese prison guards "gooks." An apology did in fact come. *Washington Post* writer Rajiv Chandrasekaran reported on February 28: "'I will continue to condemn those who unfairly mistreated us,' McCain said. 'But out of respect to a great number of people whom I hold in very high regard, I will no longer use the term that has created such discomfort. I deeply regret any pain I have caused . . . I apologize and renounce all language that is bigoted and offensive'" (2000). The apology and the protests that followed embody competing readings of the cultural memories surrounding "gook," and this is evident in the sharp disparity between McCain's representational memory and Duc's rhetorical memory.

No doubt, McCain's reliance on a modern representational understanding of memory directly contrasted with Duc's stated belief in the creative capacity of memory and the ways memories require critical interpretation. McCain composed memories in order to represent his experiences, calling up memories of war (recalling abuses), camaraderie (remembering his military friends), and new alliances (listening to South Vietnamese POWs memories). By recollecting his military service in the war and objecting to the abuses he endured, he effectively created alliances with U.S. veterans as well as many anticommunist Vietnamese Americans who shared his disdain for the North Vietnamese military. To a large extent, his rhetoric worked, in that his controversial statements were treated briefly, and in fact, an article in the *San Francisco Chronicle*, one day after the protest, proclaimed, "Little Saigon Opens Arms for McCain; Vietnamese Americans Dismiss His Use of Slur," noting that the senator was "flanked onstage by nearly a dozen former Vietnamese soldiers who also were POWs" (Marinucci 2000).

It is worth noting, however, that while McCain's statements were rhetorical in terms of speaking to the cultural expectations of his audience, his treatment of *memory* was positivist. The apology and his "straight talk" mantra indicate a modern representational conception of language. That is, McCain adopted a modern epistemology, one that thwarted the possibility of his understanding the rhetorical construction and impact of his utterance. With his brand of "straight talk," he suggested that "gook" was an objective signifier that referred only to specific prison guards who imprisoned him for five and a half years, not all Asians. He could maintain his "hate" because his apology suggested that the problem was his audience's "discomfort." Rather, I would argue that the problem went beyond the immediate exchange between speaker and audience—the problem was that each iteration of a racial epithet continues to reproduce a culture in which racializing is the norm. McCain, however, believed that the word applied only to the intended referent (specific prison guards) and to his personal memories, but for activists, the use of "gook" was tangled up in a cultural memory of American racial violence. Neither McCain's apology nor his recollection of military service acknowledged the legacy of racism and racial violence cued by the word. Asian American activists were jarred by McCain's insistent use of a racial slur, so when the senator's campaign visited southern California's Little Saigon (the largest Vietnamese American community in the country), Duc had marked "American Gook" on T-shirts and organized a protest rally.

In contrast to McCain, who characterized "gook" in purely modern representational language that recalled his war trauma, Duc recalled the word's copious meanings. Duc fervently recounted his memory of the "American Gook" protest in an interview for me two years later in 2002. By then, he was a fourth-year undergraduate majoring in political science who had been active in the Vietnamese American Coalition for several years. As a poet, a political science major, and an Asian American student activist, he understood that to remember is to create, and Asian American rhetorical memory played into the copious ways he traced past uses of "gook."

Duc began his account by recalling how he, then a student leader in VAC, had difficulty persuading other officers to challenge McCain. In this telling, he placed the word "gook" among multiple memorial traces, ranging from McCain's utterance to hate crimes that took place in 1982 and 1996, from the Vietnam War to California's Little Saigon community.

Duc: I went up to the cabinet members, and I said, "Oh, please be out here, you know, we need the numbers." And cabinet members, mostly guys, said, "We have an intramural basketball game that night." So, they can't be out there, right? Because they're playing an intramural basketball game.

HH: How did you describe this issue to them? Or did they already know?

Duc: They pretty much knew. And if they didn't, I told them that, you know, it's, it's wrong. We can't allow a public figure, any public figures, anybody that has influence upon people to use that kind of language, to use the term so casually.

And to convince our community that gook equals communist?

Because it does not. And how Vincent Chin was killed because of racial slurs and anti-people-of-color sentiment? Thien Minh Ly, you know, our own Vietnamese American brother who was killed. And how racial slurs dehumanize people and lead to hate crimes.

If VAC claims to be a political organization and represent the community, we *have* to be out there.

The word "gook," like most words, has many memorial traces that index past uses and varied signification. But what makes Duc's discourse an instance of rhetorical memory is his persuasive stitching together of a series of seemingly disparate moments and cultural sites. Each recalled moment or site contributes to a memorial composition whose sum is greater than all its parts and whose effectiveness becomes a catalyst for the group's response to McCain.

To begin, Duc called up McCain's "gook" utterance in order to reread its rhetorical impact. What McCain overlooked was what the Asian American protesters knew too well: memory confers significance on signs, especially charged ones like "gook." By identifying McCain as a "public figure," Duc not only commented on the reach and authority of McCain's speech, but also read the public figure as embodying the state, itself a site of cultural memory. McCain's representational approach to language results in a "memory that is only sometimes our own," and, in this way, the state is a site that contains struggle over cultural memories. Duc then presented a series of fragments ("*and* to . . ." ; "and how . . ." ; "and how . . .") that place the meaning of "gook" in other sites and thus destabilize McCain's statement that "gook" referred only to the North Vietnamese soldiers who kept him imprisoned.

Turning from a focus on a McCain-centered memory of war, the fragment that follows foregrounds the Vietnam War but shifts the emphasis from military conflict to the present-day Little Saigon community: "*And* to convince our community that gook equals communist?" For many in the diasporic community, "communist" signaled not simply the soldiers who imprisoned McCain but the phantom object of resentment in Little Saigon. The result was that McCain had many supporters in Little Saigon who did not know about, who forgave, or who condoned his use of "gook" to describe the North Vietnamese. Veterans of the South Vietnamese military literally stood beside him onstage during the political rally. In fact, some attendees cathected so strongly with McCain they spat on Duc and his fellow protesters, yelling, "Communist!" an incident I'll detail in the next section. But by centering the Vietnamese American community within this war reference, Duc recentered "gook" within the cultural memory of the Vietnamese American immigrant and American-born community, and he argued that this local ethnic community needed to reject such racializing language. This memorial trace begins to unseat the primacy of McCain's memories without necessarily disregarding his experiences.

Threading together these traces of "gook" into the memories of McCain's rhetoric and the diasporic community, Duc's memorial investigation turned to two other uses of racial epithets against Asian Americans, hate crimes where racial epithets aggravated and even encouraged interracial violence: the murders of Vincent Chin in 1982 and Thien Minh Ly in 1996. Vincent Chin was a victim of hate crime memorialized in the documentary *Who Killed Vincent Chin?* (Choy 1988). In 1982, in the midst of anti-Japanese attitudes resulting from the depressed auto industry in Michigan, a white employee from Chrysler and his son beat a Chinese American man to death with a baseball bat. The documentary introduces the conflict as beginning with the murderers' comments about Chin's race, which they erroneously assumed was Japanese. The more recent case of Vietnamese American Thien Minh Ly, in 1996, was also a hate crime framed by racial epithets. Gunner Lindberg and his friend beat, stomped, and stabbed Ly, a twenty-four-year-old who was rollerblading near a community tennis court in California. Greg Hernandez's "Grisly Account of Ly Killing Believed Penned by Suspect" in the March 7, 1996, issue of the *Los Angeles Times* reported that Lindberg wrote in a letter to a friend in prison, "'Oh, I killed a jap a while ago" and detailed how he had killed Ly. Hernandez continues, "In a four-page letter filled with casual mentions of birthday plans, a friend's new baby, and the need for new tattoos, Gunner J. Lindberg may have also laid out a murder confession that led police directly to his door in their search for the killer of the 24–year-old Ly."

Duc layered these racially motivated crimes in his recall of McCain's "gook" statements and thereby foregrounded the ways language racializes. These threads point to the violent anger directed against Asians and Asian Americans, as in Chin's case, and the casual dehumanizing of Asians and Asian Americans, as in Ly's case. Moreover, the threads of these memories weave back into McCain's own anger against the North Vietnamese "gooks" and his own casual use of the racial slur. Those who have seen the documentary *Who Killed Vincent Chin?* know that the atrocities of Chin's murder resulted in a national Asian American movement, indicating that racism was a national phenomenon and not the aberration of two men. The trial against Chin's murderers resulted in a three-year probation and a $3,000 finc. The ease with which two men could beat to death a Chinese American and get away with it sparked a national controversy, eventually leading to a civil rights case against the men, but both were exonerated. By alluding to this famous case, Duc invoked the Asian American activism that grew out of the trial and activists' efforts to organize against injustice.

The fabric of his recollection knits together traces of a public figure's rhetoric about war trauma, the Little Saigon community's ambivalence over Vietnamese communists, and the place of "gook" within cultural memories of hate crime—all of which seamlessly lead to Duc's final critique: "how racial slurs dehumanize people and lead to hate crimes." The composition therefore calls up a troubling association between racial slurs and hate-driven racial violence, an association that recasts McCain's war trauma in terms of the dehumanizing effects of "gookism" in the Vietnam War. According to Asian American movement scholar William Wei, the term was first used during the Philippine-American War (1899–1902) to name Filipinos with no mix of European heritage. Later, "the appellation has been applied to Haitians, Nicaraguans, Costa Ricans, and other people of color, but since the Korean War it has been used mainly by U.S. soldiers to denigrate Asian people. It implied that they were in the Vietnam War to prepare soldiers to psychologically maim and kill Southeast Asians, according to some Asian American veterans" (1993, 38). "Gookism" encouraged a psychology of racism and racial violence, but the increasing popularity of "gookism" in the late 1960s helped awaken an Asian American critical consciousness.

With this memory of "gookism," we are left with a troubling understanding of McCain's utterance, which Duc suggests continues the hateful racialization of Asian Americans. As Duc explained, "We can't allow a public figure, any public figures, anybody that has influence upon people to use that kind of language, to use the term 'gook' so casually. And to convince our community that 'gook' equals 'communist' because it does not." He was concerned that a public figure's use of a racial slur could perpetuate ongoing normalization of racializing language. Largely ignoring the memories of Vietnamese Americans and other Asian Americans, he argued, would harm our communities, aggravating the anger, violence, and dehumanization of Asian Americans. Indeed, Duc was not alone. In the March 5, 2000, issue of the *New York Times*, Anthony Ramirez writes that the controversy "flared and faded within a few days," but critiques of McCain's statement continued online. For instance, Ramirez quotes Jocilyn Dong's post to an Asian American journalists forum, "The English language is rife with words to express a former P.O.W.'s feelings toward the men who tortured him . . . [b]ut the slur he's sticking to is the racial one. Not one that zeroes in on the unconscionable cruelty of his enemies, but one that expresses hatred of 'differentness'—skin color, facial features, culture." And he cites a participant in another online forum who asked whether there would be a greater public outcry if McCain had fought in Somalia and used racial epithets to refer to Somalian soldiers.

Duc's protest against McCain's utterance teaches us that rhetorical memory can account for how the memorial sign had recurred within plural contextual memories and how writers and speakers frame signs within these contexts. Imploring his peers to take action, Duc juxtaposed copious memorial traces that decentered McCain and McCain's part in authorizing harmful conceptions of Asian Americans. This composition traversed memorial sites that are significant to historical processes of Asian American racial formation: McCain's statements on the 2000 campaign trail; the internally conflicted Little Saigon community; racial hate crimes against Vincent Chin and Thien Minh Ly; racialization during the Vietnam War; *and* the university site where Duc persuaded his peers to act. Importantly, the memorial traces did not cancel one another. Their simultaneous part in the composition worked to destabilize the primacy of any one memory. At the nexus of student activists and a prominent politician, bullhorns and mass media, grassroots protest and electoral politics, this case of Asian American rhetorical memory makes palpable memory's inseparability from ideological and social concerns. What divided McCain's perspective from the Asian American protester's perspective was not necessarily the simple question of whose memory was "right"; rather, the protest happened due to struggles over memorial entitlement and also conflicts between their understandings of memory as representational or rhetorical.

ENGAGING THE PUBLIC WITH MEMORY

As important as these memorial investigations were to recasting McCain's reference to "gooks," what mattered most to Duc was engaging the Vietnamese American community. Reflecting on the protest, he told me, "We were there to educate them." Whereas Duc began discussing the protest by focusing on the argument he offered to his peers in the Vietnamese American Coalition, he then turned my attention to the dramatic events of the protest. In addition to employing copia through his memorial investigation of the word "gook," he now employed copia by reframing the event in plural ways, each time calling attention to social interaction. His first account of the protest is framed by a conversation with his student organization and located at an educational site. His copious recounting continues with multiple frames and thus takes us to three other cultural sites of memory, all literally offstage: the protest site in Little Saigon; the site of the activists' discourse community; and the street-side contact zone of activists, opponents to the activists, and the police. These memorial reframings and Duc's movement among the cultural sites highlight the importance that he placed on social engagement and shared cultural production with his audience.

Duc's memorial account traveled to a different cultural site with each reframing, first as the persuasive dialogue with fellow VAC students discussed above. Drawing on the same memorial premises, he then reframed the narrative as a persuasive speech event in the Little Saigon rally:

> I spoke in Vietnamese on the, on the bullhorn . . . to the people at the rally, and I was explaining it to them in Vietnamese. I was saying how this term is unacceptable, how terms like this lead to hate crimes and murders, and I brought up Thien Minh Ly. I brought up how people can't tell the difference between a Vietnamese commie, or, or VC, and you or I.
>
> They were listening. They were listening. And we were rallying, too. I got, I got the bullhorn, and I was like, "Are you a gook?" to those people who were there to support McCain. And they were actually on our side. You know, we were rallying, you know?

Moving from the first site of the university student organization, he called attention to the protest site as a dynamic engagement. With the university site, Duc spent relatively more time arguing about investigating "gook" as a memorial sign, and he framed all this with an explanation of VAC officers' need for politicization. By contrast, with the protest site, Duc spent relatively less time on the premises of his argument and more time on the audience's participation. By stressing he was speaking Vietnamese in the excerpt above and several other moments in the interview and by stressing the audience's involvement, Duc emphasized that his argument was not directed at McCain so much as it was directed at the Vietnamese community members who had shown up in support of McCain. He was encouraged by community members' support for the protesters' efforts, being informed of what McCain had said and being persuaded that it was harmful. We experience not just a shift in our lens but a shift in audience.

Then, he moves us *within* the discourse community of his fellow Asian American activists when recalling a conversation he had with a disillusioned friend:

> And another thing I remember from that was a friend of mine. Everyone was really upset at the reaction from . . . the people who were Vietnamese American who went to rally in support of McCain. And one of my friends got so upset, and he, he was telling me that we just need to wait until they, being older Vietnamese Americans who don't understand or whatever, to die. And I was like, my God.

Here, Duc turned away from his audience to a fellow protester, distracted by his friend's missing the point of engaging the community. The friend, he told me, believed that only when the first-generation Vietnamese Americans—those who support McCain and continue to resent communists—die out will the entire community progress. Duc's response is telling:

> That made me very angry. That made me extremely angry. And I was trying to tell him, "No. That's not it." Because we were there to educate them, you know? We were there to educate the community. We didn't know the media was going to be, like, swarming around us.

Through these triply reframed accounts, we understand the multiple participants involved in this event: Duc and other activists, VAC student leaders, Vietnamese American community members, and a disillusioned friend. McCain, in fact, has little agency in these accounts and retreats into the background of Duc's telling. What mattered most to Duc was building solidarity with the Vietnamese American community.

The focus on offstage cultural sites decenters McCain's onstage presence, suggesting that Duc was more interested in community activism *for* the community rather than *against* McCain. For Duc, the protest was about the social effect of McCain's "gook" utterance. The community members present could respond in at least two ways: McCain and his audience would read "gook" as something innocuous, what a patriotic war hero and political authority had uttered. Or, Duc and fellow activists meant to foster social involvement, a dialogue between themselves and the Vietnamese community, in order to claim agency over the memorial sign of "gook" and its historical resonance. He urged that Asian and Asian Americans had historically been tangled up in "gookism," and, moreover, he was trying to share the memorial traces of "gookism" with the ethnic community. As philosopher Avishai Margalit aptly explains, "The significance of the event for us depends on our being personally connected with what happened, and hence we share not only the memory of what happened but also our participation in it" (2002, 53). In this sense, Duc aimed to increase community members' participation in claiming agency over "gook" as a sign with a memory. These ideas came to a head in the final cultural site within his account: a contact zone among Duc and fellow activists, opponents to the activists, and police.

In a dramatic conflict between Duc and an audience member who opposed the Asian American students' activist stance, memory became a cultural affair where Duc's purpose was to have the community jointly call attention to the harmfulness of the term "gook." Duc explained that some opposition members in the audience had started calling him and fellow protesters "communists," with the rationale that if they were opposing McCain, a former prisoner of war, then they must be communists. With the protest taking place in the commercial center of Little Saigon, to which people had fled because of North Vietnamese persecution and violence, the allegation of being "commies" had heavy consequences. The crowd became violent, pushing the protesters into oncoming traffic:

Duc: All of a sudden, it became a whole crowd of people. I don't know h—. All of a sudden, just instantly. They started *pushing* us. And then, like, a lot of my friends kind of protected me as I continued to speak. *(laughs)* And . . . and I was continuing my little spiel.

Yeah, and then we started chanting, you know. And then they continued to push us. And they poked us and they pinched us and people spat on us and they threw stuff at us.

And they pushed us into oncoming traffic on Bolsa Avenue.
And at the same time, while that was all happening—
When we first started rallying, you know, all the cameras are pointed onto the stage, onto that media press thing up high, I guess bleachers or whatever. . . .
And all of the cameras turned around. And all of a sudden, it was a mixture of people poking us and spitting on us and throwing stuff at us and yelling at us and saying we were commies and going like that *(shoots an angry stare).*

HH: In English or in Vietnamese?

Duc: In Vietnamese *and* in English. I spoke in English, too. And we weren't all Vietnamese Americans, you know. There were Japanese Americans, Filipino Americans, you know. There were Chinese Americans.

HH: Mostly college students?

Duc: Yeah, mostly students from [the university]. And a lot of people I didn't even know who got the flyer and, "Hey, you know, totally, we'll be out there" and whatever. And they showed up.
And they pushed, they pushed all of us. Some guy got arrested for, he was running, running at me to knock me over, whatever. He didn't get me, but a cop arrested him. And then we started chanting, "Do not arrest him."

HH: Why is that?

Duc: My reason was he just didn't understand. He was my same age, you know, and we could easily talk to him and he could easily understand us and easily identify why we shouldn't allow McCain to use this word or to be unapologetic about using it.

Despite the fact that a man was charging him, Duc remained steadfast in his intention to communicate with rather than defeat those who disagreed.

In this cultural site of memory, the police, though trying to protect the activists, indicate the challenges of memorial production within social structure. The police function to impose discipline, a paradigm that could not account for Duc's hope for an opening, a space to deliberately compose memory. The shifts among the cultural sites of memory—university, Little Saigon protest, activist community, and the policed society—present the complexity of Asian American memorial production within social conditions. Moreover, when Duc's recollection moves among these sites of memory, he underscores his attention to social engagement. The protest did receive brief media attention, but its departure from news accounts was quick. In any case, Duc explained that the point of the protest was to engage fellow Asian Americans in the making of memories, to compose more textured and socially responsible American cultural memories; he did not anticipate the media attention. Bringing up memory was a way of inviting participation, involvement, and solidarity among the Vietnamese and Vietnamese American community. The struggle here was about Vietnamese American and other Asian American student activists literally placing their memorial practices center stage, where only silenced memories and McCain's racial epithet had previously been recognized.

TOWARD A "DELIBERATE ACT OF REMEMBERING"

Defining an Asian American rhetorical memory requires a deep analysis of sites where Asian Americans have refashioned memory in response to histories, representations, and experiences. The "American Gook" protest and other performances of Asian American rhetorical memory suggest that the rhetorical art of memory is wedded to the social conditions in which that art is practiced. Asian American rhetorical memory thus entails investigating the memory traces that emerge from Asian American cultural sites. In composing Asian American memory, writers and speakers contribute to an American cultural production. Margalit describes this social involvement in memory as a mnemonic division of labor, where what is important is not just the memorial referent but participation in the memorial activity (2002, 51–53). Memory, then, is not just about legitimated recovery of marginalized experiences. Rather, rhetorical memory is a process of participation in a wider cultural production. Toni Morrison's reflections on her writing capture this sentiment:

> My compact with the reader is not to reveal an already established reality (literary or historical) that he or she and I agree with beforehand. I don't want to assume or exercise that kind of authority. I regard that as patronizing, although many people regard it as safe and reassuring. And because my métier is Black, the artistic demands of Black culture are such that I cannot patronize, control, or pontificate. In the Third World cosmology as I perceive it, reality is not already constituted by my literary predecessors in western culture. If my work is to confront a reality of the West, it must centralize and animate information discredited by the West—discredited not because it is not true or useful or even of some racial value, but because it is information

> held by discredited people, information dismissed as "lore" or "gossip" or "magic" or "sentiment." (1984, 388)

In the "American Gook" protest, Duc's purpose also went against this kind of "patronizing"—an attitude reflected in the disillusioned student's comments that they should wait until the older oppositional generation died. He composed memories in order to invite further memorial production, significant for social engagement, thereby working toward copia and destabilizing cultural production. And because each community member's memory is necessarily partial, such participation in memory presumes a spirit of cooperation and provisional memory work.

Reviving the art of memory matters: memory is a complex art that entails critically interpreting a sign's past and varied utterances, selectively weaving memorial compositions, and sharing cultural memories to foster social engagement. Asian American rhetorical memory, in particular, reveals how intricate layers of cultural memories are recollected into compositions and how the textured meanings that emerge from this copia foster social involvement and community solidarity. When rhetorical memory disappears, we should be wary. As Kathleen Welch warns, "It is crucial to an understanding of western literacy at this millennium to recognize that the disappearance of memory and delivery is not a benign removal; rather, it is part of a larger movement in the United States to pablumize the humanities in general and to vitiate writing in particular by behaving as if it were a mere skill, craft, or useful tool" (1993, 18). For Asian Americans, who are so often disregarded by mainstream American history, making our own memories is a critical answer to Jacqueline Jones Royster and Jean C. Williams's call to write in the "spaces left" and to resist the primacy of officialized narratives. By no means are the Asian American activists' memorial acts at the McCain protest representative of all Asian Americans, but this instance of rhetorical memory does point to the challenge broadly faced by Asian American rhetorical memory: to strategically construct collective identity, challenge racial injustice, and generally participate in American civic life.

REFERENCES

Carruthers, Mary J. 1990. *The Book of Memory: A Study of Memory in Medieval Culture.* Cambridge: Cambridge University Press.

Chan, Sucheng. 1991. *Asian Americans: An Interpretive History.* Boston: Twayne.

Chandrasekaran, Rajiv. 2000. In Vietnam, McCain Finds Unlikely Allies; Despite Ex-POW's Slur, Many Former Foes Support Candidacy. *The Washington Post,* 28 February 2000, A9. LexisNexis Academic.

Choy, Christina, director. 1988. *Who Killed Vincent Chin?* [documentary]. Detroit: Film News Now Foundation and WTVS.

Climo, Jacob J., and Maria G. Catell. 2002. "Meaning in Social Memory and History: Anthropological Perspectives." In *Social Memory and History: Anthropological Perspectives*, edited by Jacob J. Climo and Maria G. Catell. Walnut Creek CA: AltaMira.

Crowley, Sharon. 1990. *The Methodical Memory: Invention in Current-Traditional Rhetoric.* Carbondale: Southern Illinois University Press.

———. 1993. Modern Rhetoric and Memory. In Reynolds 1993b.

Fabre, Geneviève, and Robert O'Meally, eds. 1994. *History and Memory in African-American Culture.* Oxford: Oxford University Press.

Francoz, Marion Joan. 1999. Habit as Memory Incarnate. *College English* 62.1:11–29.

Havelock, Eric A. 1986. *The Muse Learns to Write: Reflections on Orality and Literacy from Antiquity to the Present.* New Haven, CT: Yale University Press.

Hernandez, Greg. 1996. Grisly Account of Ly Killing Believed Penned by Suspect. *Los Angeles Times,* March 7 2004.

Hoang, Haivan V. 2004. "To Come Together and Create a Movement": Solidarity Rhetoric in the Vietnamese American Coalition (VAC). PhD diss, The Ohio State University.

Kammen, Michael. 1997. *In the Past Lane: Historical Perspectives in American Culture.* Oxford: Oxford University Press.

Kim, Elaine H. 1982. *Asian American Literature: An Introduction to the Writings and Their Social Context.* Philadelphia: Temple University Press.

Lowe, Lisa. 1996. *Immigrant Acts: On Asian American Cultural Politics.* Durham, NC: Duke University Press.

Margalit, Avishai. 2002. *The Ethics of Memory.* Cambridge, MA: Harvard University Press.

Marinucci, Carla. 2000. Little Saigon Opens Arms for McCain: Vietnamese Americans Dismiss His Use of Slur. *The San Francisco Chronicle,* 2 March 2000, A3. *LexisNexis Academic.*

Matsuda, Matt. 1996. *The Memory of the Modern.* New York: Oxford University Press.

Morrison, Toni. 1984. Memory, Creation, and Writing. *Thought* 59 (235): 385–390.

Nora, Pierre. 1989. Between Memory and History: *Les Lieux de Memoire. Representations* 26:7–24.

Omi, Michael, and Howard Winant. 1994. *Racial Formation in the United States.* 2nd ed. New York: Routledge.

Palumbo-Liu, David. 1999. *Asian/American: Historical Crossings of a Racial Frontier.* Stanford, CA: Stanford University Press.

Ramirez, Anthony. 2000. Word for Word/Asian Americans; McCain's Ethnic Slur: Gone, But Not Quite Forgotten. *The New York Times,* 5 March 2000, sec. 4, p. 7, col. 1. *Lexis Nexis Academic.*

Reynolds, John Frederick. 1993a. Memory Issues in Composition Studies. In Reynolds 1993b.

———, ed. 1993b. *Rhetorical Memory and Delivery: Classical Concepts for Contemporary Composition and Communication.* Hillsdale, NJ: Lawrence Erlbaum.

Royster, Jacqueline Jones, and Jean C. Williams. 1999. History in the Spaces Left: African American Presence and Narratives of Composition Studies. *College Composition and Communication* 50:563–584.

Tachiki, Amy, Eddie Wong, and Franklin Odo, eds. 1971. *Roots: An Asian American Reader.* Los Angeles: Regents of the University of California.

Tran, Barbara, Monique T. D. Truong, and Luu Truong Khoi, eds. 1998. *Watermark: Vietnamese American Poetry and Prose.* New York: Asian American Writers' Workshop.

Wei, William. 1993. *The Asian American Movement.* Philadelphia: Temple University Press.

Welch, Kathleen. 1993. Reconfiguring Writing and Delivery in Secondary Orality. In Reynolds 1993b.

Yates, Francis. 1966. *The Art of Memory.* Chicago: University of Chicago Press.

4

LISTENING FOR LEGACIES

or, How I Began to Hear Dorothy Laigo Cordova, the Pinay behind the Podium Known as FANHS

Terese Guinsatao Monberg

Despite our ubiquitous presence throughout the diaspora, Filipinas remain contingently visible: as nameless, faceless overseas contract workers, sex workers, and mail-order brides scattered across the globe. We are seen as objects of a sexist, imperial ideology, yet we remain invisible as subjects and agents. Filipinas are simultaneously everywhere and nowhere.

Melinda L. de Jesús, *Pinay Power*

In reviewing the "legacies of erasure" that prevent Filipina and Filipina American women from being seen as subjects and agents, Melinda L. de Jesús reminds us that this erasure stems from other legacies, including long histories of imperialism, "further complicated by the patriarchal bias of both Asian American and Filipino American Studies" (2005a, 3).[1] But she further notes that Filipina women are also underrepresented in feminist studies—a field that includes feminist rhetorical studies, particularly feminist rhetorical history. How the historical legacies and rhetorical powers of Pinays[2] have gone unnoticed for so

1. Shirley Hune confirms that one reason Asian American women remain invisible is that race remains the dominant organizing category in Asian American studies and "the master narrative remains male-centered" (2003, 2). She also confirms that women's studies in the United States has not yet fully recognized the complexity that difference(s) bring to gender studies.
2. The term *Pinay* has a complicated history, but is often used to refer to Filipina American women. The term, along with its masculine equivalent, *Pinoy*, is thought to have its origins in the 1900s, perhaps used to denote Filipina/os living in the United States (as opposed to being seen as visitors or temporary workers). Historians Emily Lawsin, Dawn Mabalon, Dorothy Laigo Cordova, and Fred Cordova have all written about the term and the evolution of its use. See, for example, Lawsin 1996. See also De Jesús's footnote citing Dawn Mabalon in her introduction to *Pinay Power* (2005).

long—despite women rhetors like Gabriela Silang, Prosy Abarquez-Delacruz, Carol Ojeda-Kimbrough,[3] Irene Natividad, Dorothy Laigo Cordova, and countless others—is the larger subject of this essay. It is not that Pinay rhetors have not existed, have not taken up the cause, or have not made a difference; rather, it is the lens through which we have been looking for "feminist" rhetorical activity and history that requires closer examination.

Feminist historiography has long been concerned with recuperating the rhetorical contributions of women. Recuperation efforts have required feminist rhetoricians to challenge traditional masculine notions of rhetoric, including dominant assumptions about what it means to participate in public spheres, to read texts through the lens of gender (Jarrett 1990), to count something as evidence (Mattingly 2002), and to interrogate the "dynamics of suppression by which women's voices were silenced" (Campbell 2002, 45).[4] In challenging these assumptions, however, we find that certain other assumptions remain dominant in the field. Assumptions meant to recuperate women's voices intersect in complicated ways that still prevent many Asian/Asian American women from being heard. This dynamic can be seen, for example, in Hui Wu's discussion of her research on Chinese post-Mao literary women. While these women's texts directly engage issues of gender, Wu finds it difficult to justify these texts as "feminist rhetoric" using a western feminist theoretical framework defined by certain binary oppositions, including masculine/feminine, mind/body, "gender/sex, public/private, reasoning/caring, and equality/difference" (1990, 172). While many feminist rhetoricians have tried to recuperate the less valued term of the binary opposition and/or problematized the binary, as Wu demonstrates, these binaries still define the field, potentially hiding a number of non-western women and women of color from rhetoric's view.

In her study of silence as an active strategy in Asian Pacific American women's writing, Patti Duncan elaborates on the forms these binaries can take in U.S. feminist discussions:

> Such discussions have tended to either overlook the involvement of Asian American women in the history of feminist movements, or they have

3. See Catherine Ceniza Choy's important essay on Abarquez-Delacruz and Ojeda-Kimbrough (2005).
4. See Bizzell 2002.

> attempted to interpret the lives, actions, and experiences of Asian and Asian American women (and other women of color) according to disturbing stereotypes and/or categories framed in oppositional paradigms: "developed" vs. "underdeveloped"; complex, real, material subjects vs. monolithic, homogeneous, objectified nonsubjects; independent and empowered vs. oppressed, victimized, and dependent; capable of expression and possessing a feminist vision and voice vs. silent, unknowing, and unable to understand or analyze one's surroundings. (2004, 220)

Duncan reminds us that the consequence these paradigms have for Asian Pacific American women is often invisibility, not only in mainstream but also in feminist historical accounts. Thus, our methods for gathering and interpreting feminist rhetoric need further revision so we might see "Asian Pacific American women involved in movements for social change and justice in the United States, participating in activities that could easily be called 'feminist' in nature" (Duncan 2004, 221).

Building on Wu's and Duncan's arguments, this essay outlines one methodological and interpretive approach for recovering and theorizing a Filipina/o American "feminist" notion of rhetoric, an approach that has been helpful in uncovering the rhetorical legacy of Dorothy Laigo Cordova, founder and executive director of the Filipino American National Historical Society (FANHS). While Cordova is often hidden from traditional scholarly citations to FANHS, she is a central author of the spatial metaphors, methods, and pedagogical theories that structure the rhetorical activities of FANHS. This rhetorical space/structure is lost in traditional readings of FANHS texts and becomes available only through other methodological and interpretive approaches, including what Jacqueline Jones Royster, Malea Powell, Krista Ratcliffe, and Dorothy Cordova herself have each theorized as "listening." My goal, then, is not just to recuperate the voice of a single Asian Pacific American woman, but to highlight how certain approaches may prevent an entire legacy of Asian Pacific American women rhetoricians from being heard.[5] Listening as a methodology makes it possible to see and hear women who are

5. In a recent call for papers on the topic of feminist rhetoric, the editors explain that they "prefer theoretical or methodological topics to those that deal exclusively with the work of specific individuals." Similarly, a recently published essay that reviews feminist rhetoric portrayed one scholar's work (on rhetorical contributions by women of color) as not doing theory building or not explicitly reading through the lens of gender. This is one of the binaries—perhaps subtle, perhaps unintentional—that may prevent Asian Pacific American women from being heard by rhetoric.

presumed to be absent, but it also makes visible underlying assumptions in feminist historiography that reinforce those presumptions. In working toward a more culturally contingent model of feminist historiography, I argue that certain methods of listening—because they are attentive to interdependencies among rhetorical space, memory, and history—are central to the makings of an Asian Pacific American "feminist" rhetoric.[6]

LOSING SIGHT OF DOROTHY LAIGO CORDOVA

The term *listening* is a common theme among feminist scholars in the history of rhetoric. The commonsense definition of the term conjures up feminist rhetoricians struggling to hear the voices of women absent from "the" tradition. While early work in feminist historiography is not always seen as explicitly theorizing its meaning, listening has since been enacted and theorized as a method for recuperating women's rhetorical contributions, for uncovering women's intellectual genealogies, shifting interpretive paradigms, and hearing cultural difference. In recent scholarship, notions of listening have often been connected with Krista Ratcliffe's important work on "rhetorical listening" (1999, 2005). Responding to several exigencies, Ratcliffe is most interested in how listening as a rhetorical strategy might facilitate cross-cultural dialogue. This important cross-cultural dialogue, however, somewhat depends on women of color being audibly or visibly present so that others might listen to their speeches/texts alongside speeches/texts or instances of whiteness. Because Ratcliffe's model potentially reinforces distinctions between listening, theorizing, recovering voices, and creating texts, I turn instead to the ways listening has been enacted and theorized by, for example, Jacqueline Jones Royster and Malea Powell. In doing so, I implicitly argue that the making of an Asian Pacific American rhetoric benefits from the insights of other rhetorics of color, even as it requires its own culturally contingent context.

My argument begins with the premise that while most feminist historiographers in rhetoric use the term *listening*, most forms of listening have largely rested in seeing—seeing women at the podium, seeing women's texts, seeing women's words in print before they can be heard. But seeing is only one part of the dynamic equation when listening for/to women's

6. I assume that most readers are familiar with some African American and black women's reluctance to identify with the term *feminism*, preferring the term *framework* and values termed *womanist*. Similar reluctance exists among many Asian Pacific American women.

voices that have been institutionally marginalized in multiple, intersecting ways. To go beyond what is immediately visible and documented, then, requires what Jacqueline Jones Royster calls "a habit of critical questioning, of speculating in order to make visible unnoticed possibilities, to pose and articulate what we see now, what's missing, and what we might see instead" (2000, 10). Royster repeatedly resists narratives of individual exceptionalism, redirecting attention to patterns and traditions of rhetorical leadership among African American women. While this tradition of leadership is often invisible in mainstream historical accounts, she listens for the "traces" that are visible in order to reveal the larger "stream" of women in that tradition. Perhaps, then, our primary reliance on sight is skewing our focus toward identifying historically significant documents at the expense of hearing other rhetorical activities. This skewed focus, in turn, may be keeping us from "seeing" the large numbers of women who have been present and contributing all along—in ways that challenge what we think of as rhetoric and as "feminist" rhetoric. In her discussion of black women's roles in the black public sphere, Gwendolyn D. Pough reminds us: "We need to extend our interrogations and discussions in ways that validate not only the presence of women in the Black public sphere but women's roles in *shaping* that sphere. Instead of commenting on the strength of male presence in the public discourse, we need to ask what Black women were doing *to enable that presence.* We will no doubt find women like [Houston] Baker's mother writing speeches, raising funds, and *building institutions*" (2004, 37–38; emphasis mine).

Shaping public spheres, enabling the presence of others, and building institutions have not generally been recognized as rhetorical activities, particularly when texts providing evidence of these activities cannot be seen. To echo the words of Malea Powell, "this implied absence of [these] others" points more to "a space, an absence, in a particular conceptual understanding" of what rhetoric is and where we might find it (2002b, 398). Powell asks us to listen not only for these absences, but for the narratives these absences allow rhetoric to tell about itself as a discipline. In building a notion of rhetoric that "both listens and speaks" differently, Powell prompts us to imagine other "possible hearings and tellings" of rhetoric and its absences (2002a, 12; 2002b, 399).

Dorothy Laigo Cordova's case demonstrates how Filipina American "feminist" rhetoric(s) are particularly vulnerable to invisibility if we rely on methods dominated by seeing and collecting texts. These methods might uncover writing by Cordova in FANHS newsletters, announcements, an essay published in *Making Waves*, or a manuscript in progress on the history of Filipina women in the United States, but these visible texts might not illuminate her central role in shaping FANHS as a rhetorical space—or the rhetorical legacies that have informed that shaping. Cordova, a second-generation Filipina American, the eldest of nine children, was born in 1932 and raised in Seattle, Washington. Cordova and her husband, Fred Cordova, have been lifetime partners in Filipina/o American activism. The Cordovas cofounded the legendary Filipino Youth Activities, Incorporated, of Seattle in 1957; throughout the 1960s and 1970s they were active in the civil rights and Asian American movements. Dorothy is both founder and has always been executive director of FANHS; Fred is founding president emeritus of FANHS and founder of the National Pinoy Archives (NPA) associated with FANHS. Both are affiliate assistant professors in American ethnic studies at the University of Washington, and both were granted honorary doctorates by Seattle University in 1988. They have received lifetime achievement awards from numerous organizations, including the Association for Asian American Studies and *Filipinas Magazine*. But while Dorothy Cordova's achievements have been recognized, her rhetorical imaginings and capacities have not.

For more than twenty years prior to her founding of FANHS, Cordova had been writing and securing numerous grants to fund large-scale social research projects on Asian American communities, using her research findings to testify before Congress and to develop advocacy programs for these communities. Her founding of FANHS in 1982 was built on this foundation of community-based research and activism; and FANHS has since grown, with twenty-seven chapters currently active nationwide. Cordova's vision of FANHS as a rhetorical space and what this space offers Filipina/o Americans would be largely invisible to a methodology that privileges our use of sight to navigate traditional maps and catalogs of knowledge. We might *see*, for example, her husband, Fred Cordova, as the principal voice of FANHS. His book, *Filipinos: Forgotten Asian Americans* (1983)—made possible by oral histories and documents collected through the Demonstration Project for Asian Americans (DPAA) directed by Dorothy Laigo Cordova—is a foundational text in Filipina/o American historiography.[7] Fred Cordova has also published numerous

7. While Fred Cordova makes a concerted effort to credit Dorothy Laigo Cordova in his book—listing her as editor, listing the contributions of her staff, having her write the introduction, crediting her again in his prologue—academic convention requires that when the book is cited, Fred Cordova is cited as the author.

essays that we could locate in the FANHS journal, the foreword to one of the first anthologies of Filipina/o American studies (1997), and op-ed pieces in Philippine newspapers in the Seattle area. While most Filipina/o American scholars and community members familiar with FANHS recognize Dorothy Laigo Cordova as an equally key figure behind the organization, her rhetorical influence and contributions remain hidden from view, especially invisible to feminist historiographers of rhetoric who tend to privilege sight as the primary method for identifying sites of feminist rhetoric.[8]

In 1999, I had the privilege of meeting both Cordovas when two Chicago-based FANHS members and I traveled to Seattle to visit the national office and archives. Before my visit, I had performed some preliminary analyses of FANHS texts in preparation for my interviews. I noticed that in several of Fred Cordova's essays, he refers to FANHS as "a podium." When I asked Fred Cordova about this metaphor, however, he told me: "That's Dorothy's [term]" (1999). He further explained that, when it came to FANHS, he was more of the speaker and writer, while Dorothy Laigo Cordova was more of the thinker. When I asked Dorothy Laigo Cordova about this during our interview, she replied: "Yes. Probably. That's probably right. I'm more the behind the scenes person. I like to get an idea, and then I start typing it out and I'll plan it. And then I'll want to see it happen. To me, that's important. It's the execution, the carrying out, and bringing it [to] people, that's really important to me" (1999, 19).

Bringing people to the podium and having them take something away from it is what motivates Dorothy Laigo Cordova. While these rhetorical activities may not always result in (what we traditionally see as) a published document, especially of her explicit authorship—there is an important shaping of a public sphere happening here. To see this Pinay behind the podium known as FANHS, however, required different forms of data gathering and interpretation, since I was not familiar

8. Recent texts have begun to include references to Dorothy Cordova's work with FANHS. See, for example, Dorothy Fujita Rony, *American Workers, Colonial Power: Philippine Seattle and the Transpacific West, 1919-1941* (Berkeley: University of California Press, 2004); Barbara Posadas, *The Filipino Americans*, New American Series (Westport, CT: Greenwood, 1999); Peter Jamero, "The Filipino American Young Turks of Seattle: A Unique Experience in the American Sociopolitical Mainstream," in *Filipino Americans: Transformation and Identity*, edited by Maria P. P. Root (Thousand Oaks, CA: Sage, 1997), 299-315; and Nomura 2003,

with FANHS or the work of the Cordovas before I began this project.[9] And it was only through an oral history interview that I began to hear Cordova's spatial/rhetorical imaginings of FANHS as a podium, as a place where Filipina/o Americans can create new historical texts, narratives, and landscapes.

ORAL HISTORY AS A SITE FOR LISTENING

While oral history methodologies are a common preference among academic and community-based researchers in Asian Pacific American studies, feminist historiographers have not traditionally turned to oral history as a method for uncovering historical texts of significance. This may stem from disciplinary debates surrounding authorial intention and rhetorical agency, or disciplinary assumptions about what counts as history, as rhetoric, as public participation, as feminist practice, and as evidence. But our reluctance to turn toward oral history may also stem from implicit assumptions that history lives only in the past, in archival documents, and not in memories and communities. In considering the significance "feminist theories from the Third World" might have for rhetoric, Wu argues that "historical studies of rhetorical women should not be limited to the study of the deceased; living women should also be included as historical subjects as long as the study contributes to history building" (2002, 90–91). While uncovering historical texts is an important endeavor, it is just as important to document the rhetorical practices, institutions, social movements, and theories that women like Cordova have contributed. And these contributions, or traces of these contributions, may be glimpsed only through photographs or oral history interviews—if we act while these women can still share their histories. As a method and a discipline, oral history has often defined itself by its ability to give voice to populations whose perspectives and everyday experiences have been historically overlooked by histories focused on "great" men (and women). Oral histories also give us a view into the arena of lived experience where subjects actively make rhetorical choices, where categories are created, refused, and negotiated—if we are willing to really listen.

---

9. While I am a mixed-blood Pinay, I grew up in the Midwest and was trained not in Asian American studies but in rhetoric and composition. Unpacking the many reasons I was not familiar with FANHS or the Cordovas before this project confirms the perceived invisibility of Asian Pacific American rhetoric(s) and writing(s) and the need to pursue the ongoing struggle of decolonization and resistance.

To understand why oral histories hold special importance in the making of a Filipina/o "feminist" rhetorical history, I turn to Royster's discussion of how the essay, as one generic form used by the African American women she studied, was central in theorizing the ways these women used literacy for sociopolitical action. Generic features of the essay, as identified by Royster, resonate with the ways oral historians describe generic features of oral history narratives. For example, of the essay, Royster writes: "[The essay] is self-authorized; it privileges the first-person 'I' perspective; it is grounded in experience; it shows a mind at work; it is exploratory; it recognizes a listening audience and expects response; it invites skepticism; it is situated in a particular time, place, and writer; it permits the writer's knowledge, experience, and insight to emerge; it is protean in form" (2000, 232).[10]

Like the essay, an oral history narrative privileges the first-person perspective; it is situated in relationship to particular times, places, people, social movements, and historical events while allowing the narrator's "knowledge, experience, and insight to emerge." An oral history narrative can show us "a mind at work," telling us, in the words of Alessandro Portelli, "not just what people did, but what they wanted to do, what they believed they were doing, and what they now think they did" (1991, 50). Oral history narratives, then, reveal a speaking subject actively negotiating, shaping, and building spaces, institutions, and histories of rhetoric.

Generic features of the oral history narrative point to several reasons for the use of oral history methods among Filipina/o American community-based and academic researchers. Perhaps the most evident reason for turning to oral histories is that our history has been absent from the documents traditionally seen as worthy of preserving, archiving, reading, and analyzing. An equally evident reason is that these narratives place the speaking subject at the center of the narrative, as "I," as an active agent (rather than a passive recipient) of knowledge and history. But these reasons alone cannot tell us why Filipina/o American researchers might prefer this genre to others (like, for example, the essay); this requires listening to how the features of a genre or discourse are taken up, used, and performed (Powell 2002b; Royster 2000). Royster, for example, not only identifies features of the essay, she also listens closely to African American women's *performance* of the essay and highlights the

10. These features of the essay resonate with how oral historians describe oral history interviews (see, for example, Anderson and Jack 1998).

importance of the essayist tradition among African American women. In doing so, Royster reminds us that rhetorical activities only become "meaningful within systems of belief," and these systems of belief may indicate why a group might employ rhetorical *preferences* in working toward their sociopolitical purposes (43; emphasis mine).

To understand the larger sociopolitical purposes that may lead Filipina/o American scholars like myself to prefer oral history narratives, then, means understanding our strong tradition of orality, and how oral modes were put to *different uses*—especially in the face of colonization—in order to carry history, cultural memory, and tradition.[11] S. Lily Mendoza offers one example of how this preference shapes the making of rhetorical histories. In her study of the indigenization movement among Filipina/o and Filipina/o American scholars, she privileges this rhetorical preference as an important part of her data collection. She writes: "Given the strong tradition of orality in both the Filipina/o and Filipina/o American community, I took pains to trace the latest trends in theorizing not only in published texts but also in informal conversations and settings among Filipina/o and Filipina/o American academics. Included in these informal discursive encounters are face-to-face engagements in such contexts *as kapihan* (coffeeshop gatherings), *balitaktakan* (informal chats and discussions), mediated e-mail conversations, or the more structured context of conference meetings" (2002, 37).

In an endnote, Mendoza points to a larger implication of this Filipina/o tradition of orality when she notes that "some of the most influential theorists, particularly in Philippine academe, are not necessarily the most published and vice versa" (2002, 41).[12] Thus, oral histories may be particularly important to the making of a Filipina/o American rhetoric because they create spaces for dialogue, for informal discursive encounters on formal topics deemed important by community members—and these encounters have potential to enact a sense of community that is valued by members. So while an oral history narrative places the speaking subject, as "I," at the center of the narrative, like

11. I use the term *carry* in the ways that Malea Powell uses the term in her recent work on American Indian material rhetoric(s) (2002b).

12. This is not to say that Filipina/o and Filipina/o scholars do not write prolifically. I am not arguing for an essentialist or functionalist notion of oral culture. The idea of preference points to our need to take into account the complex reasons preferences take shape and how they are taken up, many times in ways that subvert the genre's perceived standard uses, to accomplish specific sociopolitical goals.

the essay, it is a genre that "recognizes a listening audience and expects response" (Royster 2000, 232). Thus, the processes and products of oral history can be used (and have been used) to facilitate and mobilize dialogues not just between interviewer and interviewee but also among real and imagined members of a larger listening audience. These dialogues are one example of the ways oral histories can be put to use; they are one vehicle through which our history, culture, intellectual and rhetorical traditions, strategies for resistance and survival are shared, performed, and carried forward (Powell 2002b). Oral history, then, not only documents but also carries/shares a form of social memory not often documented in traditional texts and tellings of history, including feminist rhetorical history.

Oral history guides emphasize listening as one of the key skills an oral historian can cultivate. The researcher must actively listen and engage the research participant in a dialogue by asking for further connections, clarifications, and elaborations during the interview process. But conducting oral history interviews with the Cordovas was only the first step in my listening process.[13] I then transcribed the interviews myself—listening, pausing, typing, rewinding, listening again. Certain passages stayed with me, I heard her voice as I read other FANHS texts, transcribed other interviews, analyzed data, and recalled other conversations we had outside of the formal interviews. I listened to my own voice as I typed my dissertation, conference papers, essays for publication, striving to resist easy generalizations and categories that academic work often fosters. As I have listened, recursively across multiple performances of FANHS's rhetoric, one segment from my interview with Dorothy Laigo Cordova has stayed with me throughout this project. In response to my question about her use of the term *podium* to describe FANHS, she shared her vision of FANHS as a rhetorical space this way:

> Yeah. I've always used that [term]. And I saw that. Especially, when you have people who are just community researchers, or students, who would never be invited to speak anywhere. We gave them the podium to share their information. And to me, I was just delighted. I mean, they were coming up with things that nobody else was coming out with. They came out of that. And so they were / what they did often times is they followed / they followed their heart, or they followed something that they knew and they just wanted to

13. It is important to note that my interview with Fred Cordova was just as significant in revealing Dorothy Laigo Cordova's role in shaping FANHS.

> find out more information about it. You know, I like to compare Filipino American history or even all kinds of history: it's like a great big beach that's not sandy. It's like the beaches we have in the Northwest are full of stone. And so, when you ask people to give you history, some of them will just tell you about a beach that's all white sand. And others will say, well, there's a beach with a whole bunch of rocks. What I want people in FANHS to do is to say, there's a beach with rocks, but under every rock, there's a different story. And to go down. And possibly even / for them to even dig down / and find what's further down. That, to me, is community research. (1999, 9; slashes indicate a pause in narration)

Cordova's description of the podium is both simple and deeply complex. It seems natural for community-based researchers and students to share their information at a podium, similar to the ways researchers share information at academic conferences. But unlike academic researchers, these community-based researchers, students, and "just plain folk" (as FANHS often calls them) wouldn't normally have a formal place to share their information. The fact that most of these researchers and students are Filipina/o Americans who are writing and speaking about Filipina/o American history complicates this desire for a place to share. Unlike other (though certainly not all) Asian Pacific American groups, multiple layers of colonization make the topic of history—for both Filipina/os and Filipina/o Americans—a continual process of excavation: we must listen to the story under every rock. To speak about Filipina/o American history, in the United States in particular, is to interrogate cultural amnesia surrounding U.S. imperialism in the Philippines and to deconstruct ideals of linear progress and individualism that permeate most popular narratives and images in U.S. history (including the history of rhetoric). Thus, oral history is not a simple solution for making new forms of rhetoric "visible." For if a "text" or rhetorical space is meaningful only within a larger system of beliefs, then we also need to rethink the interpretive paradigms we use when listening for/to, in this case, a Filipina/o American "feminist" rhetoric.

EXCAVATING SITES FOR FILIPINA/O FEMINIST RHETORIC

The role listening can play in research, as defined and enacted by researchers like Royster, Pough, Wu, Duncan, and Powell, for example, means rethinking interpretive frameworks, listening for patterns within an emerging tradition, and looking to other disciplines in a larger effort to understand the context in which words can mean. For as Royster argues, "a community's material conditions greatly define the range of what this group does with the written word and, to a significant degree, even how they do it" (2000, 5). For example, while Cordova's vision of FANHS as a podium, as a place for recovering and sharing undocumented histories and voices, resonates with the social movements of historically underrepresented groups, it's also important to note that themes of place, of home, are central to Asian American writing. As Rocío G. Davis argues, "the artistic appropriation of place ranks among the central concerns for Asian American writing" (2001, 47). This sense of place, what she calls a "simultaneous geography of space and imagination," differs from the sense of place we might get from the discipline of cultural geography—a discipline that Nedra Reynolds (2004) has characterized as "a seeing discipline." For Asian American writers, Davis elaborates, these imagined places are "not just [articulated] in geographic, economic, or planning terms, but also in terms of feeling and emotion" (2001, 48). One must listen for them, hear them, feel them, not just see them.

In Filipina/o and Filipina/o American writing, themes of place are often expressed spatially in terms of landscapes. As one Filipina writer, Marianne Villanueva, explains it: "the idea of landscape has always been a central one in my writing, perhaps because I no longer live in the country of my birth. What is this landscape that I write about? It is not only a place that exists in real time. It is something more personal and inward, a landscape of memory. . . . It is what . . . Andre Aciman calls 'the geographical frame to a psychological mess'" (2003, 12). This spatial sense of place shows that, for Filipina/os and Filipina/o Americans, places are deep, sedimented spaces marked with history. Renato Rosaldo's study of Ilongot headhunters (1980), for example, shows how Ilongots' conceptions of history are embedded in stories tied deeply to places—history is marked by recursive movements through space rather than movements through linear time. For Cordova, the recursive movements through space that rewrite the historical landscape are imagined as community-based researchers moving across the beach, listening to the story under every rock, rather than grouping rocks solely by time or waves of immigration—categories readily available in mainstream and some academic discourses.

Cordova's rhetorical imagining of the podium resonates with other writers of Filipina/o descent in their desire for a sense of place, location, history, memory, a site for relocating and rewriting cultural and historical consciousness. In rewriting this landscape, community members can reposition themselves in relationship to American culture and in relationship to the multiple cultures and languages through which they move. By essentially authoring a podium, a public space where other Filipina/o American writers can write and speak about Filipina/o American history, Cordova creates both a place and a movement through space—one Filipina/o American rhetorical tradition of many. But while Cordova's text resonates with other forms of Asian American and Filipina/o American cultural expression, what is it about this spatial text that merits its characterization as a feminist space? While oral history methods might now allow Cordova to become visible as a woman rhetor, mainstream feminist standards may keep her only contingently visible as a *feminist* rhetorician. As Wu argues, our analysis of women's rhetorical contributions must "begin with an awareness of the contingency and cultural specificity of analytical categories," including what it means to be a "feminist" in a given context (2005, 175). To look at how "feminism" might take form, then, in a Filipina/American context requires an attention to "struggles with racism, sexism, imperialism, and homophobia and struggles for decolonization, consciousness, and liberation" (de Jesús 2005a, 5). For these reasons, as de Jesús notes, Filipina and Filipina American "feminists" may prefer the term *peminism.* She writes:

> Peminism describes Filipina American consciousness, theory, and culture, with the p signifying specifically Pinay or Pilipina, terms used in referring to ourselves as American-born Filipinas. . . . Peminism thereby signifies the assertion of a specifically Filipina American subjectivity, one that radically repudiates white feminist hegemony as it incorporates the Filipino American oppositional politics inscribed by choosing the term Pilipino over Filipino. . . . peminism is an inextricable part of our decolonization as a people: far from being a slighting of Filipino American men or Filipino American culture in general, attention to Pinay voices and perspectives demonstrates our commitment to all Filipinos. (5; emphasis in the original)[14]

14. As Fred Cordova has highlighted in his common phrase "to 'P' or not to 'P,'" there is an ongoing debate (with historical roots) about whether to call ourselves *Filipinos* or *Pilipinos.* As de Jesús explains in an endnote, the term Pilipina/o is a "political and regional choice of self-naming grounded in the third world student movements of the 1960s" that helped establish the first Asian American studies programs in the United States. De Jesús explains that although the term is grounded in "specifically a California-based, working-class-identity politics," it more generally signifies an

Throughout de Jesús' collection, *Pinay Power: Peminist Critical Theory*, peminist scholars refute feminist frameworks that have neglected the complex experiences of Filipina American women. Perla Peredes Daly, for example, argues that "all forms of resistance by Filipinas against exploitation fall under the category of Filipina feminism" (2005, 233). Being Filipina and Filipina American women, by definition, says Linda M. Pierce, "means having a relationship to decolonization: whether active or passive, engaged, conflicted, opposed, or in denial, the relationship is automatic (and sometimes uninvited) by living in [the United States]" (2005, 33). So how Pinays use their relationship to decolonization may be one determining factor in how we might define a Pinay peminism. Within this framework, Cordova's metaphorical text is the making of a Pinay peminist rhetorical space that makes it possible for Filipina/o Americans to reclaim their histories and rework more dominant narratives of American and Asian American history and identity.

HEARING THE PEMINIST RHETORICAL CONTRIBUTIONS OF DOROTHY LAIGO CORDOVA

Given the history of U.S. imperialism in the Philippines and the forms of academic knowledge production that support those imperialist ideologies, Cordova's vision of research—how it should be conducted and disseminated, what purposes it should ultimately hold—demonstrates this Pinay's active resistance to colonization. Thus, listening to Cordova's community-based model of the podium within the larger context of U.S. imperialism, we might better understand why Dorothy Laigo Cordova positions community members (as researchers, as research subjects, as subjects of knowledge) at the center of the dialogue. The social distance that academics often see as necessary to produce "objective" academic knowledge has proved to be not only colonizing, but also taking knowledge from community members and producing this knowledge in forms often irrelevant to the needs of those community members. When I asked Dorothy what it meant—from her perspective, as founder and executive director of FANHS—to be a community-based

---

active resistance to the effects of multiple layers of colonization and the recuperation of "what is perceived to be the native *p* sound" over the colonizers' *f* sound (2005, 14). The *f* sound was introduced when King Philip II of Spain named the Philippines for himself, but the sound was further reinforced under U.S. colonization. This history of colonization and the importance of self-naming as a process of decolonization have also played out in debates over establishing and naming a national language in the Philippines.

research organization and how that might compare to a traditional academic model, she replied: "The academic one is very selfish. It's for them. I've worked with academics. See, in social research, I was a community person. Everybody else was the academician. I'm the one who connected with the community. We used to have fights. I'd say, 'You guys are sitting up in your ivory tower and you're looking down at these people.' One guy, the director, referred to the war brides as 'entities.' They weren't human beings, they were entities that they were documenting" (1999, 8).

Viewing the dominant academic model through the lens of Pinay peminism, community activism and advocacy, Dorothy Cordova sees academic researchers as disconnected from the community. She sees academics as sitting in their "ivory tower," looking down on Filipina/o Americans as "entities," sources of historical evidence to be mined for academic research purposes and goals. We might see how dominant academic notions of objectivity further justify (and reproduce) this social distance between the academy and the community.[15] When academics accept and perpetuate their social distance from Filipina/o American communities, they risk reproducing the colonizing ideologies found in early U.S. research on Filipina/os.[16] Community members are seen as research objects to be categorized rather than as human beings who might be affected by the methods and outcomes of academic knowledge production. Only certain details of their lives may be relevant to an academic researcher, and when little other research exists on Filipina/

15. While I agree that an assumed binary between "the academy" and "the community" is problematic, especially in Asian American studies, I also want to recognize how the academy—as an institution—privileges certain kinds of knowledge making and provides certain kinds of incentives and disincentives for knowledge-making activities. For example, Malea Powell writes about how "the 'rules' of scholarly discourse" both require and perpetuate a deeply rooted sociological distance: "Scholars are set forth on the fringes of 'the unknown' in order to stake out and define a piece of 'unoccupied' scholarly territory that, through our skill at explicating and analyzing, will become our own scholarly homestead, our area of concentration. We are trained to identify our object of study in terms of its boundaries, its difference from other objects of study, and then to do everything within our power to bring that object into the realm of other 'known' objects" (1999, 3). Powell draws a piercing analogy between claiming a scholarly territory and claiming a colonial territory. Because distance from our objects of study is what often lends us our legitimacy and authority as academic experts, we risk imposing colonizing ideologies on the people we study. The ways these forces manifest themselves can be both disciplinary specific and institutionally specific.

16. See, for example, Renato Rosaldo's discussion of early ethnographic studies of Ilongots in the Philippines (1980).

os and Filipina/o Americans, these details may come to (mis)represent "the" history of the community.

As Dorothy Cordova is a community researcher, her work has been partly motivated by distorted representations of the community perpetuated by academic experts, particularly during the 1970s and 1980s. In her early years as a community researcher, she was often confronted with academic misconceptions about Filipina women: that they were absent from the United States until 1945. Knowing they were "totally wrong," she began collecting histories on Filipina women and traced their presence in the United States to as early as 1860. In 1985, her work culminated in a series of traveling photo exhibits as part of a project entitled "Filipino Women in America: 1860–1985." Her methods for collecting history, through oral history and journal writing, have received critical acclaim in Filipina/o and Asian American studies, most recently resulting in an article by Gail M. Nomura (2003) on how Cordova uses journal writing to recover women's history.

In Cordova's work, if we listen, we can hear how her notion of the researcher moving recursively through space, across the beach, connected to the landscape, listening to the story under every rock, informs how she approaches her research on Filipina and Filipina American women. If we listen, we can hear her rhetorical/spatial imaginings textualized in a book chapter she published in *Making Waves: An Anthology of Writings by and about Asian American Women*. Her essay incorporates multiple voices—through citations of oral histories—and deconstructs assumptions about Filipina American women who came to the United States before World War II. She writes: "Though the largest group of Filipino immigrants during this period [the early 1920s and 1930s] was comprised of young single men, a very small minority were married; and a few of the more fortunate ones brought other families with them to the new land. In addition to the few women who accompanied their spouses, other women arrived to seek educational opportunities, employment, and cultural and social freedom" (1989, 42).

In this excerpt, Cordova refutes assumptions constructed through historical narratives framed by time (and primarily by male academic historians): that all the women who came to the United States before World War II were wives, mothers, and daughters of Filipino male laborers; many were, in fact. But they were also, as she told me, "more than that." In her essay, Cordova introduces us to women who demonstrated other forms of agency, women who were students and professionals, women who fled poverty and unwanted marriages.

Cordova also sees women across waves of immigration as connected to one another. She emphasizes both diversity and unity among women within the community: "The women came as war brides, students, plantation workers, teachers, housekeepers, seamstresses, wives, kitchen helpers, labor camp cooks, entertainers, and nurses. Some were small business entrepreneurs who ran pool halls, restaurants, grocery stores, beauty parlors, and gambling concessions" (1989, 49).

Cordova's approach to oral history is to document the way women (and men) have "led different lives at different times," rather than focusing narrowly on how one research participant can contribute to a narrow research project on, for example, war brides. War brides, in Cordova's model, have lives and histories that cannot be solely defined by their relationship to their husbands. In emphasizing the connections among women across immigration waves, Cordova also stresses the important role women have played in their communities: "As guardians of Filipino culture in America, the women played an important role. They sought to preserve language, traditions such as folk dance and music, and a sense of family and community" (1989, 49).

By connecting women from one immigration wave to women in other immigration waves, Cordova illustrates both the traces and the larger stream of Filipina American women. These "traces of a stream," as Royster argues, show how these women's "activities might connect . . . multidimensionally, to the practices of others both before and after them in the making of various traditions" (2000, 8).

This connection to women who came before her and women who have come after her can be seen throughout Cordova's work. During my interviews with both Dorothy and Fred Cordova, they each acknowledged their strong mothers, and the role these women played in creating strong traditions of history, identity, and storytelling in their lives and their communities. Dorothy Cordova has taken up this community preservation and advocacy role herself countless times, the most relevant for my purposes here being her shaping of the rhetorical and public space known as FANHS. She also brought together researchers who helped form the research foundation of FANHS. Research projects that served as the foundation of FANHS in its founding—research on the Manilamen who settled in New Orleans as early as the eighteenth century, the Indios Luzones who landed in Morro Bay in the sixteenth century, the oral histories of Filipina/os who (im)migrated to the United States in the early twentieth century—were research projects primarily conducted by women: Marina Espina, Eloisa Gomez Borah, and Dorothy Laigo Cordova (and her research staff made up primarily of women). Cordova has also served as a mentor for young Filipina American women. At the Eighth Biennial FANHS Conference, she awarded two young Pinays the "Young Pioneer Award" for their groundbreaking community-based efforts in promoting Filipina/o American history.

Cordova continually places herself and other women in the community within a larger legacy of community leadership among women (and men). She sees herself as part of a larger whole rather than as an exceptional individual. This deep belief, which questions dominant U.S. values of exceptionalism and individualism, may be rooted in the Filipina/o indigenous concepts of *loób* and *labás*—which add another level of complexity to Cordova's landscape metaphor of the beach. Filipina decolonization scholar Leny Mendoza Strobel explains:

> Filipino psychology and philosophy studies assert that Filipinos have a holistic worldview that is derived from the sense of the self as a whole. We perceive ourselves as holistic from an interior dimension operating under harmony (loób). We perceive ourselves as people who will, people who think, people who act as a whole. Many Filipino languages are nonlinear and vertical; there is not separation of subject and object and there are usually no gender distinctions. Filipinos use poetic speech, which is rooted in a spiritual consciousness that is affective and nondiscursive and where objective and subjective reality, the world and the soul, coexist separately. The core concept of loób has dual dimensions—loób (interiority) and labás (exteriority); these dimensions are deployed as accommodative tools under colonization. (2005, 27)

In the context of Strobel's concepts of loób and labás, we can see how Cordova's spatial notion of the podium positions any given Filipina/o American community member or researcher both as a speaker at the podium and as a rock on the beach (loób, labás). There is no separation between subject and object of knowledge. Any given rock is more than a one-dimensional source of historical evidence; each rock is a holistic being with multiple dimensions of interiority and exteriority. In conversations and during FANHS conference presentations, Cordova has often criticized the patriarchal and academic linear bias of Asian American and Filipina/o American studies—one example being how they have approached and portrayed Filipina war brides: not as "human beings," she says, but as "entities to be documented." In her own work, she counters this approach by promoting research that further promotes Filipina/o cultural values for women and men as articulated by Strobel: by seeing Filipina/o American community members, and listening to them, as holistic beings. The podium assumes a model of subjectivity that is multidimensional. The life story under every rock, in other words, reveals (and contributes to) not just one academic agenda but deeper knowledge of the community and its histories.

The rhetorical space known as FANHS is a place where collaborative forms of rhetoric, including texts, emerge from community members. Ideally, these "texts" are then carried further into the community, added to, built upon. For Cordova, a single-authored text does not necessarily benefit the community in the same way that many collaborative living texts might. Cordova's rhetorical imagining and theoretical understanding resonates with one articulated by Malea Powell; that is: "that human beings learn to produce texts through both theory and practice, *by listening and by doing*; that 'successful' texts are collaborative and meant for the community, not for the self; and that through continued textual production the community (and the knowledge of its members) survives and gives thanks for its survival" (2004, 44; emphasis mine).

Cordova's vision of FANHS articulates the kinds of listening required for working against the histories of colonization that haunt Filipina/o American history. To hear Cordova, however, also required that I listen for ways to honor her vision, not just as a practice, but also as a form of *peminist theorizing* that may not be valued under mainstream feminist standards. This form of listening includes listening for what Malea Powell calls "ghost stories." Powell elaborates: "For me, ghost stories are *both* the stories of material colonization and the webs and wisps of narrative that are woven around, under, beneath, behind, inside, *and* against the dominant narratives of 'scholarly discourse.' I think a lot about what ghost stories can teach us, how in telling them I might *both* honor the knowledge that isn't honored in universities *and* do so in a way that interweaves these stories with more recognizable academic 'theorizing' as well" (2002a, 12; emphasis in the original).

Listening for ghost stories, then, includes working against a dominant feminist framework that fails to hear Cordova and risks perpetuating colonizing narratives of our rhetorical history: seeing her work as history but not as rhetorical history; seeing her work as rhetorical practice but not as rhetorical theory; seeing her work through modes of listening but not as theorizing listening; seeing her work as decolonizing but not as feminist.

LISTENING FOR/AS THE MAKINGS OF ASIAN PACIFIC AMERICAN RHETORIC(S)

The work of Dorothy Laigo Cordova, at least as I have discussed it here, demonstrates the kinds of listening required to uncover larger legacies of Asian Pacific American women's rhetorical agency, theory, and history. While Cordova is the central author of the spatial metaphors, methods, and pedagogical theories that structure the rhetorical activities of FANHS, her rhetorical capacities might remain hidden because of a preference for sight and visible textual evidence and, as Wu (2005) suggests, by a preference for feminist frameworks that are not always culturally contingent. The making of a Filipina/o American peminist rhetoric, then, may be similar to LuMing Mao's description of the making of a Chinese American rhetoric; it "lies in reflective moments, and it finds its makings through emergent alignments and unsettled associations" (2005, 460). In many ways, the making of a Filipina/o American peminist rhetoric carries the legacy of unsettled and uneasy associations with feminist, Asian American, and Filipina/o American rhetorics. In other ways, it emerges in alliance with, for example, the makings of an Asian Pacific American rhetoric, for it requires that we listen for/to: unrecognized rhetorical capacities and imaginings, new sites for these capacities and imaginings, resonance with other rhetorics of/from color, other disciplines and knowledge-making communities that might illuminate the deeper contexts in which rhetoric(s) make meaning, and dominant assumptions that may be encouraging us to ignore (or reduce the significance of) these capacities and imaginings.

Listening is both a method for uncovering and for *making* an Asian Pacific American rhetoric, which must by necessity "explore other modes of retrieving and spatializing [rhetorical] history" (Lowe 1996, 101). Themes of space, history, and memory are central to the articulation of an Asian Pacific American rhetoric, just as they were for the very emergence of the naming of "Asian America" in the 1960s and 1970s. The rhetorical spaces where Asian Pacific American rhetorics are used/performed and contested, made and remade over time—like FANHS—are sedimented spaces that require deep excavation (125). This deep excavation for some Asian Pacific American rhetorics, like Filipina/o American rhetorics, will depend heavily on alternative forms of institutional or public memory, and different methods for re/constructing that collective memory. Perhaps this is not unlike other rhetorics of/from color; however, the contexts and ways in which these collective memories are formed, shared, and carried—if also excavated—might provide important specificities. Listening for emergent rhetorical structures and imaginings, like Cordova's notion of the podium, helps us to map our understandings of how Asian Pacific Americans use rhetoric to craft collective and political identities that perform some larger use. Listening, as I have theorized and enacted it in this essay, becomes an important part of an Asian Pacific American rhetoric—an emergent, diverse, often transcultural and transnational tradition—which is always in the process of becoming.

Thank you for listening.

REFERENCES

Anderson, Kathryn, and Dana Jack. 1998. Learning to Listen: Interview Techniques and Analyses. In *The Oral History Reader*, edited by Robert Perks and Alistair Thomson. New York: Routledge.

Bizzell, Patricia. 2002. Preface to "Feminist Historiography in Rhetoric," edited by Patricia Bizzell, special issue, *Rhetoric Society Quarterly* 32 (1): 7–10.

Campbell, Karlyn Kohr. 2002. Consciousness Raising: Linking Theory, Criticism, and Practice. *Rhetoric Society Quarterly* 32 (1): 45–64.

Choy, Catherine Ceniza. 2005. Towards Trans-Pacific Social Justice: Women and Protest in Filipino American History. *Journal of Asian American Studies* 8 (3): 293–307.

Cordova, Dorothy Laigo. 1989. Voices from the Past: Why They Came. In *Making Waves: An Anthology of Writings by and about Asian American Women,* edited by Asian Women United of California. Boston: Beacon.

———. 1999. Interview with author, FANHS National Office, Seattle, WA. September 10. In-text citations to this interview refer to page numbers from a 28–page transcript.

Cordova, Fred. 1983. *Filipinos: Forgotten Asian Americans; A Pictorial Essay, 1763–circa 1963.* Edited by Dorothy Laigo Cordova. Demonstration Project for Asian Americans. Dubuque, IA: Kendell/Hunt.

———. 1997. Foreword to *Filipino Americans: Transformation and Identity,* edited by Maria P. P. Root. Thousand Oaks, CA: Sage.

———. 1999. Interview with author, September 9.

Daly, Perla Paredes. 2005. Creating NewFilipina.com and the Rise of CyberPinays. In de Jesús 2005b.

Davis, Rocío G. 2001. "I wish you a land": Hawai'i Short Story Cycles and *aloha ´aina. Journal of American Studies* 35 (1): 47–64.

de Jesús, Melinda L., 2005a. "Introduction: Toward a Peminist Theory, or Theorizing the Filipina/American Experience." In de Jesús 2005b.

———. ed. 2005b. *Pinay Power: Peminist Critical Theory; Theorizing the Filipina/American Experience.* New York: Routledge.

Duncan, Patti. 2004. *Tell This Silence: Asian American Women Writers and the Politics of Speech.* Iowa City: University of Iowa Press.

Hune, Shirely. 2003. Introduction: Through "Our" Eyes: Asian/Pacific Islander American Women's History. In *Asian/Pacific Islander American Women: A Historical Anthology,* ed. Shirley Hune and Gail M. Nomura. 1–15. NY: New York University Press.

Jarrett, Susan C. 1990. Speaking to the Past: Feminist Historiography in Rhetoric. *Pre-Text: A Journal of Rhetorical Theory* 11 (3–4): 189–209.

Lawsin, Emily Porcincula. 1996. Pensionados, Paisanos, and Pinoys: An Analysis of the Filipino Student Bulletin, 1922–1939. *Filipino American National Historical Society Journal* 4:33–33P.

Lowe, Lisa. 1996. *Immigrant Acts: On Asian American Cultural Politics.* Durham, NC: Duke University Press.

Mao, LuMing. 2005. Rhetorical Borderlands: Chinese American Rhetoric in the Making. *College Composition and Communication* 56:426–469.

Mattingly, Carol. 2002. Telling Evidence: Rethinking What Counts in Rhetoric. *Rhetoric Society Quarterly* 32 (1): 99–108.

Mendoza, S. Lily. 2002. *Between the Homeland and the Diaspora: The Politics of Theorizing Filipino and Filipino American Identities: A Second Look at the Poststructrualism-Indigenization Debates.* New York: Routledge.

Nomura, Gail M. 2003. Filipina American Journal Writing: Recovering Women's History. In *Asian/Pacific Islander American Women*, edited by Shirley Hune and Gail M. Nomura. New York: New York University Press.

Pierce, Linda M. 2005. Not Just My Closet: Exposing Familial, Cultural, and Imperial Skeletons. In de Jesús 2005b.

Portelli, Alessandro. 1991. *The Death of Luigi Trastulli and Other Stories: Form and Meaning in Oral History.* Albany: State University of New York Press.

Pough, Gwendolyn D. 2004. *Check It While I Wreck It: Black Womanhood, Hip-Hop Culture, and the Public Sphere.* Boston: Northeastern University Press.

Powell, Malea. 1999. Blood and Scholarship: One Mixed-Blood's Story. In *Race, Rhetoric, and Composition*, edited by Keith Gilyard. Portsmouth, NH: Boynton/Cook.

———. 2002a. Listening to Ghosts: An Alternative (Non)argument. In *Alt Dis: Alternative Discourses and the Academy*, edited by Christopher Schroeder, Helen Fox, and Patricia Bizzell. Portsmouth, NH: Boynton/Cook.

———. 2002b. Rhetorics of Survivance: How American Indians *Use* Writing. *College Composition and Communication* 53:396–434.

———. 2004. Down by the River of How Susan LaFlesche Picotte Can Teach Us about Alliance as a Practice of Survivance." *College English* 67 (1): 38–60.

Ratcliffe, Krista. 1999. Rhetorical Listening: A Trope for Interpretive Invention and a "Code of Cross-Cultural Conduct." *College Composition and Communication* 51:195–224.

———. 2005. *Rhetorical Listening: Identification, Gender, Whiteness.* Carbondale: Southern Illinois University Press.

Reynolds, Nedra. 2004. *Geographies of Writing: Inhabiting Places and Encountering Difference.* Carbondale: Southern Illinois University Press.

Rosaldo, Renato. 1980. *Ilongot Headhunting, 1883–1974: A Study in Society and History.* Stanford, CA: Stanford University Press.

Royster, Jacqeuline Jones. 2000. *Traces of a Stream: Literacy and Social Change among African American Women.* Pittsburgh: University of Pittsburgh Press.

Strobel, Leny Mendoza. 2005. A Personal Story: On Becoming a Split Filipina Subject. In de Jesús 2005b.

Villanueva, Marianne. 2003. Introduction to *Going Home to a Landscape: Writings by Filipinas,* edited by Marianne Villanueva and Virigina Cerenio. Corvallis, OR: CALYX.

Wu, Hui. 2002. Historical Studies of Women Here and There: Methodological Challenges to Dominant Interpretive Frameworks. *Rhetoric Society Quarterly* 32 (1): 81–98.

———. 2005. The Paradigm of Margaret Cavendish: Reading Women's Alternative Rhetorics in a Global Context. In *Calling Cards: Theory and Practice in the Study of Race, Gender, and Culture,* edited by Jacqueline Jones Royster and Ann Marie Mann Simpkins. Albany: SUNY Press.

5

LEARNING AUTHENTICITY

Pedagogies of Hindu Nationalism in North America

Subhasree Chakravarty

For the Hindu Swayamsevak Sangha (HSS)[1] in North America, it is especially important to represent a unified Indian national experience that can be easily conveyed to a diasporic audience. In recent years, therefore, the HSS has undertaken a rigorous method of disseminating knowledge on Hindu history, society, and culture within its target groups through various forms of pedagogic practices ranging from regularly organized educational camps to meetings to publications of instructional books and pamphlets. As a continuation of this endeavor to spread knowledge of Hinduism, the HSS and affiliated organizations have now undertaken projects like the so-called California Hindu textbook controversy to ensure strict vigilance over all written materials published on Hinduism in North America. Through all this, the HSS proposes to transmit messages to awaken Hindus across the world to a realization of their current social and cultural predicament. In keeping with these sentiments, the HSS in its mission statement proclaims Hindu Jage Vishwa Jage—in the awakening of the Hindus, the world will awaken.

In my reading of the HSS texts, including pedagogic documents, pamphlets, brochures, and other print materials obtained from Web sites and various chapter offices, it has become increasingly evident that in the revival and proliferation of education on Hinduism, the HSS attempts to stimulate and reorient a certain restrictive Hindu religiopolitical sentiment for its specific diasporic audience. These attempts, I argue, can be seen as strategies on the part of the HSS to instill what I shall call here "exclusivist rhetoric." This policy, implemented through rhetorical constructions of legends concerning Hindu Indian cultural heritage, practices, signs, symbols, and images, as we

1. Roughly translated as Hindu Volunteer Corps and commonly known as the HSS.

shall examine here, eventually paves the way for mobilizing religious sentiments through cultural interpretations. The exclusivist rhetoric, therefore, successfully weaves narratives of Indian pride and supremacy directed especially at the young members of these organizations, who have not had a chance to be adequately informed about the "true" qualities of being Indian—a concept largely circulated among Hindu educational groups. The four major organizations whose contributions in promoting and educating the Hindu masses in North America have been most noteworthy are the Educator's Society for the Heritage of India (ESHI), the Hindu American Foundation (HAF), the Vedic Foundation (VF) and the HSS. Looking into the mission statements and activity reports of each of these organizations, one cannot fail to see that the current generation of Hindu Indian Americans are persistently being misled about their cultural heritage through multiple educational sources. In fact, the ESHI claims its position by asserting that "our children are the future and we do not want them to grow with embarrassment learning wrong things and lose pride. Hindu parents and the community leaders are very important since it's our children and their future" (n.d.).

LEARNING, THE HINDU WAY

The crux of the problem lies in the way Hinduism is represented in school textbooks, college/university publications and books, all forms of media representations, including radio, television, the Web, and magazines, and in libraries and museums. All these mediums of transmission of knowledge on Hinduism are, according to the above-mentioned organizations, inconsistent in their depiction of Indian cultural values and consequently fail to encourage the second generation of Hindu American children to be inspired by them. To prevent this loss of pride in Indian traditions and culture among young Hindu Americans, these educational groups have drafted agreements that declare, "[T]here is a total disconnect between what we know of India and how it is presented. The stereotypes and negativity is a very embarrassing experience to our children to an extent that they want to dissociate. Embarrassment also leads to emotional stress within our families, enhances generation gap" (ESHI n.d.).

Furthermore, the pedagogic materials supplied by these organizations treat Indian culture and heritage as synonymous with Hindu religious teachings, failing to understand that Indian heritage is not just its religious traditions. The ESHI asserts that it is both secular and religious at the same time. On one hand, it affirms its secularity and impartial position by stating that it "is an organization of academicians, professionals and other educators whose sole purpose is to help the world understand our heritage," while, on the other hand, it claims solidarity with Hindu Indian "temples, sampradays [religious sects], ashrams [monasteries] and certain other Indic religious traditions—Buddhism, Jainism and Sikhism." The duality embedded in these principles, that of dissemination of religious sentiments through secular modes, gains further prominence as organizations like the HSS, ESHI, HAF, and VF vow to provide a platform that would make "the right changes to re-establish the greatness of Hinduism, educate individuals about the divine history of India and the original teachings of Indian (Hindu) scriptures through logical, scientific, historical and scriptural evidences and to serve as an authoritative resource on authentic Hinduism" (ESHI n.d.). Establishing this "authentic Hinduism" thus develops as the main objective in educating a new generation of young Indian Hindu Americans whose pride and knowledge of their religious and cultural heritage could then successfully be used to counteract issues of multiculturalism and diasporic discontents in American classrooms and other social settings.

What is the form of this authentic Hinduism? How is it different from other interpretations of Hinduism? Since Hinduism does not provide a single authoritative scriptural text or a specific set of religious guidelines (as is the case with most other religions, including Christianity, Islam, and Judaism), it is the myriad of myths, legends, and philosophical doctrines that form the vast body of religious literature integrating a range of instructional measures. It also lends a certain flexibility to the structure of religious education, leaving it mostly to individual audience members to decide upon what values to derive from it. The adaptability of the multifarious narratives embedded in most Hindu religious texts to contemporary times makes it a highly popular pedagogic method among Hindus, especially because they mostly retain loose ends and questions regarding what could be called a quintessential Hindu religious life. It is this amorphous characteristic of Hindu religious education that makes it a fluid and widely followed body of instructions, at times devoid of dogmatic dicta. Within the diverse linguistic and social practices of India, these tales of the Hindu way of life then act as a cohesive force uniting the Hindu majority through shared religious beliefs and ethical principles that form the backbone of Hindu religion and culture. Even now, in most everyday household practices in India, myths, epics, and other similar texts are communicated orally, chiefly through a tradition of storytelling, along with the enactment of religious rituals and customs that ensure their continuity through generations, many of them providing moral guidance to their audience. In a hierarchical social setting like conservative Hindu society, these stories are probably one of those rare elements of religious literature that are made readily available to all people regardless of class, caste, or gender. Perhaps it is this accessibility of Hindu religious literature, and its universal reception across the country, that also make it the best possible instrument of ideological inculcation. The core of these narrative strategies, which usually center on some moral predicament, compels compliance. And this might go a long way toward explaining the proliferation of similar chronicles, written with the persuasive techniques adopted by contemporary Hindu fundamentalist groups. As we shall see here, these contrived accounts of what Hinduism entails function explicitly at times and implicitly at others like a rhetorical edifice, through which convictions of Hindutva[2] are filtered and molded. In the following sections, I explore how this process of constructing stories about Hinduism has been incorporated within the North American Hindu educational organization ideology as part of its fundamentalist propaganda. The chronicles on Hinduism that the HSS, ESHI, HAF, and VF conjure are relatively rigid, focusing on epics that are considered supremely authoritative texts within the organizations. Although most of these stories are still transmitted orally, occasionally in informal settings, they are motivated by a singular agenda and repeated often to fulfill the goals of the organizations.

Accounts of Hindu religiocultural values that are disseminated by the HSS and VF include verbally constructed narratives as well as a conglomeration of visual images and practices. For the most part, these narratives comprise invigorating tales of religious nationalism. The models that

2. The term *Hindutva* was coined by Vinayak Damodar Savarkar—the founder of the HSS/RSS (Rashtryia Swayamsevak Sangha; see below) group. The concept originally coincided with the concept of Hinduism, meaning people who followed Hindu religious principles. In his book *Hindutva: Who Is a Hindu?* Savarkar first distinguished Hinduism from Hindutva, associating the former with an orientalist viewpoint and validating the need for a substitution of the suffix "ism" with the Sanskrit "va" to ensure that it embraces what he understands as racially pure terminology. Subsequently, members of the Hindu nationalist movement began identifying themselves as of Hindutva origin referring to the racial identity established by Savarkar.

are set up for emulation by young Hindu Americans alternate between the lives of Hindu mystics and those of Hindu rulers and their political struggles. The luminaries in turn alternate, rather arbitrarily, between real-life historical figures like Shivaji, Rana Pratap, and Vivekananda and mythical characters such as Krishna, Arjun, Ram, and Sita. Furthermore, the morals these works promote show a gendered division. Stories illuminating public-sphere virtues such as political courage, idealism, and honesty are directed at male audiences, while women are directed toward the traditional "feminine" virtues, such as loyalty to one's husband, motherly love, patience, and similar qualities that are seen as indispensable within the domestic sphere of life. These narratives are then supplemented by the practice of yoga, meditation, and martial arts to strengthen the mind and body in defense of nation and religion. Within the verbal practices there are tales from Indian mythology, chronicles of the Indian struggle for freedom from the British, stories of Hindu rulers who fought against the Muslims, accounts of the life and works of HSS leaders, and finally, performances of songs and prayers. Although, for the purposes of our analysis here, these distinctions are crucial, it is important to bear in mind that the cultural activities conducted by both HSS and VF daily are inclusive of both verbal and nonverbal practices. It is also significant to note that most of these activities, whether verbal or nonverbal, are intended to promote a narrative of the Hindu way of life, imposing upon their audience an edifice of values and actions that constitute Hinduism for these organizations.

For instance, by way of their propaganda of Hindutva, the HSS and VF establish and utilize already established narratives from the Hindu pantheon of gods and goddesses to construct an array of neomythical narratives. In other words, primary myths are rhetorically deployed to produce a chain of narratives that achieve mythical dimensions of a secondary order within the ideological parameters of Hindutva, which is at several removes from the primary myth. I would first like to provide an analysis of the primary myths, specifically the mythical figureheads of the two Indian epics *Ramayana* and *Mahabharata*, who emerge continually within the Hindutva ideology. Widely believed to be the incarnations of Lord Vishnu—the preserver within the Hindu trinity of Brahma (the creator), Vishnu, and Maheshwar (the destroyer)—Ram was born around 5000 BCE and Krishna around 3000 BCE. The *Ramayana* is principally a story of the victory of good over evil. The basic storyline involves Ram, who goes into exile in the forest with his brother Laxman and his wife Sita (an incarnation of the goddess Laxmi) through a ploy of his stepmother Kaikeyi. In the forest, Sita is abducted by the demon king Ravan from Lanka (modern-day Sri Lanka). In order to rescue his wife and destroy the ten-headed Ravan, Ram wages a war against the demon, aided by the army of the monkey-god Hanuman. This monumental and decisive war is interpreted to constitute the core of this epic and concretize the crucial struggle between good and evil. However, later renditions of the epic, which gained popularity among groups like the HSS in the 1990s, represent Ram as an aggressive warrior. As Matthew Biju and Vijay Prashad state, this epic has been "utilized for the recreation for Hindu religious and nationalist iconography in militant ways." Significantly, the visual representation of Ram has undergone a transformation wherein he has been far removed from the earlier versions depicting "a benign and noble patriarchal civility, perhaps even humility." While the former depiction is found framed and worshipped in domestic shrines as an image of a just ruler, brother, husband, and bestower of patronage "in a tableau which contains his power within a benevolent frame," the latter image is endowed with the prowess of "a lone vengeful figure unleashing weapons" (Biju and Prashad 2000, 527). This modification of Ram exemplifies perfectly a transformation on the narrative plane and is a process that is carried out through a conjunction of verbal narratives and the production of corresponding visual rhetoric.

This transformation from the benevolent ruler to a warrior who took up arms to defend his nation, wife, and dharma is mirrored in the role of Krishna—the hero of the epic *Mahabharata*. While Ram and Krishna are the most widely worshipped among Vishnu's incarnations, with each holding prime positions in the respective epics, there are marked distinctions in their characters. While Ram symbolizes images of what is seen as the perfect son, brother, husband, and king who followed the sacred law and the path of restraint till the end, Krishna is invested with a complex and morally ambivalent personality,

> [H]is life story reveals a number of different facets; a child-god who loves playing pranks and practical jokes, a handsome dark skinned pastoral god who plays the flute and has hair adorned with peacock's feathers. His oozing melodies ravish the mind and souls of the milkmaids [gopis]. Yet another facet to Krishna's character is revealed during the moment he leaves the cowherd's settlement for Mathura and sloughs off his pastoral nature to become an accomplished ruler and statesman. He is the king of the Yadavas, and also

> the shrewd politician and philosophical counselor of the Pandavas, who play a pivotal role in the epic Mahabharata." (Dalapicolla 2003, 77)

But there are different aspects to this story, as the duality of Krishna's character illustrates most strikingly. Even as a child, Krishna evinced extraordinary skills in exercising divine powers in the face of peril. Under more normal circumstances, he displayed affection and was a most endearing child, demonstrating a childlike impishness that is characteristic of him. He is playful, mischievous, disobedient at times, and yet simple and innocent. However, this simplicity quickly gives way to superhuman strength whenever he is pitted against challenges that could cause harm to his community or countrymen. Replete with tales of Krishna wielding divine powers to fight evil, the epic constructs the climax of his potential in the narration of the Bhagavad Gita. The Gita, which is the Hindu text approximating most closely the Gospel in Judaic religions, is primarily a compilation of Krishna's sayings on matters spiritual and secular, most of which is constructed as an argumentative exchange between Krishna and his friend Arjun on the battlefield of Kurukshetra. This dual aspects of Krishna's character—the apparent simplicity and charm and other endearing qualities juxtaposed with the determination and sternness that underscore his martial endeavors—stand out as essential elements of his godliness as reflected through his human incarnation. The mysterious interplay of his anthropomorphic existence—of the myth of the human and the human God—interestingly provides a significant subset of the religious, cultural, and political aspirations of the HSS and VF. Articulating the latent martial potential in every Hindu and invoking this therefore become the primary objectives of these organizations' propaganda on Hinduism. The HSS and VF thus have been active in summoning up feelings of militant nationalism, inspiring their audience to the realization that they, too, can perform the aforementioned dual roles whenever their country or dharma so requires.

The act of transformation from benign ruler to aggressive warrior is rhetorically represented as an eye-opener, indicating the discrepancies that lurk within the character of Hindus and their enemies. Equally, the enemies of Hindus also harbor these dual qualities and may rise up in arms to defend their own religious positions. Inspired by the vast political potential of such ideologically invested rhetorical constructions, the Hindu educational organizations reinforce their political agenda of "authentic Hinduism," with the purpose of mobilizing their audience to defend an imaginary Hinduhood.

THE CONTROVERSY IN CALIFORNIA

Given the formulations of these narratives of inflexible Hindu cultural values by the HSS, along with the ESHI, HAF, and VF, to promote religious supremacy, it is not surprising that these groups would find alternative depictions of Hinduism questionable. Indeed, the construction of "exclusivist Hindu rhetoric" was most vividly articulated in North America in recent years in the issue of the California Hindu textbook controversy. What the ESHI unequivocally proclaims in contextualizing this debate is that there is a "preponderance of Hinduphobia at all academic levels in the United States" (n.d.). The material on Hinduism in sixth grade textbooks in the state of California reflects this abhorrence of Hinduism, the ESHI states. Supporting this viewpoint, the HAF insists: "We believe these comments clearly relay the urgency with which Hindus must counter this insidious Hinduphobia. With your support, we can ensure that Hinduism is represented in a fair and appropriate manner" (ESHI n.d.). The discrepancies in Hindu knowledge and education—between what the HSS and its allies deem "authentic" and the representation in the textbooks in question—are in reality microcosmic evidence of larger social, cultural, and political debates between Hindu conservative groups and other Indian American scholars, thinkers, and activists. In this case, too, representation of Hinduism becomes the pivotal point, a significant rhetorical category, which neither the conservative educational groups nor liberal Hindu scholars can effectively define. Subsequently, any imposition of an arbitrary compilation of Hindu religious ideas (regarded as authentic only by a selective minority) on sixth grade Hindu American children could incite a limited and restrictive religious, cultural, and nationalist ideology.

There are indeed a number of inaccuracies and flaws in the proposed textbooks, which the ESHI, VF, and HAF have enumerated. These grievances range from factual errors—for example, one of the textbooks notes that Hindi is written in Arabic script when actually it is written in the Sanskrit Devnagari script—to problems of "promoting colonial stereotypes" or "distortion and caricaturing of Hinduism." While many textbooks "repeat colonial equation of Hinduism with caste, cow, curry and sati or the controversial Aryan invasion theory implemented to trace the origins of Hinduism," a few of them also "describe yoga as merely a set of physical and breathing exercises and the subtle doctrine of karma is explained as a theory where if you do bad deeds you may be born as an insect or a pig." A set of comparative analytical categories is erected as well by these Hindu educational organizations to substantiate discriminatory treatment by the California Board of Education between Hinduism and other religions. As an example, VF and HAF note that "Buddhism is treated as an advance over Hinduism, whereas Christianity is never treated as an advance over Judaism." Furthermore, "Hindu scriptures are referred to as 'poems' 'stories' and 'myths' whereas the Abrahamic scriptures are called Holy Books. The latter are dealt with from an insider's perspectives, whereas Hinduism is treated often from a hostile outsider's perspective." Insensitive remarks and "obsessive negative focus" are also trademarks of discriminations meted out to Hindus: one textbook section describing the Hindu emphasis on vegetarianism has the title "Where Is the Beef?" and the Hindu goddesses Kali and Durga are referred to as "bloodthirsty" in another textbook. All the above-mentioned instances are characterized by the Hindu conservative groups as intentional and politically motivated means of ostracizing the Hindu community in the predominantly Christian western society of North America. The groups present the issue as one of a crisis of identity; Hindu American community members are encouraged to view such instances as typically indicative of an anti-Hindu stance that extends over national and religious borders. This readily distinguishes the enemies of Hindus, who lurk in all imaginable places, and demarcates their modes of oppression, establishing a perpetual state of crisis and urgency in response to which the clarion call of awakening Hindus then is asserted. Otherwise, the impact of such wrongful teaching would lead to "lack of self esteem in 11 year old children of Indic origin in California classrooms and expose them to potential embarrassment at the hands of their classmates" and would inevitably be "responsible for perpetuation of prejudices against Hindu Americans" (ESHI n.d.).

The perceived suffering of ignominy and the perpetuation of anti-Hindu sentiments form the basis for creating Hindu exclusivist rhetoric, one that is replete with narratives of a glorious Hindu Indian past that has been lost due to the infiltration of "other" religions in India—and therefore needs to be resurrected. Losing pride in Hinduism is a threat that most conservative Hindu American organizations regard as severe, especially since in a diasporic setting such losses seem to be always imminent. The California textbook controversy provided an opportunity for

Hindu conservative educational groups to fight against this perceived threat—they plunged into the debate, confirming prejudicial treatment not only by American educators in California, but also by all those Hindus who have strongly opposed any revision based solely on the recommendations of a handful of Hindu American educational groups, whose members see Hindus who disagree with them as a "[m]otley group of Indian American communists/Leftists (e.g., FOSA, 'Coalition Against Communalism' or academics such as Vinay Lal), Christian evangelical organizations such as Dalit Solidarity Forum (often pretending to represent Dalit [a minority caste in India] interests), Islamists, Sikh groups with an antipathy towards Hindus and academics with a track record of promoting stereotypes against Hindus. Interestingly these groups, often claiming to be 'South Asian peace groups,' are completely silent about the whitewashing of other South Asian religions like Islam, Buddhism and Christianity in these textbooks" (ESHI n.d.).

As a means of counteracting damaging treatment, the exclusivity of Hinduism is preached through reference to comments made by renowned western scholars and thinkers who have acknowledged the greatness of Hinduism and its position as an unparalleled ancient civilization.[3] Robert C. Rowland and Abhik Roy claim that at the core of all Hindu nationalist rhetoric one can trace a grand mythic narrative. While nationalist sentiments form the motive behind this narrative, the production of myth serves as the means through which it is enacted. Describing the rhetorical characteristics of Hindu nationalist movements in India, they suggest that "religious fundamentalists use 'myths of return' to get back to the fundamental core of the faith. The most powerful stories in any culture are myths, which define who we are by providing a narrative essence for individual and social roles" (forthcoming).

Every society, as such, is exposed to narrative sequences that establish behavioral patterns its members are expected to follow. It is worth asking why, under "normal" and "daily" circumstances, these myths of splendor and glory lead a largely inactive life and are usually contained within rhetorical practices in the private sphere of household religious performances. And yet, the power of these apparently dormant practices within the quotidian private sphere is cleverly exploited by the religious

3. For example, Mark Twain once commented, "India is the cradle of the human race, the birthplace of human speech, the mother of history, grandmother of legend and great grandmother of tradition. Our most valuable and most instructive materials in the history of man are treasured up in India only."

revivalists—to drastic long-term effects in the political constitution of the national public sphere. One probable factor behind these dichotomous existences of the dormant and active stages in the life of such narratives might be found in Partha Chatterjee's distinction between the "inner" and "outer" domain of Indian national politics. The nation was perceived to suffer successive defeats at the hands of foreign colonizers such as the Muslims and the English in the "outer" domain of statecraft and material politics. However, the spiritual and moral supremacy of the Hindu nation was seen as forever undefeated in the "inner" domain of national consciousness in spite of the material defeats. The projection of such private-sphere myths into the national public sphere is therefore part of a rhetorical aggression that underlies militant religious nationalism, which can only construct itself in terms of a historicized cultural polemic (Chatterjee 1993).

THE DIVINE HINDU AND THE OTHER

Reclaiming such a glorious past for Hindu children in North America also necessitates close monitoring of their cultural development and education. Both in the public and the private articulation of the religious nationalist sentiments, however, as Rowland and Roy (forthcoming) point out, the representation of the "powerful enemy" remains constant. Within the HSS, ESHI, VF, and HAF discourses, moreover, the image of the enemy is frequently blurred by a constant shift in position. Rather than erecting the icon of a tangible enemy with legitimate grounds for grievance, these organizations construct a synthetic image of the enemy as culled from all the forces that are historically seen as threats to Hindu culture. But even so, this archetypal image of the enemy is subjected to interesting modifications according to the territorial locations of the movement in question, most significantly between RSS[4] propaganda in India and that of its North American counterpart, the HSS. For instance, while the RSS is direct and vitriolic in its opposition to Christian missionary work in India, the HSS is far more moderate in its anti-Christian rhetoric, doubtless because of its operations within North America. At the same time, the HSS fully exploits its North American location, as the celebration of policies of multiculturalism within the United States provides new immigrants spaces to assert their cultural traditions. This is the

4. Rashtryia Swayamsevak Sangha is translated as the National Volunteer Corps—the mother organization of HSS, based in India and founded in 1927 during India's anticolonial struggle.

political juggling act forever executed by the HSS, and this is founded on its claim to be a predominantly cultural organization with no ties to Indian national politics, a claim that is hard to accept at face value.

The contemporary stories of war and sacrifice that continually resurface within the Hindu educational organizations' pedagogic discourse, needless to say, display a close affinity with the wars fought by both Ram and Krishna. The ultimate motive for such narratives, as stated earlier, is to install the logic of revenge by invoking a sense of religious and cultural ignominy suffered at the hands of followers of other religions. In the numerous biographies of great Hindu rulers and leaders, lessons on Hindu dharma and heritage, and tales of the contribution of Hindus in science and mathematics found in Hindu Right literature, there exists a metanarrative of suffering, oppression, and colonization.

For example, Balagokulam, a center for Hindu children's education in North America founded by the HSS, is devoted to the cause of raising kids in the image of Lord Krishna as well as reconstructing the mythical abodes of Hindu gods. Such a center ensures a safe haven for young Indian Americans, who are seen as unfortunate in their lack of direct access to Hindu culture. Describing it as the place where "Lord Krishna's magical childhood days were spent" and claiming that also "it was here that his divine powers came to light," the organization Web site stridently proclaims that "every child has that spark of divinity within" (*Balagokulam* n.d.). Therefore, "Balagokulam is a forum for Hindu children in North America to discover and manifest that divinity," thus enhancing their ability to appreciate their cultural roots. The pedagogic practices of teachers of Balagokulam as well as a quarterly magazine published by the organization are replete with mythic narratives indicative of passion, courage, strength, valor, and justice for men and docility, devotion, and sacrifice for women, occasionally juxtaposed with tales from the lives of HSS leaders and founding fathers. The magazine's pedagogic guidelines state the importance of presenting "role models" for children to learn and emulate, since "children learn values and habits mostly by imitating their role models. . . . Children select those people as role models whom they like, whom they respect, admire and adore" (HSS 2005).

The reconstruction of the conditions of Krishna's childhood (as in the Balagokulam centers) thus exemplifies the re-creation of the context of grand myths so that myth itself can be reproduced. In other words, the complex relationship between the texts and the audiences of the epics is translated not through the act of creating entirely new narratives, but by reproducing past and popular "myths" within a foreign cultural setting. It is usually assumed that all Hindu children growing up in India have been influenced by the myths of Krishna's childhood in shaping their identities. To be away from the land of Krishna's birth deprives second-generation Indian American children of such knowledge and influence. At the same time, in order to keep the myth of Krishna alive, one needs to construct "centers" where these children can understand the specific moments of Krishna's childhood. A reading of the texts on Balagokulam's mission and goals, intriguingly, reveals not the idyllic bliss of fifth century BC rural India, but a training institution closely resembling other HSS organizations and their methods of *Boudhik* (intellectual) persuasion. In every story narrated to the children at this center, the underlying moral lesson emphasizes the heroism of Hindu rulers and the nature of Hindu dharma. The events of any historical period of India discussed here are arranged as a chronicle by the temporal order of their occurrence. They are then further organized into a story of the rise and fall of India's glorified past, so that the arrangement of the events as a spectacle or processes of happening have a discernible beginning, middle, and end. Narrating a synchronic history of the nation, followers of HSS shape it much like a romance, where the hero of the narrative transcends his world experience and gains victory over it. The battle for political freedom is thus amalgamated with the battle for religious and cultural freedom, so Ram becomes a political icon over and above a religious one.

For instance, in the section on biographies, we find descriptions of the lives of leaders from two crucial periods of the history of India, namely, those of Mughal and British rule. Dwelling upon the courage and charisma of these personalities such as Prithviraj Chauhan, Queen Laxmi Bai, and Tanaji in the face of challenges posed by adversarial invaders and the plight of their communities under the tyrannical rules of Muslims and Christians, these accounts are in fact valorizations of Hindu cultures at the cost of intolerance for other religions. Each of the characters discussed is colored by qualities that are considered quintessentially "Hinduistic" by the HSS. These characters are united by their collective inclination toward the renunciation of worldly desires and an unquestioning dedication to traditional Hindu culture, closely followed by the virtues of prudence, diplomacy, in some cases celibacy (though mostly among men), reliance, and, of course, defiance and subversion of oppressive regimes. Tracing the roots of some of these qualities to the characteristics of the mythical figureheads of Ram and Krishna, the themes of war and sacrifice also squarely fit into the treatment of the epics in the hands of the HSS. That is to say, since the HSS analysis of the epics largely includes the decisive battles as the core of its educative features, it is not surprising to see them transplanted into the scheme of the battles fought against the Mughals and the British. The Hindu way of life therefore becomes an irreducible and insatiable "warmongering" temperament that seeks revenge for all the tortures inflicted in the past. As such, we find ourselves in the midst of leaders who, though exceptionally commendable for their actions, are limited in these organizations' depictions of them.

The first among these personalities described in the HSS literature is Swami Vivekananda, a great philosopher and spiritual leader of nineteenth century India, a social reformer who worked to liberate society from the bonds of casteism, gender discriminations, and class conflicts. He traveled to the United States in 1895 to attend the Parliament of Religions conference in Chicago and persuaded his audience to understand the spiritual aspects of Hinduism in spite of India's then contemporary colonial condition. In the HSS, VF, and ESHI pedagogic publications, Vivekananda stands apart as a Hindu preacher more than as a philosopher and social reformer. Vivekananda's attempts to uphold the spiritual legacy of India invited compassion from the rest of the world at the plight of the colonized state, which for the HSS is tantamount to the real dharma or duty of the Hindu— not only to profess and promote Hindu values but simultaneously to depict the adverse material conditions imposed upon Hindus by their foreign colonizers. The ensuing arguments thus institutionalize political conditions as fundamentally driven by moral and religious forces. As such, rarely do we see in HSS literature any mention of Vivekananda's vision of a free and secular India unified across religious borders.

Like Vivekananda, his favorite disciple Sister Nivedita has also found a venerable place in the HSS canon. The case of Nivedita is, however, somewhat different. A major transformation in her life occurred when she met Vivekananda in Ireland. Born of Irish parents, Nivedita (or Margaret Noble) was so profoundly impressed by the teachings and philosophy of Vivekananda that she joined the mission he founded to help him in his social reform movements in India. For the HSS, Nivedita's embracing of the Hindu religion brought to light the universal appeal of Hinduism that had been unfortunately suppressed by foreign rule. The following story from the HSS pamphlet describes the duty assigned to Nivedita and the way in which she performed her role:

> From Europe she went to America. Her original aim was just to raise enough funds for her small school. But, upon her arrival in America, she found that the urgent task was to educate the Americans about India and her glorious culture. A great deal of false and malicious propaganda had been carried on against India and her religions by some Christian missionaries. They had grown extremely jealous of the tremendous impact on the West of Swami Vivekananda's powerful address at the Parliament of Religions and of the growing popularity of Hinduism, especially of the Vedanta, not only in America but in Europe. They had been systematically painting a totally misleading picture of India by blowing up her poverty, ignorance and superstition out of all proportion. These evil doings of so called men of religion were, she felt, an outrage against Christ himself. Like the Master, she went on a whirlwind tour of the States and addressed huge gatherings in all the principal towns and cities in order to educate the Americans about the real state of India at the time, the greatness of her past, the sublimity of her cultural and spiritual heritage and above all, the true causes of the present degradation. She was a gifted orator. She had steeped herself in India's history, her religions and her scriptures. In living words, charged with truth and invigorated by her sincerity, she depicted India in vivid colors. The audience felt a deep regret that they had let themselves be totally misled by pious frauds. They were thankful to Nivedita for revealing to them the very soul of India. She had succeeded in making America realize that India's degradation was essentially due to her long subjection to foreign rule. But she had not gained substantial success in raising funds for her school and for her other work in India. (HSS 2005)

While both Vivekananda and Nivedita's "dharma" entailed spreading the tenets of Hinduism, the subsequent stories from the biographies section of HSS Boudhik education for its members continue with an emphasis on the oppressions of the Mughal rulers. Narrating the stories of Prithviraj Chauhan, Rana Pratap, and Rani Laxmi Bai, the HSS once again foregrounds episodes of revenge, war, torture, and unfulfilled desires. In almost all of these accounts, the Hindu ruler's attempt at revenge is thwarted by their Muslim captors, and hence the sense of failure looms heavily over these tales. Such thwarted actions thus become the site where feelings are invoked that might avenge the deaths of the Hindu rulers. To include these tales within contemporary contexts of Hindu cultural education among children of diasporic Indians provides an occasion to believe that the true nature of Hindu history is fundamentally a history of violence—of victories, defeats, or unfulfilled desires.

Contrary to the teachings of the epics of *Ramayana* and *Mahabharata*, where, in the end, the righteous prevails, with the downfall of the unrighteous, and peace is bestowed upon the commoners, the HSS treatment of the Hindu king frequently includes the failing of the "righteous" against the ploy of the "villain." Each of these defeats is hyperbolically described so as to provide supernatural explanations for historical phenomena. Falling in between the real and the imaginary, these chronicles of violence embody a life constituted partially of truth and partially of myth. Every story only strengthens the conviction within the Hindu conservative groups of the "heathenism" prevalent among the Muslims and occasionally the Christians. The unified experience of betrayal is thus elevated to larger- than-life proportions and channeled into contemporary tales of war and conflicts. The cycle of reconstructing Hindu greatness is further kept alive through passages like the following from the *Bhagavad Gita,* where Krishna stridently proclaims to return to the world every time Hindus face a crisis of "dharma": "[W]henever there is a decline of righteousness and rise of unrighteousness, then I send forth Myself . . . for the protection of the good, for the destruction of the wicked and for the establishment of the righteous, I come into being from age to age." Relating this in terms of its own Hindutva dharma, the HSS and VF especially have taken it upon themselves to provide the infrastructure necessary to surge forth with the task of liberating Hindus. The cycle of myths and remyths and neomyths of magnificence thus produced, though removed from historical reality, gathers momentum during communal controversies in both India and abroad. As Arvind Rajagopal states, "During the movement to build a Ram temple (at what was alleged to be his birthplace, on the site of a sixteenth-century mosque), in Ayodhya in India, shila pujan [brick worship] were performed not only in villages across the country. In the US too, groups in 31cities participated, sanctifying bricks through rituals and sending them to Ayodhya for the proposed Ram temple. These contributions were themselves substantial, and constituted an important financial support to the Hindu campaign" (2000, 474).

The Hindu conservative organizations' campaign against followers of Islam is also clear in documents that narrate the history of Hindu heritage. The Muslim invaders are generally held responsible for most of those ignoble Hindu social customs that continue to be harshly criticized for their discriminatory foundations. One such infamous practice was that of the self-immolation of widows, or *Sati,* which is described as an act of honor that: "[h]as to be seen in the light of the compulsions of alien rule in India during the medieval ages. From the 13th century onwards up to the coming of the British, the position of women was insecure under the rule of the Sultans of Delhi. Their insecurity increased after the demise of their husbands. This compulsion which was resultant of a particular age was by far the most important reason for the prevalence of Sati during the middle ages" (HSS 2005).

The HSS is aware that Sati is looked upon as a deplorable custom by the rest of the world, but their aim is to "highlight what kind of sacrifices have been made to keep our civilization alive." It also explains "how the system of Sati and child marriage came into being during the Islamic rule in Northern Bharat. Children in America read about these topics in their school text-books or in the western media coverage of India. This explanation would clarify some of the questions on its origin and its prevalence today" (HSS 2005). Child marriage is also promoted as a practice undertaken as a means of saving the girl-child's life, which was otherwise threatened by the promiscuous activities of the Muslims.

THE MAKING OF A HINDU DIASPORIC MYSTIQUE

In the writings of nineteenth-century German Indologists such as Max Mueller, a certain romanticized and essentialized image of Hinduism and Hindu religious texts emerged that has been readily incorporated into the Hindu Right discourse as evidence of the superiority of Hindu thoughts and customs. Adapting some of the analytical frameworks of such scholarships, the HSS reading of Hindu cultures emphasizes the idea of the Hindu ascetic endowed with mystical knowledge. This spiritual image is then paradoxically juxtaposed with the materially rooted political struggle for the establishment of a Hindu nation. This is most effectively constructed through a rhetorical reproduction of narratives conflating the accomplishments of Hindu rulers in Indian epics with tales of Hindu leaders involved in the Indian struggle for independence. On one level, the HSS propaganda hinges on ancient Vedic wisdom of detachment from material politics, while on the other it valorizes militant political conquest for the defense of one's national territory.

For the diasporic audience, moreover, an essential element of such a discourse of superiority is the contrast between Indian spirituality and the perceived materialism of postindustrial western societies. Whenever the needs of HSS propaganda require persuasive techniques to amplify the virtues of Indian spirituality, this spirituality is always favorably compared to the consumerist lifestyles of North American communities. Relating the basis of this "consumer behavior" to what it sees as "cultural" inadequacy, the HSS advocates:

> With the collapse of the Communist world, the western democracies appear to be reigning all supreme, without any other viable political-cum-economic system to challenge it. . . . However, soon enough, all that euphoria is subsided. Being open, democratic countries, impartial, critical assessments in those capitalist countries began, as days rolled by, revealing the inhuman face more and more. . . . The sole emphasis on material affluence as the source of happiness has led to unbridled consumerism leading to never-ending craze for acquiring more and more objects of material enjoyments. . . . At the root of all these problems lies a distorted and fragmented view of the world set afloat by science since the days of Darwin and Descartes. In this view, the world is conceived of as a mechanical entity, comparable to a machine whose parts, by themselves separate, have been joined together to form the whole. . . . As such, the values and views generated by this mechanical view have resulted in dealing with problems of man as if each one is distinct and separate from the other. . . . This has made the goal of human happiness and peace more and more of a distant dream. (Sakhalkar 1995, 5)

In this critique of the nature of "western democracies" by the Hindu propaganda groups, the criticism is directed toward a certain way of living, in this case, characterized as a "mechanical entity." Living according to these standards of "mechanization" entails an extreme form of individualism that results in a disintegration of communal living—a form of mayhem. Arguably, the structure of this narrative represents certain ideologically constructed notions about capitalist western culture that is part of this propaganda. Simplistically speaking, according to their agenda, all capitalist systems necessarily involve a mad scramble for material desires, which can lead only to despondency in the end. Publicizing this notion becomes doubly crucial for members of a demographic group who have left their place of ancestral origin for better material opportunities abroad. Such an audience is always reminded of their critical situation, of the complexities associated with it, and that their loyalties are always in danger of being misdirected.

In a way, the success of Hindutva ideology is contingent upon the widespread publicity of "crisis" or "fear" (threats to spiritual and cultural identity) as much as it is on the tropes of "war" and "sacrifice" crucial to its historiographic discourse. As a part of this process of intellectual interpellation, this sense of fear is mobilized among the members of its target group. Though the HSS clearly does not propose a substitute for capitalist systems—say, to the effect of reverting to a feudal society—it voices a caveat against indulgence in what it sees as western lifestyles of individualism and consumerism. Looking upon its former colonizers with suspicion, the Hindu Right reiterates the dangers of being dominated by a western culture. It goes without saying, of course, that such discourses identify the West as a seamless whole where post-Renaissance British imperialism and contemporary North American capitalism are seen as easily interchangeable. Fearing a recolonization of one's "culture" and of the sacrosanct private domain that has remained unblemished all through the history of colonial India, Hindu traditionalist texts resignify the importance of maintaining cultural superiority all the more in its diasporic contexts. At the same time, the results of an individualistic and consumerist lifestyle are counterpoised with the so-called spiritual qualities of Hindu cultural traditions to display how the latter can serve as an antidote to the former. For example, when the dejection from material interests becomes overwhelming, the ESHI proclaims, many westerners have recourse to the spiritual solace of yoga and other traditional rituals and practices. Similarly, Indians are encouraged to practice yoga to ensure that they do not fall into the traps of material desire whetted by lifestyles of consumerism.

> The solution therefore lies in expanding the awareness of one's self. And this becomes possible only when the individual is able to restrain his unbridled desires and emotions and harmonize them with the highest interests of society. And yoga is the word that signifies that restraining principle—that way of life which helps sublimating his self-centered thoughts, feelings and impulses into those of his wider personality—the society. . . . The leading physicists of the world have also started rethinking and discarding the materialistic,

> fragmented concept of the world and of man and have been echoing the words of Eastern scriptures pointing to an integrated view of human personality. (Sakhalkar 1995, 9)

On a similar note, the HSS argues for the implementation of Hindu models of economic policies as opposed to the dominant capitalist model. The author claims: "The findings of the experiments on the subatomic particles showed an unbelievable semblance with the (intuitive) findings of the ancient mystic thinkers of India and China. All these revolutionized the western Scientists' outlook, not only towards life and environment but also about the traditional wisdom and mystical writings of the Orient. . . . It is time, we have taken a second look at the basic issues in the discipline of Economics and modified it to reconcile the contradictions both at the methodological and the empirical levels. Hindu Economics rightfully provides such a modification" (Sakhalkar 1995, 3).

The very notion of Indian spiritualism here is mythologized to a scale such that it is rendered as an exclusive tradition, so much so that its meaning is changed: from reference to Indian doctrines on metaphysical objects to a body of knowledge fundamentally contradicting western cultural opinions and beliefs. Concurrently, the rhetorical success of this tradition is contingent upon similar constructions of North American diasporic identities, especially among young Indian Americans, who would now grow up to be defensive Hindus, practicing a Hinduism that seldom shows tolerance of diversity.

If these interpretations of Hinduism as written and promoted by the HSS, HAF, VF, and ESHI could successfully invoke a sense of injustice and patriotism in their audience, then we will find ourselves confronted with a group of young Hindu Americans in North America who are charged with a historically entrenched sense of grievance. Imposing upon itself the rhetoric of marginalization, which becomes doubly significant in the diasporic context, this group would then participate in a rhetoric that articulates the need to revisit history and undo the "wrong." It is as easy for the diasporic audience to authenticate its subaltern status (due to its minority position in North America) as it is empowering to be able to act on behalf of the homeland. The dichotomy of *pitribhumi* (fatherland) and *karmabhumi* (land of work) in time becomes rhetorically critical, as these immigrant groups align it with the binary of the private and public domains.

REFERENCES

Balagokulam: Online Resource on Hindu Dharma for Children, Teachers and Parents. http://www.balagokulam.org/ (accessed September 21, 2005).

Biju, Matthew, and Vijay Prashad. 2000. The Protean Forms of Yankee Hindutva. *Ethnic and Racial Studies* 23 (3): 516–534

Chatterjee, Partha. 1993. *The Nation and Its Fragments: Colonial and Postcolonial Histories.* Princeton, NJ: Princeton University Press.

Dalapicolla, A. 2003. *Hindu Myths.* Austin: University of Texas Press and British Museum.

ESHI (Educator's Society for the Heritage of India). http://www.eshiusa.org/ (accessed February 1, 2007).

HSS (Hindu Swayamsevak Sangha). http://www.hssus.org/ (accessed September 25, 2005).

Rajagopal, Arvind. 2000. *Hindu Nationalism in the U.S.: Changing Configuration of Political Practice.* Ethnic and Racial Studies 23 (3): 467–496.

Rowland, Robert C., and Abhik Roy. Forthcoming. The Rhetoric of Hindu Nationalism: A Narrative of Mythic Redefintion. *Southern Speech Communication Journal.*

Sakhalkar, Narendra. 1995. *Economics: A Hindu View Point.* Mumbai: Rambhau Mhlagi Prabodhini.

Savarkar, Vinayak Damodar. 1969. *Hindutva: Who Is a Hindu?* 5th ed. Bombay: Veer Savarkar.

6

RELOCATING AUTHORITY

Coauthor(iz)ing a Japanese American Ethos of Resistance under Mass Incarceration

Mira Chieko Shimabukuro

> To say that the War department's announcement last week opening selective service to Japanese Americans brought instant joy to the hearts of all draft-age men would be misleading and inaccurate.
>
> Many have waited hopefully for selective service to be opened. Others have hoped that it wouldn't; that it somehow would miss them and allow them to continue their pointless, purposeless lives behind the fences of relocation centers. . . .
>
> Issues will provoke some to point out "why should their parents be confined behind barbed wire while the parents of other soldiers are free to go where and as they please. Why, since they may ultimately face the supreme sacrifice for this nation, their parents can't return to their former homes." The questions will be endless.
>
> Endless questions against the inevitability of the draft are senseless. The draft is here and welcome.
>
> —*Heart Mountain Sentinel*, 1942

January 1944—two years after Pearl Harbor and the subsequent reclassification of young American male citizens of Japanese ancestry as "aliens not acceptable to the armed forces, or any group of persons not acceptable" (Muller 2001, 41), the War Department made a startling announcement: these same men, most of whom were referred to as *Nisei* (second-generation Japanese Americans) in their own communities, were now reclassified back, "on the same basis as other citizens" (64), thus making them susceptible to the draft. However, during the official U.S. involvement in World War II, the majority of Japanese Americans were not living "on the same basis as other citizens," having been incarcerated en masse into War Relocation Authority (WRA) camps after being forcibly removed from their homes along the West Coast during the spring of 1942. The news of the draft, throughout the incarcerated *Nikkei* (of Japanese ancestry) community, appeared to have been met at first with a kind of quiet resentment. But in some camps, like the one in Heart Mountain, Wyoming, the news would serve as the tipping point for an organized resistance to emerge, and with it, a resistant rhetoric that seemed to draw its authority from a multitude of both "friendly" and "hostile" sources. Amid these contending forces, several Japanese Americans stepped forward and claimed their rhetorical agency in the face of mass incarceration because they felt they had been authorized to do so.

The draft announcement was circulated to internees on January 22 via radio and camp newspapers, including the *Heart Mountain Sentinel,* which served a population of approximately ten thousand inmates. The *Sentinel*'s contradictory claims, seen in the opening quotation, were made within a week of the announcement. However, it soon became clear that questions about the draft were not "senseless," nor was the draft as "welcome" as the WRA-sponsored paper tried to proclaim. Less than three weeks after the War Department announced the draft, a committee of male, mostly Nisei, Heart Mountain residents, who would later describe themselves as a group "organized to inject justice in all the problems pertaining to our evacuation, concentration, detention and pauperization" (Fair Play Committee 1944), publicly emerged and began to speak out against the draft. These men called themselves the Heart Mountain Fair Play Committee (FPC) and went on to organize and articulate the only known collective Japanese American draft resistance during the World War II incarceration period.[1]

Over the past seven years, the resistance by the FPC has begun to gather some recognition via PBS-supported documentaries by filmmakers Emiko Omori and Frank Abe, and via writers like Frank Chin, Lawson Inada, Mike Mackey, Arthur Hansen, and Eric Muller, but the history of Japanese American draft resistance during World War II remains a

1. While the FPC was the only group to explicitly refuse induction, collective responses that questioned the government's right to draft already-incarcerated citizens actually emerged in most of the camps. I have, as of this date, come across letters, resolutions, and petitions in various community archives that were written in at least five additional camps; however, more research is needed to study the extent and impact of these documents. In addition, individual acts of draft resistance (refusals of induction) took place at camps such as Tule Lake and Minidoka, but not in the same collectively organized manner as in Heart Mountain. See Hansen 2002 and Muller 2001.

controversial subject within the Nikkei community itself, in which there is disagreement regarding what is the best image to put forth in a country still struggling with its ongoing legacy of white supremacy. Decisions over what is and what is not the most correct response to the announcement of forced military service are never easy, but perhaps become even more difficult when one's entire community remains confined by barbed wire and guarded by armed soldiers. While I cannot begin to pass judgment on those who did decide to enlist under these historical conditions, I do want to consider how under these same conditions the members of the FPC might have come to claim their rhetorical agency, or their ability to act with words, and their resistant *ethos*, or the authority to explicitly resist oppression through writing. In using the often overused terms *resistant* and *resist,* I draw upon a discussion of Roger Gottlieb's work by camp studies scholar Arthur Hansen, who writes that to "qualify as authentic acts of resistance . . . [the] motivation must be to prevent, restrict, or terminate the oppressor's group exercise of power over the oppressed . . . [or to] 'lessen the total quality of oppression, not just shift it around.'" In addition, to resist, in Gottlieb's terms, means to "place oneself in jeopardy" at the hands of an oppressor (Gottlieb, quoted in Hansen 2002, 82). In this chapter, then, claiming a resistant ethos can be understood as claiming the authority to consciously "prevent, restrict, or terminate" an "exercise of power" over one's group, and to do so at some kind of material risk (for the FPC, further imprisonment), via an act of literacy in response to a specific moment in history.

To fully understand the nature of this resistant ethos and its material embodiment in the FPC writings, we should understand the ways in which the FPC's circulated bulletins were authorized, or sanctioned, not only by members themselves but by much of the camp community, and even the broader social conditions of the exact moment in history. This collective sanctioning, or coauthorization, was key to the FPC's emerging ethos, and developed out of several competing processes working to enable or suppress its draft resistance rhetoric. As Brandt and Clinton remind us, "literate practices can be shaped out of the struggle of competing interests and agents, . . . [and] multiple interests can be satisfied during a single performance of reading or writing. . . . 'Agency' does not have to be sacrificed through such an analysis, only recognized as multisourced" (2002, 350–351).

If we understand that rhetorical agency is multisourced, then we must understand the ways in which it contains multiple contradictions.

For any given rhetorical moment, we navigate between and across "concrete" and "abstract" processes that have bumped up against our lives, some of which, intentionally or unintentionally, encourage us to speak or write, to rhetorically act, and others which, intentionally or unintentionally, discourage us. Amid these competing tensions, we may or may not come to voice, or we may come to voice in some moments and not others. For the members of the FPC, the struggle between these contradictory processes seemed to provide the energy, and a kind of permission or authorization, that they needed to rhetorically act by using literacy to "go on the record" with their resistance.

The fact that the FPC did "go on the record" has allowed many of us Japanese Americans who identify with social justice activism to better understand not only our "intellectual heritage" (Royster 2000) but our political one as well. For many Japanese Americans, the "good war" of World War II continues to be one of the events pushing against our own sense of our authority to speak or write the realities of our lives, as the legacy of mass incarceration of almost an entire community continues to weigh heavily in any sense that we may have of ourselves. This is why it is all the more important to recover moments in Japanese American history when Nikkei claimed the rhetorical agency that they *did* have and articulated an explicitly resistant ethos in the face of oppression.

By exploring this history, I am following in the footsteps of several rhetoricians of color who mine the archives for examples of how people of color have performed "rhetorics of survivance" (Powell 2002), or have "construct[ed] a sense of an empowered self amid disempowering forces and use the energy generated by this process to act" (Royster 2000, 70), or have tried to find ways to "*create respect under conditions of little or no respect*" (Cintron 1997, x; emphasis in the original). These acts of "recovered legacies" (Lawrence and Cheung 2005) are critical to developing a fuller, and more accurate, understanding of rhetorical history. For Asian Americans specifically, these acts of recovery are important in that writing like that of the FPC helps document the ways in which people of Asian ancestry chose to "talk back" to both the symbolic and material incarnation of two racialized stereotypes that continue to frame Asian American experience in the United States—the "model minority" and the "perpetual foreigner." In addition, understanding the ways in which social conditions called forth, "sponsored," or coauthorized the struggle against racism can help us imagine how the social conditions of our own time might do the same, and thus enable us to continue the resistant legacy of literacy that we have as racialized people living in a racist society. For those of us who have always hoped that our communities were not simply a group of "Quiet Americans" (Hosokawa 1969), complicit with each and every aspect of the incarceration period, recovering the written words of this resistant legacy can potentially help restore the psychic wholeness we need to engage in contemporary struggles of our own. In other words, archival recovery matters for *all* of us because we need to understand our human rhetorical heritage, but archival recovery matters for *some* of us in order to *recover* from both material and psychological damages. This is why through this research, even as many members of the FPC are still alive, I have come to claim them as *ancestors*, that is, as part of my rhetorical ancestry, *coauthor(iz)ers,* if you will, of what I am attempting to do here. It is in their name, then, that I write these words for you to recover.

THE EMERGENCE OF THE HEART MOUNTAIN FAIR PLAY COMMITTEE

The year before the draft was announced, Kiyoshi Okamoto, a fifty-four-year-old Nisei who had challenged many WRA policies since the beginning of the incarceration period, began giving talks on the Constitution to whoever would listen, calling himself the "Fair Play Committee of One." One night, after an open debate with Nobu Kawai, one of the editors of the *Heart Mountain Sentinel*, on whether or not people should answer the infamous loyalty questionnaire with qualifications,[2] several younger Nisei, including Frank Emi, Paul Nakadate, and Isamu Horino, sought him out for weekly discussions. As historian Eric Muller wrote, these "younger men were drawn to Okamoto, seeing him as a visionary and a constitutional scholar, [even though] Okamoto had no legal training and developed his rather elaborate and some idiosyncratic

2. One of the more famous aspects of the incarceration period, the loyalty questionnaire was a form distributed to all inmates, purportedly designed to see if they were qualified to receive temporary clearances for leave from camp. Included on the form were the two most controversial questions, number 27, which asked if internees would be willing to serve in the U.S. armed services, and number 28, which asked if internees (many of whom were barred from U.S. citizenship) would forswear any allegiance to the Japanese emperor. Needless to say, these questions caused much distress in the community, dividing many family members and generations. People who answered no to both questions were removed from their respective camps and segregated as troublemakers in Tule Lake. Most FPC members had answered yes, but many had written in qualifications to their answers, saying they would fight only if their present circumstances were changed.

views on the Bill of Rights and the Constitution entirely from his own study" (2001, 77).

While the younger Nisei admired Okamoto for his righteous zeal in the face of oppression, the WRA and some *Sentinel* staff often portrayed him as "an 'intellectual hobo' and a 'latrine lawyer,' a man who was 'over-radical, unreasonable, irresponsible, and verbose'" (Muller 2001, 77). While much of this perception can be assumed to stem from the political anxiety that Okamoto must have instilled in WRA authorities, former FPC members also remember him as being in love with "salty expressions" (Emi 1998). Regardless, many of the draft-age Nisei in Heart Mountain were taken with his "great passion, creativity, and willingness to speak bluntly" (Muller 2001, 77). As former Heart Mountain resistor Mits Koshiyama put it, "I heard he had coarse language, but he was eloquent in preparing people to understand and study what the government was doing" (2001).

Some internment historians contend that this "preparation" would not have gone anywhere had a concrete issue not emerged while the FPC was holding its discussions (Nelson 1976, 119). But after the draft was announced, over the course of a week, the FPC transformed from a small study group to "a formal and militant resistance movement"authorized by a sizeable number of both Issei (first-generation, noncitizen) and Nisei (second-generation, citizen) internees. According to historian Douglas Nelson, "The change came on the evening of January 26, at a public meeting attended by almost 300 evacuees. The group voted to officially dedicate the Fair Play Committee to the clarification of 'certain issues raised by the decision to draft the Nisei'" (121).

Over the course of the next two months, the FPC not only responded to practically nightly invitations to give standing-room-only talks across camp (Emi 2002, 53), but also gave open public forums where the group's position was discussed and honed among audiences as large as four hundred Issei and Nisei, including a dues-paying membership that grew to 275 young men. For those who could not attend the meetings, or perhaps felt too nervous to do so, the FPC also issued a total of three mimeographed bulletins of its evolving position, posting them on the outside walls of barracks, latrines, and the mess hall. It is in the third and final bulletin, "one for all-all for one," that we can see the FPC's conscious resistance fully articulated.

Opening their one-page manifesto with two epigraphs from the Bill of Rights, the document moves on to declare that the Nisei have been "complacent" and "too inarticulate" and that the time for "decisive action" is "NOW!" Following a sweeping detailed catalog of the ways the rights of Japanese Americans have been violated thus far, the FPC declares the draft to be the proverbial straw that broke the camel's back. It is then that the FPC openly refuses to go to war while the Japanese American community is still incarcerated en masse:

> [U]until we are restored all our rights, all discriminatory features of the Selective Service abolished, and measures are taken to remedy the past injustices thru Judicial pronouncement or Congressional act, we feel that the present program of drafting us from this concentration camp is unjust, unconstitutional, and against all principles of civilized usage. Therefore, WE MEMBERS OF THE FAIR PLAY COMMITTEE HEREBY REFUSE TO GO TO THE PHYSICAL EXAMINATION OR TO THE INDUCTION IF OR WHEN WE ARE CALLED IN ORDER TO CONTEST THE ISSUE (FPC 1944a, capital letters original[3]).

Even though the writers followed this paragraph by declaring that they were "all loyal Americans fighting for JUSTICE AND DEMOCRACY RIGHT HERE AT HOME" (FPC 1944a), it was this bulletin, and this exact wording, that eventually landed the seven-man steering committee of the FPC in prison. While sixty-three other FPC-member resistors were arrested for refusing induction, the FPC leadership was arrested, tried, and convicted for "conspiracy to counsel Heart Mountain's draft-age Nisei to evade the draft" (Muller 2001, 114). In other words, it is because of this final bulletin, the focus of my study, that the FPC leaders were convicted for their rhetorical actions.

THE COAUTHORIZATION OF A RESISTANT ETHOS

Damage as an Authorizing Force

To understand the members of the Fair Play Committee's emergence as rhetorical actors, and the simultaneous construction of their resistant ethos "amid disempowering forces," I want to first consider the role that oppression, along with its local and distant agents, plays in both "authoring" and "authorizing" resistant rhetoric.

First and foremost, "minority discourse," Abdul JanMohamed and David Lloyd assert, "is a product of damage." This damage, they go on to explain, is "more or less systematically inflicted . . . by the dominant

3. All capital letters in excerpts from the FPC manifesto are retained as they were printed in the original.

culture. The destruction involved is manifold, bearing down on variant modes of social formation, dismantling previously functional economic systems, and deracinating whole populations at best or decimating them at worst" (1990, 4).

It is in *this* context that the discourse of "minorities" is formed and expressed, articulating the pain, anger, frustration, and/or rage that boil up in oneself or in a community facing that "damage."[4] Both local and distant agents can perpetuate that damage and discourage us from claiming or locating any authority within ourselves over our actions, material and/or rhetorical. Locally, in Heart Mountain itself, the Fair Play Committee experienced one of those agents of "damage" to be the WRA-sponsored paper itself, the *Heart Mountain Sentinel.*

One week after the FPC issued its third and final bulletin, the *Sentinel* responded with a front-page editorial, "Our Cards on the Table," accusing the FPC of "deluding" Nisei youth by drawing them "unsuspecting into a tangle of intrigue" (1944). The following week FPC vice president, Paul Nakadate, accused the *Sentinel* of painting a distorted picture not only of the amount of support that the draft had throughout the camp, but also of the FPC's position itself. In doing so, Nakadate explicitly questioned the *Sentinel*'s allegiances: "With the FPC in demand for nightly educational bookings at the request of the Block, the Sentinel could have very easily learned the true stand of the organization. . . . If the Sentinel is going to be the Sentinel of this camp I should like to have it come out clean and straight. Why cannot the outside public know of our genuine feeling instead of putting an artificial front in accordance with WRA policy" (1944).

The *Heart Mountain Sentinel* did seem to be serving as a medium through which a pro-WRA policy position could be fostered, though former editors have more recently denied this accusation (see Hosokawa 1998). Whether or not the WRA-sponsored *Sentinel* stayed consistent with WRA newspaper policy to "provide a medium through which WRA can direct public opinion within the evacuee group, and stimulate reactions and attitudes desirable for the maintenance of a high morale" (quoted in Mizuno 2001, 507) is less important for the purposes of this

4. "Minority discourse is in this respect a mode of ideology in the sense in which Marx in 'On the Jewish Question' describes religion—at once the sublimation and the expression of misery—but with the critical difference that in the case of minority forms even the sublimation of misery needs to be understood as primarily a strategy for survival, for the preservation in some form or other of cultural identity, *and* for political critique" (JanMohamed and Lloyd 1990, 5; emphasis in the original).

chapter than is the reality that the FPC *perceived* that the *Sentinel* was doing so. And given the tone and attitudes professed in earlier articles and editorials leading up to the FPC's public emergence of its resistant rhetoric, this perception is more than understandable.

The week after the draft was announced, and a month before the FPC issued its third bulletin, the *Sentinel* ran a front-page story profiling a young Nisei, a former "newshound for the Sentinel," who had volunteered for the military even amid his conflicted feelings about serving while his community lived behind barbed wire. Engaging a kind of proto–model minority rhetoric, the *Sentinel* began its tale of honor: "One of the most striking proofs that America has met with success in teaching its people loyalty to democratic traditions is found, we believe, in the Japanese American evacuees whose faith in American democracy remains solid and real despite the rankling injustice of evacuation" (Kitasako 1944, 1).

Continuing, the *Sentinel* moved back and forth between acknowledging the hardship and the confusion the Nisei faced as they navigated their decision:

> The economic losses cut deep, but equally as painful was the severe beating his [the young Nisei who was the subject of the article] faith in American democracy suffered. To a youth who had been nourished on the tenets of democracy, evacuation was something which threw him way off. He found it hard to get his bearings. Things happened too fast, too crazily, too un-Americanly.
>
> Where was the sanctity of United States citizenship, where was the justice of American democracy? Was it all talk after all?
>
> It was disappointing, heartbreaking. America had rudely let him down.
>
> But in the cool light of second thought, he realized the futility of protesting. He rationalized, and decided to fall in line with what the government wanted evacuees to believe: that evacuation was a military necessity.
>
> "You can't buck the army. It's [*sic*] word is final. But I'll always feel that evacuation was not fair."
>
> But the healing salve of time went to work on his wounds, and as the months went tumbling by, even amid the penal atmosphere of this camp, his battered faith was patched up almost as good as new. . . .
>
> "It takes a maximum of faith to volunteer after you've been stuck into a camp like this, and in face of that sentiment," he said. "But if you want to be an American, you have to show it, and the best way to prove it is to offer your life for your country." (Kitasako 1944, 1, 5)

With this article, the Sentinel seems to address the "endless questions" it anticipates the Nisei having in its editorial of the week before. But the answer was simple: faith in American democracy is best shown by offering your life for your country. Certainly not by protesting what everyone, even the staff of the Sentinel, seemed to agree was an injustice. With this kind of tacit silencing of dissent, "if you want to be an American," the *Sentinel* perpetuated the idea that Japanese Americans should just accept the realities of their oppressive situation.

It's important to note, though, that the *Sentinel* was only a local incarnation of government policies put forth by the WRA and the Office of War Information policy (see Mizuno 2001). The true oppressive culprit here was not the *Sentinel* but the U.S. government, with its history and contemporary reality of institutionalized racism toward the Nikkei and other people racialized within the United States as "minorities." After all, this entire situation took place during a time of war, when racialized animosity was heightened toward people of Japanese ancestry no matter what they professed the best response to be. Eleven months before the draft announcement, the head of the western Defense Command, General DeWitt, uttered his famous words before Congress: "A Jap's a Jap. . . . There is no way to determine their loyalty. . . . It makes no difference whether he is an American citizen; theoretically he is still a Japanese and you can't change him" (quoted in Niiya 2001, 66), and the year before that, right before the forced removal was announced, the *LA Times*, which served an area of California where Heart Mountain Nisei had grown up, had written a similar argument on its editorial page:

> A viper is nonetheless a viper wherever the egg is hatched. . . . So, a Japanese American born of Japanese parents, nurtured upon Japanese traditions, living in a transplanted Japanese atmosphere and thoroughly inoculated with Japanese . . . ideals, notwithstanding his normal brand of accidental citizenship almost inevitably and with the rarest exceptions grows up to be Japanese, and not an American in his . . . ideas, and is . . . menacing . . . unless . . . hamstrung. Thus, while it might cause injustice to a few to treat them all as potential enemies . . . I cannot escape the conclusion . . . that such treatment . . . should be accorded to each and all of them while we are at war with their race. (59)

Publicly, Nikkei loyalty to the United States was continually questioned, regardless of the fact that a twenty-five-page government report had been conducted a month before the attacks on Pearl Harbor and circulated among high officials of the State and War departments prior to the incarceration decision, concluding that "there was no Japanese problem" in regard to loyalty (see Weglyn 1976). While the Nikkei community was unaware of the report at the time, it was aware of the absurdity of the mass suspicion and the effects of the racist hysteria its members continued to face even inside the camps.

Given this historical context, some might find the "advice" of the *Sentinel* editors to be reasonable. All of these processes do seem to discourage Japanese Americans from acting in any explicit opposition, especially given the cultural norms of *shikataganai* (It can't be helped) and *gaman* (Endure) which were so prevalent in the community at this time.[5] But when a newspaper that is sponsored by one's oppressors baits its readers' allegiances ("if you want to be an American"), declares the "endless questions" of the draft as "senseless," and portrays those that do question the draft as manipulative provocateurs, it does seem as if the editorial staff has become conscious or unconscious agents of the damage being inflicted. And despite all implicit and explicit warnings, the FPC was not going to remain "complacent" or "inarticulate" and instead would move to actively respond to these types of silencing processes designed to discourage it from engaging in a rhetoric of resistance via local and distant agents.

Well aware of the *Sentinel*'s position on the draft, the FPC knew that part of what was at stake in organizing an effective movement was its disagreements with the WRA-sponsored editorial staff as to the nature of *true* American behavior—that is, what being a "loyal" American entailed. Anticipating its detractors, the FPC explicitly addressed the issue in the second half of its manifesto:

> We are not being disloyal. We are not evading the draft. We are all loyal Americans fighting for JUSTICE AND DEMOCRACY RIGHT HERE AT HOME. So, restore our rights as such, rectify the injustices of evacuation,

5. In his discussion of "cultures of resistance," Takashi Fujitani cautions us to remember that all cultures are in a constant state of change, impacted by their specific historical circumstances. So while these cultural norms probably were in effect during the incarceration period, we should also understand them as kinds of "invented traditions" born from a century of competing nationalisms. We should also be aware, Fujitani argues, that the concept of *ganbaru* (to persevere in struggle), was another cultural "norm" with which some Nikkei identified, suggesting a more active engagement than is often associated, stereotypically, with Japanese Americans (2002, 24).

> of the concentration, of the detention, and of the pauperization as such. In short, treat us in accordance with the principles of the Constitution.
>
> If what we are voicing is wrong, if what we ask is disloyal, if what we think is unpatriotic, then Abraham Lincoln, one of our greatest American President [sic] was also guilty as such, for he said, "If by the mere force of numbers a majority should deprive a minority of any Constitutional right, it might in a moral point of view justify a revolution." (FPC 1944b)

Calling upon "the principles of the Constitution" and the denial of "[c]onstitutional right[s]," the FPC denied the disloyalty of which it knew it would be accused. In this way, the FPC's resistant rhetoric can be seen as authorized, or called forth, in part by the rhetorical processes of the *Sentinel*, which had encouraged Nisei to emerge from their "questioning" with a "maximum of faith" in American democracy and with the willingness to offer their lives for their country. This local position simply incensed most members of the FPC.

While it's important to avoid the oversimplification of characterizing the *Sentinel* staff as WRA "dupes," it is equally important to see how the positions set forth by the *Sentinel* were connected to distant and more "global" forces. To understand the ways in which large-scale oppression can work to coauthorize an oppressed group of people to claim rhetorical agency, we can read the FPC bulletin through JanMohamed and Lloyd's theory of "minority discourse":

> Out of the damage inflicted on minority cultures, which, as Fanon so clearly recognized, prevents their "development" according to the western model of individual and racial identity, emerges the possibility of a collective subjectivity formed in practice rather than contemplation. . . .
>
> [T]he collective nature of all minority discourse also derives from the fact that minority individuals are always treated and forced to experience themselves generically. Coerced into a negative, generic subject-position, the oppressed individual responds by transforming that position into a positive, collective one. (1990, 9–10)

This "transformation" can be seen in the first half of the bulletin. Here the FPC testifies to its given "negative, generic subject-position" of a collection of oppressed "one hundred and ten thousand innocent" individuals, who, as the FPC recounts, "were kicked out of their homes, literally uprooted from where they have lived for the greater part of their life, and herded like dangerous criminals into concentration camps with barbed wire fences and military police guarding it," and then the group transforms that position into a "positive, collective one" in the "practice" of its rhetorical act:

> *We, the Nisei* have been complacent and too inarticulate to the unconstitutional acts that we were subjected to. If ever there was a time or cause for decisive action, IT IS NOW!
>
> *We, the members of the FPC* are not afraid to go war—we are not afraid to risk our lives for our country. We would gladly sacrifice our lives to protect and uphold the principles and ideals of our country as set forth in the Constitution and the Bill of Rights, for on its inviolability depends the freedom, liberty, justice, and protection of all people *including Japanese-Americans and all other minority groups* . . . unless such actions are opposed NOW, and steps taken to remedy such injustices and discriminations IMMEDIATELY, *the future of all minorities* and the future of this democratic nation is in danger. (1944; italics added)

As one part of a body of people "forced to experience themselves generically," the FPC claims its coauthorized ethos on the grounds of that experience, employing repetition to build a sense of indignation as the particularities of both the authors' and intended audience's oppression are recounted: "Without any hearings, without due process of law as guaranteed by the Constitution and Bill of Rights, without any charges filed against us, without any evidence of wrongdoing on our part . . .". This indignation then erupts into the use of all capital letters, rhetorically symbolizing the FPC's collective rage, with which, hopefully, the audience now identifies:

> AND THEN, WITHOUT RECTIFICATION OF THE INJUSTICES COMMITTED AGAINST US NOR WITHOUT RESTORATION OF OUR RIGHTS AS GUARANTEED BY THE CONSTITUTION, WE ARE ORDERED TO JOIN THE ARMY THRU DISCRIMINATORY PROCEDURES INTO A SEGREGATED COMBAT UNIT! (1944)

Thus, in this passage, the FPC is able to rhetorically claim its experiences with racialized oppression and "[o]ut of the damage inflicted," authorize itself to claim its rhetorical agency to resist through the written word.

In order to more fully understand how the FPC did this, though, we must consider additional ways in which its rhetorical agency was "multisourced." If some experiences worked to coauthorize the FPC's resistant ethos by attempting to deny its members' right to live as full human beings, other experiences coauthorized their burgeoning ethos by doing the opposite—encouraging the Nisei to fully claim that right, and in doing so, encourage their resistant ethos. This "encouragement" can be better understood by considering some of the rhetorical choices in the final FPC bulletin.

Sponsorship as an Authorizing Force

> Accumulated layers of sponsoring influences—in families, workplaces, schools, memory—carry forms of literacy that have been shaped out of ideological and economic struggles of the past. (Brandt 2001, 567)

Having grown up as the children of immigrants during the 1920s and '30s, the majority of the FPC leaders would have been immersed in the ideology of the Americanization movement in public schools. In California, where most of the members of the FPC were from, the movement provided educators with "a rhetorical framework for those who worked with immigrants. Some general characteristics of Americanization included staunch support for democracy, representative government, law and order, capitalism, general health . . . and command of the English language. Public schools were a key component of Americanization, the aim of which was to transform immigrants into patriotic, loyal and intelligent citizens of the Republic" (Yoo 2000, 22).

According to the *Los Angeles School Journal*, by 1925, most children of immigrants in California had already become to a "considerable extent Americanized," having had "placed upon them the imprint of American citizenship" in their "desire to live as Americans" (Shafer 1925, 10). Whether this was true or not, we can certainly imagine that the discourse of American citizenship and civics education, including discussions of the U.S. Constitution, was prevalent in the public schools and thus readily available to Nisei children of the time, including future FPC leaders Paul Nakadate and Frank Emi, who played key roles in the writing of the bulletins.

Interestingly enough, in addition to their "Americanist" experiences in the public schools, the Nisei along the West Coast may have also gotten a heavy dose of Americanization through the Japanese-language schools, which were attended by almost every Nisei child during this time period. Frequently under attack by xenophobic organizations along the West Coast, the Japanese-language schools were designed by the Issei leaders as a way to teach Japanese to the second generation and instill in them cultural values deemed necessary to strengthen and maintain ethnic ties. While leaders in the community differed as to how much the schools should teach values associated with the militarism of the then Japanese empire (Azuma 2005), they also found themselves confronted with two ongoing characteristics of the American empire: white supremacy and American chauvinism. By 1921, the state legislature of California had passed laws to govern these non-state-funded community institutions, including those that would "regulate the operation of schools, the certification of teachers, and the content of instructional materials. . . . To be certified to teach in a school, all teachers had to pass a state examination in English competency (reading, writing, and speaking) as well as in American history and institutions in English. All textbooks and curricula had to be approved by the Superintendent of Public Instruction" (Ichioka 1988, 207).

By the mid-1920s, in response to the growing institutionalization of anti-Japanese racism, the language schools had revised their stated goals, now saying that they were "[b]ased on the spirit of American public schools," with their "purpose" being more to "supplement good civic education" (Ichioka 1988, 207). In other words, the atmosphere of Americanism and its discourse had been present on some level in both types of schooling available to the future FPC Nisei, both of which may have added another kind of authorization to resist the draft, both rhetorically and materially.

As "one layer" of what Brandt would call a "sponsoring influence," this kind of "Americanist" discourse can be seen throughout the FPC bulletin. The first thing Heart Mountain residents would have read in the FPC's third and final bulletin are two epigraphs from the Bill of Rights:

> "No person shall be deprived of life, liberty, or property, without due process of law, nor private property be taken for public use without just compensation." Article V Bill of Rights.

> "Neither slavery nor involuntary servitude, except as punishment for crime whereof the party shall have been duly convicted, shall exist within the United States, or any place subject to their jurisdiction." Article XIII Bill of Rights.

Continuing through the one-page mimeographed manifesto, readers would have encountered at least seven different references to the Constitution, the Bill of Rights, "constitutionality," or "unconstitutionality," including explicit reference to the ways in which the current Japanese American circumstances violated the supposed highest law of the land:

> Without any hearings, *without due process of law as guaranteed by the Constitution and Bill of Rights,* without any charges filed against us, without any evidence of wrongdoing on our part, one hundred and ten thousand innocent people were kicked out of their homes . . .
>
> WITHOUT RESTORATION OF OUR RIGHTS *AS GUARANTEED BY THE CONSTITUTION,* WE ARE ORDERED TO JOIN THE ARMY . . .
>
> we feel that the present program of drafting us from this concentration camp is unjust, *unconstitutional* . . . (*italics* added)

In addition to the constitutional references threaded throughout the bulletin, another aspect of Americanist discourse appears with the invocation of Abraham Lincoln in the fifth paragraph—one that I discussed earlier in relation to FPC's rhetorical move to appeal to the principles of the Constitution: "If what we are voicing is wrong, if what we ask is disloyal, if what we think is unpatriotic, then Abraham Lincoln, one of our greatest American President [sic] was also guilty as such, for he said, 'If by the mere force of numbers a majority should deprive a minority on any Constitutional right, it might in a moral point of view justify a revolution.'"

Clearly drawing upon Lincoln's stature as an iconic emancipator of slaves, the FPC seems to invoke Lincoln's name and words not as a kind of legal authorization, as the group does with references to the Constitution, but as a kind of moral authorization to resist when rights are clearly being denied. Whether or not Lincoln can truly be considered a "great" American president (and whether or not the FPC truly believed this to be so) matters less than the fact that the FPC knew that within the rhetorical framework of Americanization, he was *considered* a great American president, having read about him in textbooks used in either the U.S. public or Japanese-language schools.[6] Because the FPC knew that Lincoln was held in such regard within Americanist mythology, additional authorization was provided to establish a resistant ethos in its manifesto.

In addition to the more "distant" authorizing process of Americanization, though, there were also more "local" agents taking part in the enabling processes involved in the FPC's coauthorization. Nisei FPC members—275 in all—paid dues of $2 apiece, which was

6. Compilers and translators of a textbook approved by the California State Superintendent in 1923 for the state's Japanese-language schools prominently featured "[s]tories about George Washington, Abraham Lincoln, Betsy Ross and other American figures" (Ichioka 1988).

used to buy ink and paper for the mimeographed bulletins (Emi 1998). Additional financial support and authorization came from residents who were not officially members of the committee, but who seemed to at least secretly believe in its cause. Guntaro Kubota, the lone Issei on the steering committee, was responsible for drumming up Issei support, providing translation at all meetings and for all bulletins. His wife later described how important Issei sponsorship was: "[T]hat's the only way they can make the money, raise the money, 'cause the Isseis have the money, the Niseis, they're young . . . they didn't have any money." And after listening to Kubota, many Issei did authorize the committee's rhetorical and material actions. As Gloria Kubota explained, the FPC and her husband "got quite a few people, older ladies to follow him around and donate, and it was really cute how some of these old people . . . the ones that believed in him, they just followed him around . . . there were thirty blocks in our Heart Mountain, and it used to be cold but he'd go all over and they'd follow him around. Some people brought all the cash that they had and they'd give it to him" (1993).

But there was also the growing collective energy of the public meetings. By several accounts, there were approximately four hundred people present at the meeting where the decision to explicitly refuse to go was decided. While some say 99 percent voted for it, others say everyone did (Emi 1998; Nelson 1976, 122). Regardless, the FPC leaders afterward certainly would have felt authorized to incorporate explicitly resistant wording into "one for all-all for one," and they certainly would have felt authorized to claim a collective ethos, their rhetorical authority to say, "*We, Nisei* . . ." and distribute their resistant rhetoric throughout Heart Mountain, the prison home in which they found themselves placed during World War II.

ETHOS AS HISTORICAL LOCATION

In some of her early work on the "politics of place," Nedra Reynolds suggested the possibility of considering "ethos as location": "Ethos in fact, occurs in the 'between' . . . as writers struggle to identify their own positions at the intersections of various communities and attempt to establish authority for themselves and their claims" (1993, 333). Following Reynolds, we can see how the FPC's construction of a resistant ethos took place at the intersection not just of various communities, but of several processes discussed above. But in addition to these "discouraging" and "encouraging" authorizations, I'd like to extend Reynolds's point here and suggest that in considering the construction of ethos, location matters not just in terms of space, but also in terms of time—historical location matters.

In writing about Asian American literacy narratives, Morris Young describes the genre as an engagement in a metaphorical "rhetoric of citizenship" in response to the ongoing anti-Asian racism in the United States that constructs anyone of Asian ancestry as being a "perpetual foreigner," no matter how many generations his or her family has lived in the United States. For Japanese Americans during World War II, this "construction" was foregrounded in the racist rhetoric of military leaders and the mainstream press, and materialized in the mass incarceration of all West Coast Nikkei, citizen and noncitizen alike. As a group, people of Japanese ancestry were continually questioned as to whether they could be truly American (read: *human*) with "faces of the enemy" (Hayashi 1992). For some Japanese Americans, being a "loyal" American meant "cooperating" with the WRA and all government policies; for members of the FPC, being a "loyal" American meant calling upon the discourse of the American Constitution and of the Americanist ideologies in which most of them had been schooled, thus exposing the racist hypocrisy of Americanist discourse at the time.

In this age of anti-immigrant rhetoric and legislation, as in the one that brought us the mass incarceration of citizens and noncitizens alike, for many Asian Americans, a "rhetoric of citizenship" may simply symbolize the right to be treated as an equal human being. This was the rhetoric of the Americanist curriculum most Nisei had learned in school. And this was the "master's house" that they knew, the one where they lived. And these were the tools, the "codes of power," that they had.

But what remains true with the use of all codes of power remains true with the use of Americanist discourse—the relations of power tend to be reified and stay intact. When we lay claim to Americanist ideologies, all of us born with U.S. citizenship, despite any antiracist intentions we have, inherit the legacies (become the benefactors) of things done in our name, whether it has been recognized as our name or not. As Kandace Chuh asserts, "By claiming ownership of US national identity, Asian Americanists must also then claim responsibility for the cultural and material imperialism of this nation" (quoted in Fujikane 2005, 94).

Of course, this is not to argue that the FPC was wholeheartedly guilty of imperialist design via its reliance on constitutional discourse. On the contrary, there is no question in my mind that the FPC was asserting its rhetorical agency to resist racist oppression, *especially given its exact historical location.* After all, the men put themselves at material and bodily risk, with every intention of thwarting the oppressions carried out by the War Relocation Authority and were subsequently tried and convicted for conspiracy in a time of war. They enacted their agency to resist via a rhetorical act. But I am also reminded of Perry Anderson, who noted that the term *agent* "possess[es] two opposite connotations. It signifies at once active initiator and passive instrument" (1980, 18). Or, as Brandt and Clinton so ominously assert, "When we use literacy, we also get used" (2002, 350). Of this duplicitous potential, whenever we make a claim on our rhetorical agency, even if it is, in that moment, designed to resist, we should always be aware. This is the complicated path we continue to walk, even today, as we find ourselves at the intersections of many processes working to enable and disable our sense of authority to speak and write.

However, for the FPC and the construction of its resistant ethos in a time of mass incarceration, we must understand that the most pressing contradiction was the absurdity, the *audacity,* of the U.S. government stripping a group of humans of the rights they had been taught all their lives were *inalienable,* force them into so-called relocation camps, surrounded by barbed wire and armed guards, and then tell them they would restore *one* of their rights—the "right to be shot at" (Weglyn 1976, 136). It is within this historical location, this location of *damage,* this intersection of a wild mix of various, and jostling, sponsorships, or literacy authorizations, that we must understand the construction of the Fair Play Committee's resistant ethos.

So while forces like the narrow definitions of "loyalty" were being articulated through the War Relocation Authority–sponsored *Heart Mountain Sentinel,* and calls for *gaman* and *shikataganai* may have echoed from some Issei lips, and the racist rhetoric of politicians and military officials continued to circulate in the minds of many who were incarcerated supposedly for their own safety, these forces undoubtedly combined into a collective message of "Don't speak, don't write" anything that could make things worse. Things are bad enough as it is. All of the above, intentional or not, was serving to limit, serving to damage any rhetorical agency and authority that the Nisei might have claimed.

And yet, this same damage also called forth other forces, which pushed against those attempting to limit the authority that the Nisei could claim. Forces saying, *Speak, write—you must.* Issei donations, the angst and determination of 275 young Nisei men, the "salty expressions" of a "latrine lawyer," and all the aspects of Americanization itself—all of them saying, *Yes, you, Nisei, you.* You do not deserve what is happening to you. You do not deserve it, and you can change it. You must have your conscience and write it, too. You can gather up all the energy "generated by this process" to claim and name your ethos, incarcerated and incensed, because you have been *coauthorized* to do so.

CONCLUSION: RELOCATING AUTHORITY

The FPC's relocation of authority, the naming and claiming of a resistant ethos in a time of war, serves as a key part of our legacy as Asian Americans. In our own time and place, the United States of the post–9/11 world, this legacy remains important to invoke, for we have seen a new round of racial profiling and the partial rounding up of another group of racialized peoples,[7] not to mention the ongoing political justifications of what is now clearly an illegal war. In times like these, when civil rights erode, when race, gender, sexuality, and class-based inequalities deepen, when a vastly unpopular war expands, all forms of paralysis that any of us might feel are understandable. However, trite as the saying may be, wherever there is oppression, there is indeed resistance. In June 2006, another Asian American, Lt. Ehren Watada, became the first commissioned officer to refuse deployment to Iraq after he had set about to "learn all that he could about the war and what he and those he commanded would likely face" ("About" 2007). As an officer, Watada had his own form of "coauthorizations," including sanctioned time to "read widely," and he soon became convinced that the war in Iraq was illegal. And like the FPC, he decided to put himself at material and bodily risk as he publicly refused to be sent to war.[8] While Watada is only one person, he is part of a growing antiwar movement among the people of the United States' own military (Cooper 2007). Certainly information about this movement should be a larger part of mass public knowledge than it currently is; however, many of these accounts of opposition and

7. "In the two months following September 11, more than twelve hundred Muslim, Arab, and South Asian men were detained and held indefinitely" (Nguyen 2005, xvii).

8. While the parallels between the FPC and Watada are not exact, Watada himself sees the similarities: "[The resisters] said 'we're Japanese American' and we are part of this country no matter what the president says. They faced ostracization and imprisonment, but it was shown many years later that they were correct. . . . What I'm doing is no different" (quoted in Hamamoto 2006).

resistance have been written about and made available via the Internet and various print sources. These encoded acts of resistance mean that stories like that of Watada's and the FPC's hold the potential to "travel, integrate and endure" (Brandt and Clinton 2002, 337) and join a written legacy of Asian American resistance. And as long as these written accounts are not destroyed or erased, the potential remains for them to be recovered for both material and psychological purposes.

So no matter what amount of "damage" we do in fact face, one potential source of our recovery lies in our rhetorical history, our legacy of resistance encoded in our own community's "ways with words." Understanding this legacy of our written rhetoric helps us as Asian Americans, too long constructed as model minorities and/or perpetual foreigners, trace our own set of coauthorizations, our political and intellectual ancestries, which, in turn, helps make possible what we so sorely need in order to act, and write: the relocation of authority back into our bodies and ourselves.

REFERENCES

Abe, Frank. 2000. *Conscience and the Constitution* [video recording]. Hohokus, NJ: Transit Media.

About Lt. Ehren Watada. November 10, 2007. *Thank You LT.org*, January 21 (accessed July 17, 2008). www.thankyoult.org/content/view/1069/80

Anderson, Perry. 1980. Agency. In *Arguments within English Marxism*. London: Verso.

Azuma, Eiichiro. 2005. *Between Two Empires: Race, History, and Transnationalism in Japanese America*. New York: Oxford University Press.

Brandt, Deborah. 2001. Sponsors of Literacy. In *Literacy: A Critical Sourcebook*, edited by E. Cushman et al. New York: Bedford/St. Martin's.

Brandt, Deborah, and Katie Clinton. 2002. Limits of the Local: Expanding Perspectives on Literacy as a Social Practice. *Journal of Literacy Research* 34 (3): 337–356.

Chin, Frank. 2002. *Born in the USA: A Story of Japanese America, 1889–1947*. Lanham, MD: Rowman and Littlefield.

Cintron, Ralph. 1997. *Angels' Town: Chero Ways, Gang Life, and Rhetorics of the Everyday*. Boston: Beacon.

Cooper, Marc. 2007. About Face. *Nation*, January 8–15, 11–16.

Emi, Frank. 1998. Interview II by Frank Abe, January 30. Frank Abe Collection, Densho. http://archive.densho.org/main.aspx (accessed March 12, 2006).

———. 2002. Protest and Resistance: An American Tradition. In Mackey 2002.

Fair Play Committee. 1944. *Questions and Answers on the Fair Play Committee*. http://www.resisters.com/documents/FPC_Bulletin_2.htm (accessed March 23, 2006).

Fujikane, Candace. 2005. Foregrounding Native Nationalism: A Critique of Antinationalist Sentiment in Asian American Studies. In *Asian Americans After Critical Mass*, edited by K. A. Ono. Malden, MA: Blackwell.

Fujitani, Takashi. 2002. Cultures of Resistance: Japanese American Draft Resisters in Transnational Perspective. In Mackey 2002.

Hamamoto, Ben. 2006. Nikkei Army Lieutenant Calls the Iraq War Illegal, Refuses Deployment. *Nichi Bei Times*. http://www.nichibeitimes.com/articles/stories.php?su

baction=showfull&id=1150399740&archive=&start_from=&ucat=1& (accessed March 26, 2008).

Hansen, Arthur A. 2002. Protest-Resistance and the Heart Mountain Experience: The Revitalization of a Robust Nikkei Tradition. In Mackey 2002.

Hayashi, Ann Koto. 1992. Face of the Enemy, Heart of a Patriot: Japanese-American Internment Narratives. Ph.D. diss., Ohio State University.

Heart Mountain Sentinel. 1944. Our Cards on the Table. http://www.resisters.com/documents/HMS_OurCardsOnTheTable.htm (accessed March 23, 2006).

Hosokawa, Bill. 1969. *Nisei: The Quiet Americans.* New York: Morrow.

———. 1998. The Sentinel Story. In *Remembering Heart Mountain: Essays of Japanese American Internment in Wyoming,* edited by M. Mackey. Cody, WY: western History Publications.

Ichioka, Yuji. 1988. *The Issei: The World of the First Generation Japanese Immigrants, 1885–1924.* New York: Free Press.

Inada, Lawson Fusao. 2000. *Only What We Could Carry: The Japanese American Internment Experience.* Berkeley, CA: Heyday.

JanMohamed, Abdul, and David Lloyd. 1990. Introduction: Toward a Theory of Minority Discourse; What Is to Be Done? In *The Nature and Context of Minority Discourse,* edited by A. JanMohamed and D. Lloyd. New York: Oxford University Press.

Kitasako, John. 1944. Faith in American Democracy Keeps Nisei Going. *Heart Mountain Sentinel.* February 12, 1, 5.

Koshiyama, Mits. 2001. Interview by Alice Ito, July 14. Densho. http://archive.densho.org/main.aspx (accessed March 12, 2006).

Kubota, Gloria. 1993. Interview by Frank Abe, August 28. Frank Abe Collection, Densho. http://archive.densho.org/main.aspx (accessed March 12, 2006).

Lawrence, Keith, and Floyd Cheung. 2005. *Recovered Legacies: Authority and Identity in Early Asian American Literature, Asian American History and Culture.* Philadelphia: Temple University Press.

Mackey, Mike. 2002. *A Matter of Conscience: Essays on the World War II Heart Mountain Draft Resistance Movement.* Powell, WY: western History Publications.

Mizuno, Takeya. 2001. The Creation of the "Free" Press in Japanese-American Camps: The War Relocation Authority's Planning and Making of the Camp Newspaper Policy. *Journalism and Mass Communication Quarterly* 78 (3): 503–518.

Muller, Eric L. 2001. *Free to Die for Their Country: The Story of the Japanese American Draft Resisters in World War II.* Chicago: University of Chicago Press.

Nakadate, Paul. 1944. Letter to the editor. *Heart Mountain Sentinel.* March 18, 5.

Nelson, Douglas W. 1976. *Heart Mountain: The History of an American Concentration Camp.* Madison: State Historical Society of Wisconsin for the Dept. of History, University of Wisconsin.

Nguyen, Tram. 2005. *We Are All Suspects Now: Untold Stories from Immigrant Communities After 9/11.* Boston: Beacon.

Niiya, Brian. 2001. *Encyclopedia of Japanese American History: An A-to-Z Reference from 1868 to the Present.* Rev. ed. New York: Japanese American National Museum.

Omori, Emiko, and Chizuko Omori. 1999. *Rabbit in the Moon* [video recording]. San Francisco: Wabi-Sabi Productions.

Powell, Malea. 2002. Rhetorics of Survivance: How American Indians *Use* Writing. *College Composition and Communication* 53:396–434.

Reynolds, Nedra. 1993. *Ethos* as Location: New Sites for Understanding Discursive Authority. *Rhetoric Review* 11 (2): 325–338.

Royster, Jacqueline Jones. 2000. *Traces of a Stream: Literacy and Social Change among African American Women.* Pittsburgh: University of Pittsburgh Press.

Shafer, Harry M. 1925. Tendencies in Immigrant Education. *Los Angeles School Journal* 9 (5): 9–11, 46.

Weglyn, Michi. 1976. *Years of Infamy: The Untold Story of America's Concentration Camps.* New York: Morrow.

Yoo, David. 2000. *Growing up Nisei: Race, Generation, and Culture among Japanese Americans of California, 1924–49.* Urbana: University of Illinois Press.

Young, Morris. 2004. *Minor Re/Visions: Asian American Literacy Narratives as a Rhetoric of Citizenship.* Carbondale: Southern Illinois University Press.

Appendix

FAIR PLAY COMMITTEE THIRD BULLETIN[9]

FAIR PLAY COMMITTEE
"one for all – all for one"

"no person shall be deprived of life, liberty, or property, without due process of law, nor private property be taken for public use without just compensation." Article V Bill of Rights.
"Neither slavery nor involuntary servitude, except as punishment for crime whereof the party shall have been duly convicted, shall exist within the United States, or any place subject to their jurisdiction." Article XIII Bill of R.

We, the Nisei have been complacent and too inarticulate to the unconstitutional acts that we were subjected to. If ever there was a time or cause for decisive action, IT IS NOW!

We, the ~~Nisei have~~ members of the FPC are not afraid to go to war—we are not afraid to risk our lives for our country. We would gladly sacrifice our lives to protect and uphold the principles and ideals of our country as set forth in the Constitution and the Bill of Rights, for on its inviolability depends the freedom, liberty, justice, and protection of all people including Japanese-Americans and all other minority groups. But have we been given such freedom, such liberty, such justice, such protection? NO!! Without any hearings, without due process of law as guaranteed by the Constitution and Bill of Rights, without any charges filed against us, without any evidence of wrongdoing on our part, one hundred and ten thousand innocent people were kicked out of their homes, literally uprooted from where they have lived for the greater part of their life, and herded like dangerous criminals into concentration camps with barb wire fence and military police guarding it, AND THEN, WITHOUT RECTIFICATION OF THE INJUSTICES COMMITTED AGAINST US NOR WITHOUT RESTORATION OF OUR RIGHTS AS GUARANTEED BY THE CONSTITUTION, WE ARE ORDERED TO JOIN THE ARMY THRU DISCRIMINATORY PROCEDURES INTO A SEGREGATED COMBAT UNIT! Is that the American way? NO! The FPC believes that unless such actions are opposed NOW, and steps taken to remedy such injustices and discriminations IMMEDIATELY, the future of all minorities and the future of this democratic nation is in danger.

Thus, the members of the FPC unanimously decided at their last open meeting that until we are restored all our rights, all discriminatory features of the Selective Service abolished, and measures are taken to remedy the past injustices thru Judicial pronouncement or Congressional act, we feel that the present program of drafting us from this concentration camp is unjust, unconstitutional, and against all principles of civilized usage, therefore, THE MEMBERS OF THE FAIR PLAY COMMITTEE HEREBY REFUSE TO GO TO THE PHYSICAL EXAMINATION OR TO THE INDUCTION IF OR WHEN WE ARE CALLED IN ORDER TO CONTEST THE ISSUE.

We are not being disloyal. We are not evading the draft. We are all loyal Americans fighting for JUSTICE AND DEMOCRACY RIGHT HERE AT HOME. So, restore our rights as such, rectify the injustices of evacuation, of the concentration, of the detention, and of the pauperization as such. In short, treat us in accordance with the principles of the Constitution.

If what we are voicing is wrong, if what we ask is disloyal, if what we think is unpatriotic, then Abraham Lincoln, one of our greatest American President was also guilty of such, for he said, "If by the mere force of numbers a majority should deprive a minority of any Constitutional right, it might in a moral point of view justify a revolution."

Among the one thousand odd members of the Fair Play Committee, there are Nisei men over the draft age and Nisei girls who are not directly affected by the present Selective Service program, but who believe in the ideals and principles of our country, therefore are helping the FPC in our fight against injustice and discriminations.

We hope that all persons whose ideals and interests are with us will do all they can to help us. We may have to engage in court actions, but as such actions ~~require~~ require large sums of money, we do need financial support and when the time comes, we hope that you will back us up to the limit.

ATTENTION MEMBERS! FAIR PLAY COMMITTEE MEETING SUNDAY, MARCH 5, 2:00 P.M. BLOCK 6-30 MESS. PARENTS, BROTHERS, SISTERS, AND FRIENDS INVITED.

---

9. Reprinted with permission from Frank Abe, www.resisters.com. Still image from *Conscience and the Constitution,* produced by Frank Abe for the Independent Television Service, with funding provided by the Corporation for Public Broadcasting.

FAIR PLAY COMMITTEE
"one for all—all for one"

"No person shall be deprived of life, liberty, or property, without due process of law, nor private property be taken for public use without just compensation." Article V Bill of Rights.

"Neither slavery nor involuntary servitude, except as punishment for crime whereof the party shall have been duly convicted, shall exist within the United States, or any place subject to their jurisdiction." Article XIII Bill of Rights.

We, the Nisei have been complacent and too inarticulate to the unconstitutional acts that we were subjected to. If ever there was a time or cause for decisive action, IT IS NOW!

We, the members of the FPC are not afraid to go to war—we are not afraid to risk our lives for our country. We would gladly sacrifice our lives to protect and uphold the principles and ideals of our country as set forth in the Constitution and the Bill of Rights, for on its inviolability depends the freedom, liberty, justice, and protection of all people including Japanese-Americans and all other minority groups. But have we been given such freedom, such liberty, such justice, such protection? NO!! Without any hearings, without due process of law as guaranteed by the Constitution and Bill of Rights, without any charges filed against us, without any evidence of wrongdoing on our part, one hundred and ten thousand innocent people were kicked out of their homes, literally uprooted from where they have lived for the greater part of their life, and herded like dangerous criminals into concentration camps with barbed wire fences and military police guarding it, AND THEN, WITHOUT RECTIFICATION OF THE INJUSTICES COMMITTED AGAINST US NOR WITHOUT RESTORATION OF OUR RIGHTS AS GUARANTEED BY THE CONSTITUTION, WE ARE ORDERED TO JOIN THE ARMY THRU DISCRIMINATORY PROCEDURES INTO A SEGREGATED COMBAT UNIT! Is that the American way? NO! The FPC believes that unless such actions are opposed NOW, and steps taken to remedy such injustices and discriminations IMMEDIATELY, the future of all minorities and the future of this democratic nation is in danger.

Thus, the members of the FPC unanimously decided at their last open meeting that until we are restored all our rights, all discriminatory features of the Selective Service abolished, and measures are taken to remedy the past injustices thru Judicial pronouncement or Congressional act, we feel that the present program of drafting us from this concentration camp is unjust, unconstitutional, and against all principles of civilized usage. Therefore, WE MEMBERS OF THE FAIR PLAY COMMITTEE HEREBY REFUSE TO GO TO THE PHYSICAL EXAMINATION OR TO THE INDUCTION IF OR WHEN WE ARE CALLED IN ORDER TO CONTEST THE ISSUE.

We are not being disloyal. We are not evading the draft. We are all loyal Americans fighting for JUSTICE AND DEMOCRACY RIGHT HERE AT HOME. So, restore our rights as such, rectify the injustices of evacuation, of the concentration, of the detention, and of the pauperization as such. In short, treat us in accordance with the principles of the Constitution.

If what we are voicing is wrong, if what we ask is disloyal, if what we think is unpatriotic, then Abraham Lincoln, one of our greatest American President [sic] was also guilty as such, for he said, "If by the mere force of numbers a majority should deprive a minority on any Constitutional right, it might in a moral point of view justify a revolution."

Among the one thousand odd members of the Fair Play Committee, there are Nisei men over the draft age and Nisei girls who are not directly affected by the present Selective Service program, but who believe in the ideals and principles of our country, therefore are helping the FPC in our fight against injustice and discriminations.

We hope that all persons whose ideals and interests are with us will do all they can to help us. <u>We may have to engage in court actions but as such actions require large sums of money, we do need financial support and when the time comes we hope that you will back us up to the limit.</u>

ATTENTION MEMBERS! FAIR PLAY COMMITTEE MEETING SUNDAY, MARCH 5, 2:00 P.M. BLOCK 6-30 MESS. PARENTS, BROTHERS, SISTERS, AND FRIENDS INVITED

7

RHETORIC OF THE ASIAN AMERICAN SELF

Influences of Region and Social Class on Autobiographical Writing

Robyn Tasaka

As someone who has recently moved to the Midwest after living almost my entire life in Hawai'i, I have become acutely aware of how different it is to be Asian American in the two places. In some ways, this was not a surprise. I knew Hawai'i was unique and that being Asian American in the Midwest would be different, but recently I have been able to see more clearly how living in the two areas affects me. When I am in Michigan, I am often aware of how many other Asian Americans are in the room—whether it's just me, or there are one or two others a few tables away. I notice if the others are speaking English, or Korean, or Mandarin. I notice if they are with other Asians, Caucasians, or members of another racial group. After several months, there are times when I forget to notice, but still, when I am back in Hawai'i, I feel a bit more relaxed.

I guess if, in Michigan, I notice other Asians, I know that they—and others—notice me as well. In Hawai'i, I am no longer on display. Or at least not as a representative of my race. In Michigan I am more aware of myself as Asian American. If I play hip-hop or rock or show tunes in my car, I feel others reading it in connection with my Asian appearance. This experience has increased my awareness of how location affects Asian American identity.

In this chapter, I focus on how region as well as social class affect students' conceptions of themselves as Asian American and thus the ways in which they inscribe their racial and/or ethnic backgrounds in autobiographical writing assignments. I begin by describing Hawai'i's current and historical racial environment and the ways social class can influence Asian American student writing and then turn to examples of personal writing by Asian American students at the University of Hawai'i at Manoa (UH) to show how these factors may have affected the ways they communicate significant events in their lives.

HAWAI'I'S ETHNIC AND RACIAL ENVIRONMENT AND HISTORY

In Hawai'i, Asian Americans are not a minority. According to the 2004 U.S. Census Bureau estimates, the population of Hawai'i is 27 percent white, 42 percent Asian (including 17 percent Japanese, 15 percent Filipino, 4 percent Chinese, and 2 percent Korean), and 9 percent Native Hawaiian or other Pacific Islander.[1] The UH population, though slightly different, reflects this racial mix. In addition, some Asian American groups have been able to gain positions of political and economic power in Hawai'i. In this section I describe two significant elements of Hawai'i's racial history—the plantation and the English Standard education system. I then discuss the current racial hierarchy and views of race in Hawai'i in order to help illuminate the context within which Asian American students in Hawai'i write themselves.

Hawai'i's ethnic diversity is largely a result of the plantation system. Chinese, Japanese, Koreans, and Filipinos first came to Hawai'i in the mid-nineteenth century as "cheap labor" for the sugar plantations (Takaki 1989, 132). They performed backbreaking work, sometimes spending four hours bent over in order to cut rows of sugarcane, overseen by whip-bearing foremen on horseback (135–136). Plantation laborers were subject to "numerous restrictions [that] governed work, housing, and social life and were enforced through fines, docking of time and wages, imprisonment, and corporal punishment" (Okihiro 1991, 34). The Caucasian planters viewed the plantation as a "beacon in the wilderness, [which] upheld Christianity and civilization; [and] the plantation master, through discipline and paternal affection, cultivated cane and morality among his impressionable charges" (39–40). The planters' view of Asian workers as childlike led to the implementation of racist restrictions that kept Asian workers from rising to skilled positions (Takaki 1989, 138–141). Planters also encouraged workers' national pride so that when the Japanese union, for instance, went on strike, Korean workers could be counted on to work as scabs (150–151).

In 1920, however, when the workforce was ethnically diversified to the point that workers realized they needed each other in order to

1. The statistics for the remainder of the population are as follows: 2 percent African American, less than 1 percent American Indian and Alaska Native, and 20 percent mixed race (Hawaii 2004).

effectively strike, the Hawai'i Laborers' Association, the first interracial workers' union, was formed (Takaki 1989, 155). At around the same time, the International Longshoremen's and Warehousemen's Union (ILWU) aimed to register plantation workers to vote so that the unions and workers could gain control of the legislature (407). In this way, local Asian groups began to gain political power in Hawai'i. After World War II, the ILWU helped end the plantation system, and "the Democratic party in Hawai'i became the bastion of reform-minded Asian-Americans, primarily second-generation Japanese" (Hughes 1993, 84–86).

Asians in Hawai'i also faced a racist school system. From 1924 until 1948, Hawai'i's public school system was divided into English Standard and non–English Standard schools, with students ostensibly divided by English ability, but in reality segregated by race. The system was designed to allay the concerns of "Americans [who] know that their impressionable children, literally surrounded throughout the school-day and at playtime by these swarms of Orientals, will unconsciously pick up and adopt Oriental manners and mannerisms" (quoted in Young 2004, 116). Furthermore, in the non-Standard schools, "Hawai'i's nonwhite students . . . were often seen as nothing more than future plantation laborers"; educating these children past a certain level was considered a waste of taxpayers' money (115).

Today, however, some Asian ethnic groups[2] such as the Chinese and Japanese have managed to gain a certain degree of power. Based on 1990 census data, ethnic studies scholar Jonathan Okamura found these groups, along with Caucasians, "'holding dominant positions' while 'lower levels of the ethnic/racial stratification order continue to be occupied by Filipinos, Hawaiians, and Samoans'" (1998, 200–201). Okamura says, "Koreans and, to some extent, . . . African Americans" fall somewhere in the middle (201). Japanese and Chinese began to gain power after World War II, when many moved into the middle class and obtained more influential careers. Local Japanese also gained power through involvement in politics and law, some relying on the GI Bill to earn their degrees (Cooper and Daws 1985, 42).

The roster of the Hawai'i State Legislature reflects the political

2. It is important to note that in Hawai'i, different Asian ethnic groups are viewed quite distinctly. The term *Asian American* is rarely used, and individuals are more likely to identify as Chinese, Japanese, Korean, Filipino, Taiwanese, Laotian, Vietnamese, or some mix. Each ethnicity is even stereotyped differently. Chinese, for example, are said to be tight with money, while Koreans are said to have short tempers.

power of different ethnicities. Between 1960 and 1980, local Japanese "averaged 50% of the total membership of both houses" (Cooper and Daws 1985, 42). Based on self-reported responses from members of the state House of Representatives in 2005, 58 percent of the representatives were Japanese, 17 percent Caucasian, 17 percent mixed (including Chinese/Caucasian and Filipino/Chinese/Spanish/Caucasian), and 8 percent Filipino. Because representatives' racial and ethnic backgrounds are not officially recorded, this data is only partial, based on voluntary responses to an e-mail I sent to the fifty members of the Hawai'i State House of Representatives, briefly informing them about my project and asking their ethnicity. Twenty-four percent of the representatives responded. Despite the relatively small response, however, alongside George Cooper and Gavan Daws's reports in *Land and Power in Hawaii*, this data provides an idea of the relative representation of different ethnic groups in the legislature.

Race is also discussed quite differently in Hawai'i than it is in other parts of the country. There seems to be a belief that being "local" is more important than one's race or ethnicity (Young 2004, 71). This belief is expressed, in part, through a sense of pride in the local ability to laugh at ethnic differences. In one of Hawai'i's daily newspapers, for example, an article on "the king of ethnic humor in Hawaii [sic]" says that the comedian's "takes on racial stereotypes can pretty much be a gauge of residency: Laugh, and it shows you've been in Hawaii [sic] for a while. Laugh at a joke about your own race, and you've been here longer" (Kreifels 1999). Making jokes about race is seen as characteristic of local identity, while non-locals, especially those from the U.S. mainland, are viewed as being too uptight when it comes to ethnic humor.

Charles Memminger, a columnist in the same daily paper, expresses another popular Local idea about race, saying, "Hawaii's come a lot further than the rest of the country on racial relations. We take it for granted that people of different races marry, socialize, work and live together in relative harmony" (2001). While this statement is not entirely without basis, it reflects an overly self-congratulatory view of race in Hawai'i. Several scholars have pointed out the dangers of this blind faith in the local, which can make it more difficult to bring up the racial injustices one does experience (Rodrigues 2000, 202). Local unity is also used to attack the Hawaiian sovereignty movement, which is portrayed in a local daily newspaper as "a dangerous threat to ethnic harmony" (Okamura, 1994, 283). The difficulty of discussing racial problems in Hawai'i is also reflected in the caution exercised by Hawai'i journalists who do criticize race relations. One editorial, for example, which goes on to suggest ways to increase racial harmony in Hawai'i, begins with "Make no mistake. Hawaii's overall atmosphere of racial and cultural tolerance is still the envy of the rest of the world" ("How Can Schools Teach" 1999). Both these current and historical racial issues likely influence the ways in which race and ethnicity show up in the autobiographical writing of Asian Americans in Hawai'i.

SOCIAL CLASS AND EDUCATIONAL VALUES

In concert with race and region, social class may also influence the ways in which Asian American students write. According to Mike Rose, middle-class students are less likely to write about issues of race than students from less privileged backgrounds (1989, 177). Victor Villanueva (1993) also finds that social class, more than racial background, predicts the extent to which students attend to difference.

Middle-class students of color may avoid discussing race because they do not see themselves as disadvantaged or Other. According to Rose, middle-class students of color grow up seeing "people of their race exercise power. They felt at the center of things themselves . . . they felt strange about being marked as different." While they may be aware of hardships their families have faced, they perceive these events as being part of history rather than an immediate concern (1989, 178). Middle-class experience also leads some to feel that, rather than dwelling on past suffering, one should focus on the future and making a good life for oneself (179). Whether based on the lack of blatant racism in their own lives or the way they have been taught—by immediate family, the mainstream media, or both—middle-class students of color may not see themselves as underprivileged.

These students may also recognize the class-based privileges they have had and feel it would be unfair to claim hardships based on race. Villanueva, for example, describes a Japanese American student from Hawai'i he works with. He notes that she makes some errors in writing that she corrects in speech and suggests that the errors seem similar to those of English-language learners from Asia. The student denies the connection Villanueva draws between her writing and racial background, instead attributing her errors to a less race-specific cause: "I just don't worry" about it, she says (1993, 104). When reading this account, I felt that the student chose to attribute her errors to carelessness because she was embarrassed to be compared with Asian immigrants. I imagine her being embarrassed for a variety of reasons—perhaps she does not want to be associated with recent immigrants, but more than that, as a fourth-generation Japanese American with an "exclusive private school" education (102–103), I imagine she feels she has little in common with recent immigrants, and is perhaps embarrassed for Villanueva, thinking that he does not understand the difference between Asians and Asian Americans. She may also be embarrassed that she made these errors, given her expensive education and fourth-generation status. In a way, it may be a form of humility[3]—this student realizes the privileges she has had and does not feel entitled to claim hardships based on race.

Similarly, middle-class Asian American students may avoid social issues because they believe that they have a better chance of succeeding by "playing the game" than by calling attention to racial inequities. This is how Villanueva describes a group of working-class African American students' resistance to a teacher, Floyd, who uses a "Freire-like pedagogy" (1993, 53). The students resist in part, Villanueva says, because they "could reason that no matter how slight their chances of getting into college or the middle class, they did have chances, maybe better than most." Revolution is for "when there is nothing left to lose," and Floyd's students feel they have the chance to succeed (61). Like Floyd's students—perhaps even more so since their families have already achieved middle-class status—some students of color feel they can be successful; there is thus no reason to bring up the difficulties that individuals might face because of their racial background.

In addition, middle-class students may be able to avoid discussing race because of their familiarity and similarity with others in the academic community. According to Villanueva, students in a basic writing class he studies that, like many basic writing courses, enrolls a large number of working-class students, had to pay attention to difference and how it might affect the way their writing is understood. During a peer workshop, for example, one student tells her group, "[M]y experience . . . *you* guys . . . can understand. . . . Cause maybe in some way *we're* alike, but I'm not talking to *you*. I'm talking to people like *John* [the teacher] who don't move up from where we do" (emphasis in the original). On the other

3. In discussing one student's supposed humility, I do not intend to further the stereotype of the humble Asian. Nevertheless, I do believe it is a form of humility that can lead middle-class individuals who are not perceived as coming from such privilege to avoid discussing the source of their supposed setbacks.

hand, regardless of color, students in the traditional writing class feel they do not need to explain their perspectives because they all "share in the speech code of the majority" and have the same context "born of a common literate background" (Villanueva 1993, 109). The primarily middle-class students in the traditional writing course, even when faced with a text about racial difference, limit their discussion to things like word choice and mechanics rather than discuss the issues raised in the paper (114). Villanueva seems to say that issues of race and other forms of difference arise more readily among working-class students because they must think about and discuss these factors in considering how their writing will be read by others in the academic community, who they assume, often accurately, have backgrounds different than theirs. In addition, middle-class students can avoid confronting difference because, based on their greater facility with the language and values of the academic community, they can explain their perspectives without discussing factors like race.[4]

IMPLICATIONS

In the existing literature, the characteristics of the autobiographical writing of Asian Americans and other people of color are attributed not to some inherent, for example, Chinese American or African American trait, but to the role of the individual—as a person of color—in American culture. Thus, in order to more fully understand the autobiographical writing of Asian Americans, it seems crucial to pay attention to such things as region and social class and how these factors interact with race to influence individuals' roles in society and their perceptions of those roles. While Asian Americans in Hawai'i are, to some extent, aware of where we stand in mainstream American culture, Hawai'i's environment also influences our self-perceptions. An Asian American with Caucasian schoolteachers, community leaders, classmates, and neighbors is certainly going to have a different perception of herself and her race than someone who is surrounded with people who share her racial and/or ethnic background.

And, as Rose and Villanueva argue, racial differences are sometimes tempered by similarities in social class. In Hawai'i, as stated previously,

4. This claim may seem questionable, as Villanueva does not discuss other possible explanations for the difference between the two student discussions. The difference between the two groups, for example, may instead be a result of the different ways the students were taught to use peer revision groups. Villanueva's larger argument, however, that we need to pay attention to class, and not just race, is surely valuable (114).

those of Japanese, Chinese, and Caucasian ancestry occupy relatively high socioeconomic status, giving these students the privileges of social class that Rose and Villanueva describe.

Autobiographical writing, with its complex ethical issues, provides a valuable space in which to study the influences of race and ethnicity. As scholars like Ellen Cushman (Brandt et al. 2001, 57) and bell hooks (1990, 152) have argued, assigning autobiographical writing can be problematic. Asking students to earn their grade by communicating their personal lives to strangers is fraught with ethical issues—and ones closely tied to racial and ethnic difference. Are individuals from some backgrounds, for example, less comfortable sharing their private lives? How do different perceptions of the self influence how students perform on personal writing assignments? How might racial difference between the student and teacher, or the student and her peers, influence the way she writes her life? Autobiographical writing is an arena in which racial and ethnic difference can have critical consequences, and the study of these issues has been limited, particularly for Asian Americans. In conducting the research for this chapter, for example, I began by searching for literature on Asian American autobiographical writing but, when that turned up few resources, had to expand my search to include literature on other people of color as well.

In the existing literature, race is represented as, in many ways, determining what individuals write. Scholars describe the way the "ethnic" autobiographer writes and seem to assume that people of color experience "limiting social conditions" and perceive themselves differently than others do (Wong 1992, 262; Ray 2000, 94; Friedman 1998, 76). I find these descriptions to be too narrow. As Rose (1989) and Villanueva (1993) demonstrate, the experiences of students of color may not be limited in the ways we expect if they come from middle-class backgrounds. This is not meant to deny that many people of color do face "limiting social conditions," even in a place as diverse as Hawai'i, but if they do not perceive themselves as facing hardships, if they do not see race as heavily influential in their life—as the students in my research claim—they will not write in the ways that, based on the published literature, Asian Americans and other people of color are expected to write.

In the following section, I summarize the existing literature on the autobiographical writing of Asian Americans and other people of color and use samples of autobiographical writing from Asian American students at the University of Hawai'i in order to show the gaps in the published literature. The student writing shows none of the characteristics described by scholars of autobiographical writing and, in fact, includes few references to race at all. I believe this discrepancy is in part due to the effects of region and social class.

DISCUSSION OF STUDENT ESSAYS

In my analysis of the student writing, I rely on the scholarship of W.E.B. DuBois (2004), Susan Stanford Friedman (1998), Ruth Ray (2000), and Sau-ling Cynthia Wong (1992). Of these scholars, only Wong focuses specifically on Asian Americans; DuBois focuses on African Americans, Friedman studies women's autobiography, and Ray writes about Armenian and African American students. The qualities these scholars find, however, are depicted not as inherently female, Armenian, or African American, but as resulting from the writer's role outside the mainstream. Thus it seems this scholarship would apply to the autobiographical writing of other minorities as well. I also rely on these scholars because they provide descriptions of the autobiographical writing and characteristics of the writers they discuss. Based on the work of these scholars, I expected to find in the students' autobiographical writing evidence of double consciousness, social statement, and guided tours of the writers' cultures.

According to DuBois and Friedman, double consciousness results when an individual faces contradictory views of herself—"the self as culturally defined and the self as different from cultural prescription" (Friedman 1998, 76). DuBois and Friedman discuss the existence of double consciousness for African Americans and women respectively, leading me to expect that any minority or relatively powerless group in the United States—including all people of color—would also experience the phenomenon. Double consciousness is expected to appear in autobiography because the genre provides an opportunity to reconcile the writer's multiple identities.

Wong says that "ethnic" autobiographers may "capitalize on white curiosity by conducting the literary equivalent of a guided Chinatown tour: by providing explanations on the manners and mores of the Chinese-American community from the vantage point of a 'native.'" Chinese American autobiography has this inclination because Chinese culture is seen as exotic (and readers tend not to distinguish between Chinese and Chinese Americans) (1992, 262). As the guided tour is a result of western perceptions rather than an inherent Chinese

American quality, it seems the guided tour might also appear in the autobiographies of other Asian American writers, since their cultures are also often exoticized.

Another characteristic attributed to the autobiographies of nonwhite writers is the inclusion of social statement. Ray says that the elderly Armenian and African American women she works with tend toward "social documentation [through] either tacit or explicit critique of limiting social conditions" (2000, 94). I imagine that these social statements are intended to help readers understand how ethnicity informs the writer's experiences; social conditions are noteworthy elements of the writer's life, and she wants to show how they have influenced her story.

None of these characteristics, however, appears in the autobiographical writing of the three University of Hawai'i students involved in this study.

Double Consciousness

The double consciousness DuBois and Friedman describe is supposed to arise for those outside the mainstream, which may be why the student writing shows no evidence of it. In Hawai'i, Asian American and mixed race students like Brian, Christine, and John Williams[5] are the mainstream.[6] Brian identifies his ethnicity as Chinese. Christine says her mother is Chinese, Filipino, and Spanish, and her father is English, Irish, Welsh, Swedish, Scottish, and French. John describes himself as Korean and Caucasian. The students confirm, in interviews, that they do not feel like minorities in Hawai'i, where Brian and Christine have lived their entire lives, and John has lived since he was a teenager (personal communication, May 2004). These students also do not feel Other in the 300–level autobiographical writing class for which they composed the pieces they shared with me; Christine and John describe their classmates as "diverse—different ages, different races" (Williams 20004b). Christine adds, "I don't feel like I stick out any." Brian may feel like a minority in the classroom—he identifies the majority of his classmates as "probably Caucasian," but he does not feel like an outsider in the greater environment—his hometown or state.[7]

5. Participants indicated whether they wanted a pseudonym used. "Christine" and "Brian" are pseudonyms.
6. Twenty percent of Hawai'i residents count two or more races in their ancestry ("Hawaii" 2004).
7. Brian's view of his classmates' ethnicities may be a bit skewed as the instructor, like Christine and John, describes the class as "diverse" (Curry 2004).

Guided Tour of Culture

Composing guided tours as Wong says "ethnic autobiographers" do may be unnecessary for Brian, Christine, and John because they feel their audience will understand their cultures without explanation. Brian says his primary audience is the instructor. He and Christine also consider the classmates in their autobiographical writing course to be their audience. Based on the broader racial makeup of Hawai'i and the university, students can generally assume that their classmates and instructor have had many experiences with people of Chinese or Filipino ancestry; describing foods or practices is unnecessary.

Christine also says, however, that she "kind of went out of the way to mention my cultural background in there, like with the story about my grandmother and just little tidbits so that people would know a little bit more about me." In this statement, Christine seems to acknowledge that it is important for readers to know her racial background, that this can help them understand her. What Christine feels is going "out of the way" to mention race, however, is quite minimal compared to what Wong describes. She includes, for example, only two direct references to race, one to "an old Japanese man" and another to her grandmother "swearing in every dialect of Filipino she knew." While there are a few other slight references, for example, to Hawai'i place-names, overall Christine's inclusion of race is quite subtle.

John, in contrast to Brian and Christine, describes his audience more broadly, as "Everybody" (Williams 2004b). Coupled with the lack of explanation in his writing of how race plays into his experience, it seems John assumes that race does not affect his story. Perhaps this, too, stems from living in Hawai'i. While he does not specify if "Everybody" means everybody in the world or just in Hawai'i, as with Brian and Christine, John's experiences in Hawai'i, where he may not often be required to explain his race, might influence the extent to which he feels his racial background has affected his life's stories.

Social Statement

The social statements Ray describes do not show up in Brian's, Christine's, or John's writing, although all three write about situations in which it seems race may have been significant. John, in his interview, describes feeling like an outsider when he lived in the continental United States. Since moving to Hawai'i as a teenager, he says, he feels "more the majority" (Williams 2004b). The racial consciousness indicated in the interview, however, does not appear in his writing. In a piece about his adolescent friends, John focuses on one young man in particular. Near the beginning of the piece, he writes, "You meet a lot of interesting people when you move around a lot. I have had all types of different friends, and shared all types of different experiences with them." He goes on to describe a friendship in which "[t]here were a few moments . . . where we had some 'respect' issues, but all friends do" (Williams 2004a, 1). Based on the statements John made in his interview, it seems strange that this piece, which refers to both diversity and conflict—two issues that, to differing extents, are often raised when discussing racial difference—does not include any mention of the friend's race or how he reacted to John's race.

One of Christine's pieces is about a friend, also from Hawai'i, who committed suicide. Christine mentions that the young woman "had been attending Harvard University, and she had trouble making friends." While the friend's race is never identified, Harvard's racial and cultural environment is surely much different from Hawai'i's. A 2005 Associated Press article, for example, describes the difficulties that students from Hawai'i often have adjusting to life on the continent, to the "more fast-paced lifestyle and sometimes unfriendly encounters, especially in large East Coast cities." One student, for example, says, "For a Hawaii [sic] person on the mainland, the culture here is different" (Lee 2005). It seems that this kind of change, in part related to racial difference, may have affected Christine's friend, yet she does not comment on this in the piece.

Brian writes a piece on his father being shot. He expresses a sense of shock in the text; he cannot believe this is happening to him. He mentions the "faint sound of sirens" and writes, "It was the same sound I'd hear behind me in rush hour traffic, but it meant something else to me this time." These quotes and others like it indicate Brian's disbelief, his sense that "[t]his isn't supposed to happen to people like us." It seems this would lead into thoughts about who typically is involved with violent crime, which might reveal racial stereotypes that he could then examine, but Brian's story does not move in that direction. Instead, he returns to recounting the events—his conversation with the police officer, a phone call to his mother.

Issues related to race and ethnicity might also have appeared in descriptions of his characters, particularly his parents, whom Brian describes, in conversation, as first-generation immigrants. Brian says he is surprised by the shooting, but how do his parents react to this violent event in their adopted country? Does it make them question their migration? Or are the effects of immigration something they no longer think about? There are also a lot of missing details about Brian's parents—details that might have revealed their ethnicities in the service of providing a fuller picture of their characters. Brian's father, for example, is reacting to the gunshot throughout the piece, so his dialogue is limited to telling his son what has happened and directing him to call 911. Brian could have, however, included other scenes to provide background information about his father or show how the shooting affected his life. All he says about his mother is that she is not home at the time of the shooting, but where is she? At work? At a friend's or relative's house?

Omitting these details may have been a conscious decision, as Brian did indicate in the interview a concern with revealing too much about his parents. He says he would be hesitant to share his writing with his mother and father because they "might not be that comfortable knowing that this has been read by other people." On one hand, it seems this would not have affected Brian's writing, as he seems worried not about sharing his parents' stories but about having them find out he has shared them. Nevertheless, perhaps this concern did limit Brian's portrayal of his parents.

The topics John, Christine, and Brian choose to write on seem conducive to the inclusion of social statements. The absence of these statements is even more conspicuous when coupled with the students' minimal references to race overall.

Lack of References to Race

Though Brian, Christine, and John write detailed descriptions of such things as friends' bedrooms or paramedics' gear, descriptions of characters' physical appearances are lacking. In her "Fallen Friend," Christine describes her friend's room as "sparsely decorated with only a chest of drawers, a wooden desk with matching chair, and a twin bed neatly made." She says her friend was "a sweet, quiet thinker," but gives no physical description of the young woman. Brian describes the paramedics "in their white uniforms and latex gloves, shouldering duffel bags bulging with medical supplies." John does give a physical description of one of his friends, but references to race or ethnicity are still absent. John writes: "James was your average sized guy. The funny thing about him was that he was eighteen and looked like he was thirty. Seriously, when we went to parties everyone who didn't know him thought he was an undercover cop. James had a five o'clock shadow that grew back at two-thirty, with thinning hair, and a small beer belly slowly developing a large one [*sic*]" (Williams 2004a, 1).

This is a quite thorough sketch. John's description includes details about James's build, hair, and facial hair, as well as how others reacted to his appearance. What is missing is any description of James's race or ethnic background; there are not even clues like hair or eye color. Perhaps James is white, the invisible norm—but coming from a writer who is part Korean, why does John not describe how James is similar to or different from him? Or how people reacted to him at parties compared to James? Physical traits, of course, are not the only possible markers of race—things like behavior, food or eating habits, and language can also be markers. Physical traits are one racial marker, however, that these students neglect.

In addition, the students' stories can barely be placed in Hawai'i except for the faintest hint of Hawai'i Creole English (HCE) in the dialogue and a reference here and there to a character with a Hawaiian name, local food like plate lunches and *kaki mochi*, and a few place-names. In one of Christine's pieces, for example, a character slips the HCE phrase "Shame you know," indicating that she is embarrassed, into a conversation in which all other dialogue seems to be in, if not Standard English, then relatively mainstream teenage slang. In Brian's piece, his sister's boyfriend's name is Kimo, a Hawaiian name, but as far as the reader can tell, this has absolutely no effect on his experience. All Kimo does in this story is say that the robbers "asked where the girl was." One of Christine's pieces includes references to the Ala Moana Shopping Center, her hometown of Waialua, and "the island," which provide some clues about the story's setting. Christine's reference to her hometown might also lead readers familiar with Hawai'i to speculate about the writer's ethnicity.[8] These hints of the Hawai'i setting are there, but often need to be searched for carefully and are still quite minor. It is also unclear exactly what the authors' thinking processes were as they worked on these stories. Was Kimo, for example, really the young man's name? If not, how did Brian choose the name?

8. In the interview, Christine says that most people in her neighborhood are of Filipino ancestry. This is due to the town's plantation history; while workers of other ethnicities had lived and worked on the plantations in Waialua in the past, "Filipinos . . . have been the majority of the plantation workforce since 1920" (Alcantara 1972, 2). While the plantation is no longer in operation today, the town's population still reflects the makeup of its most recent plantation workers.

In John's piece about his eccentric friend, there is one clue that might point toward Asian influences. John describes a language his friend invents as part of his imaginary spy persona. His friend calls the language "Campodonese," and displays his skill, saying, "'Sudi wado Nuagaki Takmako si si Do namo'" (Williams 2004a, 3). This fictional language looks a bit like Japanese or Indonesian, and its name sounds like it might be some kind of cross between Cambodian, Indonesian, and Japanese, perhaps influenced by John's or his friend's familiarity with Asian languages. This might be seen as evidence of ethnicity and/or ethnic influences on John's writing, but again it takes quite a stretch to identify.

I recognize that the identification of "race" in writing is an extremely subjective task. I have tried to be as comprehensive as possible, hunting down the tiniest signs of race and taking the views of other readers into consideration. I am aware, however, that my analyses of these texts change from reading to reading. My understanding of this is influenced by Stanley Fish, who describes each person's reading as "a moving field of concerns, at once wholly present (not waiting for meaning but constituting meaning) and continually in the act of reconstituting itself" (2001, 2079). According to Fish, even in one reading of one piece, my understanding of the text changes multiple times.

In addition, the views of other readers, as I did not always agree with them, drew my attention to the fact that others might read race in these students' writings differently than I do. Fish also sheds light on this, discussing how readings differ from person to person, depending on the associations each reader makes (2001, 2080). Another reader who looked at the students' stories, for example, drew my attention to the invented language in John's piece as influenced by familiarity with Asian languages. We also discussed whether the characters' dialogue in that piece reflects the influences of HCE or the dialogue between young males as seen in movies like *Swingers* (1996) and *Clerks* (1994). John's characters say things like, "Man, where the hell is James at?" "[W]here you been?" and "Man, that's some bullshit, that wasn't no language" (Williams 2004a, 2–3). We were unable to come to a conclusion; in the end I do not include a discussion of John's characters' dialogue mainly because I do not feel equipped to argue its reflection of either influence. My knowledge of language patterns is based primarily on hearing—I can say what the dialogue sounds like to me, but beyond that I have no evidence.

While I did incorporate some references to race that other readers pointed out, others I omitted—either because I disagreed with them or because I do not have the disciplinary training to argue for them. Hearing other readers' views about race in these readings, however, draws my attention to the possible ways that I might be misreading race. I have tried to be as comprehensive as possible, and to take the students' views and the views of other readers into account, but ultimately, the interpretation of race in these students' writings is my own.

In interviews, however, Brian, Christine, and John also seem to believe that race is not a factor in their writing or classroom performance. When asked whether he feels his cultural background affects his experience in the class, John immediately answers negatively. Brian and Christine, while more ambivalent, ultimately seem to feel that their ethnic backgrounds have little effect on their writing and experiences. Brian, for example, when considering the way some of his classmates write about serious issues like rape while others stick to lighter topics like dirt biking, says, "I don't think that [difference in how much writers reveal] really has to do with culture. . . . Maybe it did. I think it's just the person." While some students seem more confident of their answers than others, all seem to, at the very least, downplay the effect their ethnic and racial backgrounds have on their writing and experiences.

CONCLUSION

Through the minimal references to race in their writing, these students rhetorically construct themselves as only marginally influenced by race and ethnicity. They make clear that their Asian American and mixed-race backgrounds are tangential to who they are. They construct themselves as unique, as "just" Brian, Christine, and John. In many ways, this can be seen as playing into the ideals of neoliberalism and multiculturalism. The ways that race might be said to appear in their writing, through Hawaiian place-names and diverse neighbors and languages, point to the brand of diversity celebrated by multiculturalism—in which difference is visible, but has no effect. Participants' denial in interviews of the influence of race may also reflect Local and neoliberal views that privilege "color blindness." It also reflects, however, participants' realities—they do not perceive race as influencing their or their peers' writing. Thus, Brian, Christine, and John seem to construct themselves as untouched by race. Brian specifically, in attributing differences between student writers to "just the person," emphasizes the influence of individual identity over membership in a racial group.

We might say that these students' experiences are simply different from those reflected in the published literature, that Brian, Christine, and John are lucky to have grown up or experienced living in a place where they did not feel their Asian ancestry was a liability. This is true, but I think we must also recognize that the limited references to race in these students' writing in many ways reflect their position of privilege.

Just as Caucasian is the invisible norm in many parts of North America, Asian, as described earlier, is in many ways the invisible norm in many parts of Hawai'i. In demonstrating the invisibility of whiteness, Barbara Applebaum describes a study where "both African Americans and white Americans were asked to describe them-selves [*sic*]." The study found that, "[w]hile the African-Americans used racial identity markers in their self-descriptions, most of the white Americans did not [because w] hiteness, for many white people, is not considered to be a colour, it is not even considered to be a perspective, a position" (2001, 63). I believe that as Asian and mixed-race students in Hawai'i, Brian, Christine, and John do not mention their races because, like white students in North America, they think of themselves as the norm.

Students' insistence that race does not matter also points toward their dominant position. Their statements that cultural background has little effect on their writing and experiences are quite similar to those of a white student teacher who says, "What's the hangup, I really don't see this color until we start talking about it, you know. I see children as having differences, maybe they can't write their numbers or they can't do this or they can't do that, I don't see color until we start talking multicultural. Then oh yes, that's right, he's this and she's that" (Applebaum 2001, 56). As Applebaum says, these comments, "based as they may be on lofty intentions, indicate a lack of awareness on the part of these teachers of their own dominant positions" (57). I believe that Brian, Christine, and John, in their similar responses to talk about race, may also be reflecting their own dominant positions.

These students have the privilege to avoid talking about race. On one hand, perhaps they are wise to take advantage of this privilege. When you talk about race, you are often pigeonholed, consequently seen only as "the Chinese kid." Like an academic who does not want to be known only as a Native American scholar, Brian, Christine, and

John are careful about the ways they reveal hints of their cultural backgrounds. They have this privilege because they are perceived as "typical" students. Conversely, someone who is immediately perceived as different will be pigeonholed no matter what she writes about; she, in response, might thus be more inclined to use her writing expressly to defy the stereotypes that she expects color her classmates' perceptions, perhaps invoking the characteristics mentioned in the published literature: double consciousness, social statement, and the guided tour. In a sense, Brian, Christine, and John may be attempting to defy stereotypes in their own way: by telling their stories as ones that simply happen to be part of one person's Chinese American or mixed-race experience. Brian, Christine, and John, however, have the privilege of avoiding race in their writing—in a way that students who are immediately perceived as different do not.

In addition, while ignoring race in their writing may be an attempt to defy racial stereotypes, it also reinforces the idea that race does not matter. If Brian, Christine, or John had mentioned race in their writing, they might, in class, have been called on it, and asked, "Why do you think race is important to mention?" They would be forced to defend themselves on a topic that is uncomfortable for most—to interrogate the links between race and experience. While uncomfortable, however, this would have created an opportunity in which to discuss the extent to which their racial and/or ethnic background influences their (or their peers') lives, stories, and ways of telling those stories. By avoiding discussions of race completely, the connections between race and privilege and other experiences are invisible, kept under the surface, and we have the privilege of continuing to believe that race does not matter.

The differences between the students' writing and the published descriptions point toward the underexamined complexities in the writing of Asian Americans. Perhaps, Brian, Christine, and John are constructing the influences of race in their lives in ways we are unable to see and measure given current literature on Asian American autobiographical writing. This seems a possibility particularly in Christine's case, since she claims she did try to make race evident. Despite arguments in the existing literature, however, double consciousness, foreign practices, and immediate hardship are not always significant aspects of our life stories. Depending on such factors as region and social class, "Asian American" can mean quite differently, even marking relative privilege.

An understanding of the intersection of factors like region and social class with race will help build a more comprehensive awareness of the experiences and writing of Asian American students.

REFERENCES

Alcantara, Ruben. 1972. The Filipino Wedding in Waialua, Hawaii. *Amerasia Journal* 1:1–12.

Anonymous, "Fallen Friend" (working paper, March 2004).

Applebaum, Barbara. 2001. Raising Awareness of Dominance: Does Recognising Dominance Mean One Has to Dismiss the Values of the Dominant Group? *Journal of Moral Education* 30:56–70.

Brandt, Deborah, Ellen Cushman, Anne Ruggles Gere, Anne Herrington, Richard E. Miller, Victor Villanueva, Min-Zhan Lu, and Gesa Kirsch. 2001. The Politics of the Personal: Storying Our Lives against the Grain. *College English* 64:41–62.

Cooper, George, and Gavan Daws. 1985. *Land and Power in Hawaii: The Democratic Years.* Honolulu: Benchmark.

Curry, Steven. 2004. Interview with author, Honolulu, May 3.

DuBois, W.E.B. 2004. Of Our Spiritual Strivings. In *The Social Theory of W.E.B. DuBois,* edited by Phil Zuckerman. Thousand Oaks, CA: Pine Forge Press.

Fish, Stanley. 2001. Interpreting the *Variorum.* In *The Norton Anthology of Theory and Criticism,* edited by Vincent Leitch et al. New York: Norton.

Friedman, Susan. 1998. Women's Autobiographical Selves: Theory and Practice. In *Women, Autobiography, Theory: A Reader,* edited by Sidonie Smith and Julia Watson. Madison: University of Wisconsin Press.

Hawaii: General Demographic Characteristics: 2004. 2004. *American FactFinder,* U.S. Census Bureau. http://factfinder.census.gov/servlet/ADPTable?_bm=y&-geo_id=04000US15&-qr_name=ACS_2004_EST_G00_DP1&-ds_name=ACS_2004_EST_G00_&-_lang=en&-_sse=on (accessed June 24, 2006).

hooks, bell. 1990. *Yearning: Race, Gender and Cultural Politics.* Boston: South End.

"How Can Schools Teach Tolerance?" 1999. *Honolulu Advertiser,* August 31, A6.

Hughes, Judith. 1993. The Demise of the English Standard School System in Hawai'i. *Hawaiian Journal of History* 27:65–89.

Kreifels, Susan. 1999. DeLima Reaching Out to Students. *Honolulu Star-Bulletin,* April 23. http://starbulletin.com/1999/04/23/news/story2.html (accessed June 24, 2006).

Lee, Jeanette J. 2005. Campus Hawaii Clubs Help Ease Transition to Mainland Life. *Lancaster Online,* April 26. http://ap.lancasteronline.com/4/hawaii_clubs (accessed June 24, 2006).

Memminger, Charles. 2001. Hawaii's Race Relations to the Fore. Honolulu Lite. *Honolulu Star-Bulletin,* January 15. http://starbulletin.com/2001/01/15/features/memminger.html (accessed July 16, 2006).

Okamura, Jonathan. 1994. The Illusion of Paradise: Privileging Multiculturalism in Hawai'i. In *Making Majorities: Composing the Nation in Japan, China, Korea, Fiji, Malaysia, Turkey, and the United States,* edited by D.C. Gladney. Palo Alto, CA: Stanford University Press.

———. 1998. Social Stratification. In *Multicultural Hawai'i: The Fabric of a Multiethnic Society,* edited by Michael Haas. New York: Garland.

Okihiro, Gary. 1991. *Cane Fires: The Anti-Japanese Movement in Hawaii, 1865–1945.* Philadelphia: Temple University Press.

Ray, Ruth E. 2000. *Beyond Nostalgia: Aging and Life-story Writing.* Charlottesville: University Press of Virginia.

Rodrigues, Darlene. 2000. Imagining Ourselves: Reflections on the Controversy over Lois-Ann Yamanaka's *Blu's Hanging. Amerasia Journal* 26:195–207.

Rose, Mike. 1989. *Lives on the Boundary: A Moving Account of the Struggles and Achievements of America's Educational Underclass.* New York: Penguin.

Takaki, Ronald. 1989. *Strangers from a Different Shore: A History of Asian Americans.* New York: Penguin.

Villanueva, Victor Jr. 1993. *Bootstraps: From an American Academic of Color.* Urbana, IL: National Council of Teachers of English.

Williams, John. 2004a. Bullshit. Unpublished essay.

———. 2004b. Interview with author, Honolulu, April 30.

Wong, Sau-ling Cynthia. 1992. Autobiography as Guided Chinatown Tour? Maxine Hong Kingston's *The Woman Warrior* and the Chinese-American Autobiographical Controversy. In *Multicultural Autobiography: American Lives,* edited by James Payne. Knoxville: University of Tennessee Press.

Young, Morris. 2004. *Minor Re/Visions: Asian American Literacy Narratives as a Rhetoric of Citizenship.* Carbondale: Southern Illinois University Press.

PART TWO

"Translating" and "Transforming" Asian American Identities

8

"ARTFULBIGOTRY & KITSCH"

A Study of Stereotype, Mimicry, and Satire in Asian American T-Shirt Rhetoric

Vincent N. Pham and Kent A. Ono

Prior to starting graduate school in the spring of 2004, I, Vincent, worked as a substitute teacher at a local high school. When I walked into class one day, one of the students, who apparently identified me as Asian, stood up, shook his hips, and started singing, "She-bangs, she-bangs, she moves, she moves" in broken English, mimicking the rejected American Idol participant William Hung. Coincidentally, in the spring of 2006, I entered a local grade school to help conduct interviews for a fellow graduate student; a small child, probably in first grade, noticed me in the hallway and broke into a performance of martial arts–like hand movements and facial expressions, saying, "Waaaahhh." And, after a recent funeral, my Asian American friend thanked the white host for serving rice at the reception, only to have the host say, "No problem. You know, ching chong," while using her two index fingers to pull back the corners of her eyelids, making slanted eyes.

These examples demonstrate the prevalence of racialized mimicry in private and personal settings. Instances of racialized mimicry are not limited to the private realm, however; they also occur more broadly within popular culture. For example, in 2004, William Hung became famous not for his ability to sing, but for speaking broken English, singing off-key, and lacking rhythm on the dance floor.[1] In January of 2006, Spencer's Gifts released a T-shirt that read, "Hang out with your wang out," with an accompanying image of a bucktoothed and slant-eyed Asian man wearing a rice paddy conical hat and holding his penis (Jackson 2006). Later that year, Adidas released a limited-edition shoe line called the "Yellow

1. This fame was eventually followed by the sale of a variety of William Hung–inspired merchandise and a William Hung album. Josephine Lee (2006) has attended to Hung as an example of "bad performance" that reveals the limitations of stereotype.

series," with the tongue on one shoe featuring a bucktoothed and slant-eyed "Chinaman" with a bowl haircut (BBC 2006).

The examples of William Hung, Spencer's Gifts, and Adidas are just three of the innumerable popular culture events that help demonstrate a relationship between symbolic actions and personal experiences and, for Asian American consumers, the psychic violence of repeated and accumulated instances of private and public humiliation. Repeated instances of public and private mimicry and mockery and of (mis)re-representation function together to imprint on the psyches of Asian Americans and others an indelible caricature: a powerful marker that serves as a social stigma and effective arbiter of power relations, a merging of commodification and capitalism that perpetuates a contemporary kind of racism—not one where dogs are set upon children or protestors are fire hosed in the streets, but rather where image, text, and performance psychologically attack and scar. This is what we would call a "spectacle of racism"—a (mis)represented, mocking, and commodified public performance of race and racialized communities that simultaneously impacts the psychosocial understanding within racialized communities and shapes the psychosocial understanding of those who interact with members of racialized communities and those who ultimately influence policies, structures, and institutions that affect these racialized communities. Debord suggests a spectacle is not a collection of images but a social relationship between people mediated by images (1994, 12). By using Asian Americans and their visual representations in popular culture, the "spectacle of racism" via mass-produced images and products helps mediate the relationships of non-Asians with Asian Americans and among Asian Americans.[2]

In this essay, we demonstrate that mimicry/mockery is one way the dominant white society has helped control racialized communities historically. In 2002, clothing retailer Abercrombie & Fitch (A&F) produced and distributed a T-shirt that used mimicry and mockery to poke fun at Asian Americans, hence conspicuously displaying its power to represent Asian American identities and in the process reproduce and consolidate unequal power relations between the dominant society and Asian Americans racially. In response, Blacklava, an independent

2. These examples are not the first examples of the "spectacle of racism," however. The spectacle of racism applies to many other marginalized groups, especially African Americans. Images serve as the mediating factor between social interactions where visual culture, such as television and photographs, serve as the only representation of people of color to communities that do not have many people of color.

Asian American–owned apparel company, satirically reworked A&F's representation, using the technology of mimicry of A&F's design to its own end and against A&F in an attempt to reverse the original racializing effects and hence to turn the gaze back onto A&F's original act of racial mimicry and mockery. In this case study, we argue that commodification and capitalism converge to produce a spectacle of racism, but that the cultural products that emerge do not have a singular effect and meaning; the same context allows for re-representation and refigurement of symbols with powerful effectivity. In order to understand this spectacle, we first assess this example in relation to what Said defines as Orientalism and what Bourdieu theorizes as symbolic domination; then, we evaluate A&F's mimicry and mockery of Asian Americans and Blacklava's reuse of that imagery by drawing on Bhabha's theories of mimicry and ambivalence.

Although the response to A&F by Asian Americans came in the forms of public protests, e-mail petitions, we primarily concentrate our analysis on the counter-rhetorical protest T-shirts released by Blacklava afterward.[3] Counter-rhetorical in the sense that, while it challenges an already existing rhetoric event, it is not just a response but becomes a rhetoric itself, articulating its own claims. Thus, it is not merely reactive but is also productive. By analyzing the counter-rhetorical T-shirts of Blacklava, we seek to draw attention to Asian American artists as activists whose rhetoric critiques commodification and symbolic domination through satire, recirculating the images and calling upon Asian Americans to remember, possibly prevent, and ultimately to take actions to deter future acts of commodification, while problematically using the self-same strategy of commodifying the images. We take up Chuh's (2003) challenge to Asian American studies to "imagine otherwise" and

3. In stating "counter-rhetoric" and "counter-rhetorical," we draw upon public and counter-public theories. In citing Fraser's (1993) seminal piece, "Rethinking the Public Sphere: A Contribution to the Critique of Actually Existing Democracy," Asen and Brouwer (2001, 7) argue that "counter-public spheres voice oppositional needs and values . . . by affirming specificity of race, gender, sexuality, ethnicity, or some other axis of difference" in order to highlight the multiplicity of publics. In labeling the T-shirt "counter rhetorical," we seek to highlight the recurring oscillation between encountering and countering symbolic violence and racist rhetoric and the affirming actions for counter publics, while downplaying the event that spurred the "protest," despite being located in that event. Protest might indicate a temporal dimension, whereas counter rhetorical implies a continuing struggle, one that continues after the offensive T-shirts are removed and the protests fade away. Thus, a counter rhetorical shirt deals with the racist imagery of A&F but also becomes a rhetoric against racist imagery and corporate practices beyond the A&F event.

to extend studies past topical discourse, to move beyond simple representational objectification into the realm of the epistemological, which might be considered "rhetorical."[4] Even though our chapter interrogates A&F's representational objectification of Asian Americans, we are more interested in the counterrhetoric of Asian American activists than in simply demarcating instances of racist discourse, such as A&F's T-shirt.[5] Even though the actions of A&F draw upon Manicheanistic dualities and divisions as applied to Asian Americans, the dialectical tension of art and offense emerge in A&F and then resurface within the Blacklava T-shirts under a newly reconfigured Asian American rhetoric.

Finally, the rhetoric of the Blacklava T-shirts demonstrates that we are not helpless within a world where commodified racism persists and that all is not hopelessly overdetermined. The Blacklava counter-rhetorical T-shirts demonstrate that Asian Americans can and sometimes do perform what Tina Chen (2005) calls "double agency": the critique of institutions that represent Asian Americans as "aliens," that simultaneously functions as a claim to U.S. American identity in the process. Ultimately, this chapter seeks to connect postcolonial studies, rhetorical studies, and Asian American studies through a study of the counterrhetoric of Asian American arts activism against the corporate racism of A&F and to suggest the possibility of social change regarding the positions of Asian Americans.

SYMBOLIC DOMINATION, MIMICRY, AND AMBIVALENT IMAGES

Said's (1979) well-known conception of Orientalism has implications for our theory of rhetorical discourse. In this vein, Orientalism is a communicative discourse that dominates, restructures, and maintains authority over the Orient. The Orient, figured in Said's Orientalism as the West's Other, is a historical accretion juxtaposed against the Occident that renders the tropes of Orient and Occident in a binaristic relation of power

4. Other Asian American scholars have looked beyond critical studies on topical discourse. For example, Gudykunst's (2001) book, *Asian American Ethnicity and Communication*, takes a social science perspective on Asian American communication. However, as Ono and Nakayama (2004) argue, Gudykunst's objectivist social science perspective overlooks the political and activist implications of the term "Asian American."

5. We suggest here that simply documenting how racialized and racist images relate to particular racialized bodies may, as a rhetorical move, tend to reproduce and possibly sediment social relations without the study of an actional/activist counterrhetoric. Hence, the study of activist counterrhetoric also seeks to deterritorialize and de-sediment racist social relations.

(5). This binary relation occurs through the production of Orientalist knowledge that reifies the notion of difference, the superiority of the West, and the inferiority of the Eastern Other. The production and perpetuation of Orientalist knowledge requires that the Occident, which characterizes the West as "normal," saves and civilizes the Other through ritualized and repeated acts of domination (Ono and Buescher 2001). Thus, Orientalism requires the creation of an Other, and we argue it also requires what Bourdieu (2001, 5) calls "repeated acts of symbolic domination" to help maintain power.

Symbolic domination is a result of continual and repeated symbolic violence: a violence that Bourdieu (2001, 5) states is "exerted through purely symbolic channels of communication and cognition (more precisely, misrecognition), or even feeling." Bourdieu and Passeron (1990, 5) define symbolic domination as the means by which violence is exerted and domination attained and maintained, a method that works through symbols and is "the imposition of a cultural arbitrary by an arbitrary power."[6] Within this definition of symbolic domination, racialized mimicry and stereotype serve as tools to enact symbolic violence and reify symbolic domination.

Both racialized mimicry and stereotype play a role in the history of symbolic colonial domination. Bhabha (1994, 85) states that colonialism "repeatedly exercises its authority through the figures of farce" and uses mimicry as an "elusive and effective" strategy for perpetuating colonial power and knowledge. In addition, Bhabha (70) states that "the stereotype is a complex, ambivalent, contradictory mode of representation, as anxious as it is assertive, and demands not only that we extend our critical and political objectives but that we change the object of analysis itself." Stereotype serves as the template from which racialized mimicry is performed and enacted; its representation is performed and propagated. Colonial mimicry desires a "reformed, recognizable Other *as a subject of difference that is almost the same, but not quite*" when compared with the colonial people and power (86). Thus, colonial mimicry employs the stereotype as a tool to exert power, control, and symbolic domination over its subjects through the stereotype's ambivalent and contradictory mode of representation. Mimicry is effective at contributing to an environment of symbolic domination

6. However, DeLuca and Peeples (2002, 138) interpret symbolic violence differently and define it as "acts directed toward property, not people, and designed to attract media attention."

because of its ambivalence. Ambivalence is the uncertainty and coexistence of opposing attitudes toward the subject of domination that continually produces a slippage between what is different and what is the same. Cloud (1992, 314) addresses the role of ambivalence in her study of the television show *Spenser for Hire*, stating that "these mechanisms of ambivalence" can help us "understand the discursive representations of urban blacks in the United States." Like Cloud, we study ambivalence, stereotype, and mimicry as a way to understand the representations and the rhetoric surrounding marginalized communities, in our case, Asian Americans. Thus, mimicry is a strategy of dual articulation that appropriates the Other at the very same time that it functions to visualize power through ambivalence. Mimicry signals what is inappropriate in the Other, while delineating who has power and who is dominant, thus reinforcing unequal colonial power relations. The representation of the difference of the Other becomes a process of disavowal: the Other's difference is the reason for its inferiority, but through mimicry that difference is denied and yet rendered mimickable. Young (2004, 2) states that literacy "has been key in the construction of a person's identity, legitimacy, and citizenship when that person is racially marked as 'Other.'" While Young recognizes standards of literacy proficiency as a marker of difference, we also add here the physicality and image of bodies to text: the representation of difference via mimicry articulates a discourse of reform, regulation, and difference, which attempts to control what the "Other" can and should be. Bhabha argues, however, that mimicry also provides a space of resistance for the colonized. While the colonized are well aware of the colonizers' representations of them, the colonizer, entrenched in the stereotype, does not understand that colonized representations can be flawed. In the rhetorical context, mimicry and stereotype expose a space for potential resistance from the colonized, and the colonized can use this space and knowledge of flawed colonial representations to produce a rhetoric of resistance.

In short, colonial mimicry disavows the Other's grounds for articulating a legitimate identity based on difference while simultaneously attempting to appropriate the identity of the Other. The strategic desire of colonial mimicry, however, is to have objects that represent what Bhabha (1994) calls the *metonymy of presence*, where a referent is used to identify and also to substitute for the person. A repeated stereotype, then, is metonymic: it is an inadequate substitution for the Other—and constructs discriminatory identities across "cultural norms and classification," such as the historical "Simian Black, the Lying Asiatic" or the contemporary Arab terrorist. The metonymy of presence and metonymic nature of stereotype strategically confuses the meanings and representations of the colonized. For relations established and maintained through mimicry, the Other becomes an "*object* of regulatory power" (90).

The process of mimicry creates the binary power relations of Orientalism and the construction of the "Other." Mimicry splits discourse into two attitudes and ways of thinking about the Other: one takes reality into account while the Other rearticulates a "reality" constructed by mimicry (Bhabha 1994, 91). For example, mimicry can work through language, as in the mimicking (and making a farce of) African American ghetto dialects and images. Thus, the farce of mimicry denies marginalized groups the ability to represent themselves and claims the power to represent the Other; in short, the issue of mimicry is an issue of representation.

Bourdieu (2001), Bhabha (1994), Said (1979), and others argue that the symbolic violence, Orientalism, and mimicry enacted through images work together to reify colonial power. Corporations like A&F play a particular role contemporarily in this realm of colonial power. Where colonial powers have affected national boundaries, corporations have played a larger role in shaping the transnational landscape. Corporations in this postcolonial and postmodern world have found a new place, not only as producers of products but also as ambassadors to other countries and producers and distributors of cultural products, such as music, clothing, and movies. Examples of such phenomena include the circulation of Nike and McDonalds commodities worldwide. Masao Miyoshi (1995) comments on the propagation of products by transnational corporations (TNCs), such as Nike, that dictate global economies and local industries; he explicates how these TNCs also prevent the possibilities for resistance. Instead of colonialism, we have "corporationalism," where corporations enact rules and norms that attempt symbolic domination and symbolic violence, not in the name of civilizing or manifest destiny, but rather in the name of profit.[7] Yet, as much as corporations are working in the name of profit, McMillian (1987) reminds us that they are also public and persuasive entities.

7. The documentary *The Corporation* by Mark Achbar and Jennifer Abbott (2005) traces the rise of the corporation within the United States and the global effects of the transnational corporations.

Symbolic domination by corporations does not attempt to civilize as much as to commodify the Other. The commodification of racism and attempts at symbolic domination via mimicry signal an opposition to a folkloric era of corporate social responsibility.[8]

In the case of A&F, corporate social irresponsibility is enacted through the commodification and sale of racist and offensive dominant representations of Asian Americans, thus reifying colonial relations through capitalist practices that are often seen as apolitical and race-neutral. By analyzing A&F's T-shirts, we can see the prevalence of corporate irresponsibility as a spectacle of racism. The Blacklava T-shirts as an example, however, provide us the opportunity to see how marginalized groups of people hold A&F accountable for corporate social irresponsibility. We can see how Asian American rhetoric positions itself as a mode of self-representation and as an area of artistic and cultural production and how it participates in the public and social enactment of ethics to combat corporate attempts at symbolic domination.

AN EMERGING ASIAN AMERICAN RHETORIC

In 2002, the Ohio-based clothing retailer Abercrombie & Fitch released a line of T-shirts that spurred many Asian Americans into action.[9] After much protest from Asian American student groups, A&F issued a formal apology and ultimately recalled the T-shirt line. In response to the release of the A&F line of clothing, Blacklava designed its own T-shirt using some of the same offensive images on the A&F shirts but reading "ArtfulBigotry & Kitsch" instead of Abercrombie & Fitch. Thus, Blacklava reproduced the offensive images on T-shirts and in the public

---

8. McBride (2005) criticizes A&F's institutionalization of elite whiteness and racism in its stores and manuals, albeit from a cultural studies perspective. From an organizational communication perspective, Lammers, Barbour, and Duggan (2003) argue that the organizational phenomenon of institutionalization can easily copy and propagate instances of corporate social irresponsibility, especially if they prove to be profitable. Lammers, Barbour, and Duggan (320) call for the advent of an institutional perspective that "emphasizes the rules, values, and beliefs that surround organizations and their members as critical components of behavior and communication practices," and recognize that corporate social irresponsibility can easily be copied and enacted by fellow corporations. McBride and Lammers, Barbour, and Duggan attend to the spread of corporate social irresponsibility, such as the case of Spencer's Gifts mimicking A&F's T-shirt designs, but from differing disciplinary perspectives.

9. We decided not to describe the T-shirts at this point in the essay. A brief description would not adequately illustrate why A&F's T-shirts offended the Asian American activist contingent. We present a full description of both A&F's and Blacklava's T-shirts later in the essay in the context of our analysis.

sphere but did so in order to produce an ostensibly new cultural, potentially resistant, meaning. Blacklava's T-shirt satirically mimics A&F's actions, while urging those who wear or view the T-shirt to remember A&F's original act and prevent future instances of mass-produced and mass-marketed racism.

Bhabha's (1994) notions of mimicry and stereotype and Said's (1979) "Other" demonstrate the neocolonial nature of dominant representations of Asian Americans. Mimicry and stereotype work together to exert symbolic domination (Bourdieu 2001) over Asian Americans and thus reify Asian Americans' status as the "Other." These neocolonialist tendencies are exemplified in dominant rhetoric and representations of Asian Americans, most notably the A&F shirts. In short, A&F's use of mimicry and stereotype demonstrated their colonial relationships of symbolic domination and attempted control over Asian Americans. Nevertheless, in this context, we can see the emergence of an Asian American rhetoric through the Blacklava case study.

Asian American communication studies and Asian American studies have recently highlighted the malleability of Asian American identity. As we have seen, however, Asian Americans are publicly constructed and represented by dominant discourse as a specific "Other." Thus, Asian Americanists have seldom attended to *how* Asian Americans publicly construct themselves through rhetoric. In addition, the field of rhetoric has rarely attended to communities of marginalized people through an analysis of their own vernacular discourse and public rhetoric. Through a conception of Asian American rhetoric, we can see *how* Asian Americans can publicly construct and put forth these messages in addition to seeing how these constructions were developed for and by Asian Americans through a critique of what Ono and Sloop (1995) call "vernacular discourse." A critique of vernacular discourse is a critique of the rhetoric of the everyday, including the rhetoric produced with, for, and by communities on the margins (27). By drawing upon vernacular rhetoric, we theorize Asian American rhetoric as both a resistant and self-representational discourse; Asian American rhetoric is an act of self-articulation and control by Asian Americans. Asian American rhetoric serves as a stabilizer—a fixing of a particular identity in a certain political and social context or situation. In this case, Asian American rhetoric arises as a minority discourse to fix, both spatially and correctively, the meaning and identity of Asian American activists. Asian American rhetoric resists by complicating the symbolic registers

Asian Americans inhabit, in this case by satirically reproducing the images within a politicized space of a T-shirt. In the process of resisting, Asian American rhetoric also serves as a mode of representation, positing a more complicated representation of Asian Americanness; in this case Asian American activists are cognizant of the symbolic violence being perpetrated.

"TWO WONGS MAKE IT WHITE"

A&F is a nationally known clothing retail corporation that heads four different brands: the flagship A&F; the children's version, simply named abercrombie; the surf-and-turf-themed Hollister; and the upscale adult Ruehl. A&F describes itself as an "All-American" organization, with the label dating back to 1892 (*A&F History*). A&F boasts on its website that they have outfitted numerous famous Americans, such as Charles Lindbergh, former president Teddy Roosevelt, and writer Ernest Hemingway (A&F History 2006). Since 1998, however, A&F has refashioned its image to become a "lifestyle brand"—consumers purchase the clothing for the image and lifestyle it portrays rather than for functionality.[10] Currently, the A&F corporation operates 355 A&F stores, 201 Abercrombie stores, 447 Hollister stores, and 22 Ruehl stores in the United States. For the fiscal year of 2007, the A&F corporation "reported sales of $3.75 billion, up 13% from the previous year, and net income of $475.7 million" in U.S. dollars (Abercrombie & Fitch 2006). Despite its financial success, A&F has had its share of controversy that extends beyond recent Asian American outrage. Parents were infuriated with A&F's 2003 "Christmas Field Guide" catalog, equating some of the photographs with soft-core pornography marketed to impressionable teenagers (Kadzin 2003). In November 2005, high school–aged female teenagers and others spoke out against T-shirt slogans that were emblazoned across the chest: "With These, Who Needs Brains" (Tecson 2005). Most recently, A&F was indicted for discriminatory hiring practices for denying jobs to people of color and for moving employees of color to the back to do inventory while keeping white employees on the sales floor (NewsSource13 2008).

10. Dwight McBride's (2005) "Why I Hate Abercrombie & Fitch" documents an excellent history of A&F and its shift from outdoors clothing in the early 1900 to the current brands. He also explains his disgust with A&F because of its marketing of elite whiteness. McBride cites the Asian-themed T-shirts as an example of A&F's lack of representation of people of color while demonstrating their proclivity toward whiteness.

These indictments of A&F demonstrate that A&F is explicitly engaged in creating a spectacle of racism and implicitly practicing discrimination in its policies. A&F has continued to be an emblem of fashion on college campuses and in shopping malls, however, despite these boycotts and protests.

In the spring of 2002, A&F released Asian-themed T-shirts that were "designed to appeal to young Asian shoppers with a sense of humor" (Strasburg 2002). Much to A&F's chagrin, the T-shirts infuriated many Asian Americans and resulted in a boycott of A&F and a petition to the company demanding the removal of the T-shirts. The activist movement against A&F began in California, when the China Community Development Center in San Francisco notified the Asian American Students' Association at Stanford University about the T-shirts (El Boghdady 2002). From that starting point, the story of A&F's T-shirts quickly spread around Asian American e-mail listserves and was forwarded on through people's e-mail address books (Strasburg 2002). While these e-mail notifications were being passed on, public protests were also occurring in front of A&F stores in places such as the San Francisco Bay Area of California, central Indiana, and Boston (B. Li 2002). After public e-mail protests and a deluge of phone calls by Asian American activists, A&F pulled the T-shirts from the shelves, an uncommon act for any clothing retailer (El Boghdady 2002). In addition, a spokesperson for A&F, Hampton Carney, stated, "We personally thought Asians would love this t-shirt. We're very, very, very, sorry. It's never been our intention to offend anyone" (AP 2002; Guillermo 2002). However, Carney also noted that A&F parodies all groups, not just Asian Americans, and referred to previous T-shirt designs as evidence. Despite A&F's half-hearted excuse, some Asian American activists were not satisfied with the apology, stating that a formal apology must come from the CEO, not the spokesperson.[11] The formal apology never came, however, and A&F moved on; if A&F's profits were adversely affected, any declining revenues appear to have been short-lived. There is no doubt that Asian Americans still shop at A&F (AP 2002). Indeed, current college-aged Asian Americans may have little to no recollection of the symbolic violence, racial mimicry, and stereotype that A&F invoked for humor and profit in this campaign.

11. Chia-Chi Li (2002), Bethany Li (2002), and the Asian Student Alliance (2002) are examples of Asian American activist groups that perceived the apology as half-hearted.

Protests centered on four of five different designs; the "Wok-N-Bowl," "Buddha Bash," "Wong Brothers," and "Pizza Dojo."[12] Overall, though the T-shirts vary in color, they all have the same layout: a large design on the back with a shrunken version on the front in the left upper chest area. After A&F recalled the T-shirts, Blacklava followed with a release of its own satirized version. As rhetorical artifacts, T-shirts occupy both visual and textual spaces in the form of imagetexts, where the relations between the visual and textual are inexplicably linked in their interpretation while drawing meanings from each and producing new ones in conjunction.[13] In addition, with the marketing of A&F as a lifestyle brand and the prevalence of "branding" as a function of clothing, T-shirts display the social status and/or identity that the wearer chooses to put forth for the public to see.[14] Thus, it is important to consider both the A&F and Blacklava shirts as public displays of imagetexts along with the private reinforcement of social identity. A&F T-shirts display the imagetext of dominant representations of Asian Americans and demonstrate a spectacle of racism where the imagetext serves to reify the stereotypical notions of Asian Americans. The imagetext on the T-shirts serves as a mediator of social relations with whoever comes into contact with the T-shirt, whether in the store or, more likely, on the streets. The T-shirts' commonalities lie in their display of stereotypical roles: the forever foreigner's lack of fluency in the English language, yellow peril imagery. In the following sections, we will describe A&F's four controversial T-shirts before moving on to an analysis of Blacklava's counterrhetorical T-shirt.

12. There was a fifth T-shirt, "Dragon Lady," which also drew some attention, although not as much as the four described here.

13. Art historian W.J.T. Mitchell (1995) explains the relationship between image and text by defining three terms: image/text, imagetext, and image-text. "Image/text" is the gap in presentation between the text and image, "imagetext" is the composite or synthetic works that combine image and text, and "image-text" is the relation of the visual to the textual (89). The A&F T-shirt images are not separated from text as in the "image/text"; both image and text are interconnected and require a reading that takes both into account. In addition, the A&F shirts are more than just a relation between the visual and verbal, like the caption to a photograph, which can be read separately from the image. Thus, the A&F T-shirts resemble "imagetext," where the image and text are combined.

14. Kalle Lasne's (2000) *Culture Jam* and Naomi Klein's (2000) *No Logo* explicate the nature of branding and its impact on U.S. American consumer culture. Both scholars are influential in the *Adbusters* movement, which stresses antibranding. The process of branding is so prevalent in modern advertising, however, that even logo-less brands, like American Apparel, have a reputation that functions as a brand. In the case of American Apparel, the company brands itself as a nonsweatshop, made-in-the-U.S.A. brand.

ABERCROMBIE & FITCH'S T-SHIRT RHETORIC

The "Wok-N-Bowl" T-shirt features a cartoon with a profile of an Asian man posed in a lunging position with a bowling ball in his right hand, pulled back as if he is about to swing the ball forward to let it loose. The left profile of the face shows an extended round nose, an open mouth, and a sharply slanted eye. The clothing of the Asian man emphasizes a round conical "coolie" hat, stereotypical of depictions of Asians working in rice fields, with a white T-shirt and colored pants. The image of the Asian man appears directly above a text box that displays the A&F logo, as if the box were the floor where the man is running and bowling. Below the A&F logo a line of text reads, "Chinese Food & Bowling." Directly to the left of the man is another line of text that reads, "Let the good times roll." To the right of him is an unknown Chinese character. Above the Asian man is the main text, "Wok-N-Bowl," a take on "rock 'n' roll" subtly implying an Asian and Asian American disfluency, an oral and verbal error in the use of words in the English language.[15]

The "Buddha Bash" T-shirt displays the religious figure Buddha as a proponent of partying. We see Chinese characters on the left, next to and partly covered over by the words "Buddha Bash," written in white, with the Buddha to the right of the logo. Above is the A&F logo, this time with no graphic outline, and below the words "Buddha Bash" is a line of text that reads, "Get your Buddha on the floor."

On the "Pizza Dojo" T-shirt, "Abercrombie's" appears at the top in yellow, with "Pizza Dojo" written below it in a "chopstick" font, thus indicating that it is "Abercrombie's Pizza Dojo," that A&F possesses the Pizza Dojo. Below the "Pizza dojo" lettering is an image of an Asian man wearing a robe and tight-fitting cap with his hands holding a pizza dish and fork and smiling, looking at the viewer, as if to offer the pizza to the viewer. To the left of this image is text that reads, "You love long time." Below the man is a text box that reads, "Eat in or wok out" and below that "Call us at 1–888–520–PEZA," both texts stereotypically depicting the verbal Asian accent when speaking English.

The theme of the last T-shirt is the "Wong Brothers" laundry service. In large letters appear the words "Wong Brothers." In a smaller font

15. In what Elaine Chun (2004) calls "mock Asian stylings," she gives a linguistic perspective on the mockery of Asian accents when speaking English as a second language by non-Asians. She draws upon the examples of Shaquille O'Neal, Adam Corrolla, and more recently Rosie O'Donnell, discussing their use of "Ching-Chong" language when imitating Asians.

and below that are the words "A laundry service," and below that and to the right is a phone number. Partially superimposed onto these images is an image shaped like a clothes hanger that is broken up by that text and placed among soap bubbles. On the left and right of the T-shirt are the Wong brothers, smiling and looking jovial. Both the brothers are wearing Chinese peasant clothing and conical coolie hats and are looking out at the viewer. Their faces are round and they have slanted eyes. In the space between the two brothers and connecting them is a small banner with small print that states, "Two Wongs can make it white." The A&F logo inhabits the space directly below the banner.

"ARTFULBIGOTRY & KITSCH": COUNTERING A&F

Asian American activists understood A&F's T-shirts as an act of symbolic violence. College student activists recognized the spectacle's ability to mediate the "social relationship between people" (Debord 1994, 12). Student protesters were outraged by the commodification of the Asian American experience. Austin Chang from the Asian-focused magazine Monolid put it best when he wrote, "You have to ask yourself, who benefits, who gets empowerment, from these kinds of 'images'?" (Strasburg 2002).

In the first phase of the anti-A&F movement, Asian American activists redirected consumer buying power into a boycott to pressure A&F to remove the Asian-themed T-shirts. This phase strategically utilized new media through a combination of forwarding e-mails, contacting listserves, and online petitions.[16] Although we do not focus on this part of the anti-A&F movement by Asian Americans, we do recognize that the use of technology allowed for a quick response and the application of consumer pressure, which led to an apology and ultimately the company's withdrawal of the T-shirt. What we do focus our attention on is the counterrhetoric of Blacklava's T-shirt that addresses A&F. Originally started as a surf-inspired clothing line in 1996, Blacklava is one of the leading producers of Asian American activist-inspired merchandise and clothing, primarily through consumer access to their Web site and connections with Asian American activists.[17] In an interview with an Asian

16. In her book *Digitizing Race: Visual Cultures of the Internet*, Lisa Nakamura (2007) focuses on Asian American use of the Internet when dealing with A&F and other instances of retail racism.

17. As this essay demonstrates, Blacklava is one of the more well-known Asian American–inspired clothing lines among the Asian American activist community.

American movement webzine editor, Ryan Suda, the founder and owner of Blacklava, stated that his inspiration for the turn from "cheesy logo driven artwork" to an Asian American politically conscious clothing company came from his experience in an Asian American studies class at Cal State Fullerton; his professor distributed a poem titled "Asian Is Not Oriental," which opened his eyes and helped him to "look at things in a different way" (Pangilinan 2005). From this experience, he printed a T-shirt called "Asian is NOT Oriental." Additional T-shirts were designed by other Asian American artists and then distributed by Blacklava; among them are T-shirts with a simple single line of text across the front that reads: "I suck at math," "I am not white," or "I speak English."[18] The rhetorical purpose of these T-shirts is to deconstruct stereotypes of Asian Americans; statements like "I suck at math" play against the popular stereotype that Asian Americans are inherently good at math and science. The antistereotype T-shirts, however, also have the ability to appeal to numerous groups, albeit with different associated meanings (A-zine 2004).

The counter-shirts point to the differently creative nature of Asian American rhetoric. Within two weeks of the A&F debacle, Ryan Suda had designed an anti-A&F T-shirt.[19] The front of the T-shirt is adorned with a reconfigured A&F logo; it reads "Artfulbigotry & Kitsch," a satirical mimicking of the original A&F logo. "Artfulbigotry & Kitsch" is underlined in large print with "Ignorance·Racism·Excuses" and "since 2002" appearing below it in an upside-down pyramid formation. The "since 2002" text highlights the year that A&F released their Asian-themed T-shirt. The back of the T-shirt is slightly different: the text reappears, but with A&F Asian images framed by the Blacklava text. "Artfulbigotry & Kitsch" is underlined with "since 2002" directly below it in small print. Then the four A&F images of the Wongs laundry service, the bowling Chinaman, Asian pizza dojo, and a rickshaw man are centered. Below the images, "Ignorance·Racism·Excuses" serves as the bottom border. The very bottom of the T-shirt says, "The Struggle Continues . . . Blacklava," suggesting, perhaps, that the struggle against racism toward Asian Americans and the general struggles of being an

---

18. You can see the various T-shirt designs at the Blacklava's Web site, www.blacklava.net.
19. Suda, e-mail to authors, March 25, 2006. Regarding the T-shirt's sales, Suda states, "It was definitely one of my best selling shirts back then mainly because so many people knew about the controversy and were so upset."

Front view of the Blacklava shirt. Detail of a photo by Vincent Pham; permission courtesy of Ryan Suda.

Back view of the Blacklava shirt. Detail of a photo by Vincent Pham; permission courtesy of Ryan Suda.

Asian American are continuing ones and that Blacklava supports these struggles and the movement.[20]

RHETORICAL T-SHIRTS AND RECIRCULATED IMAGES

We understand the Blacklava counter-A&F T-shirt, as a rhetorical artifact, in three ways: (1) it critiques and then reappropriates stereotypical and offensive images of Asian Americans as a tool of activist invention that recirculates in the public sphere with creative activist meaning; (2) it exemplifies the dialectical relationship between the wearer of the T-shirt and the rhetoric of the T-shirt; and (3) it satirizes A&F and resists A&F's attempts at mimicry and symbolic domination of Asian Americans.

The Blacklava T-shirt reconfigures the meaning of the original images, taking A&F's supposedly humorous Asian-themed graphics and reformulating them into a damning condemnation of A&F's cultural insensitivity, corporate colonialism, and symbolic violence against Asian Americans and their historical role in perpetuating U.S. racism. Suda states that the intention of the T-shirt was to expose A&F through satire of the A&F brand and that the use of the original images was the best

20. Suda, e-mail to authors, July 26, 2006. Suda refers to the struggle in a very general sense, indicating, "It's more of a general reference to all the things we need to continuously struggle with as Asian Americans. There will always be struggle." Suda implies that the Asian American experience is an experience of struggle.

way to document A&F's actions.[21] Using A&F's original images had a greater likelihood of evoking memories for people who had seen them. The counterrhetorical T-shirt transforms A&F into "Artfulbigotry & Kitsch," implying that one only needs to interpret the company's message in a slightly different way to gain new meaning, that "Abercrombie and Fitch" is only a step and a mispronunciation away from the true discriminatory corporate identity, and that A&F is a euphemism and alias for corporate practices of bigotry and tastelessness.

The counterrhetorical T-shirt also takes A&F's images and recodes them within a new text and transformed context: instead of standing alone with A&F's supposedly humorous text, the new text repositions the images within a discourse of bigotry, tastelessness, ignorance, racism, and excuses. By positioning the images between words, also from A&F's original T-shirt, the Blacklava T-shirt problematizes the images themselves: arguing that the images and the excuses for the images perpetuate racism and bigotry through offensive and tasteless "art" or "humor."

While the image and text work together to create a new meaning, the Blacklava T-shirt recirculates the images that A&F previously tried to hide. After the debacle, A&F pulled the Asian-themed T-shirts off the shelves and thus withdrew the images from public view. Word of mouth and e-mail forward chains became the means of documenting A&F's acts of symbolic violence, while the T-shirts and their images were found only on Internet search engines. The original A&F T-shirts have become collector's items, fetching upwards of $100 on Ebay (as of April 26, 2006), and are no longer worn by the general public. Moreover, A&F has yet to give us approval to reproduce the images, so we are left directing readers toward where the images continue to exist.[22] Blacklava's counterrhetorical T-shirt, however, reintroduces the images into and recontextualizes the images for the public sphere and thus allows the public to view the images that A&F constructed for profit. Furthermore, the counterrhetorical T-shirt exposes those images as acts of symbolic domination and not as hip, humorous, and edgy designs.

The counterrhetorical T-shirts re-mimic and resignify the original images. Blacklava's remimicry inhabits Bhabha's "space of resistance"

21. Ibid.

22. It is more than likely that A&F will not give us permission to use the images since they are no longer on its Web site. However, a quick Internet search of "Abercrombie & Fitch Asian American shirt" will bring up results.

that can occur through the flawed stereotype. Blacklava mimics the stereotype with recognition of the stereotype's flaws. By doing so, Blacklava's counterrhetorical T-shirt inhabits the space of resistance, resignifying and transforming the colonial images, exposing A&F's symbolic violence.

When the counterrhetorical T-shirts reintroduce the original and offending images back into the public sphere, primarily through consumers wearing the Blacklava T-shirts, T-shirt rhetoric employs the body as a metaphoric public billboard through which the rhetoric is publicized, acknowledging that the site is both mobile and discursive when worn by a person. The relationship between the body of the wearer of the T-shirt and the T-shirt's rhetoric is a dialectical one. By wearing the shirt, the person embodies and occupies the space of the activist and connects him- or herself to the satirical text on the shirt. The wearer thus occupies the position of an Asian American activist who is also anti-A&F. The T-shirt creates, maintains, and reifies the activist spirit for the wearer. In addition, the public nature of the T-shirt invites other people, who may or may not know of A&F's practices, to engage the wearer of the T-shirt, encouraging them to inquire as to its meaning. If the outsider engages with the wearer and shares the same activist mentality, then it may become a site for discussion and dialogue. If the outsider is not aware of A&F's practices, then the wearer may assume the role of educator or radical activist. If the outsider agrees with A&F's practices and chooses to engage with the wearer of the countershirt, then a dialogue and/or dispute may also ensue. That person may also choose not to speak with the wearer of the T-shirt, however, knowing that the wearer of the T-shirt is an activist. Thus, the circulation of the counterrhetorical T-shirt continually produces a discourse around A&F's attempts to commodify an Asian American persona while subjecting the Asian American to a rhetoric of self-representation.

The T-shirt challenges A&F's representations and functions as ground-level vernacular rhetoric for those in and outside the Asian American community. This vernacular discourse may spread throughout the Asian American community and encourage Asian Americans to remember and resist mass-produced and mass-marketed racism. The counterrhetorical T-shirt itself is an artifact of Asian American resistance to symbolic domination by a predominantly white corporation; the countershirt also illustrates rhetorical inventiveness through the use of satire when responding to commodifying images and the commodification and mass marketing of racism. Admittedly, the satirical act also commodifies activism and markets political beliefs; however, the marketing and commodification of activism requires an activist ethos and a commitment to supporting the activist movement of those who contribute to the resistance.[23] Hence, in this instance, arguably commodification occurs in the service of activism. In addition, satirical countershirts respond to instances of symbolic domination, mimicry, and media exploitation through self-identification with activist and political ideas. Here, Asian American activists created rhetoric through products, such as T-shirts, to complicate the symbolic terrain while self-identifying and self-representing in manners and voices that likely would be difficult for corporate clothing companies to co-opt. Blacklava also produced a T-shirt responding to the media exploitation and corporate mimicry of William Hung. This T-shirt, adorned with the text "hung over...," compares the mimicry and mockery of William Hung to past figures like Buckwheat from *The Little Rascals* or Long Duk Dong from *Sixteen Candles*.[24] As someone who experienced a mimicking performance of William Hung as an attempt to enact symbolic violence against me, I, Vincent, appreciate Blacklava's attempt to challenge, critique, and make publicly known the problematic rhetorical effects of such mimicry through the creation of a T-shirt designed to be worn by people who find this kind of mimicry offensive and see its racial and colonial implications. Here, Asian American rhetoric, in reaction to public misrepresentations, seeks to right media wrongs by setting forth a more complicated image that both supports and represents Asian Americans. In this case, the mode of self-representational discourse occurs through the rhetorical acts of producing and wearing activist counterrhetorical T-shirts that require knowledge of Asian American history in connection to current Asian American public humiliation; thus Asian Americans are not represented as quiet and passive "model minorities" but rather as activist and political participants.

23. The marketing of political beliefs is similar to bumper stickers on cars. In both instances, political beliefs are commodified and sold to activists. However, we believe that T-shirts and bumper stickers differ slightly in their communication interactions. We suspect bumper stickers are often seen from a perspective of a car or in a parking lot, where the ability to interact with the activist is often inhibited. However, the T-shirts are usually worn, and thus the opportunity to communicate with the activists is more of a possibility. Documenting whether or not this happens is beyond the scope of this essay.

24. This comparison is argued in the description of the "Hung Over" T-shirt on the Blacklava Web site ("Hung Over Unisex T" 2006).

LOOKING FOR ASIAN AMERICAN RHETORIC

While Blacklava's counter-A&F rhetoric is satirical and productive, it defines Asian American rhetoric and activism as oppositional, a limited strategy against symbolic domination by corporate entities, such as A&F, or general cultural trends, such as the media exploitation of William Hung, and replaces one form of commodification and consumption with an alternative, yet activist, one. While instances like A&F and William Hung are important and notable, they shift attention away from the lack of media representation by Asian Americans in general; as a friend once said to one of us to justify A&F's representation of Asian Americans: "At least they're showing Asians."[25]

Corporate attempts at symbolic domination and corporate mimicry exemplify the continual struggle over symbols, where the spectacle mediates the reality in which social relationships are based. Potential for creative acts does exist but is often strongly circumscribed by options and strategies existing within our contemporary cultural commoditized environment. While A&F intended the Asian-themed T-shirts to connect with the Asian American demographic, the T-shirts demonstrated A&F's (representational) power over the Asian American minority and simultaneously, through misrepresentation, displayed Asian Americans' lack of power to create, produce, mass market, and distribute self-images and, even more broadly, the overall lack of representation of Asian Americans in U.S. popular culture and politics. A&F's decision to release the T-shirts communicated an act of symbolic violence that targeted Asian Americans. Instead of connecting with the Asian American demographic, the shirts had the reverse effect of alienating part of the demographic A&F sought. A&F's T-shirts also register the metonymy of presence, in which the Asian is always the laundry man, the rice field worker, or the submissive restaurant worker. A&F's T-shirts evoked images of Asians against which the student protesters quickly acted. From the University of Michigan, sophomore Stephanie Chang stated that the A&F images depicted Asian Americans as "uncultured foreigners who can't speak English right" (Khatri 2002). Other one-dimensional stereotypes that the images propagated were Asians as oriental houseboys (Bronski 2002), dorky-looking slanted-eyed men, or as affable, passive, and apathetic workers. This metonymy of

25. Harris (1999) draws upon Clark's four stages of minority portrayal; the first being nonrecognition and the second being ridicule. In this case, the friend seems happy enough with the second stage of portrayal as a display of progress.

presence is evident in the "Wok-N-Bowl" T-shirt, in which the Asian is forever a coolie with a rice hat or a "forever foreigner" who cannot pronounce "rock 'n'roll" correctly but rather does so with an Asian or Asian immigrant accent, thereby marking the Asian's forever "otherness" within the United States.

Neocolonialism seeks to dominate ideological and pedagogical spaces of visual representations of the colonized, employing mimicry and stereotypes as tools of domination and symbolic violence. A&F exerts its symbolic violence through the propagation of stereotypical images, promoting and reproducing a caricature of Asian Americans reminiscent of nineteenth-century America. A&F's T-shirt production is an act of mimicry: the Asian is the "subject of difference that is almost the same but not quite" when compared to the A&F's traditional clientele. Thus, the T-shirt visualizes the power of A&F; the company is able to commodify the Asian American image and situate it within text that belittles the Asian American experience. When clothing corporations seek to commodify Asian Americans and marginalize their voice in the process of gaining profits, they exemplify neocolonial power. However, Asian American rhetoric arises through activist organizations and their specific response to corporate mimicry and their continual advancement of Asian American self-representation. Asian American rhetoric consists of both the public context of the time and a deconstruction of and attempt to uproot historical stereotypes currently functioning as methods of symbolic violence and eventual domination. Thus, as in the e-mail activism and the countershirts, Asian American rhetoric addresses the here and now while simultaneously complicating the past and future of Asian American representation and public identity.

REFERENCES

A&F History. 2006. August 14. www.abercrombie.com, "career" or "diversity" link, "history" tab (accessed April 5, 2008).

Abercrombie & Fitch. 2006. New York Jobsource, February 15. http://nyjobsource.com/abercrombie.html (accessed April 4, 2008).

Achbar, Mark, and Jennifer Abbott. 2005. *The Corporation*. Zeitgeist Films.

AP. 2002. Abercrombie & Fitch Asian T-shirts Trigger Boycott: Shirts Depict Stereotypes of Asians. April 18. http://www.nbc4.tv/news/1406052/detail.html (accessed April 4, 2008).

Asen, Robert, and Daniel C. Brouwer, eds. 2001. *Counterpublics and the State*. Albany: SUNY Press.

Asian Student Alliance. 2002. Abercrombie & Fitch Sells Racism with T-shirts. *Mac Weekly*, May 3. http://www.macalester.edu/weekly/050302/quietly.html (accessed April 4, 2008).

A-zine. 2004. Questioning Society One T-shirt at a Time: Interview with Ryan Suda, Founder of Black Lava T-shirts. *Asian American Movement Ezine: Azine,* February 9. http://www.aamovement.net/community/ryansuda.html (accessed April 4, 2008).

BBC. 2006. Adidas Hit over "Racist" Trainer. April 10. http://news.bbc.co.uk/2/hi/business/4895898.stm (accessed April 4, 2008).

Bhabha, Homi. 1994. *Location of Culture.* New York: Routledge.

Bourdieu, Pierre. 2001. *Masculine Domination.* Translated by R. Nice. Stanford, CA: Stanford University Press.

Bourdieu, Pierre, and Jean Claude Passeron. 1990. *Reproduction in Education, Society, and Culture.* Chicago: University of Chicago Press.

Bronski, Michael. 2002. *Sense and Sensitivity.* Phoenix Media Communications Group. http://www.bostonphoenix.com/boston/news_features/other_stories/documents/02261125.htm (accessed April 4, 2008).

Chen, Tina. 2005. *Double Agency.* (Asian America series). Stanford, CA: Stanford University Press.

Chuh, Kandice. 2003. *Imagine Otherwise: On Asian Americanist Critique.* Durham, NC: Duke University Press.

Chun, Elaine. 2004. Ideologies of Legitimate Mockery: Margaret Cho's Revoicing of Mock Asian. *Pragmatics* 14 (2/3): 263–289.

Cloud, Dana L. 1992. The Limits of Interpretation: Ambivalence and the Stereotype in *Spenser for Hire. Critical Studies in Mass Communication* 9 (4): 311–324.

Debord, Guy. 1994. *The Society of the Spectacle.* Translated by D. Nicholson-Smith. New York: Zone.

DeLuca, Kevin Michael, and Jennifer Peeples. 2002. From Public Sphere to Public Screen: Democracy, Activism, and the "Violence" of Seattle. *Critical Studies in Media Communication* 19 (2): 125–151.

El Boghdady, Dina. 2002. Tshirts' Ethnic Jokes Flop. *Washington Post,* April 19, E01.

Fraser, Nancy. 1993. Rethinking the Public Sphere: A Contribution to the Critique of Actually Existing Democracy. In *Habermas and the Public Sphere,* edited by C. Calhoun. Cambridge, MA: MIT Press.

Gudykunst, W. B. 2001. *Asian American Ethnicity and Communication.* Thousand Oaks, CA: Sage.

Guillermo, Emil. 2002. Humoring Ethnic America: Abercrombie & Fitch Still Doesn't Get It. *San Francisco Gate,* April 23. http://www.sfgate.com/cgi-bin/article.cgi?f=/g/archive/2002/04/23/eguillermo.DTL (accessed April 4, 2008).

Harris, R. J. 1999. Portrayal of Groups: A Distorted Mirror. In *A Cognitive Psychology of Mass Communication.* Mahwah, NJ: Lawrence Erlbaum.

Hung Over Unisex T. 2006. http://blacklava.net/store/product_info.php?cPath=1&products_id=167 (accessed March 5, 2008).

Jackson, Camille. 2006. Spencer Gifts: Racist Shirts for Sale. Tolerance.org, January 19. http://www.tolerance.org/news/article_tol.jsp?id=1348 (accessed April 4, 2008).

Kazdin, Cole. 2003. Have Yourself a Horny Little Christmas. *Salon,* November 11. http://dir.salon.com/story/sex/feature/2003/11/26/abercrombie/index.html (accessed April 4, 2008).

Khatri, Shabina S. 2002. Abercrombie and Fitch Offends Asian American Community. *Michigan Daily,* April 30. http://www.michigandaily.com/media/paper851/news/2002/04/30/News/Abercrombie.And.Fitch.Offends.Asian.American.Community-1403194.shtml?norewrite200603270045&sourcedomain=www.michigandaily.com&sourcedomain=www.michigandaily.com (accessed April 4, 2008).

Klein, Naomi. 2000. *No Logo.* New York: Picador.

Lammers, John C., Joshua B. Barbour, and Ashley P. Duggan. 2003. Organizational Forms of the Provision of Health Care: An Institutional Perspective. In *The Handbook of Health*

Communication, edited by T. Thompson, A. Dorsey, K. Miller, and R. Parrot. Mahwah, NJ: Lawrence Erlbaum.

Lasne, Kalle. 2000. *Culture Jam: How to Reverse America's Suicidal Consumer Binge—and Why We Must.* New York: Quill.

Lee, Josephine. 2006. New Directions in Asian American Performance: The Problem of Bad Acting. Keynote address, "Bodies and Spectacles: A Conference on Asian American Performance." University of Illinois at Urbana-Champaign, October 26–27.

Li, Bethany. 2002. Racial Inequality Not a Laughing Matter. *Amherst Student,* April 24. http://halogen.note.amherst.edu/~astudent/2001–2002/issue24/opinion/03.html (accessed April 4, 2008).

Li, Chia-Chi. 2002. Boycott Abercrombie & Fitch. Artifice, Inc. http://www.petitiononline.com/BCAF/petition.html (accessed April 4, 2008).

McBride, Dwight A. 2005. Why I Hate Abercrombie & Fitch. In *Why I Hate Abercrombie & Fitch*, edited by D. A. McBride. New York: New York University Press.

McMillan, Jill J. 1987. In Search of the Organizational Persona: A Rationale for Studying Organizations Rhetorically. In *Organization <—> Communication: Emerging Perspectives II*, edited by L. Thayer. Norwood, NJ: Ablex.

Mitchell, W.J.T. 1995. *Picture Theory: Essays on Verbal and Visual Representation.* Chicago: University of Chicago Press.

Miyoshi, Masao. 1995. Sites of Resistance in the Global Economy. *boundary 2* 22 (1): 61–84.

Nakamura, Lisa. 2007. *Digitizing Race: Visual Cultures of the Internet.* Minneapolis: University of Minnesota Press.

NewsSource13. 2008. Abercrombie and Fitch Settle $40 Million Discrimination Suit http://yellowworld.org/civil_rights/280.html (accessed April 4, 2008).

Ono, Kent A., and Derek Buescher. 2001. Deciphering Pocahontas: Unpackaging the Commodification of a Native American Woman. *Critical Studies in Media Communication* 18 (1): 1–21.

Ono, Kent A., and Thomas K. Nakayama. 2004. The Emergence of Asian American Communication Studies. *Review of Communication* 4 (1/2): 88–93.

Ono, Kent A., and John M. Sloop. 1995. The Critique of Vernacular Discourse. *Communication Monographs* 62 (1): 19–46.

Pangilinan, Erin.2005. You Are What You Wear: Asian Pacifica Islander (APIA) Themed Tee-shirts: A Movement. March 29. http://www.aamovement.net/viewpoints/2004–2005/apiawear.htm (accessed April 4, 2008).

Said, Edward W. 1979. *Orientalism.* New York: Vintage.

Strasburg, Jenny. 2002. Abercrombie & Glitch: Asian Americans Rip Retailer on Stereotypes on T-shirts. *San Francisco Chronicle,* April 18, A-1.

Tecson, Brandee J.. 2005. Abercrombie Pulls T-shirts After Teen Girls Launch Boycott. November 7. http://www.mtv.com/news/articles/1513153/20051107/index.jhtml?headlines=true (accessed April 4, 2008).

Young, Morris. 2004. *Minor Re/Visions: Asian American Literacy Narratives as a Rhetoric of Citizenship.* Carbondale: Southern Illinois University Press.

9

BEYOND "ASIAN AMERICAN" AND BACK

Coalitional Rhetoric in Print and New Media

Jolivette Mecenas

During the summer of 2003, I worked as a volunteer organizer for an annual arts festival in San Francisco called APAture, a program of the Kearny Street Workshop (KSW). The KSW office was housed in a warehouse with other community arts nonprofits in the South of Market neighborhood, and often we had to raise our voices over the African drumming in the room next door, or the hammering of a new group show being installed in the gallery. The volunteers met at night, after our day jobs as journalists, college students, corporate cubicle dwellers, Web designers, nonprofit junkies, and teachers like myself. I think some of us were still reeling in the post–dot-com era, trying to figure out how to fund our socially conscious art habits after the generous venture capitalists had fled town. As for myself, I was trying to reconnect with the city after a couple of isolated years in grad school, desperate for a community of heady idealists who also liked to have a good time. And so I found myself at KSW with the other volunteers, all of us responsible for selecting and curating submissions from musicians, performance artists, poets, fiction writers, spoken-word collectives, photographers, painters, dancers, and filmmakers from throughout the Bay Area. We were responsible for putting on a good show, and that's exactly what we did: one and a half weeks of sensory overstimulation in our warehouse gallery and performance space.

APAture is a play on the word *aperture*, the opening through which light passes onto a lens of a camera. While the wordplay may seem a bit enigmatic, the "APA" clearly stands for Asian Pacific American. This makes sense if you are familiar with the nonprofit's thirty-plus years of "arts activism," beginning in its original location in the International Hotel, or the I-Hotel, a well-known flashpoint of the Asian American movement during the 1970s. KSW is a grassroots neighborhood arts program, its mission to build coalitions of local activists, writers, artists, performers, and students that are intergenerational and multiethnic.

While aware of KSW's activist history, I never really gave the "APA" or Asian Pacific American part of APAture much thought. "APA" seemed to be more of a pragmatic title rather than an actual identity—no one *I* knew would ever call him- or herself an Asian Pacific American. At KSW I made friends with people who were Vietnamese, Japanese, Korean, Filipino, South Asian, of mixed ethnicities, Taiwanese, and so forth. It wasn't until I read through the submissions for the literary category that I began to think about what we were trying to achieve as a multiethnic coalition of artists and community leaders under the somewhat ambiguous title "Asian Pacific American." After the nth spoken-word piece utilizing food as a metaphor for an essential Filipino-ness, or expressing grievances because the author felt he could never be "American enough" by virtue of being Chinese, I began to experience what I call *identity fatigue*—a weariness brought about from prolonged exposure to others' nonimaginative representations of their cultural and/or ethnic identity. This condition was not felt only by members of the literary committee; the film committee was also heavily hit. Soon, organizers in performance and visual arts also began to express the question on my mind: Why were so many young artists so focused on rigidly constrained representations of racial identity? And why were many of the very same proclamations and grievances surrounding an "Asian Pacific American" identity repeated year after year? It became clear to us that we were not the only audience adverse to this type of art, and we began to advise each other to curate pieces that "didn't focus so much on identity."

But that advice didn't make sense, because in some of the most magnificent pieces, the artist's identity was teased out with the subtlest word, fragmented in colors, or self-mocked in song. The problem that then stymied us was how we could encourage and nurture artists and performers who were truly visionary in articulating the endless permutations of what it means to be human, let alone "Asian American." A collective of such people, I imagined, would no longer be ruled by the need to represent positive images nor respond to negative stereotypes in mainstream media. Instead, we might acknowledge the instabilities of both as part of an ongoing, complex conversation in which identity is treated like an open-ended question, the answer to which is ephemeral, and the pleasure is in the pursuit.

Now, as I pursue my research interests in rhetoric and composition, at the forefront of my inquiries are how collective subjects mobilize public articulations of identity as rhetorical practice. Identity claims such as those that I observed as an APAture organizer engender a rhetoric that seeks to create coalitions among otherwise unlike people, typically for specific political ends. And yet I have observed that, much like some of the young artists in APAture, those who purport an authoritative Asian American identity foreclose what such an identity might mean, and coalitions that once sought political agency under the aegis of Asian American are frightfully constrained. What I would like to examine in this analysis of Asian American discourse is the effectiveness of different rhetorical approaches in creating coalitions with political agency. In my reading of Judith Butler's seminal text, *Gender Trouble: Feminism and the Subversion of Identity* (1999), I was struck by how her post-structuralist approach to language, subjectivity, and political agency resonated with my own observations and thoughts of how Asian American identities are articulated through rhetorical practices. Thus influenced, I decided to apply Butler's theory of performativity to my analysis of Asian American discourses, and such is the methodology of my argument.

If the specter of a post-structuralist analysis sends rhetoric and composition specialists questioning the relevance of this argument for the field, let me suggest to the reader that a post-structuralist or deconstructive reading is "supremely rhetorical," as Stanley Fish asserts, in that such a reading questions the underlying structure of assumptions that naturalizes or legitimates hegemonic power (1998, 53). Such a reading practice is useful in interrogating the coalitional rhetoric that is mobilized by social movements based on cultural identity, such as Asian American activists. Stuart Hall maintains that there are at least two different ways of thinking about cultural identity. The first view proposes that people affiliate with one another based on a common understanding of race and ethnicity that is fixed and stable, defined by "one, shared culture, a sort of collective 'one true self.'" The second view purports that cultural identity "is a matter of 'becoming' as well as of 'being.'" Summing up these two perspectives, Hall writes: "Perhaps instead of thinking of identity as an already accomplished fact, which the new cultural practices then represent, we should think, instead, of identity as a 'production' which is never complete, always in process, and always constituted within, not outside, representation" (2003, 234–236). In the analysis to follow, I focus on two case studies of rhetorical practices that illustrate both of Hall's perspectives of cultural identity.

Using Judith Butler's concepts of performativity and parodic subversion as a framework for further discussing identity, subjectivity, and agency, I focus this discussion on two contemporary magazines devoted to Asian American or Asian cultural production: *Hyphen* and *Giant Robot*. Drawing on examples from both the print and online versions of the two publications, I examine the rhetorical approaches to building coalitional readerships—or publics—organized around particular narratives of Asian and Asian American identities. My reason for doing so is to examine rhetorical practices enacted under such political and cultural identities for ways they may engender viable and inclusive coalitions. In order for Asian American coalitions to attain the liberatory aims they often claim as a goal, they must shift away from a rhetorical approach that tries to prescribe and represent a fixed "truth" about an Asian American identity and experience. Rather, agency is gained through rhetorical practices that resignify cultural identities through shared practices of popular culture, in ways that endlessly create and contest the possibilities of what is intelligibly Asian American.

ASIAN AMERICAN PUBLICS

Before I look more specifically at *Hyphen* and *Giant Robot*, it is necessary to explain why I focus this analysis on print and new media rather than other cultural objects such as music or film. Earlier, I mentioned how the magazines' readership also constitutes a public. To clarify, I am drawing from Michael Warner's definition of publics: a public is a space of discourse that comes into existence "only in relation to texts and their circulation"—an audience that comes into being by virtue of being addressed, self-organized around discourse and comprised primarily of strangers (2005, 66–67). Jürgen Habermas, whose analysis of the public sphere has become the classical reference for all subsequent revisions in public sphere theory, connects the formation of modern publics with the onset of modernity in seventeenth-century Europe. Prior to that time, the ancient notion of the public was one of citizens administering legal and military affairs. However, with the onset of Enlightenment ideals, including an emphasis on individual reason, this administrative function shifted to the modern formulation that focused on private citizens debating on civil society. Habermas attributes this shift in large part to the evolution of literary journalism. In British magazines such as the *Tatler* and the *Guardian*, for example, representations in mass media articulated the bourgeois society's relationships to family, private property, culture, and social conventions in dealing with others in the middle and merchant classes—representations in which the reading public recognized itself and accepted this portrayal as reality. This mutual recognition between readers and culturally sanctioned texts, through which "the public held up a mirror to itself," constitutes the formation of the bourgeois subjectivity within its corresponding ideology (1989, 41). In other words, there was no such thing as a bourgeois subject before literary culture (an extension of the British Empire) described individuals—readers of the *Tatler* or the *Guardian*, for example—as such, and the public accepted this identity.

Since then the magazine genre continues to focus on contemporary discourse—news, trends, interviews, gossip—the temporal flow of which is organized by punctual circulation patterns: daily, weekly, monthly, quarterly. The twenty-first-century online equivalent complicates circulation with a more continuous, incessant flow. Readers may post their responses to articles on most sites whenever they want, to be read by others throughout the world, creating a new vitality and tempo in public discussion. Discussion boards and blogs have expanded opportunities for dialogic exchanges and public claims of identity, as I will look at more in depth with the illustrations I provide for my argument. *Publicness* describes our relations with strangers within these discursive spaces of dialogue, and our participation in the public sphere constitutes us individually as much as we constitute the public sphere by virtue of addressing it.

This illustrates Butler's famous argument undermining the logic of identity politics, or the idea that an individual must claim an essential "true" identity before she can take political action. Butler argues that "there need not be a 'doer behind the deed,' but that the 'doer' is variably constructed in and through the deed"(1999, 181). Let me rephrase her argument so that it may apply to this analysis of Asian American discourse: there is no true "Asian American" identity behind the articulation of one. Rather, Asian American identities are constructed in various ways through the act of articulation. *Hyphen* and *Giant Robot* and their readerships are examples of Asian and Asian American publics that are mutually authoring in this way. However, before a closer look at the publications, let us return to Judith Butler's theory of performativity and subversion as a framework for thinking about subjectivity and agency.

TROUBLING RACE: WHAT RHETORIC AND COMPOSITION MAY LEARN FROM GENDER TROUBLE

Since its original publication in 1990, Butler's *Gender Trouble* has had tremendous impact on feminist and queer studies and how we think about gender, identity, and political agency. At the heart of *Gender Trouble* is Butler's examination of a universal understanding of gender, specifically of "woman," that has prevailed as a main point of contention in feminism. Butler employs a post-structuralist approach to think critically about the basic vocabulary used in feminism, and the conditions in which certain vocabulary maintains positions of power. We can, for example, speak of gender in descriptive accounts that take into consideration what is possible, or we can speak of gender in normative accounts that mandate which expressions of gender are acceptable and which are not. Normative descriptions, Butler asserts, operate within existing power regimes that are often implied and thus necessitate further interrogation, as normative behavior renders all other behavior marginal or even unintelligible and therefore powerless. Such a construction is supported by the subject/object binary of traditional western ontology, the history of which Butler delineates as a "distinction between soul (consciousness, mind) and body [that] invariably supports relations of political and psychic subordination and hierarchy." Within this binary, the mind is associated with masculinity, while the subordinate body is associated with femininity. Given this, Butler calls for "any uncritical reproduction of the mind/body distinction . . . to be rethought for the implicit gender hierarchy that the distinction has conventionally produced, maintained, and rationalized" (1999, 17). The problem this binary presents is that what is normal or "intelligible" becomes naturalized against what is not; identity thus becomes fixed in nondiscursive language of the prevailing discourse, and reproduces the conditions of power regimes. How we come to know accepted understandings of "woman," for example, may be constructed in patriarchal terms, consequently reproducing the conditions of female subjection to male dominance as an accepted, uncontested "reality," thereby closing off the potential for agency.

The goal for examining the intersection between identity and politics from this post-structuralist approach is to identify ways that the articulation of identity creates the agency to meet political goals. To this end, Butler describes her theory of performativity, in which identity is constituted through language and other signifying acts. In

Gender Trouble, Butler contends that gender is constructed through language, is brought into being through language, as identity is an effect of these signifying practices. Furthermore, there is no a priori subject who "chooses" an identity; rather, identity is constituted through language within a preexisting ideology of culture, economy, family, etc. We can think of an example that Butler uses in *Bodies That Matter,* her follow-up to *Gender Trouble:* the doctor exclaims, "It's a girl!" when an infant is born. The doctor's language is the first in a lifelong chain of signifying practices that prescribe the gender identity of "girl" to the infant, according to the norms of what constitutes such an identity as intelligible. Throughout its childhood, the subject will be compelled to reiterate this identity by, for example, compulsively walking through doorways marked "Girls" rather than "Boys"; if she does not, she will be subject to disciplinary measures from the school or other institutions, as well as being ostracized by her schoolmates.[1] This institutional and ritualistic rendering of gender is what naturalizes it in culture, while the disruption of this ritual is the potential site of agency, which is "located within the possibility of a variation on that repetition" (Butler 1999, 185). A subversion of this repetition through signifying practices is an act of agency because it iterates new possibilities of what is intelligible in culture. To illustrate a subversive act, Butler uses the example of drag performers, whom she describes as revealing the imitative and unstable nature of gender through parody.

This bare-bones explanation of performativity serves to lay the framework for thinking about what may constitute an Asian American identity and the type of agency it engenders. Of the relation between performativity and race, Butler clearly states that identity must be examined through multiple lenses that acknowledge the coexistence of racial, gender, and sexual categories, and how they articulate and reproduce institutional models of power and control (1993, 116–117). To the effect that race is performative, she replies in an interview that since it has no biological basis, then the concept of race is produced through language in the service of institutional racism. However, she also clearly asserts that we cannot afford to dismiss racial categories as purely linguistic constructions with no material consequences, as doing so "would

1. Butler explains the performative and citational power of "girling": "This is a 'girl.' However, who is compelled to 'cite' the norm in order to qualify and remain a viable subject" (1993, 232). The second example, regarding the bathroom doorways marked "Girls" and "Boys," is a famous example from Lacan (1957).

misrecognize the power that the category wields, but also the possibilities of resignification that is has and does carry" (Blumenfeld 2005, 11). Butler furthermore states that although she is always skeptical of rigid uses of racial identities, she must insist that "racial identifications and identities have to be mobilized against the racism by which they were spawned" (11–12). Clearly, Butler identifies a situation in which the most effective rhetorical approach would be to organize around an identity politics–based articulation of race as a strategy to counter the institutions that created race in the first place. This position illustrates that the debate surrounding articulations of identity—here let us think of Asian American identity—is not a matter of identity politics vs. post-structuralist approaches. Rather, the question must be reframed so that we begin to ask: What rhetorical approaches will best serve to meet the political goals of Asian American coalitions?

IDENTITY POLITICS AND HYPHEN

The term "Asian American" was first and foremost a political identity constructed during the civil rights movement and student struggles during the 1960s–1970s (Chin, Feng, and Lee, 2000, 274). Historically, Asian American cultural production has sought to establish a collective, pan-ethnic voice and presence in mainstream American culture, challenging both the exclusion of Asian Americans from mass media and stereotypical representation. One prevailing stereotype challenged was that of the "model minority"—a concept that in itself implies a hierarchal dynamic in which the "minority" is seen as exemplifying model behavior as regulated by the "majority." In this model, mainstream media concede portrayals of Asians as educationally and economically successful, usually illustrated through portrayals of Asians as producers and consumers of technology and electronics; yet at the same time the intimate portrayal of family life and individual particularity remains lacking in mass media.[2] Considering this, it is no wonder that contemporary approaches to production and analyses of Asian American culture continue to evoke what Chin, Feng, and Lee call "the rhetoric of liberation, visibility, presence, voice, and consciousness-raising"—reflecting the prevalent belief in Asian American communities that cultural representation is an effective means of countering nationalist portrayals of

2. For content analysis research on the portrayals of Asians in American-market magazines, see Taylor, Landreth, and Bang 2005.

Asian Americans as threatening and foreign (272).[3] Rhetorically, the strategy of representation seeks to give marginalized subjects visibility and legitimacy as political agents—an empowering strategy considering the historical elision of Asians in U.S. mass media.

A corollary to this is the focus on representation in the feminist movement, which Butler acknowledges as a necessary and empowering political act. However, she also warns: "It is not enough to inquire into how women might become more fully represented in language and politics. Feminist critique ought also to understand how the category of 'women,' the subject of feminism, is produced and restrained by the very structures of power through which emancipation is sought" (1999, 4). Butler urges women to focus their political goals beyond seeking recognition within a patriarchal structure, for this will only reproduce their conditions of subordination. Likewise, racialized minority groups must not focus on greater representation if liberation from racist structures is their end goal; rather, they must also understand how their racialized identities are produced so that they may find the agency to disrupt the very conditions that constrain life. Returning to an examination of *Hyphen,* I would like to keep in mind how Butler's warning may inform a critical examination of representation in Asian American–produced media.

Since its launch in 2003, *Hyphen: Asian America Unabridged* has evoked the rhetoric of liberation through positive representation; the editorial from issue 6 (Summer 2005) encourages readers to "take action." What is striking in Editor in Chief Melissa Hung's editorial is her articulation of the magazine's intention: "We seek to change the way that America looks at its Asians." It seems that *Hyphen* is producing the magazine for "America" for the purpose of changing the way that (non-Asian?) *America sees its Asians.* The last four words denote a dynamic that positions "America" as a subject with agency ("sees") and "Asians" as its object ("its Asians"), reflecting the subject/object hierarchal power structure positioning "Asians" as subjugated to a central, powerful "America," a prevailing nationalist ideology that is both the effect and cause of cultural and institutional racism. Yet the editors and readers of *Hyphen* not only accept this position, they also recognize themselves in this dynamic as a necessary condition of being Asian American, and much of the magazine's content focuses on justifying and defending this rigid racial identity.

3. Also, in her notes, Parikh (2002) cites a survey of scholarship that addresses the topic of the "foreign" and "unassimilable" Asian, including works by Lisa Lowe, David Leiwei Li, and David Palumbo-Liu.

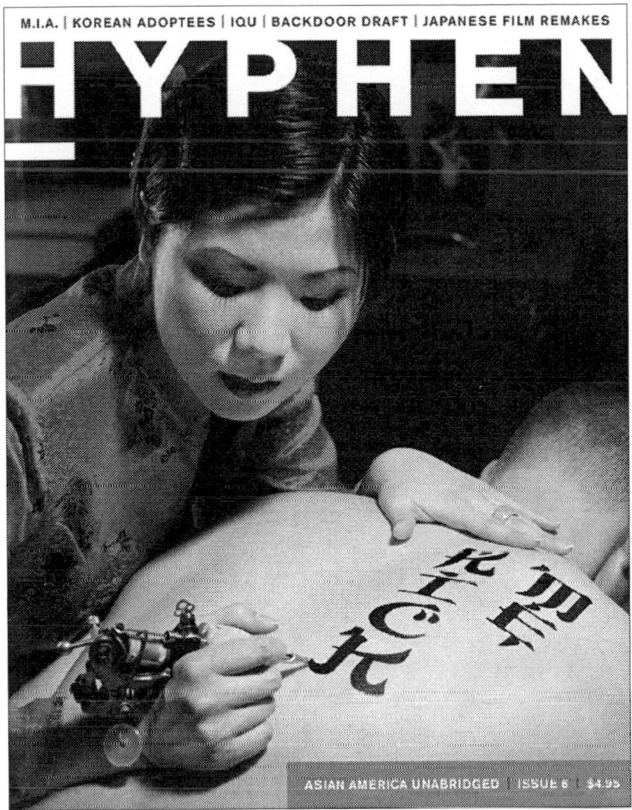

Hyphen, no. 6 (Summer 2005). Reprinted by permission.

Take, for example, an article on a Seattle-based stage production, "Sex in Seattle," which dramatizes relationships from "an Asian American perspective." One of the show's creators, Serin Ngai, is quoted as saying, "We wanted to infuse the idea that Asian Americans have love lives and normal lives just like everyone else, which is rarely displayed in mainstream media" (*Hyphen* 2006, 17). On one level, the production company seeks to represent Asian Americans in a way they find missing in mainstream media—as the subjects and objects of romantic and sexual desire—an important goal in legitimating and describing the intersections of race, sexuality, and desire when such language is lacking in theater as well as in mass media. Yet Butler exhorts us to go beyond an identity politics rhetoric; if we follow her interrogation of the relationships between representation and power, then we see that the desire to be seen (by the State, by an all-powerful Other, by "America") as having "normal lives just like everyone else" reproduces the same power structure that subjugates Asians in the first place, one that mandates what can and cannot be described as a "normal" life. In this sense, the identity politics rhetoric does not lead to the liberatory goals of Asian Americans, but instead replicates the very same power structures from which they seek freedom. Furthermore, such rhetoric is exclusionary (who will be described as normal?) rather than truly coalitional.

NEW MEDIA SPACES: WHEN IDENTITY POLITICS WORKS

The question then arises: What identity does an Asian American "voice" circulate throughout mass media? Toward what political goal does such a rhetoric work, that a unitary voice is needed to represent a varied coalition of ethnicities? This representational voice is extended into the online version of *Hyphen*, as editor in chief Melissa Hung blogs, "[*Hyphen* is] trying to sell the idea . . . that this world needs a progressive, independent Asian American magazine. That we need a voice to represent us" (2006). The identity politics approach of representing positive stories and regulating negative representations of Asian Americans is as prevalent on the Web site as it is in the print version. However, the *Hyphen* blog space and discussion board also allow an active public, through actual voices, to organize and create itself around participative dialogue. In this way, an identity politics rhetoric is successful in inviting collective discussion of the issues and challenges of race relations throughout the country under the umbrella term "Asian American"—a worthy political goal in itself in that it generates and organizes civic discussion in specific American polities in a way that is easily accessible from home or office on a daily basis.[4]

New media also open up a space that allows for new articulations of identity. One thread that demonstrates this is titled "Hawaii's Unique State" (fourteen posts from July 13, 2006, to July 24, 2006). The original poster, "Harry," a journalist from the San Francisco Bay Area, blogs about his experience attending the 2006 Asian American Journalist convention in Honolulu, and his impression of "how well the various racial

4. February 2007 was an active month for the *Hyphen* blog: archived stories include a detailed report of a forum on ethnic media and their role in reporting race relations, organized by the Chinese American Citizens' Alliance in San Francisco; a documentary on U.S. Army first lieutenant Ehren Watada, the first commissioned officer to resist deployment to Iraq; and interviews of Japanese Americans who refused the draft during WWII on the basis that their constitutional rights were taken away during their "relocation" in Japanese internment camps.

and ethnic groups who have landed on the islands have intermingled, intermarried and intermixed" (Hawaii's Unique State 2006). Such an impression sparked a dialogue among readers living in the continental United States and those with ties to Hawai'i as either former or current residents. What I find interesting are articulations from readers who counter the unitary Asian American identity ("intermixed") reflective in the editorial voice of *Hyphen*. Furthermore, the correct definition and usage of the identity *kama'āina*—a Hawaiian word that means "native born" (Kahananui and Anthony 1987, 407)—is debated, as well as the usage of the term *Hawaiian*, which is frequently misused to refer to anyone from the state of Hawai'i, much as one would refer to native Californians or Texans. The following are examples of identity claims made by participants:

> *Response to Harry from "local girl" regarding his use of "kama'āina":* Coming from someone who was born and raised in Hawaii and of Japanese [descent] . . . kama'āina does not mean "not a native, but someone who's lived in Hawaii a long time."
>
> *Response to local girl from "mainland asian":* So, local girl, what is your opinion? I'm not sure what you're getting at, except that there is a wrong definition of a word.
>
> *Response from "K. Kamasugi":* I was born and lived 30 years in Honolulu. I'm also a fourth-generation Japanese American. "Kama'aina" is used to describe both people who were born in Hawaii, but also residents, no matter how long they've lived in the state. And you can still be kama'aina even if you don't live in Hawai'i anymore.
>
> *From "Haoleboy":* I'm a kamaaina and a caucasian with native hawaiian blood.
>
> *"M. Louie," who describes herself as "a quasi- kama'āina who's comfy in both Hawaii & the 'mainland,'" clarifies:* "Hawaiian" should only be used to describe Native Hawaiian (the AP Stylebook finally just made that an official rule a few months ago).
>
> *Finally, "L. Liet" writes:* I was raised a Jersey Asian. (*Hyphen* 2006)

This is a dialogue between people who state that they were born in Hawai'i and are of specific ethnicities (and therefore are *not* "Hawaiian") and people from other states, often referred to as "the mainland." "Local girl" introduces to the thread two identity categories that are not familiar to most people outside of Hawai'i: *local* and *kama'āina*. Her critique of Harry's misuse of *kama'āina* causes "mainland asian" to reply, somewhat aggressively and dismissively, that her point is lost on him, except to say that "there is a wrong definition of a word." "K. Kamasugi" names a specific identity of "fourth-generation Japanese American," then clarifies the criteria for which one can properly be described as *kama'āina.* "Haoleboy" immediately responds by claiming the identities of *kama'āina* and Caucasian (reflected in his name, *haole* being the Hawaiian word for "Caucasian") (Kahananui and Anthony 1987, 404). Through the performative force of their claims, each participant brings into being the identities they name in this new media discussion space, an important rhetorical move given that such identities are little known outside of Hawai'i. In this way, identity politics is used as an empowering rhetoric to articulate the nuances of race and race relations as lived in the geopolitical and neocolonial context of Hawai'i. The bloggers from Hawai'i actively resist being subsumed under a unitary and homogenizing Asian American identity, successfully employing identity politics as a political rhetoric to voice *variation.* Perhaps following suit, one blogger from "the mainland" also subverts the essentialist Asian American identity by claiming to be a "Jersey Asian," pricking the imagination with the fascinating possibilities of what this may mean.

GIANT ROBOT: PARODY, POP CULTURE, AND POLITICAL AGENCY

"Once upon a time there were magazines that tried in vain to define what it means to be Asian American, rather than simply experience what is really out there." So begins coeditors Eric Nakamura's and Martin Wong's editorial for *Giant Robot,* issue 41 (2006). Whether or not this is a direct reference to Hyphen is unclear; it is apparent, however, that Nakamura and Wong set their own editorial mission apart. First of all, the tagline of *Giant Robot* reads "Asian Pop Culture and Beyond"—opening up coalitional possibilities that go beyond racial and nationalist identities and extend into the transnational. Specifically, Nakamura and Wong's editorial vision is a survey of Asian-produced or Asian-inspired popular culture—a landscape of ever-shifting and morphing acts of signification. Perhaps this has been the persuasive appeal of *Giant Robot* since Wong and Nakamura first began publishing it as a punk zine in 1994: the endless variety of "what is really out there" as opposed to constraining definitions of what is Asian American. In this way, readers of *Giant Robot* align with each other in their quixotic practice of pop culture and form a readership that engenders agency through variation.

Giant Robot, no. 42 (July/August 2006): the "Fearless" issue. Reprinted by permission.

Earlier, I described Butler's theory of performativity as the construction of identity through repetitive, signifying acts sanctioned by the prevailing power structures of culture or the law. Identities are thus normalized through repetition according to the discourses that govern what constitutes legitimate and intelligible humanity—the "reality" that is invoked when people desire to be "just like everyone else." However, subjects are not "fixed" in these discourses, but may find agency in signifying practices such as parody. Butler writes that through parody, what is "authentic" and "natural" is juxtaposed with its failed imitation. The resulting effect is the destabilization of the "original" or the "real," exposing the illusion of naturalized identities as performative as well. Parody becomes subversive because it forces us to question what is normative and proposes variations of the possible. The implications for thinking about gender, Butler explains, expose the idea of fixed or natural gender identities as illusory. She writes: "As the effects of a subtle and politically enforced performativity, gender is an 'act,' as it were, that is open to splittings, self-parody, self-criticism, and those hyperbolic exhibitions of 'the natural' that, in their very exaggeration, reveal its fundamentally phantasmatic status" (1999, 187). All gender identities are thus performative and, I suggest in this section of my argument, all racial or cultural identities are performative as well.

Parody is a common feature of *Giant Robot* issues, often as a technique used by the artists that they feature. In issue 42, for example, Hong Kong actor Daniel Wu pens a how-to article for those interested in forming a "boy band," based on his experience with his own band, Alive. He writes: "Although we are all in our 30s, being Asian and still passing for 18 was a definite plus for us" (2006, 33). In a photograph accompanying the article, members of Alive (Hong Kong actors Conroy Chan, Andrew Lin, Terence Yin, and Daniel Wu) are dressed in costumes that clearly reference the Village People, the 1970s disco ensemble famous for their hit songs of gay flirtation ("Y.M.C.A," "Macho Man") as well as their overtly gay camp personas (leatherman, construction worker, police officer). Alive is similarly costumed in hot pants, fringed boots, chaps, and—my personal fave—Daniel Wu's sequined underwear emblazoned with a dollar sign on the crotch. Wu's acknowledgment that they may still pass for adolescent boys despite being well into their thirties lacks the indignant preoccupation with "positive" representations of masculinity that is prevalent in Asian American culture. And clearly, they relish the opportunity to parody what is probably one of the most iconographic bands in western gay culture, embracing nonheteronormative gender performance as part of their boy band shtick. Wu ends his article by offering this advice to readers of *Giant Robot* (and boy band wannabes): "I can't guarantee boy band success, but if you're prepared to follow these steps, work yourself to the bone, and maintain metrosexual cool, you'll be fending off teenage groupies before you know it" (34). *Metrosexual* in the popular culture lexicon refers to "straight urban men willing, even eager, to embrace their feminine sides" (St. John 2003), and Daniel Wu's willingness to embrace his fringed chaps-wearing self exposes the "phantasmatic" status of a "true" Asian masculinity through his parodic performance.

For several issues of *Giant Robot*, Kiyoshi Nakazawa penned a column called "Fight Back!" in which he dispensed self-defense tips (of a dubious martial arts tradition) to readers. A lighthearted romp, the column both pokes fun at and embraces the cultural stereotypes that Asians are inherently facile in the martial arts *and* in personal technology usage. Issue 42 features techniques for using your cell phone as a weapon, with photos to demonstrate such techniques as "The Eye Jab," "The Cell Phone Tracheotomy," and "Call 911." Nakazawa instructs readers to "[p]unch your cell phone into the attacker's trachea, right around the Adam's apple. Find the trachea with the sharpest edge of your phone and keep pushing. . . . Tell the attacker it's a tazer while you make electric sounds with your mouth" (2006, 25). The silliness of the column

Members of the Hong Kong–based "boy band" Alive (from left to right): Conroy Chan, Andrew Lin, Terence Yin, and Daniel Wu. Although this photo is not the same that accompanied Wu's article "Born to Be Alive" in issue 42 of *Giant Robot*, it likewise showcases the spandex- and sequin-heavy wardrobe that seems, as the *Giant Robot* caption notes, "styled by Tom of Finland." This photograph is a still from the film *The Heavenly Kings* (2006), the mockumentary on Alive and the Cantopop music industry directed by Daniel Wu. Reprinted by permission from Man 5 Production Ltd.

works to expose the idea that both stereotypes are rooted in performance. Racial stereotypes, like gender-based stereotypes, are "acts" that Nakazawa parodies in his so-called advice column, in which he hyperbolically embraces popular representations of Asians, rather than decrying them as "negative" representations. Other Asian American media, such as *Hyphen*, often decry what they see as "false" representations that are not reflective of an implicit "true" Asian American voice. Such protest only serves to ratify and reproduce the logical framework in which these racialized stereotypes find agency and circulate. Nakazawa's parody breaks from this repetition by articulating a variant perspective: the stereotype and his imitative parody are *both* absurd performances.

The above are examples of *Giant Robot*-style parody, but are they subversive? Butler acknowledges that there are distinctions in parody: "Parody by itself is not subversive, and there must be a way to understand what makes certain kinds of parodic repetitions effectively disruptive, truly troubling, and which repetitions become domesticated and re-circulated as instruments of cultural hegemony" (1999, 177). The examples cited may not fall under the category of "truly troubling," but they do disrupt the powerful binaries upon which identity politics is based: object/subject, Asian/American, negative/positive representation, and so on. These parodies are disruptive because they imitate popular nationalist stereotypes of Asians perpetuated in mass media, the main forum of the U.S. national public sphere. The parody intervenes in the popular stereotypes of the emasculated Asian male and of the ruthless, often devious martial arts villain who often acts as the foil for the courageous, "true" American hero.[5] Through these types of parodying imitations, the "natural" identity of Asian Americans is revealed as fundamentally false, an identity constructed by a racializing and heteronormative ideology that serves to naturalize this hierarchy. The "reality" of this cultural identity is destabilized through parody in *Giant Robot.*

In the end, does this type of parody and pop culture play create any real political force to effect change? Here is where we must rethink our objectives for deploying a coalitional rhetoric, and I reiterate my argument that the pressing debate is not whether identity politics is more effective than a post-structuralist approach or vice versa. Rather, perhaps we have to make distinctions in our political goals, and which rhetorical means would best serve the ends. As I have shown with my examples from the print and new media versions of *Hyphen*, there are specific rhetorical situations that call for the articulation of identity from an identity politics approach; the performative force of this speech act brings into being what it names ("local girl" or "kama' ina") to counter its elision in dominant discourses. However, we must not stop with "representation" as our ultimate goal, as forming coalitions that focus on regulating what is "real" about Asian Americans operates under assumptions that place a specific, exclusive idea of "American-ness" as the central model against which Asian Americans must constantly prove

5. Tasha Oren cites Susan Jeffords's *Hard Bodies: Hollywood Masculinity and the Reagan Era* in her explanation of the emasculation trope: "Masculinity—even in its purely physical expression of power, speed, and size—functions as a complex signifier that, as Susan Jeffords has argued, speaks to contemporary definitions of nation and citizenship. As Jeffords argues, cultural articulations of national identity and politics are often bound up in representations of masculinity as their fixation over lost and regained control consistently stage interrogations of race, masculinity, and difference" (2005, 343).

themselves, their worthiness, and their authenticity. A coalition formed around this focus must first presume that its members agree upon a stable and unified identity which they will then uphold with positive representations, and against which they will decry negative representations. This becomes problematic when we question what becomes intelligible in this approach to representation; by its normative function, this type of Asian American coalition is exclusionary. Furthermore, operating from this approach also presumes that we accept our subjugation to the powerful institutions that pit us in this binary dynamic, and in doing so, we forego any true hope of agency and liberation.

What if we form coalitions that focus not on articulating a shared identity as the *end goal*, but on making meaning through shared practices such as producing films, making music, publishing comics, curating art shows and so forth? On the rhetorical effect of such practices, I draw on Barry Brummett's definition of popular culture: "If culture means those objects and events that nurture, shape, and sustain people, then popular culture must be those artifacts that are most actively involved in winning the favor of the public and thus in shaping the public in particular ways. . . . The work of popular culture is therefore inherently rhetorical, and it is an arena in which rhetoric as the management of meaning must be most actively engaged" (1991, xxi).

Under the above premises, engaging in pop culture clearly has a political goal, and that is to subvert the prevailing ideology that limits what is intelligible about an Asian identity, in effect redirecting rhetorical practices toward creating coalitions of creative and nonracist people.

CONCLUSION: READING AND WRITING SUBVERSIVELY, ACTING COLLECTIVELY

The implications of this analysis for the field of rhetoric and composition are perhaps strongest for those who read popular culture as a vibrant civic space where people engage in political work in creative and subversive ways. Furthermore, key scholars in the field such as Min-Zhan Lu (2006) and Bruce Horner and John Trimbur (2002) argue that it is imperative to address how globalization and diasporic publics, such as the many ethnicities subsumed under the term "Asian American," impact our scholarship and teaching. These scholars are at the forefront of a movement in the field to decenter U.S. rhetoric and composition as a globalizing force and instead relocate the teaching and study of writing and rhetoric in English within the wider circulation of people and languages. Other composition theories, such as place-based writing, likewise situate public argumentation within the dialectic of local and global discourses. These movements are among those in the field that are often categorized under the broad rubrics of "civic engagement" and "public writing." Given this, we need strategies for analyzing the rhetorical practices of social movements, in which people form coalitions with one another on the basis of cultural identities, and for the purpose of civic engagement and public protest.

Judith Butler's theories of performativity and subversive parody offer a method for analyzing the ideological framework that underlies the rhetorical practices of any social and political movement. Rhetorical practices based on identity politics work to bring cultural identities into being through language and other signifying language. Such an approach empowers subjects by representing them in popular culture when they have been previously subordinated and/or excluded. By reading the online *Hyphen* blogs for implied assumptions deployed by the "mainland" Asians, I observed that readers resisted a unifying "Asian American" identity and sought instead to articulate identities more central to life in Hawai'i, such as *kama'āina* and the distinction between native Hawaiian and *local* Asian identities—a distinction that is commonly ignored in the continental United States. On the other hand, when collective subjects employ rhetorical practices that forego a closure of identity, they destabilize naturalized identities based on race, gender, and sexuality, thereby questioning power structures that rely on these assumptions. Parody is an especially effective method for exposing the fragilities of normative identities, and for opening up spaces for alternative ways of being and belonging.

In my analyses of the rhetorical approaches of *Hyphen* and *Giant Robot,* I employed a post-structuralist reading of the texts, particularly Butler's theory of performativity, to show how identities are constituted as well as destabilized through language and other symbolic use. Even a minimal understanding of performativity is useful when analyzing how articulations of identity are mobilized as rhetorical practice in the public sphere. I end this analysis on Asian-produced media in high hopes, as it has helped me clarify for myself why I continue to work with cross-cultural organizations that focus on the arts. Asian American coalitions may gain true agency through shared practices of popular culture in ways that create and contest the possibilities of what is intelligibly Asian American.

REFERENCES

Blumenfeld, Warren J., and Margaret Sonser Breen. 2005. "There Is a Person Here": An Interview with Judith Butler. In *Butler Matters,* edited by Warren Blumenfeld and Margaret Sonser Breen. Aldershot, Hampshire, England: Ashgate.

Brummett, Barry. 1991. *Rhetorical Dimensions of Popular Culture.* Tuscaloosa: University of Alabama Press.

Butler, Judith. 1993. *Bodies That Matter.* New York: Routledge.

———. 1999. *Gender Trouble: Feminism and the Subversion of Identity.* 10th ed. New York: Routledge.

Chin, Soo-Young, Peter X. Feng, and Josephine Lee. 2000. Asian American Cultural Production. *Journal of Asian American Studies* (October): 269–282.

Fish, Stanley. 1998. Rhetoric. In *Rhetoric in an Antifoundational World: Language, Culture, and Pedagogy,* edited by Michael Bernard-Donals and Richard R. Glejzer. New Haven, CT: Yale University Press.

Habermas, Jürgen. 1989. *The Structural Transformation of the Public Sphere: An Inquiry into a Category of Bourgeois Society.* Cambridge, MA: MIT Press.

Hall, Stuart. 2003. Cultural Identity and Diaspora. In *Identity: Community, Culture, Difference,* ed. Jonathan Rutherford. London: Lawrenc and Wishart Ltd; 2 Rev Ed. ,

Horner, Bruce, and John Trimbur. 2002. English Only and U.S. College Composition. *College Composition and Communication* 53. 4:594–630

Hung, Melissa. 2005. *Hyphen's* Makeover. *Hyphen: Asian America Unabridged* (Summer) 2005, Issue 6. 4.

———. 2006. The Not-So-Glamorous Life of Publishing. *Hyphen: Asian America Unabridged,* June 1. http://www.hyphenmagazine.com/blog/archives/2006/06/ the_notsoglamor.html (accessed June 21, 2006).

Hawai'i's Unique State. July 13, 2006. *Hyphen: Asian America Unabridged.* http://www.hyphenmagazine.com/blog/2006/07/hawaiis-unique-state.html#comments (accessed July 13, 2006)

Kahananui, Dorothy, and Alberta Anthony. 1987. *E Kama'ilio Hawai'i Kakou: Let's Speak Hawaiian.* Honolulu, University of Hawai'i Press.

Kiu, Gena. 2005. Sex in Seattle. *Hyphen: Asian America Unabridged,* no. 6. 17

Lacan, Jacques. 1957. The Agency of the Letter in the Unconscious. In *The Norton Anthology of Theory and Criticism,* edited by Vincent Leitch. New York: Norton.

Lu, Min-Zhan. 2006. Living-English Work. *College English* 68 (6) 605–618.

Nakamura, Eric, and Martin Wong. 2006. Launch. *Giant Robot,* Issue 41, 10.

Nakazawa, Kiyoshi. 2006. Fight Back! *Giant Robot,* Issue 42, 25.

Oren, Tasha. 2005. Secret Asian Man. In *East Main Street: Asian American Popular Culture,* edited by S. Dave, L. Nishime, and Tasha Oren. New York: New York University Press.

Parikh, Crystal. 2002. Blue Hawaii: Asian Hawaiian Cultural Production and Racial Melancholia. *JAAS* (October): 199–216.

St. John, Warren. 2003. Metrosexuals Come Out. *New York Times,* June 22.

Taylor, Charles, Stacy Landreth, and Hae-Kyong Bang. 2005. Asian Americans in Magazine Advertising: Portrayals of the "Model Minority." *Journal of Macromarketing* 25 (2): 163–174.

Warner, Michael. 2005. *Publics and Counterpublics.* New York: Zone.

Wu, Daniel. 2006. Born to Be Alive. *Giant Robot,* Issue 42, 32–35.

10

ON THE ROAD WITH P. T. BARNUM'S TRAVELING CHINESE MUSEUM

Rhetorics of Public Reception and Self-Resistance in the Emergence of Literature by Chinese American Women

Mary Louise Buley-Meissner

In 1834, the first Chinese woman arrived in the United States, taking her place almost immediately as the main attraction of a foreign costumes display in the American Museum of New York City. At shows staged for the next three years, crowds gathered simply to watch her sit at a table set for a Chinese tea service, wearing her traditional embroidered gown and hand-stitched slippers. Afong Moy spoke no English, for the Chinese Beauty's foreign tongue added immeasurably to her appeal as "the real thing," a woman as curiously enticing as the porcelain, jade, and tapestries that ornamented her showroom.[1] In 1850, P. T. Barnum's traveling Chinese Museum offered Americans the spectacle of seventeen-year-old Miss Pwan-ye-koo, who soon drew the biggest crowds on Broadway.[2] The *New York Sunday Times* praised her as a true "Chinese lady . . . prepared to exhibit her charming self, her curious retinue, and her fairy feet . . . to an admiring and novelty-loving public"(Ten Thousand Things 1850, 206), while the *New York Express* proclaimed that "P. T. Barnum's enterprise stops short of nothing that is strange or wondrous"(205).

Indeed, travelers, missionaries, and diplomats had brought back such splendid tales of China's treasures that "an oriental craze" swept the East Coast from the mid-eighteenth to the mid-nineteenth century. Scrolls, rugs, furniture, lacquerware, ivory chopsticks—whatever could be imported, wealthy Americans were pleased to buy.[3] In this experience

---

1. Firsthand accounts of Afong Moy's performances are rare; general descriptions can be found in Haddad 1998; Ling 1990; and Moy 1993.
2. Haddad (1998) points out that P. T. Barnum tried to discredit Afong Moy's earlier appearance in the United States by accusing her of being no more than a peasant, while promoting Miss Pwan-ye-koo as "the first Chinese lady."
3. Informative books on the history and forms of chinoiserie include *Cathay* 1966;

of the exotic, acquisition of "chinoiserie" (things Chinese) became a mark of upper-class aspirations, leisure culture, and familiarity with a foreign world that very few Americans would ever see for themselves. What could be more gratifying? Only, perhaps, to gaze upon the lovely painted face of an Afong Moy at her tea table or to marvel at a genuine "Chinese lady" whose only desire is your pleasure.

My interest in P. T. Barnum's traveling Chinese Museum comes from teaching at a Midwest public university, where undergraduate students often take one of my Asian American literature courses to fulfill the "cultural diversity" requirement for graduation.[4] Students across majors fill these courses, and most of them have not read any Asian American literature before. Yet nearly all of them arrive with a keen curiosity about (in their words) "Asian ways of life" and "people who are very different than those we get to read about in other English courses." In teaching Chinese American women writers, I have found that students are likely to be looking for (again in their words) "glimpses of a culture we otherwise wouldn't get the chance to see" and "an experience of venturing into the unknown." What is the source of such expectations? Many possible reasons could be given, among them the power of popular culture in shaping their reading experience. For as Diana Fuss observes: "There is no 'natural' way to read a text: ways of reading are historically specific and culturally variable, and reading positions are always constructed, assigned, or mapped" (1990, 35).

Consider, for example, how the general public has learned to read Amy Tan's *The Joy Luck Club* (1989) through reviews of her novel in popular magazines and newspapers (quoted on the book cover or its front pages): "[Tan's] Oriental orientation is an irresistible magnet" (*Publishers Weekly*); "[*The Joy Luck Club* is] snappy as a fortune cookie" (*New York Magazine*); "[This book] is like a Chinese puzzle box—intricate, mysterious" (*Cosmopolitan*); "[Tan offers an] intimate glimpse into a way of life and a culture seldom explored by western literature" (*San Diego Union*); and "[Hers is] an exotic new voice" (*Washington Post*). Even students new to Asian American literature are likely to recognize *The Joy*

Edwards 2000; and Jacobson 1993.

4. Undergraduates across majors must take a three-credit "cultural diversity" course to meet the General Education Requirements for graduation; the course can be selected from an array of humanities and social science courses dealing with ethnic and/or racial topics.

Luck Club as a *New York Times* best seller, a novel compared in the popular press to the finest Chinese porcelain, painting, or tapestry—publicity which I imagine P. T. Barnum would appreciate. Could Tan be unique in prompting this kind of response?

On the contrary, my research on the public reception of Chinese American women writers indicates that reviewers frequently participate in what Edward Said (1978) terms "Orientalism," particularly when they emphasize the "exoticism" of writers' perceived cultural origins. The twist on Said, of course, is that "the Other" exists within multicultural American society. In this situation, mainstream reviewers exercise the power through mass-circulation magazines and newspapers to influence not only the marketability of single books, but also public perceptions of how an emerging body of work by "minority" writers contributes (or is marginal) to "majority" literary interests. This is a perspective that I bring to my teaching with the aim of encouraging students to become more aware of how the significance of literary texts and the historical contexts of their reception always are interlinked. As Amy Ling points out: "What is written, what is published, what is read, what makes the best-seller lists, what is forgotten, what is rediscovered, has much to do with the political, social, and emotional climate of the day" (1990, 19). In the rhetoric of public reception, "authenticity" may be valued above artistry—and certainly is assumed to make "genuine" artistry possible.

Here I would like to look at the roots of this rhetoric in turn-of-the-century popular American culture; its manifestation in popular reviews of pathbreaking authors such as Sui Sin Far in the 1900s, Jade Snow Wong in the 1950s, and Maxine Hong Kingston in the 1970s; and its continuing influence in the public reception of contemporary Chinese American women writers. In particular, I am interested in pursuing the possibility that "Orientalism"—in the form of chinoiserie connoisseurship—has maintained its hold on American audiences ever since the *New York Express* in 1850 urged its readers not to miss the "strange and wondrous" performance of an authentic "Chinese lady." Why, for example, do reviewers today so often describe books authored by Chinese American women as works of Oriental art? What do these reviewers imagine they possess–and assess for the public–when they refer to a novel as "a delicate Chinese brush painting" or to a short story collection as an "exquisite Oriental water color"? From the 1990s to the present, talented Chinese Americans such as Amy Tan, Fae Myenne Ng, Aimee Liu, Sara Chin, Lan Samantha Chang, Christine Chiu, Andrea Louie, and Mei Ng have been drawing an increasingly wide readership. At the same time, they and their books often are described by reviewers in identical terms, such as "delicate," "lyrical," "mysterious," and "enchanting." Are these the ideal qualities of authors who provide the exotic experience that reviewers continue to seek? By looking back to the early twentieth century, I believe we can begin to trace out possible answers.

In this essay, I also investigate how Chinese American women writers have developed rhetorics of self-resistance to counter public displacement and diminishment of their achievements. By rhetorics, here I mean strategies of authorship that intentionally enact (whether implicitly or explicitly) the roles and responsibilities that they are committed to fulfilling in their work, including distinctly individualized, persuasive appeals (thematic and stylistic) for reader engagement with that commitment. Although this insistence on self-determination generally has been overlooked in the popular press, women writers consistently have exercised their right to speak in their own voices—in deliberately chosen and carefully crafted literary forms—about the social and cultural realities of their lives and times. As Kenneth Burke points out, "the range of rhetoric" (1969, 20) extends far beyond argumentation to complex processes of identity formation and reformation that take place not only individually, but also socially and culturally. Moreover, acts of reading and writing become meaningful within a "wider context of motives" (31) that is rhetorically mediated through the symbolic use of language, a Burkean understanding of discourse that has proven useful across academic disciplines. (See, for example, Crusius 1999; Stob 2005; and Wess 1996.) Chinese American women writers, in my view, employ rhetorics of the self in active resistance to others' attempts to deny their individuality, their artistry, and their shared commitment to truthful storytelling.

In the rhetoric of public reception, their work has been decontextualized, regarded as politically and historically innocent. This has enabled reviewers to inscribe their own intentions on writers' texts—to assume, for example, that nothing would please writers more than to gain approval and acceptance from the dominant culture, to be assimilated into already familiar ways of knowing and being. Rarely do reviews admit the possibility that writers such as Jade Snow Wong and Maxine Hong Kingston could be challenging readers through cultural critique, particularly through investigations of identity and difference that resist rather than reaffirm Orientalist stereotypes. However, I am convinced that Chinese American women writers have achieved their own authority in articulating complex bicultural realities. As Lisa Lowe (1991) points out, "The making of Chinese-American culture—how ethnicity is imagined, practiced, continued—is worked out as much between ourselves and our communities as it is transmuted from one generation to another" (27). Across generations, women writers are not politically or historically innocent, but acutely aware of social conditions influencing response to their interpretations of identity, difference, and community. In the 1900s, for example, journalist and short story writer Sui Sin Far clearly understood what the popular press expected of her: "They tell me that if I wish to succeed in literature in America I should dress in Chinese costume, carry a fan in my hand, wear a pair of scarlet beaded slippers . . . and come of high birth" (1995, 230). She knew that a "Chinese lady"—like Pwan-ye-koo of the Barnum exhibition—was what the public expected her to be, and still she chose to identify herself as "Eurasian" (the daughter of a Chinese mother and English father) and to ally herself with the working poor of Chinatown, whose stories no one else would tell. Looking back at that time, I realize how eagerness for the exotic has persisted in popular culture, a fascination heightened at the turn of the twentieth century by popular fiction and the press.

On the one hand, Chinese people were widely despised, as epitomized by the Chinese Exclusion Acts of 1882 and 1892.[5] On the other hand, in the early 1900s, "the oriental craze"—the American fascination with cultural curios—extended to a popular craving for Chinatown pulp fiction and revelations of what Chinese people were "really like." Thus, it would not be unusual for a popular magazine such as Collier's to publish all of the following in one issue: an editorial calling for the expulsion of Chinese from the West Coast; an excerpt from the latest Chinatown thriller, complete with opium-smoking villains; a review of Chinatown restaurants; and ads for "oriental" products such as tea, perfume, and face powder. Researching this phenomenon, Rachel Lee (1997) observes: "Clearly, magazines felt no sense of incongruity in circulating ads that promoted desire for a commodified Asiatic body yet printing [stories] and editorials that voiced loathing for Asian peoples" (254). In effect, commodification became containment: the exotic was domesticated, the foreign was made familiar, and any threat posed by "the yellow peril" was abated.

5. Immigration legislation targeting Chinese Americans is addressed in Chan 1991; Lai, Lim, and Yung 1990; Okihiro 2005; and Palumbo-Liu 1999.

One writer in the early twentieth century did venture to describe Chinese immigrants in very different terms. From 1896 to 1912, journalist Sui Sin Far interviewed Chinatown residents in Seattle, San Francisco, and other U.S. cities to understand their lives "from the inside" (see, for example, Far 1898,1903, and 1909). Moreover, in 1912 she published the first major work of fiction by an Asian American, the short story collection *Mrs. Spring Fragrance* (see Bo Wang's extensive treatment of Sui Sin Far's achievements in the next chapter). What I would like to underscore is how reviews of *Mrs. Spring Fragrance* at the time of its publication consistently emphasize her success (or failure) in explaining Chinese to Caucasians. For example, the *New York Times* ("A New Note" 1912) comments: "The thing she has tried to do is to portray for readers of the white race the lives, feelings, sentiments of the Americanized Chinese. . . . It is a task whose adequate doing would require well-nigh superhuman insight and the subtlest of methods." Because "these unusual and exquisite stories . . . open an entirely new world for many readers" (McClurg 1912), Sui Sin Far must prove herself to be a trustworthy guide. Similarly, the *Boston Daily Globe* ("Book Reaches the Heart" 1912) surmises that Sui Sin Far's stories must be translations of Chinese into English (rather than original works in English) because otherwise it would not be possible for her to present the "delicate sensibilities" of Chinese people, including those "who have come, dazed, into the ways of a western civilization."

The reductive rhetoric of public reception surely contributed to the displacement of Sui Sin Far from American literary history; in fact, not until the 1980s did scholarly consideration of her importance begin, mainly undertaken by Sol Solberg (1981, 1982), Amy Ling (1983, 1990), Annette White-Parks (1995).[6] Yet, Sui Sin Far's legacy of self-resistance endures to the present day through her efforts to develop a counter-rhetoric, a transgressive rhetoric of the self that is both personal and political as it calls into question the entire popular enterprise of essentializing Chinese identity. In her autobiographical essays, for example, she claims neither a yellow nor a white identity, but instead asks readers why such a high price must be paid for insisting on individuality: "I give my right hand to the Occidentals and my left to the Orientals, hoping that between them they will not utterly destroy the insignificant 'connecting link'" (1995, 230). Moreover, as a short story writer, she creates Chinese characters who are complicated, unpredictable, and indelibly

6. Critical commentary on Sui Sin Far's work also includes Ammons 1991; Ferens 2002; Lee 1997; Leonard 2001; and Ling and White-Parks 1995.

individual, such as a young woman who chooses deportation to China over exile in the United States ("Tian Shan's Kindred Spirit"); a prostitute who does not want to be freed from the life she has chosen for herself ("Lin John"); a factory worker who can escape slavery only by dying with her child ("The Prize China Baby"); and a mother who ends her son's life rather than lose his spirit ("The Wisdom of the New"). In clearing a path for the emergence of Chinese American women writers, Sui Sin Far truly is a pioneer.

In contrast to Sui Sin Far, who was for many years effaced in misreadings of her work, Jade Snow Wong won immediate, widespread acclaim in 1950 with the publication of her autobiography, *Fifth Chinese Daughter*. The first Chinese American author to win a large readership, she tells the story of her life from 1922 to 1945 in and out of San Francisco's Chinatown, where her parents immigrated in the early 1900s. They believe that a woman's place in life is to serve her family: to obey her father, yield to her husband, and provide for her sons. When Wong insists on following a different path in life, she is forced to leave home. She moves out at age fifteen, supports herself by working as a housekeeper, and earns a college scholarship. When she tries to tell her parents that she is an individual as well as a Chinese daughter, her father admonishes her: "You are shameless. Your skin is yellow. Your features are forever Chinese. . . . Do not try to force foreign ideas into my house" (1999, 130). Nonetheless, she graduates from college at the top of her class, starts her own pottery business, and vows to become a successful writer. At last, even her father must acknowledge her achievements. As he explains to her: "You do not realize the shameful and degraded position into which Chinese culture has pushed its women. Here in America, the Christian concept allows women their freedom and individuality. I wish my daughters to have this Christian opportunity" (246). Finally Wong is again welcome in her family, where she resumes the role of obedient daughter while leading an independent professional life.

Reviews of *Fifth Chinese Daughter* upon its initial publication were overwhelmingly positive, emphasizing the inspiring example set by the author in bridging two cultures. Translated and reprinted in nine countries, the book made her famous, but in what terms? In "The Colorful Home Life of a Chinese Girl," a *Chicago Sunday Tribune* review (Judson 1950), the book is admired for being "like a piece of Chinese brocade—gay, colorful, charming, but woven with a strength that gives it lasting quality"(5). The reviewer also is pleased to find "in easy reading form . . . a true picture of contrasting cultures"; best of all, she discovers "an understandable recipe for 'sweet sour,' my favorite Chinese dish" (5). In the rhetoric of public reception, Wong is cast as a quintessentially Asian female, graciously welcoming her Caucasian readers into her exotic world. Reviews from the *New York Times* to *Commonweal* describe her as if she is a hostess, a tour guide, a goodwill ambassador. For example, she is praised for "[a] glow of being at once Richer by Asia, and Richer by the West . . . warm[ing] those with whom [she shares] her experiences" (Evans 1950), while her book is admired because "[it] exudes the delicate femininity only the Asiatic women possess" (Geary 1950).

Completely overlooked in such reviews is the pain that she feels in leaving her family and the deep disequilibrium that she experiences in becoming an American success. Likewise, her self-determination and liberation from an oppressive, traditional Chinese culture are emphasized, but nowhere do reviewers acknowledge the harsh realities of Chinatown life in the United States when she was growing up and coming of age, including poverty, substandard housing, segregated schooling, high suicide rates, alcoholism, sweatshops, and dead-end jobs even for college graduates. Wong does not directly address these issues, but they strongly color her writing, as shown by childhood talks with her maternal grandmother, who warns that society "discard[s] the weak ones" (1999, 32). To survive, Wong is told that she "must study [her] books very hard" (36), intensifying her drive to succeed.

In this context, Wong's rhetoric of the self in *Fifth Chinese Daughter* can be read as both politically imperative and socially incisive. In effect, her autobiography is a declaration that second-generation Chinese Americans and their families—who were doing their best to be self-sufficient in very limited circumstances—should not be denied the rights accorded other citizens. That these rights were held only tenuously by Asian Americans was everywhere evident with the outbreak of World War II. *Time* magazine (1941), for example, reassured readers in "How to Tell Your Friends from the Japs" that the typical "Chinese expression" was "placid, kindly, open," in contrast to the "dogmatic, arrogant" look of the Japanese; also marking the Chinese were "an easy gait and sometimes a shuffle," while Japanese had a walk "stiffly erect, hard heeled." *Life* (1941) similarly reported in "How to Tell Japs from the Chinese" that Chinese people have a "parchment yellow complexion" and a "longer, narrower face," as compared to the

Japanese "earthy yellow" and "broader, shorter face" (81–82). In a public service comic strip featuring the American hero Captain Terry, *Life* (1943) informed readers that Chinese eyes "are set like any European's or American's—but have a marked squint" and that "the Chinese smile easily," unlike Japanese, with their more obviously slanted eyes and generally suspicious appearance.

Confronted with this kind of racism in everyday life, Wong develops a rhetoric of self-resistance by deliberately constructing alternative portraits of what makes people individuals as well as responsible citizens. Her mother working sixteen hours a day on bound feet, her father exhausting himself in service to their community, neighbors helping each other in hard times, even "outsiders" becoming friends with her family—all of these people and many more are portrayed with respect and compassion. Indeed, from her family Wong derives the strength of character to prove *Time* and *Life* wrong in their assessments of human nature. "It is good to have you home again!" (1999, 246) are the most welcome words she hears in her life, spoken by her parents, whose own examples have helped her to see—and to insist to her readers—that "the great people of any race" (173) are those who know their own self-worth and honor that of others.

In the emergence of Chinese American women's writing, Wong's lasting achievement is to craft a public voice to tell a story long excluded from American literary history. Inseparable from that voice is a rhetoric of self-resistance that draws readers into a complex, conflicted story of attempting to achieve an integrated bicultural identity in a society where doing so could be a very lonely enterprise. Acutely aware that her success is so highly acclaimed because it is so unusual, Wong tells readers in the final chapter of her autobiography that she has become "a wonder in the eyes of the western world" (1999, 244) and a strange creature to the people of Chinatown. In fact, "Chinese and Americans alike acted as if they thought she were deaf or dumb or couldn't understand their language" (245) while watching her work at her pottery wheel. As Wong attempts to bridge cultures, she clearly shows that doing so exacts a high personal cost.

Ironically, *Fifth Chinese Daughter* is now criticized for the same qualities that reviewers praised in the 1950s, particularly its apparent subscription to a "model minority" view of American success.[7] As Leslie Bow

7. Takaki (1998) indicates that San Francisco's Chinatown in 1940—five blocks by four blocks in total area—held fifteen thousand Chinese, who lived mostly in sub-

puts it, "The opposition between what is Chinese and what is American is bridged through a blend of Christian ethics and Chinese American capitalism" (1993, 165). Chin et al. (1974) have gone so far as to dismiss *Fifth Chinese Daughter* as nothing more than assimilationist "propaganda" (xx). The reality that naturalized citizenship was not granted to Chinese Americans until 1943 (and to Japanese Americans in 1952) may suggest the limitations of an assimilationist assessment of the book. Acting to "correct a historic mistake," President Roosevelt repealed the Chinese Exclusion Act in 1943. However, with the onset of the Korean War, the Chinese became the enemy, and in 1950, Congress passed the McCarran Internal Security Act, authorizing detention of anyone suspected of, or likely to engage in, subversive activities. Could what happened to Japanese Americans during World War II have happened to Chinese Americans during the Cold War? As Wong's rhetoric of self-resistance underscores, Chinatowns and internment camps are no further apart than the laws justifying their existence.[8]

Maxine Hong Kingston's *The Woman Warrior: Memoirs of a Girlhood among Ghosts*, first published in 1976, has made her the most famous and controversial author of Chinese American literature. She has received countless awards and has been named a Living Treasure of Hawaii. In the 1980s, *The Woman Warrior* was one of the most frequently assigned books on college campuses nationwide. However, the "authenticity" of Kingston's work frequently has been called into question, most infamously by Frank Chin (1991), who has accused her of producing nothing except "fake work" for readers who know nothing about "real" Chinese traditions, history, and culture (3). Indeed, concerns about authenticity are pervasive in scholarship on Asian American literature. For example, Mingshui Cai (1995) goes so far as to insist, "Cultural authenticity is the basic criterion for evaluating multicultural literature" (3). Moreover, the authority to claim an "insider" perspective, in Cai's view, depends on clearly recognizable, "culturally specific ways of living, believing and behaving" (5). In contrast, John Hutnyk (2000) asserts that "there is no need to posit a fixed and authenticated Asian 'Culture' as the benchmark for critique"

standard housing and had a tuberculosis rate three times that of the general city population.

8. Literary criticism of *Fifth Chinese Daughter* also includes Blinde 1979; Kim 1982; Lim 1992; Ling 1990; and Yin and Paulson 1982. Tributes to Wong as a potter and enamelist as well as a writer are included in Kingston et al. 2002.

(39) in postmodern analyses of ethnic, national, and global identities. In the middle of this critical spectrum, Sau-ling Cynthia Wong (1993a) cautions literary scholars to recognize the limited applicability of "culturalism," which she defines as the "tendency to exaggerate exoticism and the determining role of culture in Asian American life, allowing a facile concept of cultural difference to arrest inquiry into the complexities of the Other, and thus inadvertently perpetuating Otherness" (117). Debates on the meaning and significance of "authenticity" in Asian American literature include influential essays by Cheung (1990), Chin (1991), Lim (1993), Ling (1987), and Lowe (1991).

During the past thirty years, most sharply contested has been Kingston's authority to tell her own story. In the rhetoric of public reception, Chinese American women writers still are expected to take the stage and display their desire to please one and all in the audience. Nevertheless, much like Sui Sin Far at the turn of the century and Jade Snow Wong in the 1950s, Kingston defiantly claims a place at the center of American literary history. Through a speculative, richly imaginative rhetoric of the self, she also speaks for Chinese American women writers today, who refuse to be silenced or suppressed by others' expectations of their cultural roles. *The Woman Warrior* describes her California childhood in the 1940s and 1950s, when her immigrant parents struggled to support six children through their laundry business and their sheer will to survive. Incorporating biography, myth, legend, folklore, and fantasy, the book presents the main character, Maxine, trying to understand her bicultural heritage. Most of all, she wants to invent an identity and develop a voice that will enable her to speak out against injustice—including racism and sexism—wherever she encounters it. At times, her mother, Brave Orchid, seems to oppose her, insinuating that girls are worthless, fit to be slaves, and complaining that "stupidity . . . comes from reading too much" (1977, 194). Yet at other times, Brave Orchid inspires Maxine with stories of courageous woman warriors who have stormed across China to avenge their families' honor. For many years, their relationship is marked by misunderstanding, bitterness, pain, and confusion. Finally, however, they are able to "talk story" together, their voices bringing to life the hopes and fears of women across generations.

Kingston has said that in *The Woman Warrior* she deliberately tried not to play into popular images of China as mysterious and Chinese people as inscrutable (Kingston 1982, 55). However, most of the book's early reviews praised it in exactly such terms, highlighting its "exotic" qualities. In fact, Kingston's work in 1976 was subjected to the same Orientalist attitudes as Sui Sin Far's had been in 1912. For example, a review of *The Woman Warrior* in *Publishers Weekly* points out, "Rarely does East meet West with such charming results . . . [with] Oriental myth and Occidental reality somehow blended." Moreover, the book is praised for being "as rich and varied as Chinese brocade" and for "prose that often achieves the delicacy and precision of porcelain. An unusual and rewarding book for a specially attuned audience." Why, again, is it assumed that it requires extraordinary insight to understand Chinese American lives? Why is such a talented artist as Kingston reduced to playing the part of cultural emissary or entrepreneur?

Part of the answer is that from 1949 to 1972, China had been largely closed to westerners, a period when images of the Yellow Peril and the Red Threat coalesced in American international policy and public opinion. When *The Woman Warrior* appeared—only four years after President Nixon's historic meeting with Mao Tse-tung and Zhou Enlai—readers were eager to rediscover the China of Cathay, the timeless land of their dreams. Reporting on China in the popular press at that time included travelogues of its "changeless" beauty next to critiques of its political system. Thus, through *The Woman Warrior*, readers may have hoped to glimpse what China and the Chinese were "really like," regardless of the Cultural Revolution and other social upheavals. As reviewers readily admitted, the "inscrutably foreign, oriental" life of others certainly was an attraction (Manning 1982).

Popular reviews of *The Woman Warrior* in the 1970s and the 1980s rarely mentioned its insightful depictions of U.S. social inequities. However, in a rhetoric of self-resistance deploying a voice empowered by a compelling social conscience, Kingston turns her readers' attention again and again to the painful reality of a country divided by fear, ignorance, and poverty. As she makes vividly clear throughout *The Woman Warrior*, she abhors the racism of modern America as much as she opposes the sexism of feudal China. For example, when Maxine's boss at an art supply store tells her to order "nigger yellow" paint, she refuses and loses her job. In the ghetto, she has seen corpses "rolled and dumped, sad little dirty bodies covered with a police khaki blanket" (1977, 51). When an Asian neighbor is stabbed and the police find Japanese words pinned to his clothes, her father is quick to tell them, "No read Japanese. . . . Me Chinese" (52). In Kingston's rhetoric of self-resistance, however, it is impossible to escape racism through such distinctions. When Maxine imagines herself as the female avenger Fa Mu Lan (a legendary warrior), "the words at her back" (carved into her skin) forever remind her to oppose tyranny. "'Chink' words and 'gook' words too" (53) drive her to defend her sisters and brothers, who could be anyone deprived of their dignity.

Continuing debates over Kingston's writing have centered on whether or not she authentically, accurately documents Chinese culture. In the rhetoric of public reception from the 1970s until now, her artistry often has seemed incidental. Yet Kingston herself has defied attempts to categorize her writing by race or ethnicity. Her concerns are first and foremost those of an artist. As "an American writer" of "an American book" (1982, 57–58), she asks: "Why should I be denied an individual artistic vision? . . . Readers can see the variety of ways for Chinese Americans to be" (63). When Kingston published *The Woman Warrior*, the Immigration Act of 1965 had been in effect for ten years, finally abolishing national-origin quotas. During the 1960s and 1970s, the United States also was transformed by civil rights protests, women's liberation movements, and antiwar demonstrations. In 1968, at San Francisco State College, the Third World Liberation Front (a multicultural student coalition) led a four-month strike that helped to bring about the first ethnic studies program in the country. In its own way, Kingston's writing bears witness to the powerful force of the human voice in effecting social change. As she has said, *The Woman Warrior* is "a world book" whose interpretation calls for recognition of its "many layers, as human beings have many layers" (65).[9]

When *The Joy Luck Club* was published in 1989, Orville Schell in the *New York Times Book Review*, like many other reviewers, accentuated generational conflicts in Tan's novel, paralleling mother vs. daughter and Chinese vs. American understanding of concepts such as family responsibility and personal freedom. However, the cachet of connoisseurship belonged to Schell in particular because he could parlay his reputation as a well-seasoned "China hand" into redoubtable credentials as a literary critic. Accordingly, his readership was prepared to accept as authoritative his assertion that Tan's novel was to be especially prized for its "recherches to old China . . . so beautifully written that one should just allow oneself to be borne along as if in a dream" (1989, 3). Is this possibly the dream of "Cathay," the vision of a China endlessly appealing to

9. Among many informative studies of Kingston are Cheung 1993; Skandera-Trombley 1998; Wong 1992, 1993b, 1999; and Yu 2001.

westerners in its changeless beauty and wisdom? In the early nineteenth century, as John Haddad (1998) describes it, "Cathay" in its myriad imagined forms became "an idealized conception . . . that took the place of actual knowledge of China's country and people," so "mysterious and charming" that "porcelain painters" were admired as its "most reliable topographers." Similarly in the popular press of the twentieth century, Chinese American women writers such as Tan are praised as artisans of Orientalism, providing a discerning public with glimpses of a land and people that "foreign experts" such as Schell know best.

Critical studies of Tan during the past fifteen years indicate that she, too, is a controversial figure in the emergence of Chinese American women's writing. Garrett Hongo (1995), noting that ethnic writers are expected to fulfill a wide range of responsibilities—to their art and craft, to their ethnic communities, to their readers at large, to their societies, to the development of literary traditions—advises against assuming that "ethnic topics, ethnic identities, and the literary portrayal of ethnic voices" should be "the *exclusive cultural properties* of a group that would somehow be deemed 'authentic,' licensed with the cultural 'right' to represent itself as the *ethnic Other*" (31; emphasis in the original). Yet criticism of Tan's writing frequently has taken exactly that form, as when Sheng-mei Ma (2000) claims that "someone like Tan whose cultural arsenal . . . is circumscribed by her American identity . . . is bound to duplicate Orientalist practices as often as she repudiates them" (110). Similarly, Cai (1995) argues that "cultural authenticity" is the most important literary standard to uphold because none of us should "overestimate the power of imagination to close cultural gaps" (3).

For Tan, however, imagination explores what cannot be explicated, illuminating identity as a process of discovery rather than as an authentic or inauthentic state of being. Accordingly, Tan's rhetoric of the self in *The Joy Luck Club* is double-edged, an assertion of authorship that breaks down popular stereotypes of how she should perform for the public. On the one hand, she draws readers into her fictional world by making surface appearances alluring; sensory details, for example, abound in nearly every scene. On the other hand, once she has brought readers close enough to think they know what is happening, Tan turns the tables on them; appearances prove to be deceiving, or at least to be only the first of many layers of possible significance. Chinoiserie connoisseurs among book reviewers seem to have delighted in referring to her writing as a display of oriental treasures. However, Tan's rhetoric of self-resistance in *The Joy Luck Club* warrants a different kind of appreciation for her presentation of stories within stories exploring the complex history of her characters' emotional, social, and cultural lives.

One of the most memorable characters is Ying-Ying, a woman who has lost and is trying to recover herself in a world that seems at every turn to tell her that her efforts are hopeless. How she gains the inner strength to save her daughter from the same fate is dramatized by Tan through compelling scenes of lifelong confrontations with challenging moral questions. One of the most intriguing of these confrontations comes when, at only five years old, she happens upon the hired help preparing a banquet for her family on a pleasure boat: "I stayed as if caught in a good dream. . . . I watched as she took out a sharp, thin knife and began to slice open the fish bellies, pulling out the red slippery insides and throwing them over her shoulder into the lake. I saw her scrape off the fish scales, which flew into the air like shards of glass. And then there were two chickens that no longer gurgled after their heads were cut off. And a big snapping turtle that stretched out its neck to bite a stick and—whuck!—off fell its head. And dark masses of thin freshwater eels, swimming furiously in a pot. And then the woman carried everything, without a word, into the kitchen. And there was nothing left to see" (1989, 75)

The violence of this scene erupts through a day on which Ying-Ying has been expected to take her place as an obedient, well-trained daughter of the upper class. Standing in her elegant, handmade clothing, she is splattered with blood, a picture sharply contrasting any orientalist fantasies of delicate, feminine sensibility. Moreover, in an attempt to hide herself from her anxious amah, Ying-Ying reaches into the "crimson red" of the turtle's blood to smear it on her silk and satin brocade, an outfit meant to mark her as a daughter of a first wife rather than of a concubine. However, Tan presents the possibility that it is the blood that sets Ying-Ying apart, for many others suffer to provide what her family takes for granted. In the same chapter, as the family pursues its privileged pleasures, their rickshaw drivers are described as "soaked with sweat . . . their mouths . . . open and panting like horses" (1989, 72), while peasant families are no more real to Ying-Ying than "poor-looking people" (73) without faces or feelings. Ironically, Ying-Ying's own amah, who daily meets her every demand, is part of this lower class, for she is a widow who has given up her only son to become a servant. When Ying-Ying falls off the boat, fishermen rescue her and row her around the lake, calling out to rich people on barges to see who will claim her, but no one does:

> "Have you lost a little girl, a girl who fell in the water?"
>
> There were . . . shouts from the floating pavilion, and I strained to see the faces of Amah, Baba, Mama. . . . A little girl pushed her way through some legs.
>
> "That's not me!" she cried. "I'm here. I didn't fall in the water." The people in the boat roared with laughter and turned away. (79)

Hearing this reaction, realizing she is completely alone for the first time in her life, Ying-Ying is terrified at the prospect of being "lost forever," turned into a beggar girl with no one ever to care for her again. Consistent with Tan's authorial rhetoric of the self, the reality of the world outside Ying-Ying's gated compound comes to her—and the novel's readers—not as an orientalist dream of pagodas and pavilions, but as sudden, self-shattering knowledge of how precarious identities can be. This theme continues throughout the novel as Ying-Ying marries and leaves an abusive husband, exiles herself to the countryside for ten years, survives the mean streets of Shanghai, and comes to the United States as a displaced person with a new husband who cannot speak Chinese, but who does not hesitate to change her name on her immigration papers. Relentlessly, the shadow of the lost girl pursues Ying-Ying, never letting her forget that no one knows who Ying-Ying is inside her roles as wife, mother, and outcast, whether in China or the United States. After the loss of two children, Ying-Ying nearly despairs of being found by anyone, but finally, in her daughter Lena's face, she sees their shared longing to speak out without fear of the world's retribution. "I must tell her everything" (1989, 274) are words which set Ying-Ying free to welcome back the "dark shadow" that has held her inner truths for so many years.

While Tan's work has been orientalized by the popular press and deauthenticated by some literary critics, she has cut through that double bind with a double-edged rhetoric of self-resistance. In my view, this is why her contribution to Chinese American women's writing is significant. As Wendy Ho emphasizes, "Chinese exotica" is not the focus of *The Joy Luck Club*; accordingly, "As teachers, we need to seek out new and empowering interpretive strategies for reading [Tan] rather than appropriating . . . ways of reading our emerging writers that are based on racist, sexist stereotypes" (1996, 327). Insisting that the meaning of any story is the whole story, Tan's work values above all else language itself as potentially radically transformative of our perspectives on identity, society, the entire world created by human relationships.[10]

An interesting turn away from orientalist public reception of Chinese American women's writing can be seen in response to the novel *Bone* (1993) by Fae Myenne Ng, whose literary skills have persuaded critics that she has as much in common with canonical authors such as F. Scott Fitzgerald as she does with other emerging talents in multicultural literature. Reviewers sometimes have pictured Ng (who is second-generation Chinese American) as an "Asian woman" crossing East-West divides (Stephenson 1994), or they have overlooked her San Francisco setting in search of an "ancient" China hidden beneath the modern city (Pintarich 1993). Sometimes, too, reviewers admit that they enjoy the book because in it they find "an exciting insider tour of Chinatown" (Johnson 1993), regardless of the book's clear message that tourists never know who lives there. More often, however, she has been acclaimed as a singularly gifted writer whose characters—mother, father, three daughters—become so real that their voices call out to readers long after the last page. In my view, Ng's literary achievement is made possible by a uniquely creative rhetoric of the self that finds identity in absence as much as presence. Much of her story concerns the family's response to the suicide of the middle daughter, Ona, whose reasons for leaving them are never made completely clear. Trying to bring Ona's heart into their home again, her parents and sisters realize that bloodlines are not necessarily the way to trace the truth of family connections. Instead, they see that history—recovered, revised, remembered and lived together—becomes their source of individual and collective identity. All of them have suffered, too much to bear alone, and so they cannot turn away from what hurts: how the father, Leon, arrived as a "paper son" at Angel Island, labored a lifetime for less than minimum wages, and was betrayed in a business deal by his best friend; how the mother, Dulcie, found her own American dreams dissolve into the despair of raising a family in insurmountable poverty; how the daughters sought escape from their parents' anger and shame at being denied the chance to do better. Learning to listen to each other, however, is such a painful experience that for much of the book, "the ghost, the guilt" of Ona's absence becomes a potent symbol of a "too dark" place (15), where they are afraid the failure of the family resides.

10. Scholarship on Tan is increasing, including Bloom 2000; Bow 2001; Ho 1999; Huntley 1998; Wong 1996; and Yuan 1999.

In the emergence of Chinese American women's writing, one of Ng's most important contributions is a rhetoric of authorial self-resistance that engages readers in experiencing the impossibility of anyone fully interpreting a language, a culture—or indeed an individual human being—for another. This is shown most clearly through *Bone*'s narrator, Leila, the oldest daughter, who becomes physically and emotionally exhausted from "dealing with death in two languages" (1993, 15). A teacher-parent liaison at a Chinatown school named Edith Eaton (Sui Sin Far's English name), Leila finds that both at work and at home, "I have a whole different vocabulary of feeling in English than in Chinese, and not everything can be translated" (18). After Ona's death, Leila takes her place in the middle between the parents and their younger daughter, Nina, who has moved from California to New York, giving up guilt for anonymity. Attempting to retrieve the memories and honor the sacrifices that can keep her family together, Leila searches for the lost bones of Grandpa Leong, who claimed Leon as his son at Angel Island. As a community elder tells her: "Sometimes it takes a generation, like you, but eventually somebody comes. Tomorrow, or another generation's tomorrow. . . . Blood is blood" (77). However, Leila is a "paper daughter" of a "paper son," Leon's child by marriage, not birth. (Leila's biological father has nothing to do with her or Dulcie for most of her life.) For Leila—and for Ng—"Family exists only because somebody has a story, and knowing the story connects us to a history" (36). Moreover, because "One truth open[s] another" (19), a single language or a single viewpoint can never achieve the "completion" (105) of identity, family, or community. As Ng underscores, survival depends upon being able "*to get long* . . . to make do . . . [to have] a long view, which [is] endurance, and a long heart, which [is] hope" (176)—all of which are made possible by listening to many voices, past and present, which speak in Chinese, English, and as many other languages as there are dreams.

Early reviews suggest that Ng's themes and narrative style elude any easily available categories of chinoiserie collection. Michiko Kakutani (1993), for example, notes in the *New York Times* that *Bone* is an "incantatory first novel . . . [Ng] is blessed with a poet's gift for metaphor and a reporter's eye for detail"; while Michael Upchurch (1993) in the *Seattle Times/Post-Intelligencer* calls the novel "[b]rutal and poignant, dreamy and gritty, specific to its place and resonant in its implications about what it means to be an American." Established writers of the time clearly welcome her work, as seen in these book cover endorsements: "*Bone* is the result of many years of hard work and experience. It is tough and real . . . , mark[ing] the debut of a writer whose literary skills are fantastic" (Ishmael Reed); "Ng is tough and smart, unflinching in her portrait of two generations, Chinese and Chinese-American. . . . There's a sense of history that can't be escaped by will or wit or wish" (Rosellen Brown); and "[*Bone* is] full of feeling and the sound of the streets . . . sensitive and truthful . . . there is no doubt that a new voice has come into American letters" (Frank MacShane).

Clearly, *Bone* is being read as an American book by an American writer from the onset, definitely a different kind of reception than Kingston received years before. Equally important, Ng is being respected for contributing to American literary heritage in ways transcending nationalized definitions of literary merit. As Ho (1999) asserts, Ng composes "not Chinese stories . . . but *Chinese American* and *Asian American* stories, which are in the process of being lived, contested, and constructed in the flux of U.S. culture and society" (211; emphasis in the original). Moreover, as Lowe (1991) notes, Ng is not trying to "represent an essential authenticity" (125) that she can explain through her characters. Instead, I recognize that Ng deliberately deploys an authorial rhetoric of the self that draws readers' attention to what precedes and exceeds representation. In the emergence of Chinese American women writers, Ng stands out for integrating a minimalist prose style with a deeply compassionate portrayal of intensely individual people, whose search for home and history parallels Ng's own commitment to the art of storytelling itself. In the language of emotion—fear, rage, guilt, love, desire—Leila and her family find release from trying to express everything in words. Then, out of the depths of their feeling for each other, they shape an understanding of belonging together that will allow them to live again with hope after Ona's death. As Leila affirms at the end of *Bone*, "even the unspoken between us is a measure of our everyday promise to the living and to the dead. All of our promises, like all of our hopes, move us through life with the power of an ocean liner pushing through the sea" (1993, 193). Rather than crossing the Pacific from China to America with tales of the fantastic and faraway, Ng—like Kafka—takes an ax to the "frozen sea" within us all.[11]

11. Other literary criticism on Ng includes Gonzalez 1996; Huang 2003; Kafka 1997; Sze 1994; and Yen 2000.

Ng deserves recognition for opening more literary and cultural space for other writers to be seen for their own accomplishments. Orientalist tendencies, however, are still evident in contemporary reception of Chinese American women writers' fiction. For example, in a review of Sara Chin's short story collection, *Below the Line* (1997), she is praised for "poetically draw[ing] aside the literary bamboo curtain on a culture too often silenced by its own stoicism" (Beck 1998). Potential readers also are told that they will directly experience "China and the Chinese" through her writing, "staring straight into the heart of an ancient culture," as if Chin is a trustworthy travel guide in a foreign land. Praised for their "Chinese-Cantonese flavor" (Quan 1997, 78), Chin's stories actually are set mainly in the United States, not China, and their narrative viewpoint is fixed firmly in modern urban life. A father is lost on the DC beltway, driving in endless circles, until realizing that no one else can find the way home. Watching American television to learn English, a mother becomes fascinated by the power of violence, onscreen and off. Growing up "where there were no Chinatowns" (Chin 1997, 126), a sister and a brother share an unspoken lifetime bond: "What holds us together, different as we are, is that we have survived the same metaphors . . . commies, pinkos, japs, and every now and then they got it right: chink" (127). An audio technician and sound designer for documentary films, Chin is a well-practiced listener—an artist attuned to emotions and events occurring "below the line," that is, outside the range of what dominant culture tends to value. Through her stories, readers have the opportunity to hear "the past percolat[ing] up" (55) through the buried lives and broken dreams of immigrant Americans. Across generations, Chin also carefully attends to silences underlying fears and desires, including the wariness of Asian Americans who are all too familiar with the relentless risk of being "caught on the wrong side of a word" (128). Resisting expectations that she assume the role of multimedia cultural entrepreneur, Chin instead shows that both "China" and "America" are complex categorizations of experience, each holding concepts of history, society, and culture that are individually as well as collectively defined. As one of her narrators, a young Chinese American woman visiting China for the first time, puts it: "I love the low ground, the things that people pushed offstage. . . . the heart, the trashy heart of my own history. After all, wasn't that where the unknown leaped out at you?" (57).[12]

12. Critical commentary on *Below the Line* includes Cokal 1998 and Fachinger 2005.

In the mid-nineteenth century, P. T. Barnum dreamed of acquiring Nathan Dunn's "Ten Thousand Things on China and the Chinese," a collection and exhibition including not only fifty-three glass cases of oriental treasures, but also over three hundred paintings of China and fifty life-size statues of Chinese people (Haddad 1998). Invited to the opening reception was "a goodly representation from all the learned professions" (including the "literati"), whose enthusiastic response helped to generate astounding public interest (Wines 1839, 10). From 1838 to 1841, fifty thousand copies of thc 120–page catalogue were sold as hundreds of thousands of people from across the city and state (and other parts of the country) made their way to a display and documentation of oriental lifeways so amazing that, as advertisements promised, they would gain more pleasure from the experience than any actual visit to China could provide. Finally acquiring the lease for a road show in 1850, Barnum knew what was needed to make his traveling Chinese Museum complete: he "secured and attached to [the collection] . . . the celebrated Chinese Beauty, Miss Pwan-ye-koo, and her suite" (Ten Thousand Things 1850, 6).[13] As he proclaimed, "it is a pleasure for people of taste to be associated with" such an educational enterprise (204). Thus, everyone who entered the Chinese Museum could leave a chinoiserie connoisseur.

Are Chinese American women writers still valued more for their authenticity than their artistry? Across a range of current reviews, I notice recurring imagery: on the one hand, Chinese American women writers are characterized as "captivating," "enchanting," "enthralling," "mesmerizing," and "spellbinding"; on the other hand, they are extolled as "graceful," "guileless" storytellers, born to cross cultures. In other words, they must be "the real thing," the modern version of "the Chinese lady" who performs for our pleasure.[14]

13. This group included five other Chinese, ranging in age from five to thirty-two, including a "maid-servant," a "professor of music," his daughter and son, and an interpreter. Miss Pwan-ye-koo, according to Barnum, "will be pronounced peculiarly prepossessing . . . artless, refined . . . delicate in her deportment. . . . a capital specimen of a Chinese belle"; while her servant, a "fair specimen of the Chinese women of her class . . . comely and agreeable" also will offer "quite a study . . . for a curious observer" (6).

14. In "The Next Amy Tan," Nguyen (1997) reports that "the book publishing industry employs almost 85,000 men and women, from managerial to clerical to service positions. Only seven percent are blacks, while two percent are Asian American." Very few Asian Americans hold editorial positions at major publishing houses. As agent

Perhaps the endless intrigue of discovering and possessing a culture through its curios is why so many of my students expect Chinese American literature to be "strange and wondrous," revealing East to West, making the foreign familiar. However, Tan (1996) tells us: "I write because there is a lot I don't understand about life and death, myself and the world, and the great in-between. . . . I write to find the questions I should ask. And for me, stories are possible answers" (5). Finally, this may be what is most marvelous: the shared truths that writers and readers discover as they come together through language. For as Said (2000) observes in "The Politics of Knowledge," the great literature of the world is to be appreciated across cultures "as literature, as style, as pleasure and illumination . . . [as part of] the large, many-windowed house of human culture as a whole" (372).

Students in my Asian American literature courses consistently find it eye-opening to consider how the significance of literary texts and the historical contexts of their reception are interlinked. Respect for the diversity and complexity of human identity is what they value in *The Woman Warrior*, what they look for in *Fifth Chinese Daughter*, what they find affirmed in Sui Sin Far's essays and short stories. As students analyze the rhetoric of public reception, they realize how orientalist reading diminishes the possibility of such discernment. However, they also come to appreciate the rhetorics of self-resistance that Chinese American women writers have developed through their individual creativity, their social conscience, and their bold stance on questions of identity, difference, and community. As bell hooks emphasizes, deciding to "talk back"—in literature as in life—"challenges politics of domination" through the refusal to be "nameless and voiceless" (1994, 8). Contrary to the rhetoric of public reception, Chinese American women writers speak to us not from the distant East, but from the immediacy of multicultural American life, where they continue to contribute to the ongoing formation of our literary heritage.

REFERENCES

Ammons, Elizabeth. 1991. *Conflicting Stories: American Women Writers at the Turn into the Twentieth Century*. New York: Oxford University Press.

Beck, Catherine. 1998. Review of *Below the Line*, by Sara Chin. *Rain Taxi Review of Books* 3 (2): 11.

Blinde, Patricia Lin. 1979. The Icicle in the Desert: Perspective and Form in the Works of Two Chinese American Women Writers. *MELUS* 6 (3): 51–71.

Sandra Djikstra notes, publishers keep asking, "Where is the next Amy Tan?"

Bloom, Harold, ed. 2000. *Amy Tan*. Philadelphia: Chelsea House.

Book Reaches the Heart. 1912. *Boston Daily Globe,* June 29.

Bow, Leslie. 1993. The Illusion of the Middle Way: Liberal Feminism and Biculturalism in Jade Snow Wong's *Fifth Chinese Daughter*. In *Bearing Dreams, Shaping Visions: Asian Pacific American Perspectives*, edited by Linda A. Revilla. Pullman: Washington State University Press.

———. 2001. *The Joy Luck Club* by Amy Tan. In *A Resource Guide to Asian American Literature,* edited by Sau-Ling Cynthia Wong and Stephen Sumida. New York: MLA.

Burke, Kenneth. 1969. *A Rhetoric of Motives*. Berkeley: University of California Press.

Cai, Mingshui. 1995. Can We Fly across Cultural Gaps on the Wings of Imagination? Ethnicity, Experience and Cultural Authenticity. *New Advocate* 8 (1): 1–16.

Cathay Invoked: Chinoiserie, a Celestial Empire in the West. 1966. San Francisco: California Palace of the Legion of Honor.

Chan, Sucheng. 1991. *Asian Americans: An Interpretive History*. Boston: Twayne.

Cheung, King-Kok. 1990. *The Woman Warrior* versus the *Chinaman Pacific:* Must a Chinese-American Critic Choose between Feminism and Heroism? In *Conflicts in Feminism,* edited by Marianne Hirsch and Evelyn F. Keller. New York: Routledge.

———. 1993. *Articulate Silences: Narrative Strategies in Hisaye Yamamoto, Maxine Hong Kingston, and Joy Kogawa*. Ithaca, NY: Cornell University Press.

Chin, Frank. 1991. Come All Ye Asian American Writers of the Real and the Fake. In *The Big AIIIEEEEE! An Anthology of Chinese American and Japanese American Literature,* edited by Jeffery P. Chan, Frank Chin, Lawson Inada, and Shawn Wong. New York: Meridian.

Chin, Frank, Jeffrey Chan, Lawson Inada, and Shawn Wong, eds. 1974. *AIIIEEEEE! An Anthology of Asian American Writers*. New York: Penguin.

Chin, Sara. 1997. *Below the Line*. San Francisco: City Lights.

Cokal, Susann. 1998. Review of *Below the Line,* by Sara Chin. *Review of Contemporary Fiction* 98 (18): 2.

Crusius, Timothy. 1999. *Kenneth Burke and the Conversation after Philosophy*. Carbondale: Southern Illinois University Press.

Edwards, Holly. 2000. *Noble Dreams, Wicked Pleasures: Orientalism in America, 1870–1930.* Princeton, NJ: Princeton University Press with Sterling and Francine Clark Art Institute.

Evans, Ernestine. 1950. A Chinese-American Girl's Two Worlds. *New York Herald Tribune Book Review,* September 24, 4.

Fachinger, Petra. 2005. Cultural and Culinary Ambivalence in Sara Chin, Evelina Galang, and Yoko Tawada. *Modern Language Studies* 35 (1): 38–48.

Feldman, Gayle. 1989. The Joy Luck Club: Chinese Magic, American Blessings, and a Publishing Fairy Tale. *Publishers Weekly* 236 (7 July): 24–26

Ferens, Dominika. 2002. *Edith & Winnifred Eaton: Chinatown Missions and Japanese Romances*. Chicago and Urbana: University of Illinois Press.

Fuss, Diana. 1990. *Essentially Speaking: Feminism, Nature & Difference*. New York: Routledge.

Geary, Joyce. 1950. A Chinese Girl's World. *New York Times Book Review,* October 29, 27.

Gonzales, Begona Simal. 1996. Translating Cultures through Narrative: From *Bone* to *Un padre de papel*. *Hitting Critical Mass* 4 (1): 47–68.

Haddad, John. 1998. The Romantic Collector in China: Nathan Dunn's "Ten Thousand Chinese Things." *Journal of American Culture* 21 (1): 7–27.

Ho, Wendy. 1996. Swan-Feather Mothers and Coca-Cola Daughters: Teaching Amy Tan's *The Joy Luck Club*. In *Teaching American Ethnic Literatures,* edited by John R. Maitino and David R. Peck. Albuquerque: University of New Mexico Press.

———. 1999. *In Her Mother's House: The Politics of Asian American Mother-Daughter Writing.*

Walnut Creek, CA, and Oxford: AltaMira.

Hongo, Garrett, ed. 1995. *Under western Eyes: Personal Essays from Asian America*. New York: Anchor/Doubleday.

hooks, bell. 1994. *Teaching to Transgress: Education as the Practice of Freedom*. New York: Routledge.

How to Tell Japs from the Chinese. 1941. *Life,* December 22, 81–82.

How To Tell Your Friends from the Japs. 1941. *Time,* December 22.

Huang, Guiyou, ed. 2001. *Asian American Autobiographers: A Bio-Bibliographical Critical Sourcebook*. Westport, CT: Greenwood.

Huang, Su-ching. 2003. Fae Myenne Ng. In *Asian American Short Story Writers,* edited by Guiyou Huang. Westport, CT: Greenwood.

Huntley, E. D., ed. 1998. *Amy Tan: A Critical Companion*. Westport, CT: Greenwood.

Hutnyk, John. 1999/2000. Hybridity Saves? Authenticity and/or the Critique of Appropriation. *Amerasia Journal* 25 (3): 39–58.

Jacobson, Dawn. 1993. *Chinoiserie*. London: Phaidon.

Johnson, Pamela. 1993. Chinese Family's Tragedy Buried in Bones. *Albuquerque Journal,* February 21.

Judson, Clara Ingram. 1950. The Colorful Home Life of a Chinese Girl. *Chicago Sunday Tribune,* October 1, 5.

Kafka, Phillipa. 1997. Fae Myenne Ng, *Bone*: "Nina, Ona, and I, We're the Lucky Generation." In *(Un)doing the Missionary Position: Gender Asymmetry in Contemporary Asian American Women's Writing*. Westport, CT: Greenwood.

Kakutani, Michiko. 1993. Building on the Pain of a Past in China. *New York Times,* January 29, C26.

Kim, Elaine. 1982. *Asian American Literature: An Introduction to the Writings and Their Social Context*. Philadelphia: Temple University Press.

Kingston, Maxine Hong. 1977. *The Woman Warrior: Memoirs of a Girlhood among Ghosts*. New York: Knopf.

———. 1982. Cultural Mis-readings by American Reviewers. In *Asian and western Writers in Dialogue,* edited by Guy Amirthanayagam. London: Macmillan.

Kingston, Maxine Hong, et al. 2002. *Jade Snow Wong: A Retrospective*. San Francisco: Chinese Historical Society.

Koenig, Rhoda. 1989. Heirloom China. *NewYork Magazine* (20 March): 82–83.

Lai, Him Mark, Genny Lim, and Judy Yung, eds. 1991. *Island: Poetry and History of Chinese Immigrants on Angel Island, 1910–1940*. Seattle: University of Washington Press. (Orig. pub. 1980.)

Lee, Rachel. 1997. Journalistic Representations of Asian Americans and Literary Responses, 1910–1920. In *An Interethnic Companion to Asian American Literature,* edited by King-Kok Cheung. New York: Cambridge University Press.

Leonard, Shannon. 2001. Edith Maude Eaton (Sui Sin Far). In Huang 2001.

Life. 1943. Untitled public service comic strip, March 1, 12.

Lim, Shirley Geok-Lin. 1992. The Tradition of Chinese American Women's Life Stories: Thematics of Race and Gender in Jade Snow Wong's *Fifth Chinese Daughter* and Maxine Hong Kingston's *The Woman Warrior*. In *American Women's Autobiography: Fea(s)ts of Memory,* edited by Margo Culley. Madison: University of Wisconsin Press.

———. 1993. Assaying the Gold: Or, Contesting the Ground of Asian American Literature. *New Literary History* 24:147–169.

Ling, Amy. 1983. Edith Eaton: Pioneer Chinamerican Writer and Feminist. *American Literary Realism* 16 (2): 287–298.

———. 1987. I'm Here: An Asian American Woman's Response. *New Literary History* 19:1–16.

———. 1990. *Between Worlds: Women Writers of Chinese Ancestry*. New York: Pergamon.
Ling, Amy, and Annette White-Parks, eds. 1995. *Mrs. Spring Fragrance and Other Writings,* by Sui Sin Far. Chicago and Urbana: University of Illinois Press.
Lowe, Lisa. 1991. Heterogeneity, Hybridity, Multiplicity: Marking Asian American Differences. *Diaspora: A Journal of Transnational Studies* 1 (1): 21–44.
Ma, Sheng-mei. 2000. *The Deathly Embrace: Orientalism and Asian American Identity.* Minneapolis: University of Minnesota Press.
Manning, Margaret. 1982. Review of *The Woman Warrior: Memoirs of a Girlhood among Ghosts,* by Maxine Hong Kingston. In Maxine Hong Kingston, Cultural Mis-readings by American Reviewers, in *Asian and western Writers in Dialogue,* edited by Guy Amirthanayagam. London: Macmillan. (Orig. pub. 1976.)
McClurg, A. C., and Co. 1912. Advertisement for *Mrs. Spring Fragrance. New York Times Book Review,* July 7, 405.
Moy, James. 1993. *Marginal Sights: Staging the Chinese in America.* Iowa City: University of Iowa Press.
A New Note in Fiction. 1912. *New York Times,* July 7, 405.
Ng, Fae Myenne. 1993. *Bone.* New York: HarperPerennial.
Nguyen, Lan. 1997. The Next Amy Tan. *A. Magazine,* (Feb/March), 46–51.
Okihiro, Gary, ed. 2005. *The Columbia Guide to Asian American History*. New York: Columbia University Press. (Orig. pub. 2001.)
Palumbo-Liu, David. 1999. *Asian/American: Historical Crossings of a Racial Frontier.* Stanford, CA: Stanford University Press.
Pintarich, Paul. 1993. *Bone* Pits Ancient Chinese Traditions against Modern American Life. *Oregonian,* February 5.
Publishers Weekly. 1976. Review of *The Woman Warrior: Memoirs of a Girlhood among Ghosts,* by Maxine Hong Kingston. August 9, 72.
Quan, Shirley. 1997. Review of *Below the Line,* by Sara Chin. *Library Journal,* November 15, 78.
Said, Edward. 1978. *Orientalism.* New York: Vintage.
———. 2000. *The Politics of Knowledge: Reflections on Exile and Other Essays.* Cambridge, MA: Harvard University Press.
Schell, Orville. 1989. Your Mother Is in Your Bones. *New York Times Book Review,* March 19, 3ff.
Skandera-Trombley, Laura, ed. 1998. *Critical Essays on Maxine Hong Kingston.* New York: G. K. Hall.
Solberg, Sol. 1981. Sui Sin Far/Edith Eaton: First Chinese-American Fictionist. *MELUS* 8 (1): 27–39.
———. 1982. Sui, the Storyteller: Sui Sin Far (Edith Eaton), 1867–1914. In *Turning Shadows into Light: Art and Culture of the Northwest's Early Asian/Pacific Community,* edited by Mayumi Tsutakawa and Alan Chong Lau. Seattle: Young Pine.
Stephenson, Heather. 1994. Out of the Kitchen and Traveling On: New Fiction by Asian Women. *New England Review of Books* 16 (Winter): 169–176.
Stob, Paul. 2005. Kenneth Burke, John Dewey, and the Pursuit of the Public. *Philosophy and Rhetoric* 38 (3): 226–247.
Streitfeld, David. 1989. The 'Luck' of Amy Tan. *Washington Post* (8 October): F1 ff.
Sui, Sin Far. 1897. The Chinese Woman in America. *Land of Sunshine* 9 (October): 225–228.
———. 1903. Chinatown Needs a School. *Los Angeles Express,* (14 October 1903): n.p.
———. 1909. The Chinese in America: Intimate Study of Chinese Life in America, Told in a Series of Short Sketches. *westerner* 10–11 (May–August).
———. 1995. Leaves from the Mental Portfolio of an Eurasian. In *Mrs. Spring Fragrance and Other Writings,* edited by Amy Ling and Annette White-Parks. Chicago and Urbana:

University of Illinois Press. (Orig. pub. 1909.)

———. 1912. Mrs. Spring Fragrance. Chicago; A.C. McClurg

Sze, Julie. 1994. Have You Heard? Gossip, Silence, and Community in *Bone. Critical Mass: A Journal of Asian American Cultural Criticism* 2 (1): 59–69.

Takaki, Ronald. 1998. *Strangers from a Different Shore: A History of Asian Americans.* Boston: Little, Brown. (Orig. pub. 1989.)

Tan, Amy. 1989. *The Joy Luck Club.* New York: Putnam.

———. 1996. Required Reading and Other Dangerous Subjects. *Threepenny Review* (Fall): 5–9.

Ten Thousand Things on China and the Chinese: Being a Picture of the Genius, Government, History, Literature, Agriculture, Arts, Trade, Manners, Customs, and Social Life of the People of the Celestial Empire, as Illustrated by the Chinese Collection. 1850. New York: J. S. Redfield.

Upchurch, Michael. 1993. Chinatown, Her Chinatown—A Luminous First Novel. *Seattle Times/Post-Intelligencer,* January 17. http://archives.scattletimes.nwsource.com/cgi-bin/texis.cgi/web/vortex/display?slug=1680529&date=19930117&query=bone+ng.

Wess, Robert. 1996. *Kenneth Burke: Rhetoric, Subjectivity, Postmodernism.* London: Cambridge University Press.

White-Parks, Annette. 1995. *Sui Sin Far/Edith Maude Eaton: A Literary Biography.* Chicago and Urbana: University of Illinois Press.

Wines, E. C. 1839. *A Peep at China in Mr. Dunn's Chinese Collection.* Philadelphia: Ashmead.

Wong, Jade Snow. 1999. *Fifth Chinese Daughter.* Seattle: University of Washington Press. (Orig. pub. 1950.)

Wong, Sau-ling Cynthia. 1992. Autobiography as Guided Chinatown Tour? Maxine Hong Kingston's *The Woman Warrior* and the Chinese-American Autobiographical Controversy. In *Multicultural Autobiography: American Lives,* edited by James Robert Payne. Knoxville: University of Tennessee Press.

———. 1993a. Promises, Pitfalls, and Principles of Text Selection in Curricular Diversification: The Asian American Case. In *Freedom's Plow,* edited by Theresa Perry and James Fraser. New York and London: Routledge.

———. 1993b. *Reading Asian American Literature: From Necessity to Extravagance.* Princeton, NJ: Princeton University Press.

———. 1996. "Sugar Sisterhood": Situating the Amy Tan Phenomenon. In *The Ethnic Canon: Histories, Institutions, and Interventions,* edited by David Palumbo-Liu. Minneapolis: University of Minnesota Press.

———, ed. 1999. *Maxine Hong Kingston's "The Woman Warrior": A Casebook.* New York: Oxford University Press.

Yen, Xiaoping. 2000. Fae Myenne Ng. In *Asian American Novelists: A Bio-Bibliographical Critical Sourcebook,* edited by Emmanuel Nelson. Westport, CT: Greenwood.

Yin, Kathlee Loh Swee, and Kristoffer Paulson. 1982. The Divided Voice of Chinese-American Narration: Jade Snow Wong's *Fifth Chinese Daughter. MELUS* 9 (1): 53–59.

Yu, Su-lin. 2001. Maxine Hong Kingston. In Huang 2001.

Yuan, Yuan. 1999. The Semiotics of China Narratives in the Con/Texts of Kingston and Tan. *Critique: Studies in Contemporary Fiction* 40 (3): 292–330.

11

REREADING SUI SIN FAR

A Rhetoric of Defiance

Bo Wang

Sui Sin Far, or Edith Eaton (1865–1914) has been recognized as the first Chinese American writer to depict truly the Chinese in America with empathy.[1] Certainly in her own day she was a well-known author and her works were carried by major literary journals and newspapers in both Canada and the United States, including the *Montreal Daily Star, Los Angeles Express, Independent, New England Magazine*, and *Boston Globe.* Yet, like many other women who wrote and published in earlier times, she was almost forgotten after her death. Little was written about her until the 1970s, when first the editors of *AIIIEEEEE! An Anthology of Asian American Writers* (1991), and then later literary critics S. E. Solberg (1981) and Amy Ling (1983) brought her to the attention of Asian American literary scholars.

In recent years, and especially since the publication of Annette White-Parks's biography of her (1995b), the importance of Sui Sin Far to the development of Asian American literature has been increasingly recognized. Literary scholars have examined Sui Sin Far's work using different approaches, such as multiculturalism, feminism, and postmodernism (Solberg 1981; Ling 1990; Yin 2000; Ammons and White-Parks 1994; White-Parks 1995a; Diana 2001; Beauregard 2002; Li 2004). But from a rhetorician's point of view, the most significant aspect of her work is the innovative rhetorical strategies she utilized to inform and persuade her dual audiences so that changes could be made to transform a racist society. Although literary scholars have done important critical work recovering Sui Sin Far's works from oblivion, few have provided in-depth analyses of the rhetorical strategies she employed in her fiction and

1. In this essay, I refer to Sui Sin Far as a Chinese American writer for the purpose of situating her rhetorical practices within the context of Asian American rhetoric study, though she had a multifaceted identity and lived and published in both Canada and the United States.

nonfiction pieces. It is necessary that we reread her work from a rhetorical perspective to include her contribution to Asian/Chinese American rhetoric. In a letter Sui Sin Far wrote to the editor of the *westerner* in November 1909, she mentioned: "[M]y stories and articles in 'The westerner,' 'Out West' and 'Post-Intelligencer' accomplish more the object of my life, which is not so much to put a Chinese name into American literature, as to break down prejudice, and to cause the American heart to soften and the American mind to broaden towards the Chinese people now living in America—the humble, kindly moral, unassuming Chinese people of America" (quoted in White-Parks 1995b, 154).

Saliently, she had a clear political and antiracism agenda when writing stories and articles about Chinese immigrants in America. Whether she was challenging the cultural norms in the late nineteenth and early twentieth century or protesting against institutionalized racial discrimination against the Chinese in North America or intentionally revealing to the public her identity as a Chinese Eurasian, Sui Sin Far consistently used writing rhetorically to speak for the silenced and the downtrodden and to fight for racial equality.

Some literary critics have faulted Sui Sin Far for portraying the Chinese with a certain "orientalism" in the author's tone and displaying Asian immigrants to the critical white gaze (Dong and Hom 1987).[2] Yet we must read her work in its own social, historical, and cultural context. She wrote in an era when racism was rampant in North America. Not only Chinese immigrants, but also African Americans and other people of color were cruelly persecuted. The 1880s saw the aftermath of the American Supreme Court's crashing down of the Civil Rights Act and the staggering heights of lynching and murder of African Americans. While African American women rhetors such as Frances E. W. Harper, Ida Wells, and Fannie Barrier Williams were speaking against racism and the practice of lynching, Sui Sin Far fought against racial discrimination in her own way, using literary and journalistic writing as a means to the practical ends of changing social conditions and

2. In his book *Orientalism*, Edward Said defines Orientalism as "a style of thought based upon an ontological and epistemological distinction made between 'the Orient' and 'the Occident'" (1979, 2). According to Said, this kind of distinction derives from a western projection of political dominance and academic authority in relation to the Orient. In addition, oriental methodology used in the study of the Orient produces problems of essentialism and ethnocentrism, which tend to create distorted and inaccurate views of non-western ideas and traditions.

unjust laws.[3] By initiating a dialogue between Chinese and European Americans, Sui Sin Far became a rhetor for the Chinese immigrants of her time, who were segregated and silenced. She deserves our respect for her courage to speak out against racial discrimination in an era when racism shaped not only the thinking of her time but national policies as well.

My analysis of Sui Sin Far is based on an assumption that as contemporary readers we are in dialogue with her work as we try to understand her positions, her strategies, and the consequences of her work. As I see it, such an analysis necessarily generates an argument for considering her short fiction not merely as aesthetic undertakings, but as rhetorical texts in themselves. These imaginative writings, together with her autobiography and journalistic articles, reveal her personal struggles as a biracial writer, her particular rhetorical strategies, her breaking of the stereotypes of silences and invisibility, and her commitment to the change of that racist society. Through a rhetorical analysis, I will show how Sui Sin Far used stereotyped characters, irony, personal experiences, and other rhetorical strategies to raise readers' consciousness of the irrationality of racism. Specifically, I will use narrative criticism to analyze the rhetorical dimension of Sui Sin Far's short fiction. I will examine the specific rhetorical strategies she employed in both her fiction and nonfiction to change the attitudes of her audience. I will also contend that Sui Sin Far's texts could be read along with the theoretical work of Kenneth Burke to complicate our understanding of the canonical notion of identification.

Given that Sui Sin Far was writing to dual audiences of both Protestant white readers and later some middle-class members of Chinese American communities in North America, she was facing tremendous rhetorical obstacles—she had to negotiate the difficult process of achieving her purposes without compromising her principles—which often forced her to be resourceful in delivering her message. As a consequence, her writing reflects, however subtly, the social tensions surrounding racial relations. It is only natural that some readers would resist or have doubts about Sui Sin Far's message due to the constraining function of cultural norms on people of color. Thus, this study draws attention to how a rhetor from a marginalized group and in a border position uses creative strategies to circumvent various social forces to inject her voice in the

3. For detailed analyses of 19th-century African American women rhetors, see Logan 1999.

dominant discourse. My goal is to be mindful of the distinctive rhetorical obstacles she encountered and to describe the particular rhetorical strategies she used to reach her audience.

Though Sui Sin Far's work touches various aspects of the social life of the late nineteenth and early twentieth centuries—including racial relationships, interracial marriage, acculturation, and women's status—in this essay, I will focus on her ideas about racial issues. And I will examine some representative pieces of her work as they fall in categories of genre: short stories, autobiography, and journalistic essays, discussing them in terms of the ideology they imply and the rhetorical strategies they employ as a way to achieve their goals of making changes in belief and attitudes.

BREAKING STEREOTYPES

In the late nineteenth century, after the United States completed its transcontinental railroad, racist laws and policies were implemented to drive the Chinese people out of the country. The 1882 Chinese Exclusion Act stopped legal immigration of all Chinese; Chinese immigrants already in the United States became the target of racism, being driven into segregated urban areas—the Chinatowns in large cities like San Francisco, Seattle, and New York. Accompanying this anti-Chinese wave, magazine stories and news articles against the Chinese pervaded the media with the purpose of rationalizing the ill treatment of Chinese immigrants. During this period, Chinese Americans were frequently depicted as the "yellow peril" in American fiction, which fostered stereotyped images of the Chinese as alien, even nonhuman, others.[4] In such a hostile racist atmosphere, Sui Sin Far began writing about Chinese immigrants and Chinatown life.

Sui Sin Far's task is one of writing against essentialist racism and breaking the unjust but socially accepted stereotyped images of Chinese immigrants in North America. Alongside her message that racial discrimination is unjust and irrational is the often recurring argument that it is a person's humanity and the environment in which he or she is brought up that form character rather than the accidents of race or nationality. Individuality, she insists, is more important than nationality. The depiction underlying this argument can be found in many of her short stories collected in her book *Mrs. Spring Fragrance*. Here, I will use narrative criticism to examine two short stories in this collection.

4. Wu 1982 provides an in-depth analysis of how Chinese Americans were represented in American fiction between 1850 and 1940.

Narrative criticism provides an analytical approach that can illuminate the persuasive power hidden in Sui Sin Far's fiction. Based on rhetoric theorist Walter Fisher's narrative paradigm, critics such as Robert C. Rowland and Robert Strain have developed a method that emphasizes the way that narrative functions persuasively (as opposed to analyzing a narrative by transforming it into an argument that can then be tested by the standards appropriate for rational argumentation). The three-step approach proposed by Rowland, which "moves from the *form* of the narrative, to the *functions* fulfilled by the particular story, and to an *evaluation* of how persuasive the narrative is with a given audience," offers a systematic and flexible way to examine the rhetorical function of both fictional and nonfictional narratives (2005, 143). Such an approach helps me to bring out the rhetorical dimension of Su Sin Far's short stories.

In "The Story of One White Woman Who Married a Chinese" and its sequel, "Her Chinese Husband," Sui Sin Far tells of a white woman who divorces her abusive white husband and marries a kindhearted Chinese man. The narrator, a working-class white woman named Minnie, has been deserted by her Caucasian husband James Carson, who dislikes her because she is too unsophisticated and ignorant of politics. When she attempts to commit suicide, she is rescued by Liu Kanghi, a Chinese merchant who shelters her later and marries her. Liu comforts her and supports her so that she finally recovers from her trauma and starts a new life with regained confidence. After they are married, Liu treats Minnie with reverence and respect and cares for her with tenderness and love, forming a sharp contrast to the cold and cruel behavior of her ex-husband James Carson. However, their marriage transgresses a forbidden area and breaks the taboo of miscegenation; the story ends tragically with Liu Kanghi being murdered.

Though the story is fictional, it can be considered as a narrative that has a rhetorical dimension. Minnie and Liu Kanghi, the protagonists of the narrative, play a heroic role, for they defy the forbidden ground in American society: interracial marriage between Chinese and European Americans was viewed as a threat to the survival of the American nation. Liu Kanghi as a protagonist is endowed with another layer of symbolic meaning, which turns over the stereotypical expectations: "There was nothing feigned about my Chinese husband. Simple and sincere as he was before marriage, so was he afterwards. As my union with James Carson had meant misery, bitterness, and narrowness, so my union with

Liu Kanghi meant, on the whole, happiness, health, and development. Yet the former, according to American ideas, had been an educated broad-minded man; the other, just an ordinary Chinaman" (Sui 1995, 79). Contrary to the stereotypical depictions of the Chinese at that time, Liu Kanghi presents a new image, an image of a man who has deep feelings toward his wife and children, and does everything he can do to support his family.

An analysis of the narrative forms of the story can reveal its rhetorical dimension. In the story, there are two different, but related, antagonists. At one level, the role of antagonist is played by James Carson, who first abandons his wife Minnie and later threatens and insults her when he knows that she is with Liu Kanghi. In Sui Sin Far's narrative, James Carson, the white man, is described as brutal and cruel, which flips over the stereotypical depiction. At a second level, the antagonist is the social bias against interracial marriage, and this is represented through both James Carson's remarks about Minnie's relationship with Liu Kanghi and Liu's tragic death toward the end of the story.

The primary setting of Sui Sin Far's narrative is in a Chinatown in the United States. The Chinese family with which Minnie stays are "kind, simple folk" (1995, 72). Minnie's experience living with the family teaches her that "the virtues do not all belong to the whites" (74). The major plot devices in the story involve betrayal and commitment. Minnie is betrayed by her ex-husband James Carson. In sharp contrast to Carson, Liu first kindly supports Minnie and later marries her and treats her with love and respect until the end of his life. The author's feeling about him is clearly expressed by Minnie, the narrator of the story: "[H]e is always a man. . . . I can lean upon and trust in him. I feel him behind me, protecting and caring for me, and that, to an ordinary woman like myself, means more than anything else" (77). There is a clear relationship between the two plot devices. Sui Sin Far's narrative challenges the racist stereotypes of Chinese Americans and showcases the preposterous nature of racial prejudices through the narrator's experience. The major theme of the narrative concerns racial discrimination and interracial marriage. The author argues that just like the white people, the Chinese are human beings and are capable of experiencing love. The author also tries to persuade the audience that an interracial marriage can be a happy and healthy union, though the end of the story casts a pessimistic shadow over such a union.

Viewed from a narrative perspective, Sui Sin Far's story fulfills the basic rhetorical functions of narrative. The story is well designed to attract the reader's attention with its vivid depiction of a Chinese-Caucasian marriage. The story creates identification between the audience and the major characters Liu Kanghi and Minnie. Implicitly, the author tells her readers that Chinese characters are people just like them, having their faults but also loving and caring about their families and friends. This type of identification persuades at an unconscious level, subtly leading the audience to associate with the characters through their shared humanness. Sui Sin Far utilizes the power of narrative to transport the reader to a different place and time. This function can be seen clearly in her detailed descriptions of Minnie and Liu Kanghi's daily lives in a Chinatown in the late nineteenth century, which reinforces her message that the Chinese are normal human beings just like the whites, and a mixed marriage can be a happy one if it is based on love. The story also taps into the values and beliefs of the audience in its theme of the basic human need for family and children, and therefore creates an emotional reaction by appealing to the reader's sense of empathy. Sui Sin Far's story has, in Robert Rowland's words, "narrative credibility" (2005, 145).[5] Her story is coherent to a certain degree. The action of the characters is consistent, which is reflected through the interactions between Minnie and Liu Kanghi and the attitudes of the whites toward the Chinese in the story. However, it is difficult to estimate whether the story is consistent with the reader's experience because not all readers had experience interacting with Chinese immigrants in the late nineteenth century. To the readers of her time, her story must have sounded quite different from the stories perpetuating stereotyped images of the Chinese told in the dominant discourses.

The difficulty in evaluating the story's narrative credibility, nevertheless, points to the rhetorical obstacles Sui Sin Far encountered in the late nineteenth-century in North America. The literary journals she wrote for were targeting an audience that expected to have its preconceived stereotypes about Asians confirmed rather than challenged in the stories it read, because such stories, as Elaine Kim notes, "provide literary rituals through which myths of racial supremacy are continually reaffirmed, to the everlasting detriment of the Asian" (1982, 20). Considering the rhetorical situation in which she wrote, it is small wonder that Sui Sin Far

5. Rowland uses "narrative credibility" to refer to whether a narrative is coherent in itself and consistent with the personal experience of an intended audience, which improves the narrative paradigm first developed by Walter Fisher. See Rowland and Strain 1994 and Fisher 1987.

would have to use character types and conventions from the mainstream discourse in order to disarm hostility and resistance. Take, for example, Minnie's account of James Carson as a "more ardent lover" than Liu Kanghi (1995, 78). To some scholars, this seems to be an orientalist description that conceives the Chinese man as inferior to the white man in terms of masculinity. The death of Liu Kanghi at the end of the story also seems to fall into a set pattern of the then- popular American fiction in which Chinese-Caucasian marriages often ended tragically. However, this kind of reading misses the intricacies of various social and political forces that constrained Sui Sin Far's writing. The brief description of James Carson's physique and the ending of the story may be deliberately designed by the author to appease the reader's appetite for stereotyped images and his/her concern about miscegenation. As Annette White-Parks observes, "these were mainly camouflage, under which the writer could slip in her message" (1995b, 116). I would further propose that in Sui Sin Far's text orientalism is a masquerade—a rhetorical strategy she employs to "support the fulcrum by which [s]he would move other opinions" (Burke 1962, 56). In other words, stereotyped images are used as a means of identification to change the audiences' attitudes, though this strategy involves yielding to the audience's opinions in some respects. In a culture characterized by a rigidly stratified racial hierarchy, to directly argue for egalitarianism would be fruitless, verging on disregarding the white supremacy that has been well constructed in the dominant discourse. Sui Sin Far was aware of these limits and took advantage of literary conventions and formulas, turning them into a rhetorical strategy to fulfill her own purpose. At a deeper level, her story is different from those in the mainstream discourses in that she puts Liu Kanghi at the center of her narrative and portrays him as a man with "great" soul, which is an unusually positive image of the Chinese at that time. Though the story ends with Liu's death caused by his own countrymen, her narration shows how racial prejudices devour innocent individuals in interracial marriages, thus appealing to the readers' sympathy to change their attitudes toward miscegenation. In this sense, Sui Sin Far's work challenged the stereotyped representations of Chinese Americans and went beyond, in Jeffrey Partridge's words, a literary Chinatown—"a community imagined by [European Americans]—for their own purposes and their own pleasures" (2007, ix).

Even more important, Sui Sin Far's employment of Standard Written English and the fact that her characters' development coincides in part with stereotyped images complicate Kenneth Burke's notion of identification. For Burke, identification is essential to persuasion. Creating identification entails the rhetor leading the audience to identify or be "consubstantial" with her. The rhetor can succeed in changing an audience's opinion only in one respect, and only insofar as she "yields to the audience's opinions in other respects" (1962, 55–56). In other words, the rhetor persuades members of her audience by building common ground with them, which may include origin, background, interests, shared experiences or attitudes. Although Burke's conception of identification provides a general guideline for analyzing rhetorical actions, it doesn't attend to the particularities of rhetoric's function or to what a rhetor from a marginalized social group has to do to achieve her purpose through identification. Sui Sin Far's mastery of Standard Written English and fluent prose did show her audiences that like them, she had a decent education, which might have won over some readers, though this gesture alone could hardly lead her audience, particularly Protestant white readers, to her side on such a sensitive issue in an extremely racist society.

Restricted by the larger social context and literary conventions, she had to resort to other strategies, particularly forms and character types within the genre of sentimental fiction or "Chinatown tales," to achieve her purpose.[6] In her texts, we can see how she uses the humanity of the major character Lui Kanghi to create identification between readers and character who, as humans, have similar needs for family and children. We can also see how she uses stereotyped images, the very form she intended to break through, to appease readers' appetite for exotica. The latter points to the delicate and complicated process through which a rhetor builds identification with her audience. Her employment of a literary form to identify with her audience so as to challenge the very idea embodied by the form can be viewed as an important way in which a rhetor uses identification to persuade her audience when caught in asymmetrical power relations. This innovative strategy, or what I call "forced identification," may lead to a persuasion subversively. In this sense, Sui Sin Far's work represents a special case of persuasion and sheds new light on the basic ways identification functions.[7]

6. Solberg 1981 categorizes Sui Sin Far's short stories as "Chinatown tales." Other literary scholars, such as Vanessa Holford Diana (2001) and Min Hyoung Song (2003), identify Sui Sin Far's stories as sentimental fiction, a genre employed by many American women writers in the nineteenth century.

7. For Kenneth Burke's discussion of identification, see Burke 1962, 21-24, 46, 55-56; 1966, 301; 1972, 28; and 1951, 203.

Another narrative feature—irony—is also a rhetorical strategy Sui Sin Far used to reach her audience in the late nineteenth and early twentieth centuries. In many of her stories, she adopts a strong ironic tone to speak against racism through her characters. In a short story titled "In the Land of the Free," Sui Sin Far writes against racist policies, particularly the Chinese Exclusion Act, through a strong ironic tone. The protagonists of the story are a little Chinese boy and his parents, who are separated by immigration officials just because the boy was born in China. Although the parents believe that "there cannot be any law that would keep a child from its mother," it takes almost a year for the "great Government" to clear the case (1995, 96–97). In the process, a white lawyer unscrupulously charges the parents over $500, an enormous figure at that time, to "hurry the Government" to bring the child back (99). When the boy is finally released, he has forgotten his Chinese name and cannot recognize his mother. The author casts immigration officials and the white lawyer as the antagonists who victimize Chinese immigrants, which again breaks the stereotypical expectations. In addition to detailed descriptions of the agonizing pain the separation causes the mother, Sui Sin Far uses irony as a rhetorical strategy to criticize racist policies.

An irony is built up through both the title and the plot of the story. The author's play with the word "free"—what the U.S. government professed and what a Chinese immigrant family discovered—incisively points to the fact that the government's practice was contradictory to its promise. Or in other words, this land is free only to certain people, depending on their racial identity. The parents' assumption that "there cannot be any law that would keep a child from its mother" and the ten-month separation from their child enhance the irony and reveal the dehumanizing nature of the racist policies, which appeals strongly to the rational side of the reader. The irony is further developed through the use of "the great Government" to refer to the U.S. government and a description of the legal document as "the precious paper which gave Hom Hing and his wife the right to the possession of their own son" (1995, 101). Through these descriptions, most readers of her time would have been able to detect the incongruity between the words and the author's intended meaning, or at least sympathize with the pain of the family. Thus, this seemingly casual and informative short story of a Chinese immigrant family is embedded with the author's political agenda, a rhetorical move not unfamiliar in Sui Sin Far's work. Sui Sin

Far's story illuminates the rhetorical function of irony. In other words, irony can be used as a logical proof to connect to the audience because it often exposes the illogical and contradictory aspects of human action. Further, her use of irony showcases the kind of rhetorical choices a writer has to make to deliver her message when writing within the constraints of unfavorable social and political conditions. During the time period in which she wrote, the irony Sui Sin Far used in her story would have been more effective in debunking racist policies than direct criticism.

Although Sui Sin Far's short stories are often categorized as sentimental fiction or "Chinatown tales," I view them as important articulations of her ideology, showcasing the way she dissipates the fear and misunderstanding that contribute to racial prejudice. If her characters bear traces of a certain orientalism, they are always used as a rhetorical strategy to circumvent social constraints against refuting racial stereotypes, thus reflecting the larger political ends of Sui Sin Far. Examining her stories in light of their antiracism aims, we can see that the rhetorical obstacles she encountered demanded that she use creative strategies to connect the reader to her characters, who are often designed to subvert stereotypical expectations.

LIVING AND WRITING "BETWEEN WORLDS"

During her rather short life, Sui Sin Far published two autobiographical essays, in 1909 and 1912. The essay that has brought the most attention from literary scholars is "Leaves from the Mental Portfolio of an Eurasian," in which she presents herself as a Chinese Eurasian and writes from an insider's viewpoint. The other essay, titled "Sui Sin Far, the Half Chinese Writer, Tells of Her Career," was published as a promotional piece for her book *Mrs. Spring Fragrance.* These essays offer an invaluable glimpse into Sui Sin Far's life as a writer and artist; written in a genre that blends truth and fiction, they enable her to express, in a more explicit way, her personal struggles in a racist society and her constant search for her identity. As the literary critic Janet Varner Gunn points out, autobiography is "a cultural act of self reading" done both by the autobiographer, who is "reading his or her life," and by the reader, who interacts with the text and finds his or her own meaning in the story of the author's life. Gunn also states that two-dimensional reading acts happen in the "autobiographical situation," which includes the author's impulse to write and respond to a problem, his/her perspective, and the reader's interpretation of the work (1982, 12–13). Thus, Gunn's conception of autobiography, though formed through the lens of literature, views the narrator in an autobiography as a rhetorical construction that conveys the author's intention and purpose. To appropriate Gunn's concept for a rhetorical perspective, I would say that autobiography as a genre enables the author to respond to both internal and external exigencies by telling a life story.[8] In other words, the author selects details and scenes from his/her life experiences to tell a story not only to express him/herself but also to influence the reader within a larger social and historical context. In this sense, Sui Sin Far's autobiographic writing can be seen as part of her rhetorical practices, showing the irrationality of the color line through a life story.

Though both autobiographic essays deserve an in-depth analysis, here I will focus on "Leaves from the Mental Portfolio of a Eurasian," a rather short but intense first-person narrative, structured as a series of vignettes out of memory in a more or less chronological order. In "Leaves," the narrator describes some selected life experiences with both white and Chinese communities, expressing her inner struggle as a child and later as an adult of Chinese and English heritage in the late nineteenth century. Dialogues and descriptions of the major incidents in her life provide a relentless account of an unbending, strong female whose external circumstances help shape her character, changing her from a naïve, vulnerable young girl to a woman who fought openly against racism. Faced with insulting, sometimes torturing treatment because of her identity as a biracial child—often being gazed upon, hooted at, beaten—the narrator does not so much overcome the events as internalize them to become more attuned to the pain and plight of Chinese people living in North America. Through reading, writing, and traveling, she works to immerse herself with the Chinese, and finally commits to defending the Chinese—her mother's people. In fact, to show her struggle and her determination, the narrator depicts a typical incident she experienced as a Chinese Eurasian. During a dinner the narrator

---

8. Janet Varner Gunn's conceptualization of "autobiographical situation" focuses more on the autobiographer's need to respond to an inner crisis that affects her own life and her desire to invite the reader to find a meaning in her life story. In terms of analyzing the rhetorical dimension of autobiography, Gunn's theory complements Lloyd Bitzer's (1968) concept of "rhetorical situation," which pays more attention to a crisis or an exigency in the outside world that prompts a rhetorical response. Here, I use Bitzer's term "exigency" to refer to crises the autobiographer faces in both her own life and the outside world, emphasizing her agency in reacting to a rhetorical situation.

attends in a "Middle West" town where she works as a stenographer, her employer casually mentions: "Somehow or other, . . . I cannot reconcile myself to the thought that the Chinese are humans like ourselves. They may have immortal souls, but their faces seem to be so utterly devoid of expression that I cannot help but doubt." A guest, the town clerk, echoes: "Souls, . . . Their bodies are enough for me. A Chinaman is, in my eyes, more repulsive than a nigger." Then her landlady declares: "I wouldn't have one in my house." The narrator records her inner struggle at this moment: "A miserable, cowardly feeling keeps me silent. . . . If I declare what I am, every person in the place will hear about it the next day. The population is in the main made up of working folks with strong prejudices against my mother's countrymen. The prospect before me is not an enviable one—if I speak. I have no longer an ambition to die at the stake of demonstrating the greatness and nobleness of the Chinese people" (1995, 224).

But instead of remaining silent, the narrator speaks out. When her employer asks, "What makes Miss Far so quiet?" she raises her eyes "with a great effort" and tells him: "Mr. K., . . . the Chinese people may have no souls, no expression on their faces, be altogether beyond the pale of civilization, but whatever they are, I want you to understand that I am—I am a Chinese" (1995, 225). The movement from being silent through fighting her fear to breaking silence and speaking out, in fact, becomes the narrator's primary mode of action. By speaking out, the narrator refuses to accept the humiliating remarks made by racist whites. Moreover, the narrator's action of speaking out allows her to articulate her thoughts and gives her power to persuade people that racism should be eliminated because it is wrong, unjust, and irrational. In other words, the narrator, given the cultural norms and racial prejudice she faces, feels that she has no choice but to break silence because speaking out is the only way to possibly change people's attitudes.

Throughout "Leaves," the narrator is in a constant search for an identity—one that resists any simplified or reduced representation. As a child, she feels bewildered and confused: "I do not confide in my father and mother. They would not understand. How could they? He is English, she is Chinese. I am different to both of them—a stranger, tho their own child" (1995, 222). As an adult, she straddles and struggles, pondering who she is. She writes: "When I am East, my heart is West, When I am West, my heart is East. Before long I hope to be in China. As my life began in my father's country it may end in my mother's. After all I have no nationality and am not anxious to claim any" (230). On the one hand, this expresses the narrator's feelings of being an exile, a rootless wanderer, and a lonely searcher caught "between worlds" (Ling 1990, 20). On the other hand, in refusing to claim any nationality, the narrator makes a symbolic move toward breaking down the color line—the racial and cultural hegemony that divided and discriminated people according to their skin color. What she searches for seems to be a multifaceted identity that is both Chinese and western, and that is ambivalent, contradictory, and ever-changing. She expresses such a tendency at the end of "Leaves": "I give my right hand to the Occidentals and my left to the Orientals, hoping that between them they will not utterly destroy the insignificant 'connecting link'" (230).

Sui Sin Far's narration of her life story suggests that she uses her life both as evidence of the ubiquity of racism in North America and as a demonstration of how an individual could react constructively to that racism. By describing the painful incidents she experienced both as a child and as an adult, she appeals to the emotional side of her dual audiences of both white readers and Chinese communities. Her background as a well-educated professional writer of fluent and eloquent prose would help her create identification in certain areas with her white middle-class audience, and consequently exert some influence upon it. Specifically, her courage and integrity as a human being and her literary talent would help her persuade her white readers, identifying her ways with theirs by using their language, gestures, and some shared cultural values. Actually, she mentions in "Leaves" that her employer apologized for making prejudiced remarks after she declared her Chinese heritage to the people at the dinner table in that small "Middle West" town. Yet, considering the extremely hostile racist backdrop against which Sui Sin Far wrote, it would be presumptuous to conclude that she could reach all her white audience. Her depiction of how she broke silence and confronted racism is rhetorically significant, for she models how a person from a marginalized group can resist social norms. Though faced with no small barrier in reaching out to the Chinese people, her painful life experiences and her rather explicit political stance would enable her to build common ground with the Chinese communities through a two-way identification in terms of fighting against essentialist racism. In other words, Sui Sin Far as an author uses her life experiences to identify with Chinese Americans, who in turn identify with her for both her personal struggle as a Chinese Eurasian and her courage to speak out.[9] This kind of identification would create a close union between her and Chinese communities. We can see this clearly in "Leaves" as Sui Sin Far records her sense of accomplishment: "My heart leaps for joy when I read one day an article by a New York Chinese in which he declares, 'The Chinese in America owe an everlasting debt of gratitude to Sui Sin Far for the bold stand she has taken in their defense'" (1995, 223).

As mentioned earlier, blending truth and fiction, the form of autobiography entails the author's selection and rearrangement of his/her life experiences to convey a particular message that is important to him/her. The narrator, as a rhetorical construction, enables the author to establish a public persona, which is often hidden in fiction, poetry, and other literary genres. In the case of "Leaves," Sui Sin Far effectively uses the form to achieve her purpose in this respect. Through her descriptions, we can see her struggle as well as her courage to defy racism. Despite her frequent confrontations with racial prejudice and discrimination, she retained her personal dignity and integrity. By showing how she struggled, and how she conquered her temptation to remain silent, Sui Sin Far builds up her public persona as a dignified speaker and writer who consistently seeks to break down the color line.

SPEAKING FOR THE SILENCED

Finally, I want to consider as part of her antiracism purposes and rhetorical practices Sui Sin Far's journalist articles, though these articles have been read largely as background material in analyses of her fiction. During her career as a writer, Sui Sin Far penned a large number of articles either to introduce Chinese communities to the wider public or to defend them at some difficult moments. I intend to look at her journalistic articles not as a background for her fiction or as a fully separate category, but as another equally important genre in which she speaks openly for Chinese people living in North America. In that light, they are rhetorically important and ideologically sound. Just as she believes she should use literature to break down racial prejudice, Sui Sin Far argues for the rights of the Chinese in her journalistic articles.

In the late nineteenth century, accompanying the anti-Chinese movement were news reports of the vices that Chinese immigrants brought to North America, which were used by the media to legitimize racial

9. Sui Sin Far's use of two-way identification further illuminates the ways in which identification functions; in this case, her writing is empowering, not only to herself but also to Chinese American communities.

discrimination against the Chinese. In response to the aggravated social abuse of Chinese immigrants in both Canada and the United States at that historical juncture, Sui Sin Far published a series of short sketches and reports about the life of Chinese immigrants, in which she often uses personal experiences, irony, comparisons, and other rhetorical strategies to achieve her political purposes.

Here, I will examine a journalistic article Sui Sin Far published in Canada. In 1882, the U.S. government passed the Chinese Exclusion Act to prevent Chinese from entering the country. Meanwhile, the Canadian government gradually increased head taxes on the Chinese. In 1896, there was a petition to impose a tax of $500 upon each Chinese entering Canada. To counter the charges against Chinese immigrants, Sui Sin Far published an article titled "A Plea for the Chinaman: A Correspondent's Argument in His Favor" in the *Montreal Daily Star* on September 21, 1896. In her article, which was composed as a letter to the editor of the newspaper, she argued against a Mr. Maxwell, the representative of a commission from British Columbia that was organizing the petition at the time.

She starts her letter by relating to the reader's basic values about how to treat other human beings: "Every just person must feel his or her sense of justice outraged by the attacks which are being made by public men upon the Chinese who come to this country. It is a shame because the persecutors have every weapon in their hands and the persecuted are defenseless." Obviously, she builds her argument on the assumption that it is unfair and unjust to abuse and attack human beings who are defenseless. Then she defines the major issue under discussion: "It is proposed to impose a tax of five hundred dollars upon every Chinaman coming into the Dominion of Canada" (1995, 192). She looks at the major charges the commission made against the Chinese and refutes them one by one. Disregarding the letter form, one may recognize an organization that is logical rather than chronological. She examines the grounds on which those charges against the Chinese were based and points out their illogical and immoral nature.

Sui Sin Far establishes her credibility as an author by bringing in her personal experience as a journalist who lived and worked with Chinese immigrants in their own communities in Montreal. She uses personal experiences and irony as her primary means of support; in fact, most of her claims are backed up by personal experiences combined with interpretative explanations. For example, countering the charge that the

Chinese are "immoral," she responds in the tone of a professional who knew the Chinese community very well: "They are mostly steady, healthy country boys from the Canto district. . . . They come here furnished with a modest sum of money and with the hope of adding thereto by honest labor" (1995, 195). Drawing on her personal experience to illustrate her point, she describes her visit to the Chinatown in New York, where she was received "by the Chinese . . . with the greatest kindness and courtesy," which disproves the warnings that "Chinatown was a dangerously wicked place" and if she went there she "would never come out alivc or sound in mind or body" (196). This indicates that she was conscious of the importance of credibility, especially in addressing a sensitive topic under such adverse conditions.

In addition to personal experiences, Sui Sin Far uses irony and comparisons to appeal to both the sentiments and the rational side of the reader. She mentions satirically that "Mr. Maxwell ought to be ashamed of himself" for sneering at the Chinese "for being docile and easily managed" because "a Chinaman . . . will stand for reason, but unless forced, though by no means a coward, he will not fight." Then, she further explains her point: "In China a man who unreasonably insults another has public opinion against him, whilst he who bears and despises the insult is respected. There are signs that in the future we in this country may attain to the high degree of civilization which the Chinese have reached, but for the present we are far away behind them in that respect" (1995, 195).

She develops an irony through juxtaposition of "civilization" and "barbarism"—the very terms Mr. Maxwell used to describe himself and his colleagues in relation to Chinese immigrants. By pointing out that this Mr. Maxwell actually knew nothing about China and its culture and that he and those of the same mentality who abused the Chinese shamelessly put the blame on their victims, she exposes the immorality and irrationality of their behavior. In addition, she uses her knowledge of the Chinese culture to challenge the accusers' assumption that only westerners contributed to the world civilization, which is a rather audacious action for her time.

She also employs comparisons to refute the charges against the Chinese. In debunking the hypocrisy of accusers' claim that the Chinaman "comes here to make money and with the intention of returning sooner or later," she writes: "In that he follows the example set him by the westerners; . . . The ports of China are full of foreign private adventurers.

After they have made their 'pile' they will return to their homes—which are not in China"(1995, 197). The comparison between what Chinese immigrants encountered in Canada and what westerners were doing in China further reveals the racist nature of those charges. These strategies are especially effective in the context of her letter because it is clear where she stands in relation to the issues under discussion. Unlike many of her early journalistic pieces carrying no byline, this letter is signed with the initials of her English name—Edith Eaton. This signature, together with her claim in the letter that "[i]t needs a Chinaman to stand up for a Chinese cause," shows her identity as both an insider and an outsider of the Chinese community, and therefore can be viewed as a rhetorical strategy Sui Sin Far used to enhance her credibility.

In her other journalistic articles that were published later, she committed herself to introducing Chinese communities as she perceived them to continue breaking down stereotypes. Her enthusiasm as a journalist and rhetor can be seen from titles such as "Chinatown Needs a School," "Chinese Workmen in America," and "The Chinese in America." Certainly, Sui Sin Far addressed the issue of racism repeatedly in her fiction and autobiography; the attitudes she conveys in her journalistic articles do not differ substantially from those she expressed in her literary writing. But the venue of journalism provided her with additional possibilities to communicate her ideas. While we can speculate about the rhetorical effects of her articles, we should bear in mind the obstacles she was facing in that dark era. Some readers might question or disregard her message simply because hers was different from those based on racist assumptions usually found in the media. However, Sui Sin Far's tone and persona are crucial to her effectiveness in responding to racism in her journalistic articles. As I have shown in the above analysis, sometimes she openly argues against racial discrimination with specific evidence and personal experiences, appealing to the rational side of the reader. Sometimes she reports events with an ironic tone, which often covertly touches and tests the foundations of the reader's values and beliefs. Though her journalism presented a lonely voice at the time, her rhetorical prowess would enable her to plant new ideas in people's minds.

CONCLUSION: CUTTING A PATH AT BORDERLANDS

In "Leaves from the Mental Portfolio of an Eurasian," Sui Sin Far wrote these words: "I believe that some day a great part of the world will be

Eurasian. I cheer myself with the thought that I am but a pioneer. A pioneer should glory in suffering" (1995, 224). Indeed, Sui Sin Far was a pioneer, personally and rhetorically. She was the daughter of a Chinese mother and an English father, who lived in England, Canada, and the United States. She did not marry. She worked and supported herself as a journalist, a stenographer, and a fiction writer. Though she could pass as a white, she chose to reveal her identity as a Chinese Eurasian, a splendidly dauntless move in her time. Above all, she had great talent and courage to break silencc and speak out for justice. As Elizabeth Ammons states, "That Sui Sin Far invented herself—created her own voice—out of such deep silencing and systematic racist repression was one of the triumphs of American literature at the turn of the century" (1982, 105). I would say that her achievement was also one of the triumphs in Asian American rhetoric.

Sui Sin Far contributed tremendously to the Asian/Chinese American rhetorical tradition. She was the earliest Chinese American writer who consciously used writing to fight against essentialist racism. Most significant among her contributions was the leading role she played in exposing the social abuses inflicted on Chinese people living in North America in the late nineteenth and early twentieth centuries. This is demonstrated by the short stories, autobiographical essays, journalistic articles, and other texts she has left behind. Writing, obviously, was a powerful weapon she used to battle against racial prejudice and discrimination.

Sui Fin Far was one of the earliest proponents of the cause of racial equality. In an era when racism was well constructed in the dominant social discourses and supported by a race theory that was based on pseudoscience, her idea that individuality is more important than nationality was far ahead of her time and incredibly contemporary. And her courage to openly express her idea regardless of danger and risk set up a model for people in Asian/Chinese communities. According to Annette White-Parks, in the fall of 1992, about three hundred Chinese Canadians fought to be reimbursed for the head tax that was imposed upon Chinese immigrants who entered Canada between 1885 and 1923. Many of the protesters carried with them a copy of Sui Sin Far's 1896 letter to the *Montreal Daily Star.*1995, 239). Saliently, Sui Sin Far's legacy still inspires and empowers her mother's people eighty years after her death.

Sui Sin Far's work illustrates the rhetorical choices Asian/Chinese Americans made (and make) in the Asian American rhetorical tradition under adverse social and political conditions. As a Chinese American writer, she was obliged to be particularly innovative because she faced obstacles unknown to white middle-class men. She was a rhetorical figure unique in rhetorical history because the central element of racial oppression was the silencing of her voice. Just like white and African American women rhetors who had to invoke a certain feminine style or appeal to biblical scriptures to speak for gender and racial equality during the nineteenth century (see Campbell 1989, 12–15), Sui Sin Far had to resort to various strategies including stereotyped images, irony, sarcasm, and personal experiences to reach her audiences. Her writing indicates that Asian/Chinese American writers can use literary genres and conventions rhetorically to resist and defy cultural norms when they have little access to political arenas. Sui Sin Far's rhetorical practices also reveal that the reshaping of literary genres, conventions, and character types can create rhetorical spaces where Asian/Chinese Americans are able to disseminate their ideology and have their voices heard.[10] In such a space, stereotyped characters, irony, sarcasm, personal experiences, accented language, incongruities, and tricksterism, to name a few, are all rhetorical strategies they can use to overcome social restrictions and break silence. Sui Sin Far's writing has directly or indirectly influenced Chinese American writers and rhetors of later generations. Some of her rhetorical moves can be found in the work of contemporary writers such as Maxine Hong Kingston, Gish Jen, and Shawn Wong. The connection between Sui Sin Far and contemporary Chinese American writers could serve as an important site for further rhetorical inquiry. Such inquiry would offer new insight into the rhetorical strategies Asian/Chinese American writers and rhetors used (and use) in their writing to resist and challenge the dominant discourse.

Her work also suggests that the ways identification functions inside the Asian/Chinese American rhetorical tradition complicate our understanding of the canonical conception of identification. While Kenneth Burke's notion of identification applies to the rhetorical actions of many rhetors, Sui Sin Far's use of stereotyped images, along with other narrative features to build identification with her dual audiences, certainly presents a particular way a writer from a marginalized social group induces identification. Her work shows that the canonical conceptions

---

10. Here I use the term "rhetorical space" to refer to the effect created through reshaping genres and textual features such as character type and format in a communicative event. For a detailed discussion of the concept of rhetorical space, see Mountford 2001, 41-71.

of certain rhetorical modes can be revisited and revised. Sui Sin Far's rhetorical practices exemplify the liberatory potentials of identification as a means to subvert cultural norms and interrogate power.

Though Sui Sin Far penned a large number of short stories and essays to fight against essentialist racism and speak for the Chinese Americans of her time, her name is almost forgotten. Not only she, but also many other accomplished Asian/Chinese American writers and rhetors, can hardly be found in anthologies of rhetoric. As we rebuild the canon and "remap rhetorical territory," in Cheryl Glenn's words, it is important that we include Asian American writers' work in dialogue with their historical, cultural, and social contexts and with writers and rhetors of other ethnicities (1997, 17). To do otherwise is to participate in the perpetuation of the values and beliefs that are silencing.

REFERENCES

Ammons, Elizabeth. 1982. *Conflicting Stories: American Women Writers at the Turn into the Twentieth Century.* New York: Oxford University Press.

Ammons, Elizabeth, and Annette White-Parks, eds. 1994. *Tricksterism in Turn-of-the-Century American Literature: A Multicultural Perspective.* Hanover, NH: University Press of New England.

Beauregard, Guy. 2002. Reclaiming Sui Sin Far. In *Re/Collecting Early Asian America: Essays in Cultural History,* edited by Josephine Lee, Imogene L. Lim, and Yuko Matsukawa. Philadelphia: Temple University Press.

Bitzer, Loyd F. 1968. The Rhetorical Situation. *Philosophy and Rhetoric* 1:1–14.

Burke, Kenneth. 1951. Rhetoric—Old and New. *Journal of General Education* 5:203.

———. 1962. *A Rhetoric of Motives.* Berkeley: University of California Press.

———. 1966. *Language as Symbolic Action: Essays on Life, Literature, and Method.* Berkely: University of California Press.

———. 1972 *Dramatism and Development.* Heinz Werner Series, vol. 6. Barre, Mass.: Clark University Press.

Campbell, Karlyn Kohrs. 1989. *Man Cannot Speak for Her: A Critical Study of Early Feminist Rhetoric.* New York: Praeger.

Chan, Frank, Jeffery Paul Chan, Lawson Fusao Inada, and Shawn Wong, eds.1991. *The Big AIIIEEEEE!: An Anthology of Chinese American and Japanese American Literature.* New York, NY: Meridan.

Chin, Frank, Jeffrey Chan, Lawson Inada, and Shawn Wong, eds. 1991. *AIIIEEEEE! An Anthology of Asian American Writers.* New York: Mentor. (Orig. pub. 1974.)

Diana, Vanessa Holford. 2001. Biracial/Bicultural Identity in the Writings of Sui Sin Far. *MELUS* 26 (2): 159–186.

Dong, Lorraine, and Marlon K. Hom. 1987. Defiance or Perpetuation: An Analysis of Characters in *Mrs. Spring Fragrance.* In *Chinese America: History and Perspectives,* edited by Him Mark Lai, Ruthanne Lum McCunn, and Jud Yung. San Francisco: Chinese Historical Society of America.

Fisher, Walter R. 1987. *Human Communication as Narration: Toward a Philosophy of Reason, Value, and Action.* Columbia: University of South Carolina Press.

Glenn, Cheryl. 1997. *Rhetoric Retold: Regendering the Tradition from Antiquity through the Renaissance.* Carbondale: Southern Illinois University Press.

Gunn, Janet Varner. 1982. *Autobiography: Toward a Poetics of Experience.* Philadelphia: University of Pennsylvania Press.

Kim, Elaine. 1982. *Asian American Literature: An Introduction to the Writings and Their Social Context.* Philadelphia: Temple University Press.

Li, Wenxin. 2004. Sui Sin Far and the Chinese American Canon: Toward a Post–Gender-Wars Discourse. *MELUS* 29 (3–4): 121–131.

Ling, Amy. 1983. Edith Eaton: Pioneer Chinamerican Writer and Feminist. *American Literary Realism* 16 (2): 287–298.

———. 1990. *Between Worlds: Women Writers of Chinese Ancestry.* New York: Pergamon.

Logan, Shirley Wilson. 1999. *"We Are Coming": The Persuasive Discourse of Nineteenth-Century Black Women.* Carbondale: Southern Illinois University Press.

Mountford, Roxanne. 2001. Gender and Rhetorical Spaces. *Rhetoric Society Quarterly.* 31 (1): 41–71.

Partridge, Jeffrey F. L. 2007. *Beyond Literary Chinatown.* Seattle: University of Washington Press.

Rowland, Robert C. 2005. The Narrative Perspective. In *The Art of Rhetorical Criticism.* edited by Jim A. Kuypers. Boston: Allyn and Bacon.

Rowland, Robert C., and Robert Strain. 1994. Social Function, Polysemy and Narrative-Dramatic Form: A Case Study of *Do the Right Thing. Communication Quarterly* 42:213–228.

Said, Edward W. 1979. *Orientalism.* New York: Vintage.

Solberg, S. E. 1981. Sui Sin Far/Edith Eaton: The First Chinese-American Fictionist. *MELUS* 8 (1): 27–39.

Song, Min Hyoung. 2003. Sentimentalism and Sui Sin Far. *Legacy* 20 (1–2): 134–152.

Sui, Sin Far.1995. *Mrs. Spring Fragrance and Other Writings.* eds. Amy Ling and Annette White-Parks. Urbana: University of Illinois Press.

White-Parks, Annette. 1995a. A Reversal of American Concepts of "Otherness" in Fiction by Sui Sin Far. *MELUS* 20 (1): 17–34.

———. 1995b. *Sui Sin Far/Edith Maude Eaton: A Literary Biography.* Urbana: University of Illinois Press.

Wu, William F. 1982. *The Yellow Peril: Chinese Americans in American Fiction, 1850–1940.* Hamden, CT: Archon.

Yin, Xiao-huang. 2000. *Chinese American Literature since the 1850s.* Urbana: University of Illinois Press.

12

MARGARET CHO, JAKE SHIMABUKURO, AND RHETORICS IN A MINOR KEY

Jeffrey Carroll

Whenever one tries to "territorialize" a rhetoric—whether it is Soviet, for example, or conservative or male—one is, at the same time, ineluctably tying to that territory a certain population of rhetors. One can imagine a "rhetoric machine" that could uncover the vernacular examples of rhetoric that we might associate—even divorced from context—with a certain collective, while missing or overlooking other rhetoric that is intentionally in the dominant mode. If we move this tentative assumption to a rhetoric of Asian America, then we should be able to discover those dominant modes that model for its users a rhetoric that is indistinguishable from its inspiration: the vast, standard medium and method of western argumentation that is, roughly speaking, the basis for a democratic approach to citizenry in America. The proprieties, in other words, are largely encoded in everyday discourse, decoded by the discourser, and forever attended to in civic or public functions.

To discover the deliberate deviation that a Russian formalist approach might yield is not necessarily enlightening as to specific racial characteristics—for *Asian* "is a vastly heterogeneous category that masks differences in ethnicity and social and economic status" (Lee and Bean 2002, 58)—but begins to separate the core from the margin, or the dominant from the minor. A contemporary example of the rhetoric of a racial entity, however loosely identified, is the recent immigration marches by millions of mostly Hispanic Americans, which were rhetorically effective simply as *performance* or, to use a term for the fifth canon of classical rhetoric, *delivery* (following invention, arrangement, style, and memory)—as bodies in motion with intentional effect, extralinguistical in the sense that the march itself is a forward-driving argument, like a collective fist-raising that followed much rhetoric of closed spaces with the enormous sculptural dance of a collective body. This mass gestural rhetoric, an enunciation of the collective, is at least as forceful as the words of the speakers, and recalls the words of Cicero, who writes that delivery is the "language of the body," "which displays the feelings of the soul" (2001, 294, 295). Quintilian would take the sense of the body's importance, beyond words, a step further; he argues that "the nature of the material we have composed in our minds is not so important as how we deliver it" (2001, 11.3.2) and references Cicero specifically in suggesting that delivery is action, citing Demosthenes, according to some the greatest orator of his time, as giving "the palm to delivery, and . . . second and third place as well" (11.3.5–6).

Yet the rhetoric of "mass gesture" is hardly assignable to any ethnic group; it is more a contingency open to all, and one that depends on a confluence of historical conditions and people who are in a position to respond. It is easier, often, to see the negative, and to derive from certain absences a rule or rules about those collectives that decline that act or functioning. One might begin, in response to the impressive collectivity of the immigration marches, by suggesting that Asian Americans do not *favor* public demonstration, even though there has been a public perception for centuries—as fantasy or Orientalist dream, it hardly matters—of an Asian "collectivity" of thought and behavior. Asian *American* demonstration—whether of the body or voice or both—is still largely unperceived by mainstream America.

It isn't in *protest* rhetoric, however, that we need to invest too exclusive an analysis. If we look at the mass media, a similar absence exists—and by mass media I refer to those contexts that allow for a full participation of the rhetor's identity: not by name alone, or by authorship, but by a material, bodily presence that does not allow for any easy avoidance by the audience of the rhetor's *Asianness.* Here the rhetorical is recaptured in classical or traditional terms involving the body, the gestural or elocutionary individual beyond the mere linguistical "tip" of the communication art. This is not to overlook the accomplishments of writers like Lois-Ann Yamanaka or Maxine Hong Kingston, but to look at popular culture's link to rhetoric as having a powerful, supplementary element of the gestural or performative.

If one accepts this stipulation, exemplars of Asian American rhetoric continue largely to elude popular perception. I am not so much interested in the Why? of this argument; rather, I want to assume the negative and argue that this cannot possibly be true to the pure degree that Zhou and Lee say it is (2004b, 17–19). I am not looking for "exceptions," as if a model minority of good Asian American rhetors exists somewhere in the mass media. There are, however, performers (or entertainers, to use a marketing term that is not necessarily pejorative but does locate its object in a context of pop culture) who have managed, against industry odds or racial odds, or both, to create a particular sense of the Asian American rhetorical position—a position that will be defined as these two performers' rhetoric is explored in this essay not as a way to exclude what is surely a complex of relations that exist between Asian American performers and their material and audience, but as a way to display a modality in that position that may, in fact, be a marker of what is possibly "Asian" about Asian American rhetoric in relation to the "American" of American rhetoric. One risks here a simple substitution of a binary for a unitary; if the latter is illusory, most likely the former is, too. But to begin with this double label is only a starting point for working further into the hidden complexities of cultural and social identities.

Such a complexity is hidden, for example, in our discussions of the English language—the definite article suggesting something fixed, stable, and unitary. But the language's users share the common knowledge of its being a supremely unstable medium, fluid in its textures, made up of dialects that work with and against each other in a jockeying of prestige and function. We can consider these territorial rhetorics of the Asian and the American in just such a way, with the purpose of understanding their use by individuals as a matter of rhetorical exigency.

The result may be what is a creolization of the two, as if dialects, in immediate and competitive contact—traces of both recognizable in the product—but a real instrument of communication that resists dissection or a binary analysis based on a mere conflicted double-voicedness. While creolization is associated most commonly with island cultures, like Jamaica and Hawai'i, we might extend the metaphor of islands to those performers who, in the very audiences they face (as well as in those communities from which they have sprung), seek identification with a new, organic identity, in the process of its own synthesis. Bhabha calls this process "how you negotiate between texts or cultures or practices in a situation of power imbalances in order to be able to see the way in which strategies of appropriation, revision, and iteration can produce possibilities for those who are less advantaged to be able to grasp in a moment of emergency, in the very process of the exchange or the negotiation, the advantage" (quoted in Olson and Worsham 1999, 39).

The performer's *intent to negotiate* is key here, because it is not so much an accident of contact—as in the fact of creole or pidgin—as a rhetorical strategizing, to turn one's disadvantage, or what Robert Young calls the "countersense of fragmentation and dispersion" (1995, 4), into a new synthesis. Bhabha insists that hybridity is about the subject who is "enunciatory" and "in performance and process," who is not working in a "politics of recognition" (Olson and Worsham 1999, 19). The identity *worked for*, then, is not an identity to be found but to be created anew, what Mao in his work on Chinese American rhetoric calls "promising because it represents a hybrid that serves to blur the boundary and to destabilize the binary between the dominant and the subordinated" (2006, 32).

Margaret Cho would be distressed, at least for the time it takes to deliver the next line, to be called the godmother of Asian American stand-up comedy. But her turning distress into pride is a feature of her comedy, a reverse self-deprecation that is characteristic of her work since her start in the early 1990s, the heart of which is a cold-eyed, hot-voiced look at inequality and prejudice that is overcome through a rhetoric of self-delineation and pride. Her stand-up work is raucous, hyperbolic, and explicit. Cho is so firmly canonized that her television series, a disaster by all accounts, both historic and contemporary, is hardly an asterisk in her long career of recordings and staged and filmed concerts. She remains, well into her second decade of public performance, virtually the only Asian American comic of any solid reputation or "draw," but one who has not opened up or begun a tradition the way one can clearly see, for example, Richard Pryor doing for African American comics—or Freddie Prinze for Hispanic American comics.

Cho's first video, *I'm the One That I Want*, a filmed 1990 concert from the Warfield in San Francisco, suggests a persona that has attracted an audience looking for laughs. (As an expectation, the comic effect is one most crudely drawn in terms of rhetorical consequences: none but the phenomena of the mouth opening and the peculiar sound of laughter erupting from it, with social commentary a somewhat nebulous secondary aim whose consequences are much harder to predict, let alone imagine.) Her audiences reflect a contemporary preference for a darkness of conditions out of which laughter can be worked. These conditions—or the field or situation that the audience itself feels a part of—are contemporary America, largely middle class, of mixed neighborhoods but an idealized, assumed, almost dystopian purity: a simplicity of ethnicity or race that allows for the dramatic conflict of a good story or tale, or episode, or song, or myth. Cho's Korean roots are shakily buried in San Francisco's famously confused hybridities in which, for example, Cho finds Koreans even meaner than whites, and where even her given name, Moran (pronounced "moron") is a joke for everyone to share and enjoy—even, in the reversal I noted above, as Cho turns the abuse into a self-anointing cry of individuality, of a process of negotiating a performer's solitude out of a solidarity with the audience's own insecurities.

Cho's comedy routines are really a panoply of prejudice, much of it about sexual identities and their everyday appearance in terms of work, dating, relationships, and marriage. In these routines Cho is not really acting out onstage anything particularly "Asian American," yet in her aloneness (or sovereignty) as an Asian American comic, she does appear in a kind of heroic pose (as she does in her posters and book and video covers, for *Revolution* and *Assassin*, especially, as a descendant of Che Guevara and Patty Hearst). Her "Asian Chicken Salad" performance in her film *Revolution* (2004) is a case in point: dressed in an antebellum gown of white, and barefoot, and with hair in a single braid, Cho delivers, even visually, a heterogeneous image of old, new, formal, informal, occidental and oriental fragments that are underscored through the comic recounting of a meal on an airplane that carries this sense of the confused dichotomy, of the contact dialect of modern American thought that is designed to undercut the simple binary of the contributing cultures, and to create a new emergent rhetoric of the hybrid. To the individual who admits that he cannot tell Asians apart, Cho responds, "Why do you have to tell us apart?" She adds, "*I* can't tell us apart," turning the confessional of the audience into an admission of similarity with it, a hint of identification with an audience of multiple kinds, multiple identities. After doing a comic series of Kim Jung-il's facial impressions, she remarks, "I forget I'm Asian," in contradiction to her sensitivity to that North Korean leader's visage somehow standing in for some implied insanity in the Korean heritage, or the West's perception of that heritage. The paradoxical acceptance of the face and its forgetting suggests a crisscross of competing valences, or pulls, leading to the explicitly linguistic play on "Asian Chicken Salad," a phrase spoken by a flight attendant until her Asian face requires the deletion of "Asian" when the dish is named in her presence. The deletion suggests the falsity of the label—or perhaps only its obviousness—when spoken to Cho, a gesture of simultaneous rejection and embrace by the voice of the attendant, a confusion when confronted by the factness of the Asian in view. But the burden of this emergent paradox of response is immediately taken up by the rhetor, by Cho, who does an uber-Chinese riff on the "oriental" mask, squatting and transforming her face into an "inscrutable" meditation upon the salad. Cho finally evaluates the object by saying, "This is not the salad of my people," in a hoarse and passionate whisper, adding "in my homeland" to drive home the absurdity of the artificial context of naming the authentic. She then caps the tirade by objecting to the absence of "crispy won ton crunchies"—a turn to the everyday English of foodstuffs that again undercuts any emerging gestalt around the impressive theatrics of this outraged Asian figure. She concludes, "That, my friend, is an Asian chicken salad!" with a delivered flourish of the imaginary sword across the body of the offending flight attendant. The syntax and delivery (the exaggerated movements of Cho's coup de grace) recall a cooking show, throwing once again the dialect of this hybrid rhetoric into a compelling spiral of influence, of a negotiated complexity that draws meaning out of its mixed parts, its awareness of those parts, and its comic undercutting of a fixed sense of center—much as the creoles of regions recall, like mimicry, but do not copy the master or standard tongue.

The move from the colloquial narratives of prejudice and humiliation to a working out of pride and inner strength is a rhetorical turn, and tradition, that is not unfamiliar to American audiences, although they will find this turn cast in very different language, and in very different place: for example, Abraham Lincoln's Gettysburg Address, which is, at its heart, the American story of hurt and renewal, or *The Autobiography of Malcolm X.* The "darkness" of the American imagination that I am conjoining here across centuries and discourses may, on the surface, seem tenuous, but Cho herself understands it. Her more recent performances—and the accompanying book with the echoes of another age, *I Have Chosen To Stay and Fight,* her concert recordings *Notorious C.H.O.* and *Revolution,* her blogging for the *Huffington Post* and her engagement with the daily ups and downs of a political race for president—are further condemnations of both self and nation in a kind of scorched-earth rhetoric of complete withdrawal from any position of safety, while at the same time suggesting a settled positionality of the clear-eyed compassionate. This, too, is not a unique or new attitude—Richard Pryor comes to mind and, yet earlier, Lenny Bruce—but Cho's racial content remains significant in her playing to mostly white audiences (who seem, as one listens to and watches reactions and responses, most appreciative of her material on gender and gender politics) who have far less knowledge of the Asian American experience than the African American experience, by which they are entertained almost daily on radio and television, in concert, and on recordings, especially through rap and hip-hop artists. Cho still charts very much alone, so that her routine on Hello Kitty artifacts—Kitty has no mouth—comes across as fresh and funny and countervalent to the whole ideology of the comedy of social critique. A perceived absence invites a filling of the vacuum, an infusion of language that will open the mouth, a dialect of contact—of the dominant and subordinate—emerging.

Cho's modulation to a minor key of the dominant comic rhetoric of the stand-up is to feature routinely her own humiliating experiences, to disappear within the persona of the classic American misfit model—but to imbue it, loudly and with a full physical repertoire that is against type: the quiet Asian American woman. This last turn, against one's own racial or cultural learning, is the turn from the collective to the individual that Cho uses to channel the familiar into her own emerging life, that processional Bhabha suggests is the performance itself, so that she can "fight" and "stand" and "change" by her own rules.

This "minor modulation" in Cho's comic rhetoric is "getting deeper into my own heart," for which the "getting" is a critiqued experience derived from a particular racial context that has few parallels, unless one wishes to consider the literary texts of authors like Amy Tan and Yamanaka. Cho's crypto-Marxist symbology of the last five years or so does suggest an interest more in class than race, but there is really no separating content when it is delivered in this rhetoric of lived experience as "my own quest for truth" (2005, 235), an expressive *and* purposeful rhetoric that has as much rage, outrage, and heroic purpose. Cho has conjoined the classic "double evil" of Cicero's "actors or day laborers" (2001, 10) as a kind of vulgar emotionality, a "grossness" that effectively seals up conventional identifications with traditional Asian rhetorics and opens instead a new world of contact with the language of comic performance rooted in the soil of the everyday.

Performance allows the artist to underscore the force of the word with the force of the body—or to guide an interpretation of it. Such interpretations, if so guided, become more a transparent argument, a rhetorical text, so that the performer's elocutionary talents can be brought to bear on what, on paper, might appear only despairing, or ironic, distanced in some way from the consequences of one's own stories. Stand-up is a one-person drama of the highest order, its practitioners rightly some of our favorite actor-performers. When this drama—this ability to hold and transport, to make an audience rapt with one's tales and analyses—is achieved by the Asian American performer, the minor modulation of a small collectivity of experience is recognized as sufficient for the whole to hear and recognize. The minor key of prejudice and humiliation is suddenly familiar to all. It speaks in a dialect, a creole of contact English that springs with rare power from a situation of rhetorical complexity: hybrid audiences looking to figures like Cho and Jake Shimabukuro for texts that speak these new complexities of surprise and exigencies.

Margaret Cho may be the most familiar of all living Asian American performers in America. Her commitment to social issues make her rhetoric especially felt, recognized, and accepted by mass audiences. In American music, however, there is no such figure. There are Asian musicians like Yo-Yo Ma and Keiko Matsui who are popular, and many American bands, Hiroshima, for example, have Asian American members, yet for the numbers of Asian American consumers, there is an astonishing dearth of Asian American performers of popular music, when other minorities like Hispanics and blacks have enormous presence. It is true that not all of this presence can be considered a rhetorical one, but in the broadest sense of rhetoric as the symbolic "formulations of reality" (Berlin 2003, 34) and its significance for designated audiences (through the industry, or marketing), this Asian American presence is remarkably small.

Why this is true is not so much the focus of this essay—although the success of Cho suggests that it has to do with the elements of performance that may not be common to Asian traditions of the ensemble and the mask: the solo, naked performer is as American as pie—yet is far less familiar to Asian performance traditions. *Musical* performance is an understood rhetoric when, for example, a folksinger performs an antiwar song. This is obvious—it is lyric, melody, voice, instrument, arrayed in real time by the performer in order to communicate anger or sadness and, at times, solution, as in the folk traditions of Guthrie, Seeger, and Dylan.

The performance is less obviously rhetorical the more it moves along a continuum into the instrumental (that is, when lyrics are absent there can be less linguistic content except in the sense of the "program" offered by titles or subheadings of the work, as in the movements of symphonies). All of popular music, however, can be considered at least partly rhetorical if one accepts the premise that popular music exists for the purpose of engendering a response, often collective, often unending, often combative—and always resulting in a social discourse about ourselves, or "uses of culture which are 'empowering,' which bring people together to change things" (Frith 1996, 20).

It isn't surprising to find so few Asian American voices in American popular music if one accepts the Cho analogy: Kitty has no mouth, and barely suggested hands. She cannot speak. She cannot play. Exceptions are present, of course: Mia Doi Todd, for example, is a Los Angeles–born singer-songwriter, Ivy League educated, who has been recording and performing songs with Asian allusions for years. And as soon as one mentions a Todd, a greater presence does rise up in view—Vienna Teng, for example, James Iha, Jin Ah-Yeung, Amerie—all, however, with a status somewhat better than "cult," a potent status for any performer, yet pointing again to the near invisibility of Asian American music in popular form, and suggesting a difficult career arc.

Jake Shimabukuro is remarkable for his instrumental performances and recordings without vocals (which place him in a small circle that would include silent virtuosi like Bela Fleck in jazz and bluegrass, or Jerry Douglas in bluegrass, or Derek Trucks in blues); he is a Japanese American who, as he turns thirty, finds himself the world's greatest virtuoso of a stringed instrument, the 'ukulele, which is itself a model of hyphenation: Portuguese in origin, yet thoroughly assimilated into Hawaiian music and made popular in the greater world of pop culture by two disparate men two generations apart and a world apart in place and values: Arthur Godfrey (on television in the 1950s) and George Harrison (who would not travel without one). Shimabukuro took up the 'ukulele when, he says, he found he couldn't play sports in high school (although he wrestled) (Tsai 2006, D1). In fifteen years he has recorded a half dozen albums, performed around the world, and earned the repeated accolade of being the Jimi Hendrix of the 'ukulele.

Unlike Cho, Shimabukuro has never achieved anything like star status except in his home state of Hawai'i, where the 'ukulele has a special place in the local culture, rather like the banjo or mandolin in the mountain music of the southeastern United States. His "star" quality at home is based very much on his being a virtuoso on the instrument, meaning not that he plays *like* Jimi Hendrix, but that he has taken the instrument far beyond where it had been taken before by moving it into genres like jazz, bluegrass, smooth jazz, rock, and blues, so that the genre conventions associated with those fields (and the audience expectations in performance context) are met in such a way as to enlarge the visual "slightness" of the instrument—and, metonymically, the performer himself—into a sound of utter freedom, possibility, and unexpected communication.

In these ways he is like Cho in that he has not so much enlarged a tradition but taken it and critiqued it, intentionally toying with audience expectations of propriety (the good Korean girl, the good Japanese boy) and then, through a virtuosity of voice, either natural or instrumental, shown a total command of the American *amplitude*: its freedoms of speech. This is a creole that is a generation beyond pidgin, or the accident of contact, becoming a legitimate language of the hybrid, working a sense of rigor, rules, and the technique of the virtuoso. His repertoire is eclectic, ranging from Irving Berlin's "God Bless America" (Shimabukuro 2002a) to a Paganini *Caprice* (2002b) to George Harrison's "While My Guitar Gently Weeps" (2004). He performs these particular pieces with solemn tempi and little playfulness; the Berlin piece is especially striking in its extended, nearly five-minute treatment of a Kate Smith specialty associated with flag waving and saluting. The classical piece, like the first, seems to try to establish an ascendancy for the instrument, putting it in the circle of human voice and piano. The latter piece is a tribute to George Harrison, a lover of the 'ukulele, but whose piece is specifically about the guitar, a register and timbre that Shimabukuro subverts, or at the very least transforms, into the 'ukulele's trebly range—again as a rhetoric of changing the key if not the melody while retaining a formal rigor.

Shimabukuro's stage presence is ebullient, demonstrative—in short, physical in a way that, if not recalling Cho's love of the spotlight, shares with Cho an understanding of the need to be gestural as well as linguistical. Shimabukuro does play his instrument like a guitar—he cradles, dotes upon, and displays it—while acknowledging the audience's expectations: the occasional pretty strum, simple chording, and melodic familiarity. Built around, or upon, this formal base is a wildly imaginative enlargement of the instrument's possibilities, moving its rhythmic and melodic features into the realms of improvisation, a feature that may draw Shimabukuro close to the stand-up routines of Cho.

While improvisation is a keystone of jazz performance, it has also a strong traditional presence in comic performance, especially stand-up, in that it appears, or sounds, spontaneous, and is unforeseen. It takes from the audience's knowledge of music and song and gives it back, "improv"-ed and, as expected, improved because of "instantaneous decision-making in applying and altering musical materials and conceiving new ideas. Players distinguish such operations during solos from the recall and performance of precomposed ideas, those formulated outside the current event in the practice room or in a previous performance. From this standpoint, unique features of interpretation, embellishment, and variation, when conceived in performance, can also be regarded theoretically as improvised" (Berliner 1994, 221–222).

Improvisation is a rhetorical gesture meant to throw off, while simultaneously acknowledging, the past, the expected, and to underline the momentousness, the "now" of the act of communication, fresh and deliberate in the moment in this place, between you and me, a moment of the creolization of musical language, not only as the audience understands it, but as the rhetor shapes a performance out of a repertoire of gestural and extralinguistical choices that will suggest, performance to performance, that "endless and excessive transformation of the subject positions possible within the hybridised" (Griffiths 1995, 241).

From this severe sampling of Asian American performance, one is hesitant to draw any generalizations about millions, but one can venture to assert that a rhetoric that both acknowledges and critiques tradition, one that is identified with one's very body and voice (or its instrumental surrogate), is interested in a self-revealing individuality and pride. There is always that: the individual speaking to many, a classical concept that elides modern understandings of self, so that Cho and Shimabukuro, if they were to speak to each other, might see many in one, in fact: these hybrid presentations of many roots, voices, techniques, and purposes that are emerging formulae for finding meaning in these times.

What is "minor" modulation in Cho is the descent into a nightmare of identity politics as she negotiates her way out of a tangle of Korean roots so that she can literally feel them and use them as a key to mastering them, or at the least interrogating their presence, their hold on her thinking and feeling. For Shimabukuro, a modulation into specific Asian musical performance is more subtle, since he stands before (and behind) a tradition of western music and uses the 'ukulele to voice this modulation, this sense of the hybrid musical voice (rather than, for example, a thoroughly Asian musical tradition like the *shakuhachi* or the *koto*). Shimabukuro gives us a transparent example with his composition, and performance, of "Ehime Maru" (2001).

This solo piece for 'ukulele was composed in response to the sinking of the Japanese training vessel the *Ehime Maru* by the USS Greeneville, a U.S. Navy submarine off the coast of Hawai'i in February of 2001. It was performed a month later by Shimabukuro for the families of the survivors of the nine men who were lost in the accident: "The song is meant to give the listener insight of what it must have felt like to be aboard the fishing ship during the tragic accident. The song is based on 'minor add 9' chords to represent the missing four students, two teachers, and three crewmen. It begins subtle and unsuspecting, then transcends to an intense middle section. As the song progresses, the intensity grows symbolizing the crashing of the two vessels, the chaos and confusion before coming to a climactic halt. The final section of the song includes subdued tension becoming very melancholy to symbolize the unfortunate fate of the *Ehime Maru*" (Shimabukuro 2001, liner notes).

While "program music" such as this is a western as well as an Eastern tradition, what is most strikingly rhetorical about its initial *performance* is that Shimabukuro kneels directly in front of the survivors' families, and plays it solo with head bowed. The posture is associated with Asian traditions. One doesn't *see* this in the recorded performance on compact disc (offered as a gift to the families, and also marketed to raise funds for them), but the specificity of the program is also surprising: the retelling of the accident is, for western observers, a far cry from the western rhetorical eulogy that typically employs devices of past exploits, triumph, glories, and lasting legacies—in short, an avoidance of the actual demise of the eulogy's subjects. Also, the "minor add 9" chords are, for a layperson, probably unidentifiable, but Shimabukuro, a virtuoso musician, has chosen them to indicate how the language of music can itself hold figures, a rhetorical force, that transcend themselves: the ninth note, the nine men. The interval created by the addition of this note "can produce chords of startling beauty, especially on the guitar" (Denyer 2001, 130).

That startle is the audience's gift to the performer—a bodily response, unreflective, whether from tragic or comic thrust: what one can see and hear with accomplished performers like Cho and Shimabukuro, an "unforeseenness" that is anticipated and yet unknown, the modulation from the key we know, from that of convention, the usual voice of the traditional voicings, to the sudden relocation to the unseen roots of a San Francisco childhood, or death in American waters. The rhetor turns a compassionate yet unflinching eye upon the self, the event, the audience, and does not give it only an aesthetic gloss (but which virtuosi in voice and instrument can do) but an unforeseen immediacy, an improvised integration of the public and the personal, in which, in Bhabha's words, is not recognition but surprise and "a moment of emergency." It may be in this ability, and this need, to modulate from the major to the minor, from the standard to the dialect of hybridity, that Asian American rhetoric finds its beauty and strength.

REFERENCES

Berlin, James. 2003. *Rhetorics, Poetics, and Cultures: Refiguring College English Studies.* Lafayette, IN: Parlor.

Berliner, Jay. 1994. *Thinking in Jazz: The Infinite Art of Improvisation.* Chicago: University of Chicago Press.

Cho, Margaret. 2001. *I'm the One That I Want.* Directed by Lionel Coleman. New York: Winstar TV and Video.

———. 2004. *Revolution.* Directed by Lorene Machado. New York: Wellspring.

———. 2005. *I Have Chosen to Stay and Fight.* New York: Riverhead.

Cicero. 2001. *On the Ideal Orator.* Translated by James M. May and Jakob Wisse. New York: Oxford University Press.

Denyer, Ralph. 2001. *The Guitar Handbook.* New York: Knopf.

Frith, Simon. 1996. *Performing Rites: On the Value of Popular Music.* Cambridge, MA: Harvard University Press.

Griffiths, Gareth. 1995. The Myth of Authenticity. In *The Post-colonial Studies Reader,* edited by Bill Ashcroft, Gareth Griffiths, and Helen Tiffin. New York: Routledge.

Lee, Jennifer, and Frank D. Bean. 2004. Intermarriage and Multiracial Identification: The Asian American Experience and Implications for Changing Color Lines. In Zhou and Lee 2004a.

Mao, LuMing. 2006. *Reading Chinese Fortune Cookie: The Making of Chinese American Rhetoric.* Logan: Utah State University Press.

Olson, Gary, and Lynn Worsham, eds. 1999. *Race, Rhetoric and the Postcolonial.* Albany: State University Press of New York.

Quintilian. 2001. *The Orator's Education.* Translated by Donald Russell. Cambridge, MA: Harvard University Press.

Shimabukuro, Jake. 2001. Ehime Maru. In *Ehime Maru.* Four Strings Records FSCDS 7492.

———. 2002a. God Bless America. In *The Art of the Solo 'Ukulele.* Tradex Records 1.

———. 2002b. Selections from Caprice no. 24. In *Sunday Morning.* Four Strings Records FSCDS 7493.

———. 2004. While My Guitar Gently Weeps. In *Walking Down Rainhill.* Hitchhike Records HRCD 1103.

Tsai, Michael. 2006. Jake Shimabukuro Slows Down the Pace. *Honolulu Advertiser,* July 16, D6, D8.

Young, Robert. 1995. *Colonial Desire: Hybridity in Theory, Culture, and Race.* New York: Routledge.

Zhou, Min and Jennifer Lee, eds. 2004a. *Asian American Youth: Culture, Identity, and Ethnicity.* New York: Routledge.

———. 2004b. Introduction: The Making of Culture, Identity, and Ethnicity among Asian American Youth. In Zhou and Lee 2004a.

13

"MAYBE I COULD PLAY A HOOKER IN SOMETHING!"

Asian American Identity, Gender, and Comedy in the Rhetoric of Margaret Cho

Michaela D. E. Meyer

> *The genius of Margaret Cho, like Lenny Bruce, Richard Pryor and Robin Williams before her, is that she has turned the world into her own personal psychotherapist. Cho gets paid for telling audiences what mere mortals have to pay their shrinks to listen to.*
>
> James Verniere

Following her first film, *I'm the One That I Want*, Margaret Cho and director Lorene Machado filmed Cho's second major motion picture, *Notorious C.H.O.*, in November of 2001. The film grossed more than $1 million at the box office within six months of its release on June 28, 2002, and grossed more in its video release. In Cho's ninety-minute stand-up, monologue performance, she explores the tragedy of 9/11, racism, women's issues, sexuality, and self-esteem. Cho's rhetorical subtext challenges dominant ideological constructs that proliferate racial, ethnic, and sexual oppression in American society. As an Asian American rhetorical figure, Margaret Cho is worthy of scholarly attention because she is rather open about her intention in creating her one-woman shows. Not only has she been quoted in numerous interviews as trying to change the standards for Asian Americans in the entertainment industry, she incorporates her stance on contemporary social issues throughout her performance. She offers a serious cultural critique of the representations of Asians and women in popular media, as well as comments on various social and political issues.

As she is a rhetor and cultural critic, Cho's high degree of polysemy presents an interesting rhetorical case study. In the late 1980s and early 1990s, communication scholars demanded a recognition of "the potential for polysemic rather than monosemic interpretation" of rhetorical texts (McKerrow 1989). Leah Ceccarelli (1998) situated discussions and uses of polysemy by identifying three types of polysemic interpretation: resistive readings, hermeneutic depth, and strategic ambiguity. Ceccarelli defines strategic ambiguity as "a form of polysemy [that] is likely to be planned by the author and result in two or more otherwise conflicting groups of readers converging in praise of a text." In other words, when rhetorical texts can contain multiple meanings for different types of audiences, the ambiguity of meaning is controlled primarily by the author. In this type of polysemic interpretation, "the power over textual signification remains with the author, who inserts *both* meanings into the text and benefits economically from the polysemic interpretation" (404).

As a result, rhetorical and media studies scholarship interested in strategic ambiguity often focuses on the political economy surrounding the marketing of mediated texts. For example, Naomi Rockler (2001) examines the use of strategic ambiguity in the film *Fried Green Tomatoes,* finding that the film transforms a fairly unambiguous lesbian relationship into a relationship that can be defined by different viewers as either a lesbian relationship or a close female friendship. Ultimately, the film became an economic success because heterosexual audiences could define the relationship between the protagonists as friendship. Similarly, Sut Jhally and Justin Lewis (1992) read *The Cosby Show* as strategically ambiguous because viewers could define the Huxtables from multiple standpoints. The show was economically successful because white viewers could define the family as financially well off, while black viewers could define the text as a statement on race relations. These kinds of studies have illuminated the intersections among rhetor, audience, and economics in mediated texts.

For the purpose of this chapter, I examine strategic ambiguity within the text of Cho's performance rather than from the standpoint of political economy. I argue that Cho's unique position as an Asian American, queer, female allows her a certain rhetorical voice on issues of race, class, and sexuality. By offering an analysis of Cho's performance in *Notorious C.H.O.* from both "western" and "Eastern" rhetorical perspectives, I illustrate unique features of marginal rhetoric and provide implications for future rhetors. Most importantly, Cho's identity is malleable as part of the comedic rhetorical situation, and as a result, her rhetoric offers us the ability to think of women's rhetorical strategy as *intentional* rather than simply a strategic function of mediated political economy.

READING MARGARET CHO FROM A "WESTERN" PERSPECTIVE.

To a critic schooled in western rhetoric, one interpretation of *Notorious C.H.O.* is that Cho is acting from her Asian identity to provide a critique of racism in America. First and foremost, she challenges the binary associated with her Asian identity in an American context. While Cho's physical appearance is stereotypically Asian—she has dark black hair, small brown eyes, and a facial composition that is East Asian in orientation—she establishes early in her film that she views herself as American. She explains that she was rejected by the entertainment industry at first because, as one agent told her, "Asian people will never be successful in entertainment." Cho's critiques of the entertainment industry stem from her own early experiences in television. In her earlier film, *I'm the One That I Want,* Cho interrogates her experiences in the maligned and woefully mishandled ABC sitcom *All American Girl* in the mid-1990s. Media executives were unfamiliar with how to market an Asian American female as a lead character and thus forced Cho to lose weight and manage her identity in a manner more consistent with mainstream white actresses. When the show was cancelled, Cho lost her identity, drowning in a pool of drugs, alcohol, and promiscuity. As a result of her experiences and her identity searching, Cho's found that her Asian heritage could be a powerful tool for devising an argument about her subject position as created by mainstream American media. She claims, "I never saw an Asian on television or in the movies, so my dreams were somewhat limited. I would dream maybe someday I could be an extra on *M*A*S*H.* Maybe someday I can play Arnold's girlfriend on Happy Days. Maybe I could play a hooker in something. I would look in the mirror and practice 'me love you longtime.'"

Cho's emphasis on race in this passage illustrates how the lack of representation of Asian American women in the entertainment industry stunted her ability to envision herself in anything other than very limited roles. Similarly, Nayda Terkildsen and David Damore (1999) posit that racialized representations in the media, both visual and written, provide the viewing audience with powerful cues for identity formation, particularly when marginalized ethnic groups are rarely represented in a positive manner in mainstream media. Furthermore, the passage explains how Cho's girlhood dreams are racialized by providing her with a binary option—emulate white roles that are inaccessible to her or fulfill the stereotypical Asian roles that society deems fit for her (hooks 1996; Orbe and Hopson 2002). Instead of accepting this binary, she immediately shifts out of the narrative by commenting that "I'm fucking American!" This statement specifically challenges the binary associations that are placed on Cho's multiple identities—Asian *and* American. In essence, she does not understand why both identities cannot exist simultaneously. In an interview about the film she comments, "There are so few Asian Americans being presented in the media and the ones that are, are placed under so much scrutiny . . . it's not politically correct to say this, but why does a Korean have to play a Korean? In the mainstream world, an actor of English descent can play someone who is Irish, and there are all kinds of conflicts between those two identities, but it's okay. I think that minority performers are held to a higher standard" (Herren 2001).

Cho's arguments mimic scholar Chris Berry (2001), who argues that minority representations in media are often created without family context, and as a result depict minority group members as "loners without kinship ties of any kind." In other words, Asian actors are often cast as Asian characters amid the white American cultural standard. However, Cho's argument about white actors, while valid in pointing out that minority actors are often more heavily scrutinized than white actors, fails to recognize that Asian actors are typecast across identity barriers almost as often as white actors. While white actors can cross identities among British, Irish, and other European identities, recent casting decisions in Hollywood suggest that Asian actors can play any Asian role—Japanese, Chinese, Korean, Taiwanese—without addressing the potential conflict between those identities. For example, the casting of Chinese actress Ziyi Zhang as a Japanese geisha in *Memoirs of a Geisha* caused controversy given the historical relations between Japan and China, yet the fact that Zhang was at least "representative" of Asia allowed the studio to produce the film successfully. Although this certainly does not address the issues of visibility inherent in Asian American representation in media, it does serve to illustrate that the political economy of entertainment media is reductionist with regard to racial and ethnic identity.

Cho seems to embrace these challenges, however, by embracing her Asian American identity and using it to expose problems she perceives as important to the Asian American community. The film begins with a cartoon challenging stereotypes of Asian and blacks. The skit is based on physical stereotypes such as overemphasized lips, cornrows, slanted eyes, and broken English. The setting is a small market owned by a

Korean woman. A black man comes into the store, and their encounter displays mistrust in their interaction. The scene includes drawing guns, live bombs, and cannons on one another. A moment later, we see them in group therapy, where they engage in words that reveal the larger issues of representation: the black man calls the Korean woman a "broke-down, slanty-eyed, Ching-Chong ho!" and the Korean woman sarcastically criticizes the black man for using too many words to insult her and includes the message "Korean people and black people don't get along. This needs to end right now!" Using this kind of skit opens up space for Cho not only to deconstruct misrepresentations of blacks and Koreans in general but also to draw attention to a particular kind of intergroup struggle in America. Scholarly research exploring interactions between black and Asian cultures in America has shown that these groups entered into competition in order to make societal gains that would elevate them in the social hierarchy (Brah 2000). Historically, Korean immigration in the 1980s displaced many urban black communities, contributing to the hostility between the two ethnic groups (Waldinger 1999), and was further confounded by the possessive investment in whiteness that American culture espouses (Lipsitz 2000). Thus, Cho recognizes that even economically oppressed groups engage in contributing to the reproduction of patriarchal ideologies—it is not simply an issue of political economy restricting access to the means of cultural production.

Cho further complicates the audience's perception of race and ethnicity by presenting a segment on September 11. Within this discussion, she pushes the envelope by indirectly focusing on the relations between East and West: "It's been an interesting time for our country, a very tragic time, a very difficult time. These last several months have certainly been very hard. I've been to New York a lot, and I actually got a chance to go down to Ground Zero. And I was there day after day giving blow jobs to the rescue workers . . . Yeah . . . Because we all have to do our part." Cho's attempt at humor here could be considered morally reprehensible in the wake of such tragedy, but Cho quickly defends her comic choice by adamantly refusing to be terrorized. Cho's linking of Ground Zero to sexual acts transports cultural critics back to the wars in both Korea and Vietnam. In these wars, terrorist acts, including the rape and murder of women in these countries, occurred conjointly with conflict between the East and West (see Chalk 1998; Hyun 2001; Matsui 2001). Considering this history, one must ask whether Cho's link between war and sex was meant to be a political statement on the mistreatment of Asian women during periods of war? Scholars note that media representations of Asian women as prostitutes are prolific, and that this practice "perpetuates a colonial group fantasy, in which the Asian woman embodies 'service,' especially for the white man" (Ling 1999). Cho's use of this stereotype is then transformed into several arguments. First, after her commentary about going to Ground Zero, she justifies her (hypothetical) sexual action by saying "because we all have to do our part" and then argues strongly against the victimization mentality propagated by terrorism. Thus, by using the term "we," along with an earlier reference in the monologue to "our country," she creates a sense of patriotism and American identity in the face of terrorist acts. Moreover, she later returns to this stereotype of Asian women as prostitutes to discuss Asian representation in American media. She discusses the fact that while she was growing up, she thought "maybe I could play a hooker in something," but then uses this observation to critique the entertainment industry. Before one can question her intent, she again boldly declares, "I am an American!" Just as the audience recognizes the positioning of herself as Asian, she quickly repositions herself as American. Thus, her "playfulness" with her own identity allows her access to rhetorical options that would perhaps fall flat if utilized by white comediennes.

Similarly, in the example of the cartoon, Cho utilizes stereotypes of black men and Korean women to further the argument that ethnic groups should be uniting against common oppressors rather than struggling with one another. During the skit, Cho frequently interrupts the narrative with a voice-over that provides a kind of flashback that allows the characters to play the interaction over again. Each time the interaction is replayed, it is resolved a way that dispels the traditional stereotypes of blacks and Koreans. Obviously, Cho uses these stereotypes in a transformative way to critique the dominant ideological structure. Therefore, Cho's conscientious use of strategic ambiguity allows her to create a space from which to critique the structure of racism in American society, and invites audience members to share in this critical thinking process.

READING MARGARET CHO FROM AN "EASTERN" PERSPECTIVE.

An important component of the polysemic nature of a rhetorical text is the ability of the text to convey multiple meanings simultaneously. While a western critic can read Margaret Cho as a statement on racial discourse in the United States, there is an Eastern alternative for reading her rhetoric. On stage Cho is American culture: she speaks fluent English without an Asian accent, she talks about the social phenomena of race relations, gender identity, and sexuality in the United States, and screams that she is "fucking American!" In other words, while American audiences might view her as speaking from an Asian perspective, she is not necessarily representative of Asian culture. She violates the expectations and norms associated with Asian identity, thus making her rhetoric appealing to both western and Eastern audiences.

For western audiences Cho might be "Other" (hooks 1992) simply because she looks Asian. However, Cho's knowledge and experience within American society, coupled with fluency in a language familiar to western audiences, simultaneously positions Cho as both insider and outsider. For Asian audiences, this same standard applies. Cho's ethnic identity may make her part of the Asian group, yet her performance is potentially foreign to Asian culture. Thus, in many ways she is not Asian. Instead of claiming either Asian or American identity as primary, she rejects the binary definitions of what it means to be Asian and American. From an Eastern perspective, the people of Asia have often been viewed as a cultural entity offered up in ratings by the European colonial community (Foss, Foss, and Griffin 1999). Moreover, postcolonial theory stresses that Asian women in western subjectivities are often used as exotic images constructed for the imperial gaze and ultimate conquering. Therefore, cultural representations of Asian women often construct them as oppressed victims in racialized patriarchal structures. Even in feminist studies, western feminists tend to legitimize an implicit western agenda of white feminists "saving" their non-western, nonwhite sisters (Ling 1999). Cho, however, situates herself in between the extreme of westernized domination and Asian subjectivity, thus disrupting the western gaze (Minh-ha 1991).

For example, Asian women have been traditionally stereotyped as diminutive and passive. As a result, Asian women have historically been robbed of voice. Cho's performance challenges these traditional Asian stereotypes, because she uses her voice to critique western ideologies. Cho is also larger than Asian women "should be," but she uses her size as a way to disrupt the colonizing gaze. She wears clothing that is too small for her, talks about herself as part of a "chubby gang," and criticizes western culture for continually emphasizing thinness as a prerequisite for beauty. Scholars Katherine Frith, Ping Shaw, and Hong

Cheng (2005) conducted an analysis of advertisements for women's beauty products in both the United States and Asia, ultimately finding that Asian advertisements contained a large proportion of cosmetics and facial beauty products whereas American advertisements were dominated by clothing. Their findings suggest that female beauty in America may be constructed more in terms of "the body," or physical weight, whereas in Singapore and Taiwan the defining beauty factor for women is a "pretty face." Applying these finding to Cho, her Asian body, coupled with American social mores, becomes a rhetorical site of embodiment, opening a space for discourse. As Raymie McKerrow (1998, 319) observes, individual "bodies are trapped inside cultures, and exhibit those acts promoted within the culture," which ultimately allows or prohibits our ability to know the "Other" in an embodied, corporeal way. Thus, Cho exercises a unique "cultural rhetoric" in her everyday performances.

Cho further uses an Eastern style to critique western cultures' claims to intellectual superiority. In one passage, Cho describes a conversation with her mother about gay people. She recounts, "I always thought my mother was conservative but she had a really interesting attitude toward gays: *Because, I think everybody a little bit gay. You know, if you have a friend and you like your friend so much you don't know what to do, that's kind of gay.*" When Cho speaks as her mother (italics), she employs an "Asian" accent and does not use her fluent English. She also uses her facial expressions to convey a stereotype of Asian women with slanted eyes. This particular example deals with the representation of Cho's mother, a stereotype premised on the representation of Asian women as unintelligible when given voice. In essence, Cho positions herself as American by contrasting her position with her mother, who becomes the typical "Asian woman." Just as the audience is associating Cho with Asian ideologies, she redirects the narrative to position herself as an American in relation to her conservative Asian mother. This move, however, is still a subversive strategy. From a postcolonial perspective, western people tend to think about Eastern countries as noncivilized, barbaric societies (Gandhi 1998), and Cho's commentary about her mother thinking everyone is "a little bit gay" resists colonial ideology. Cho's characterization of her mother is stereotypically Asian, yet her mother is portrayed as more open-minded than contemporary western culture regarding homosexuality. Thus, the portrayal depicted by Cho is one that privileges *Asian cultures* as more sophisticated and intelligent than western cultures. In essence, she is able to renegotiate stereotypes of Asian women by repositioning them as individuals capable of critiquing social domination. Similarly, Cho's representation of herself as "a person of size" challenges not only Eastern stereotypes of diminutive and submissive Asian women, but simultaneously critiques western cultures' insistence on thinness and beauty in the entertainment industry.

THE PERFORMATIVE RHETORIC OF MARGINALITY AND GENDER

Cho's comedic choices offer implications for the rhetorical construction of gender, marginality, and identity. Through a close reading of Notorious C.H.O., it is obvious that Cho's identity is central to the content of her performance, and that she explicitly uses her subject position as Asian American to shape her comedy. In this sense, Cho's performance is not unique. Joanne Gilbert observes that "marginal comics often construct themselves as victims. In doing so, however, they may subvert their own status by embodying the potential power of powerlessness. Their social critique is potent and, because it is offered in a comedic context, safe from retribution as well" (1997, 317). In other words, marginalized subject positions related to race, ethnicity, class, gender, or sexuality can be powerful rhetorical tools within the context of comedy. Joseph Boskin and Joseph Dorinson claim that ethnic humor is intrinsically subversive as a means of surviving the difficult political economy that surrounds comedy. When examining the rhetoric of African American comics, they describe their routines as "inwardly masochistic, indeed tragic, externally aggressive, even acrimonious" (1987, 174). Cho's rhetoric functions in a similar capacity—trading on ethnicity, gender, and sexuality in order to level scathing social critiques. Elsewhere, Boskin argues that "American humor of the twentieth century is the humor of the urban, alienated minority groups whose experience has largely been that of outsiders" (1979, 49). As a rhetorical "outsider within" (Hill Collins 1990), Cho successfully performs marginality through self-deprecation.

Although Cho's ethnicity clearly contributes to her rhetoric, it is important to consider self-deprecation and perhaps autobiographical sketch comedy as its own rhetorical form. Cho's use of her own experiences with sexuality, gender, and mediated reality provide an autobiographical context to her humor. By referring to herself as a lifetime member of the "chubby gang" or saying she needs to check out the sadomasochist scene because women need to "throw themselves into a scene like that," Cho challenges our cultural standards for women.

In many ways, this self-deprecating humor is a safe choice—it does not abuse or offend the audience, but rather *appears* to reinforce the hegemonic values of American culture (Gilbert 1997, 327). In other words, as a polysemic rhetorical text, Cho's performance can resonate on different levels with audiences. If an audience member is offended, s/he can simply dismiss Cho's message because of her marginality. If an audience member identifies with the performance, s/he may identify through a number of subject positions: Asian, American, woman, queer. Scholars have noted that the backlash to the feminist movement has created a hostile environment for feminists who wish to speak in a public sphere (Faludi 1992). Since marginalized groups, particularly women, have often had limited access to the public sphere, more often than not they enter the sphere as *debatable* speakers (Calhoun 2000; Meyer 2003). As debatable speakers, women often use ambiguity within their arguments because ambiguity affords women a space from which they can address dominant epistemologies (Dow and Boor Tonn 1993). On one level, then, Cho's comedic ambiguity regarding her identity opens a discursive space from which she can challenge contemporary American culture. Thus, self-deprecation becomes a strategy of the marginalized rhetor, not simply an economic tool.

The larger implication here is one between the intent of the rhetor and the political economy of the entertainment industry. While the use of strategic ambiguity as a frame for analyzing Cho is beneficial, we must ultimately question whether the use of the term "strategy" is appropriate for marginal rhetoric. The problematic nature of using the term "strategic" as a polysemic rhetorical device is that the word itself has a long history of cultural assumptions in rhetorical discourse that associate it with masculinity. For example, the term "strategic" connotes cunning, trickery, and war—discourses that we culturally associate with masculinity, and specifically *white* masculinity. Ceccarelli defines strategic ambiguity as "a form of polysemy [that] is likely to be planned by the author and result in two or more otherwise conflicting groups of readers converging in praise of a text" (1998, 404). In Ceccarelli's assessment, the goal of strategic ambiguity is to "win over" as many audience members as possible by diluting the message enough that it appeals to the lowest common denominator. This certainly parallels arguments about the political economy of public discourse, particularly in mediated contexts; however, it is then problematic to explain ambiguity as a strategic device, particularly when discussing feminist messages. While on the surface women rhetors may seem to employ strategic devices, the use of the terminology "strategic" in relation to women allows the dominant ideology to dismiss the message on the basis that it is coercive and/or manipulative. As Helene Shugart notes, "submerged groups take a significant risk with regard to challenging their oppressors on the latter's terms because those terms have been used historically to oppress them; that history may carry more weight, ultimately, than innovative, irregular use of those terms" (1997, 211). Thus, Cho's use of her own identity as a strategy for opening discourse is conceptualized by many feminist critics as simply reifying the status quo and lending power to dominance.

In terms of strategic ambiguity, Cho's choices as a comedienne are constrained by her ethnicity and gender in such a way that even her comedic choices are regulated by the larger political economy of comedy: her message is a direct result of what she can *sell* rather than what she *actually wants to say*. By focusing almost exclusively on the political economy of a message, strategic ambiguity as a rhetorical category erases the potential for rhetorical intent, particularly from marginal rhetors. One way to perhaps resituate our discussions of agency with regard to rhetorical intent is to adopt the term *intentional ambiguity* instead of the popular term *strategic ambiguity* in rhetorical criticism (Meyer 2007). The overarching goal of intentional ambiguity would be not to *dilute* the message, but rather to purposefully *use* ambiguity in a way that *creates a space for discourse that did not exist before*. In creating that space, the ambiguity delivers an invitation to audience members to participate in the newly created discourse. In this sense, intentional ambiguity would allow the rhetor a degree of control over the message that is not necessarily present in the way scholars conceptualize strategic ambiguity at this point. Intentional ambiguity provides rhetors a way to begin a dialogue from marginalized social positions—and comedy seems to be a ripe context from which rhetorical alliances between groups can be built. Forming alliances between oneself and others with different cultural knowledge is one way to recognize that "challenging domination *without* means identifying the dominator *within*" (Johnson and Bhatt 2003, 241). In other words, through these rhetorical forms, individuals unfamiliar with specific racial, ethnic, gender, or sexual histories can participate in a nonthreatening environment—and hopefully learn something in the process.

Therefore, the greatest advantage intentional ambiguity brings to our rhetorical discourse is that over time skilled rhetors will be able to successfully challenge and invite audience members into their worldview in ways that allow audience members a sense of agency in the message itself. Cho even expresses this desire when she observes, "If there are straight white male millionaires who want to get into Asian-American women's queer culture, they are invited too" (Fowler 2000). Instead of alienating dominant groups as the problem, she rejects the idea that men (particularly straight white men) are to blame for the ills of society, "I don't criticize anybody for being straight. It's not even as if I think anything is wrong with it. . . . To just blame everything on straight [white] men is to simplify it" (Mervis 2003). Cho's work provides scholars with an example of rhetorical discourse that clearly marks the progressive intent of the rhetor while also adhering to traditional comedic rhetorical forms such as self-deprecation. Cho herself seems to recognize the intentionally ambiguous nature of her rhetoric, noting, "I write it all in advance. It may seem improvised, but it is very structured" (Savage 2002). As Joanne Gilbert observes, "Female comics negotiate myriad selves as they commodify both insights and insults, reminding audiences that to be human is to be involved in power relationships—a reality that shapes and defines who we are, what we believe and even why we laugh" (1997, 328). Cho's stand-up routine offers a clear example of polysemic rhetoric, one that enlightens audiences about Asian American identity, gender, and comedy.

REFERENCES

Berry, Chris. 2001. Asian Values, Family Values: Film, Video and Lesbian and Gay Identities. In *Gay and Lesbian Asia: Culture, Identity, Community,* edited by Gerard Sullivan and Peter A. Jackson. New York: Harrington Park.

Boskin, Joseph. 1979. *Humor and Social Change in Twentieth-Century America.* Boston: Trustees of the Public Library of the City of Boston.

Boskin, Joseph, and Joseph J. Dorinson. 1987. Ethnic Humor: Subversion and Survival. In *American Humor,* edited by Arthur P. Dudden. New York: Oxford University Press.

Brah, Avtar. 2000. Difference, Diversity and Differentiation. In *Theories of Race and Racism,* edited by Les Back and John Solomos. New York: Routledge.

Calhoun, Cheshire. 2000. *Feminism, the Family and the Politics of the Closet: Lesbian and Gay Displacement.* New York: Oxford University Press.

Ceccarelli, Leah. 1998. Polysemy: Multiple Meanings in Rhetorical Criticism. *Quarterly Journal of Speech* 84:395–415.

Chalk, Peter. 1998. Political Terrorism in South-East Asia. *Terrorism and Political Violence* 10:118–135.

Cho, Margaret. 2002. *Notorious C.H.O.* Directed by Lorene Machado. Cho Taussig Productions.

Collins, Patricia Hill. 1990. *Black Feminist Thought: Knowledge, Consciousness and the Politics of Empowerment.* Boston: Unwin Hyman.

Dow, Bonnie J., and Mari Boor Tonn. 1993. "Feminine Style" and Political Judgment in the Rhetoric of Ann Richards. *Quarterly Journal of Speech* 79:286–302.

Faludi, Susan. 1992. *Blacklash: The Undeclared War against American Women*. New York: Anchor.

Foss, Karen A., Sonja K. Foss, and Cindy L. Griffin. 1999. *Feminist Rhetorical Theories*. Thousand Oaks, CA: Sage.

Fowler, Geoffrey A. 2000. Making a Cho-full Noise. *U.S. News and World Report*, August 21, 66.

Frith, Katherine, Ping Shaw, and Hong Cheng. 2005. The Construction of Beauty: A Cross-Cultural Analysis of Women's Magazine Advertising. *Journal of Communication* 55:56–70.

Gandhi, Leela. 1998. *Postcolonial Theory: A Critical Introduction*. New York: Columbia University Press.

Gilbert, Joanne R. 1997. Performing Marginality: Comedy, Identity and Cultural Critique. *Text and Performance Quarterly* 17:317–330.

Herren, Greg. 2001. Fag Hag. *Lambda Book Report* 10:10–12.

hooks, bell. 1992. *Black Looks: Race and Representation*. Boston: South End.

———. 1996. *Bone Black: Memories of Girlhood*. New York: Henry Holt.

Hyun, Sook Kim. 2001. Korea's "Vietnam Question": War Atrocities, National Identity and Reconciliation in Asia. *Positions: East Asia Cultures Critique* 9:621–637.

Jhally, Sut, and Justin Lewis. 1992. *Enlightened Racism. "The Cosby Show," Audiences and the Myth of the American Dream*. Boulder: Westview.

Johnson, Julia R., and Archna J. Bhatt. 2003. Gendered and Racialized Identities and Alliances in the Classroom: Formations in/of Resistive Space. *Communication Education* 52:230–244.

Ling, L.H.M. 1999. Sex Machine: Hypermasculinity and Images of the Asian Woman in Modernity. *Positions: East Asia Cultures Critique* 7:277–307.

Lipsitz, George. 2000. The Possessive Investment in Whiteness: How White People Profit from Identity Politics. In *The Meaning of Difference: American Construction of Race, Sex and Gender, Social Class and Sexual Orientation*, 2nd ed., edited by Karen E. Rosenblum and Toni-Michelle C. Travis. Boston: McGraw-Hill.

Matsui, Yayori. 2001. Women's International War Crimes Tribunal on Japan's Military Sexual Slavery: Memory, Identity and Society. *East Asia: An International Quarterly* 19:119–135.

McKerrow, Raymie E. 1998a. Corporeality and Cultural Rhetoric: A Site for Rhetoric's Future. *Southern Communication Journal* 63:315–328.

———. 1989b. Critical Rhetoric: Theory and Praxis. *Communication Monographs* 56:91–101.

Mervis, Scott. 2003. Notorious Cho Spends a Weekend on the Waterfront. *Pittsburgh Post-Gazette*, January 24, W1.

Meyer, Michaela D. E. 2003. Looking Toward the InterSEXions: Examining Bisexual and Transgender Identity Formation from a Dialectical Theoretical Perspective. *Journal of Bisexuality* 3 (3/4): 151–170.

———. 2007. Women Speak(ing): Forty Years of Feminist Contributions to the Field of Rhetoric and an Agenda for Feminist Rhetorical Studies. *Communication Quarterly* 55:1–17.

Minh-ha, Trinh T. 1991. *When the Moon Waxes Red: Representation, Gender and Cultural Politics*. New York: Routledge.

Orbe, Mark P., and Mark C. Hopson. 2002. Looking at the Front Door: Exploring Images of the Black Male on MTV's *The Real World*. In *Readings in Intercultural Communication: Experiences and Contexts*, edited by Judith Martin, Tomas Nakayama, and Lisa Flores. Boston: McGraw-Hill.

Rockler, Naomi R. 2001. A Wall on the Lesbian Continuum: Polysemy and *Fried Green Tomatoes*. *Women's Studies in Communication* 24:90–106.

Savage, Dan. 2002. Margaret Cho: Gets a Dose of Savage Love. *Mother Jones* 27:80–82.

Shugart, Helene A. 1997. Counterhegemonic Acts: Appropriation as a Feminist Rhetorical Strategy. *Quarterly Journal of Speech* 83:210–229.

Terkildsen, Nayda, and David F. Damore. 1999. The Dynamics of Racialized Media Coverage in Congressional Elections. *Journal of Politics* 61:680–699.

Waldinger, Roger. 1999. When the Melting Pot Boils Over: The Irish, Jews, Blacks and Koreans of New York. In *Rethinking the Color Line: Readings in Race and Ethnicity*, edited by Charles A. Gallagher. Mountain View, CA: Mayfield.

14
LEARNING ASIAN AMERICAN AFFECT

K. Hyoejin Yoon

It is through the terrain of national culture that the individual subject is politically formed as the American citizen: a terrain introduced by the Statue of Liberty, discovered by the immigrant, dreamed in a common language, and defended in battle by the independent, self-made man. The heroic quest, the triumph over weakness, the promises of salvation, prosperity, and progress: this is the American feeling, the style of life, the ethos and spirit of being.

Lisa Lowe, *Immigrant Acts*

MARCH MADNESS

In March 2006, Kristi Yamaoka, a sophomore cheerleader for the Southern Illinois University basketball team, fell fifteen feet from the top of her squad's human pyramid and landed on her head. She suffered a concussion, fractured a neck vertebra, and bruised her lungs. The Southern Illinois University Salukis were less than four minutes away from their 59–46 victory over Bradley University (Ford 2006). But Yamaoka's fall suspended everything in a tense and freighted fermata: the fourteen thousand fans, her squad, the basketball players, the coaches all watched as the paramedics immobilized Yamaoka's head and neck in a brace and lifted her onto a stretcher. A roar rose up from the bleachers when Yamaoka waved to the crowd, assuring it that she was okay. The band began to play the fight song and the cheerleading squad commenced its routine as if to confirm the collective relief. Then, as Yamaoka was rolled across the floor, still strapped to the gurney, she began thrusting her arms in the air in automaton precision, joining her squad in the fight song. The television cameras captured this emotional drama as it unfolded: from the audience's stunned and anxious reaction to its triumphant cheers; the worried cheerleaders and coaches touched by the display of devotion, proud, some teary-eyed.[1]

1. The video footage captured by the local television news station is available online: see "Kristi Yamaoka Falls" 2006.

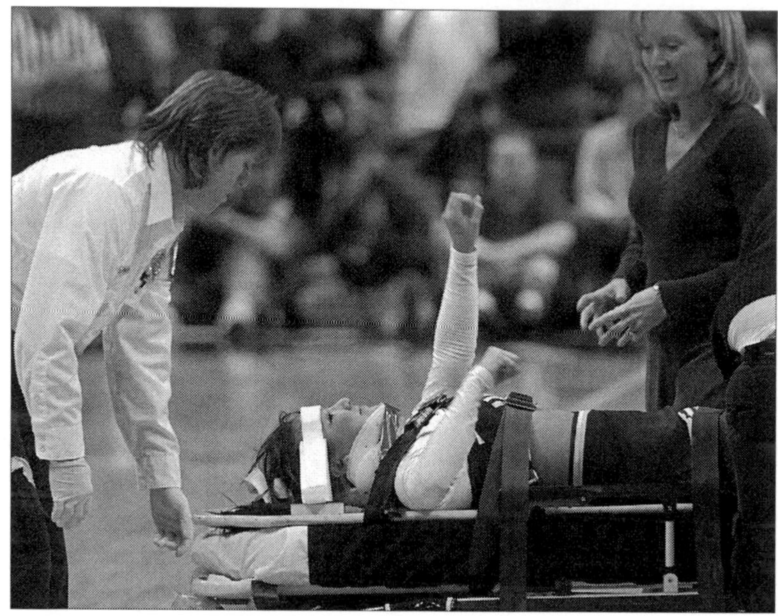

Kristi Yamaoka. AP photo 2006, used by permission

More remarkable than the accident itself is the discourse that was generated by and about it in the weeks that followed. Two days after the accident, Yamaoka appeared as a guest on the *Today Show* with Katie Couric. Dressed in her cheerleading uniform and a neck brace, Yamaoka said, "My biggest concern was that I didn't want my squad to be distracted, so that they could continue cheering on the team, and I didn't want my team to be distracted from winning the game." Her injuries and pain could not suppress her "super spirit," as the tagline for the show's segment affirms—the spirit that the cheerleader is trained to perform and instill in others. Yamaoka told Couric (a former cheerleader), "I'm still a cheerleader—on a stretcher or not. So, as soon as I heard that fight song, I knew my job and just started to do my thing" (Yamaoka 2006). Through this testimony, we celebrate Yamaoka's identification with her "job": to cheer and please regardless of her own condition.

This lesson in cheerful self-sacrifice was circulated by major news and sports media outlets, including Fox, ABC, NBC, CNN, ESPN, and *Sports Illustrated.* Even President George W. Bush and Diane Sawyer (also a former cheerleader) personally telephoned Yamaoka to relay their good wishes, reinforcing what Robert Paul Reyes (2006) exalted as

Yamaoka's "courage and willing[ness] to sacrifice [her]self for a noble cause." Touting her as a "genuine heroine," Reyes put Yamaoka on a par with the lone student facing the column of tanks in Tiananmen Square in the summer of 1989. This writer's historical and cultural conflation is an example of the often indiscriminate mapping of "official" (if exaggerated) knowledge and popular imagery onto diverse Asian American cultures and people.[2] Considering Yamaoka's accident as part of a larger lexicon of cultural representations of Asian American female bodies, we can analyze Yamaoka's cheer as a model of idealized gender performance, with her model minority body serving to discipline the citizen-subject through a national pedagogy of affect.

Yamaoka's cheer is a kind of "symbolic communication" that Tom Kerr (2003) describes: a "rhetoric of the body . . . that relies on signs and representations" (26). The communication of emotion-as-"spectacle," borrowing from S. Michael Halloran (2001), is a "rhetorical transaction" that intercedes between Yamaoka's actions and the desires and compulsions of public discourse (6)—this process of mediation and projection is evinced by the nationwide conversations about Yamaoka's accident and how she overcame (or disavowed) her injuries. Such narratives are cultural and discursive productions that function as "a form of education . . . [that] generates knowledge, shapes values, and constructs identity" (Kincheloe 2005, 58). In other words, the spectacle of cheer is a "dominant pedagogy," described by Lynn Worsham (1998), that deploys emotion to "bin[d] the individual . . . to the social order and its structures of meaning" (216). Indeed, Halloran asserts that the spectacle is a particular kind of "enactment of the social order" reflected, in this case, in Yamaoka's emotional display and gender performance, which bolster hegemonic views of citizenship and subjectivity, and provide a particular body to serve, in David Palumbo-Liu's term, as a "blueprint" that others are supposed to model themselves upon (Palumbo-Liu 1999, 415).

Indeed, *Sports Illustrated* columnist Phil Taylor (2006) gushed, "They're cute, but cheerleaders are also tough, gutsy." Extolling Yamaoka's "feisty" spirit and fearlessness, Taylor suggests that even the toughest sports players who played despite dismemberment and broken bones "owe Yamaoka a we-are-not-worthy salute. All of those supposed tough guys managed to perform in pain, but did any of them gut it out

2. Oliver Wang (2006) plays off the pun in his comment, titled "Inspir-Asians," to respond to Reyes's exaggeration: "This piece is so over-the-top that I can only assume it's satire, but I'm kind of scared that it's not."

while maintaining a perky smile, a la Kristi? Didn't think so." In this all-American sports story, Yamaoka picks herself up by her pom-poms—a model athlete able to overcome her injuries by sheer will and cheer.

This set of discourses crystallizes a lesson in the public sphere about "the Asian American woman" hailed as an embodiment of "the American feeling" that Lowe (1996) writes about in the epigraph. My contention is that Asian American female subjects are often hailed to perform a crucial form of affective cultural labor, with cheerleading being a standard of this type of work.[3] The cheer Yamaoka performs is an example of the cultural labor exacted of Asian American women to conceal the contradictions embedded in narratives of citizenship and nation—that they exclude even as they claim to include Others and, at the same time, discipline dominant subjects to maintain the polite and cheerful veneer that supports the American Dream ideology. In exchange for a conditional status, Asian American "model minorities" perform cheer, dedication, and team spirit to maintain the affective economy in which dominant notions of citizenship, belonging, and identity circulate.[4]

The lessons of "dominant pedagogies" or "emotionologies" are nowhere more evident than in the classroom and in the ways they set the stage for the pedagogical relationship between teachers and students.[5] Feminist and critical pedagogy theorists have illustrated how anxieties and assumptions about race, gender, sexuality, class, and able-bodiedness

3. Various ways of articulating this type of cultural labor have been explored in terms of "immaterial labor" (Negri 1999), "mental labor" (Ross 2000), "communicative labor" (Greene 2004), "free labor" (Terranova 2000), and "affective labor" (Hardt 1999), all of which share a common presupposition: that acts of discourse, including interpretation (Maxwell and Miller 2005) and even racial politics and signification (Hancock 2005), are forms of work. According to Hardt, affective labor is the work of producing and manipulating various affects or feelings, to generate "social networks, forms of community, biopower" (95-96). Also see Arlie Hochschild's (1983) definition of "emotion work" as the harnessing and performance of particular affects aimed at eliciting specific reactions in others, usually constituting some greater or lesser part of one's labor, and sold as exchange value for wage, for cultural capital, etc.

4. Bourdieu's (1986) concept of embodied cultural capital, elaborated by Reay (2004) and Allatt (1993), is useful here. Allatt defines emotional capital as "emotionally valued assets and skills, love and affection, expenditures of time, attention, care, and concern" (quoted in Reay 2004, 61). Jo (2003-2004) also discusses the displays of "national capital" reflected in "dominant linguistic, physical and cultural dispositions" (39), which act as a" badge of group membership" (38).

5. Carol Z. Stearns and Peter N. Stearns's(1988) term "emotionology" provides a useful way to think about social attitudes or "standards" regarding "basic emotions and their appropriate expression" as well as "the ways institutions reflect and encourage these attitudes in human conduct" (813).

infiltrate the classroom—these broader cultural discourses affecting instructional efficacy and laying bare the ideological nature of the classroom and the dynamic and fluid nature of power.[6] Scholarship on multicultural teaching, in particular, has provided insights into the intense affective responses that critical teaching by non-dominant teacher subjects can elicit from students. Indeed, students' suspicion, distrust, and hostility toward female teachers, teachers of color, lesbian and gay teachers have been well documented.[7]

These examples show the effects of student power as it is exercised through emotionologies, and that the power of the supposed "authority" in the classroom (i.e., teacher) can be undermined and resisted by the interaction with students—a perspective that highlights students' power, expectations, and performance and how they shape prevailing emotional standards and construct teacher and student identities in the classroom. I propose that by theorizing "model minority" emotionology, we can better understand and navigate the flows of power that slide in, around, and through expressions and expectations of emotional display, particularly in the space of a critical classroom. These dynamics become imbricated with the emotion work and labor of teaching, and create particular racialized and gendered expectations of Asian American female teachers. I explore these dynamics by analyzing the affective constitution of Asian American female subjectivity and, in the later part of this essay, by reflecting on classroom pedagogy and interaction with students.

MODELING "THE AMERICAN FEELING"

Inquiry into Asian American pedagogical affects must include an examination of the mutually informing elements that make up the model minority subject,[8] including racialized affect, gender performance,

6. For feminist analyses of power relations in the classroom, see Payne 1994; Friedman 1985; Ferganchick-Neufang 1996; and Chatterjee 2000. For analyses by critical pedagogues, see Giroux 1983 and McLaren 1991. Also see Luke and Gore 1992; Gore 1992; and Worsham 1998 for critiques of critical pedagogy's understanding of power.
7. See Kopelson 2003 for an especially succinct review of this scholarship.
8. The "model minority" cognomen was first bestowed upon Japanese Americans by a white male journalist in the 1960s (Petersen 1966). Its origins make this an ambivalent term, much criticized for its patronizing as well as mystifying effects (Suzuki 1977; Hu 1989; also see Lee 1999). Nevertheless, it has become a central topos in the rhetoric and constitution of Asian American subjects as well as Asian American criticism, imbricated in the discourse produced about and by Asian Americans in ongoing struggles to define their roles as citizens, workers, cultural producers (and objects) and to negotiate their various representations in the cultural imaginary.

discourses of citizenship, and the concept of modeling that is implicit in the constitution of a "model minority." In their analyses of the model minority figure, Asian Americanists Lisa Lowe (1996), David Palumbo-Liu (1999), and Anne Anlin Cheng (2000), in particular, have set the stage for more explicit discussions of racialized affect.[9] Asian Americans are called upon to internalize the myth of meritocracy and thereby perform "appropriate" or normative emotional dispositions: diligence, self-sacrifice, political passivity, and acquiescence. While these affects may not at first appear to line up with traits belonging to America's pioneering individual, according to Palumbo-Liu, they represent an ideal American disposition—"identificatory lures" that outsiders, in particular, may style themselves after in efforts to accrue symbolic capital. Model minorities are seen to adapt themselves quite readily to such ideals, praised for their easy assimilation to American ideologies of hard work and self-determination, ostensibly confirming their "recovery from racism." Ironically, rather than evince "Asian/American" assimilation, these largely passive traits serve best the interests of hegemony by ensuring their marginalization from full civic and political participation (Palumbo-Liu 1999, 399).[10]

As models, they are made exemplars of the national ideal, used to promote and discipline particular subjectivities. At the same time, their model status functions to keep Asian Americans in line, while pitting them against other, seemingly less compliant, minority groups who do not graciously leave inequality and oppression aside, and whose very grievances are seen as evidence of individual failings in comparison to Asian American "success" (Palumbo-Liu 1999, 400). As the spectacle of Yamaoka's body illustrates, Asian American bodies as texts represent "particular subject positions as (objectified) pedagogical models for future subjectivities" (465n24). In the days leading up to the nationwide immigration rallies in March 2006, with Mexican American and other immigrants asserting their rights, what better than a dose of model minority cheer in the media, extolling the virtues of self-sacrifice and forbearance?

Palumbo-Liu (1999) further theorizes that the modeling function also applies to dominant groups; with reference to the popularity of

9. See Sianne Ngai's (2002) work on racialized affect, in particular the concept of animation and its connotations of "spirit" and "excessive emotion."

10. Palumbo-Liu's use of the virgule in the term "Asian/American" is meant to symbolize an "undecidability" about the two terms and their relationship to each other; it "marks *both* the distinction installed between 'Asian' and 'American' *and* a dynamic, unsettled, and inclusive movement," a "sliding over" between the two terms (1).

Asian American literature among dominant audiences, Palumbo-Liu argues that it is due, at least in part, to the particular types of subjects it constructs for consumption. Asian American literature "solicits a particularly strong identification from a *general* audience predisposed to seeing . . . a displaced image of its own ideological presuppositions." In the case of Yamaoka, media discourses make her into an example to discipline "supposed tough guy" athletes, "reinforc[ing] dominant culture's notion of model minorities . . . and underwrit[ing] a larger ideology of individuation," as Palumbo-Liu would put it (409). The model thus reifies how "real" Americans are supposed to behave.

For Asian American women, the modeling function takes on a gendered aspect as well, delineating an ostensibly ideal femininity that western discourse interprets as "traditional": meek, docile, passive, manipulable (Prasso 2006, 162). This projection is used to discipline women in general who may be tempted to follow more independent and "feminist"-minded ways of the liberated West.[11] Critical race theorist Sumi K. Cho (2000) points out, "the gender stereotype of Asian Pacific women . . . assumes a 'model minority' function, used to 'discipline' White women, just as Asian Pacific Americans in general are frequently used in negative comparisons with their 'non-model' counterparts, African Americans" (535).

The goal of such disciplining is to produce idealized feminine subjects whose qualities best support and valorize white patriarchy. These

11. This comparison is vividly enacted in a scene from Jerry Lewis's 1958 film, *Geisha Boy* (much could be made of the title alone). A female officer, portrayed as the white American working girl, was spurned by her "Joe" for a Japanese woman. When she discovers that Jerry Lewis's character is also enamored with a Japanese woman, she exclaims bitterly, "What is it about these oriental girls?!" The story would persuade us to believe that those "oriental girls" would never speak so loudly or exclaim so publicly, and that the American woman's failure in keeping her man must be due to her independence and brashness. Orientalized femininity is promulgated in another film almost fifty years after Lewis's foray into the Far East. The recent film *Memoirs of a Geisha,* directed by Rob Marshall (2005) is an adaptation of the novel of the same title by American author Arthur Golden (1997). With pleasing performances by several beautiful and talented Asian female leads, the film is on a par with the much-written-about *Flower Drum Song* (1961), the Rogers and Hammerstein musical made into a film, in both the prevalence and display of Asian female bodies and the fetishization of beauty and femininity as contained, unattainable, yet ultimately exploitable: the western myth of Madonna and whore wrapped up in luxurious silk kimonos. Also see Marchetti's (1993) brief cinematic history of Hollywood's geisha fetish in her chapter "The Return of the Butterfly." Also see Prasso's (2006) chapter "Memoirs of a Real Geisha" for her attempt to debunk popular stereotypes, in particular through her interview with Mineko Iwasaki, the "real" geisha upon whose life Golden based his novel.

discourses play a key role in developing Asian American women's subjectivity and their internalized ideals, goals, and self-perceptions that intervene with projections of western, masculinist cultural fantasies (see Pyke and Johnson 2003; Ho 2003; and Chan 1987).

Model minority discourse, generally, and the conversations that specifically emerged from Yamaoka's accident can be considered "regimes of truth":[12] sets of practices and discourses that coalesce power and knowledge and which, according to Jennifer Gore (1993), rely on "technologies of the self which are actualized and resisted . . . through the body" (55). The modeling function, therefore, is not just an imposition of power, but rather a technology of self, a process of self-disciplining: the self-styling of behaviors by which "individuals constitut[e] themselves as moral subjects of their own actions."[13] As an essentially pedagogical discourse, the model minority myth is an ethical regime of truth according to which individuals hone their "gestures, postures, and attitudes" (53). For Asian Americans, this reinforces self-styling techniques that include the denial and displacement of their paradoxical position in relation to narratives of citizenship and belonging: both "forever foreign" and at the same time able to achieve an "honorary whiteness" (Tuan 2001).

Cheng (2000) finds Asian Americans' ambivalent relationship to dominant discourses expressed in a psycho-social dynamic of both "delight and repugnance" in the American racial imaginary, which she captures in her analysis of euphoria. The model minority represents "the figure who has not only assimilated but also euphorically sings the praises of the American way" (23). However, this is a conditional and contradictory expression, for the injunction to sing is undergirded by one's assumed outsiderness, which reveals that full assimilation is ultimately untenable, thus illuminating how Asian American subjectivity is constituted in a dialectic of melancholia and euphoria. This ostensibly private psychic coping is, for Cheng, part of a national affective economy that "conditions life for the disenfranchised, and indeed,

12. Gore (1993) modifies Foucault's "regimes of truth" by bringing together his discussions on power/knowledge, discipline, and "technologies of self" (Foucault 1977, 1980, 1983a, 1983b, 1988).

13. For Gore, critical and feminist pedagogies are themselves regimes of truth that prescribe certain ways of feeling and being that are deemed appropriate and necessary to achieving their pedagogical and ideological goals. Gore deconstructs these pedagogical discourses for what is said and how it is said, and illustrates the sometimes normative effects of ostensibly progressive intentions. Using Michel Feher's (1987) delineation of political and ethical regimes of truth, Gore opens up the possibility of analyzing cultural and pedagogical discourses in local instances.

constitutes their identity and shapes their subjectivity" (23–24). Asian Americans are caught up in a performance, a kind of mimicry of the American feeling that will always fall short. Theirs is the job of tending the "terrain of national culture," an affective terrain that they can never fully inhabit. Yet, this unveils a mythical ideal, a simulacrum, if you will, of individuality that is unattainable even for the dominant subject. This rift necessitates the installation of the minority subject in order for the dominant subjects to disavow their own alienation from authority. The model outlines the possibility of the ideal and establishes an incongruence against which the dominant subject can define itself, enacting the affirmation and the threat of sameness and/as difference that Homi Bhabha (1984) theorizes in the concept of mimicry and its potential to deconstruct dominant authority.

Leslie Bow (2001) argues that "[f]or women, citizenship is inseparable from the performance of femininity and, in turn, femininity mediates women's identification with the nation." In other words, citizenship is a racialized and gendered technology that predicates Asian American women's incorporation into the national body upon their sexual availability—the Asian American woman as a synecdoche of the feminized Orient seen in a passive and receptive relation to penetrating, masculine, western economic and military forces (42). Asian American women must perform a racialized and gendered display of national fidelity to make up for what is considered their predisposition to treachery and betrayal. This threat is branded into nationalist memory, according to Bow, in the figures of Yoko Ono and Tokyo Rose, who were constructed as traitors whose racialized, outlaw femininity "corrupt[ed] men's identification with other men, undermining allegiance to the group or the nation," be it the Allied Forces or the Fab Four (7).

According to Bow (2001), "the public display of the body [is] one of the few avenues through which women can attest to communal fealty" (42). Yamaoka's cheer from the stretcher is emblematic of such public display that signals loyalty, and indeed (over)compensates for her always already deficient service to lord and master (as connoted in the term "fealty").[14] Cheng (2000) also argues that Asian American women

14. The contradictory meaning(s) of such displays can be discerned in racialized and sexualized media representations of Asian American ice-skaters Michelle Kwan and Kristy Yamaguchi. Representations of Kwan and Yamaguchi in the highly nationalistic discourse of the Olympics is emblematic of Asian American women's ambivalent position, according to Mia Tuan (2001). During the 1998 Olympic Games, an MSNBC headline reported, "American beats Kwan," though both the gold winner,

are situated in an especially conflicted manner to narratives of citizenship, in which feminine beauty works in "service of creating an image of the ideal citizen, making femininity at once the very sign and excess of ideal national subject" (35). Therefore, performance of femininity and notions of beauty and the body further reinforce Asian American women's roles as ideal figures, their otherness both mitigated by and at the same time exceeding their model function, with cheer functioning as both an ideal and excess of American emotional standards.

"SOOOO CUTE . . . A BIT ODD": AN AMERICAN EMOTIONOLOGY

To more fully appreciate the significance of Yamaoka's cheer, we can draw from Christina Kotchemidova's (2005) succinct social history of cheer from the eighteenth to twentieth centuries, which lays out the conditions that undoubtedly inform our present-day understandings of something like Yamaoka's ostensibly unique and excessive expression. Of particular relevance is the role of cheer in shaping the emerging American middle class in the 1800s, with cheer taking on symbolic value "in relation to building a social identity and attaining status in capitalism." The emotionology of cheerfulness was seen as a particularly American "liveliness" or "excessive vivacity" and a concern with displaying happiness (not to mention virtue, courage, and self-reliance) that was in keeping with "the national paradigm of happiness and prosperity."[15] In late capitalism, Kotchemidova observes "a real pressure on the average American to construct himself/herself as cheerful in order to get a job." This has extended to the commercialization of emotion in one's work in the service economy, documented by Arlie Hochschild (1983) and others in the sociology of emotion, where the worker must manage his/her feelings such that cheer is "not only institution-dictated but also autonomously performed." By the late twentieth century, cheer had become ingrained in the dominant culture as a standard of one's social, cultural, and economic fitness, hearkening back to its associations in the

---

Tara Lipinski, and Kwan, who took the silver, were American. Such slips represent a broader tendency to associate Asian Americans as not American (40).

15. An emblem of individual success, cheer was also deployed as a tool of social cohesion (and exclusion) among the middle class to define itself and discipline various social constituents. Cheer was a way to discipline the rude and uncivil masses, as well as the snobbish upper class. In the nineteenth century, cheer came to seen as an emotion that could "serve both self and others" and informed "an ideology helping to construct women's domestic happiness," with middle-class women "fostering the culture of cheerfulness" in the United States well into the twentieth century, a phenomenon most notably critiqued by Betty Friedan (Kotchemidova 2005).

Victorian era, as "a sign of managing problems well and being in control of the situation, which creates an aura of success" (Kotchemidova 2005).

Rather than an "outlaw emotion,"[16] Yamaoka's model cheer reflects a deep internalization and a proliferation of the pedagogy of cheer that has been an integral part of the American affect: from her claim that she "knew her job" and happily "did her thing" to her physical assertions of her continuing fitness despite the injuries to the media's association of her with courage and virtue. Yet, Yamaoka's arguably "excessive vivacity" makes apparent Asian Americans' "manic relation to the American Dream," a relation that is expressed as "an involuntary delight that finds itself slightly unseemly" (Cheng 2000, 31). Yamaoka's performance of "insistent jubilance" (52) represents a paradox of Asian American belonging: as both the means for her to (re)claim her fitness and control over the situation and, at the same time, a disavowal of her alienation from full enfranchisement, which the unseemly excess of her cheer only further highlights (23). In such cases, manic or pathological euphoria is "a means of alleviating the pains of exclusion" rather than a celebration of inclusion (42).

Competing discourses of belonging and exclusion can be seen wrangling with each other in the *Today Show* interview as well, which attempts to frame the story as that of an "Injured Cheerleader [Who] Keeps Her Spirit" (Yamaoka 2006). Such titles obscure the racial subtext that is, to my mind, the heart of the story: the visual rhetoric of an Asian American female vested in the accoutrements of mainstream, all-American cheerleading creates a dissonance that has, at its core, a racial element.[17] My

16. See Allison Jaggar (1989) on "outlaw emotions" as those that would threaten the status quo.

17. It is worth noting that cheerleading is itself a contested social practice. An increasingly profitable commercial industry for outfits and paraphernalia, cheerleading elicits contradictory responses from the public. It is championed as the image of innocent (white) girlhood in pigtails and censured for being too sexual and suggestive; promoted as a legitimate athletic endeavor and derided as ditzy fluff (or, as is become increasingly the case, condemned as too dangerous). It is viewed by some as a key strategy for future success in the heterosexual, middle-class romance and, at the same time, as the province of domineering, hysterical mothers willing to kill for their daughters' ensured success and popularity (Humphrey 1998; Well 2006; Richmond 2005; and Suhr 2006). Also see Elaine Scarry's (1985) discussion of the military origins of cheerleading as part of morale-boosting and a justification of violence. See Schwalbe's (2006) discussion of sports in general as a project of nation-making, a point I extend here to include cheerleading, which I see playing a central role in the defining of nation and citizenry, despite its seemingly peripheral, supporting role.

point is that it is precisely her social position and history as an Asian American woman that set her up for her performance and created the exigency for the laudatory discourse. As one Asian American blogger remarked, "It must be that Asian in her who can't disappoint anyone. Well, Kristi, you continue to represent! I am proud of you even though I think you're a tool" (Daughter of YipYee 2006). Yet, the official narrative about a generic cheerleader disavows what makes the story noteworthy: that is was an "outsider" playing an "insider" role, almost passing in her remarkable, laudable performance.[18] The story constructs and solicits a patronizing and conflicted reaction expressed quite succinctly in Couric's concluding remark on the somewhat surreal and unexpected moment caught on film: "Soooo cute . . . a bit odd."[19]

Lowe (1996) argues that Asian Americans are seen as both objects of assimilation and "contradictory, confusing, unintelligible elements" that must be marginalized (4). Indeed, the official story cannot repress the anxiety that is provoked when outsiders come too close. In the *Today Show* interview, this anxiety is displaced onto Yamaoka's Asian surname, which Couric trips over twice during the show. Near the end of the interview, Couric asks Yamaoka if she pronounced it "correctly," Yamaoka signaling her ostensible satisfaction. Couric's belabored and excessive discomfort with the difference signified in Yamaoka's name highlights the confusing, unintelligible elements that threaten the integrity of this all-American story.[20]

18. In this context, the cheerleader, an already iconic sexualized stereotype, must fairly bedazzle the male gaze with its multilayered connotations when occupied by an Asian American body. My first Google search for "Asian cheerleader" resulted in a list littered with porn sites. The Asian American cheerleader figure generates a tension of exoticization and disavowal of otherness.

19. The public discourse about Katie Couric provides an interesting subtext of emotion, race, gender, and performance. Soon after the interview with Yamaoka, Couric took the much-celebrated position of anchor for *CBS Evening News*. Couric said, "I'm thrilled to become part of the rich tradition of CBS News." She replaced Bob Schieffer, who remarked, "I think we're going to love Katie, and I think Katie's going to love us" ("Katie Couric" 2006). In the context of Darrell Hamamoto's (1994) discussion of the "Connie Chung syndrome," Couric can be seen as a much-needed cheerful antidote to the last female anchor, Connie Chung, who was often criticized as too hard-driving, a veritable network Dragon Lady. (I would like to credit my colleague Rodney Mader for helping me make this connection.)

20. This reflects an overdetermined moment itself, which mimics an almost clichéd classroom interaction between teachers and students with "foreign" names. The discomfort of the teacher and the student's often uncomfortable, sometimes feigned, expression of satisfaction or resignation is a familiar script. (I would like to credit my colleague Rodney Mader with this insight.) The anxiety is expressed in the curious reading and speaking strategies I've observed from first-year stu-

The excess is not necessarily something that the interlocutor can control to his/her liking. As much as Yamaoka is an (albeit contradictory) emblem of citizenship, belonging, and the morale of "the team," she is also a floating signifier. As a case in point, John Lofton (2006), editor of the *American View*, a right-wing Christian Web site, revises the story of the exceptional, model cheerleader-citizen-worker to send a warning, if not outright threat, against itinerant sycophants lacking a proper (Christian) moral compass—a warning explicit in the title of his opinion piece, "A Cautionary Tale for Kristi Yamaoka and Jay Sekulow: Cheerleading Can Be Hazardous to Your Health." In finding enough commensurability between Yamaoka and Sekulow, the writer reinstantiates Yamaoka's relevance as a model, in this case, an explicitly negative one: her story becomes a parable of succumbing to worldly temptations.[21] Yamaoka becomes the siren that entrances and entices us from the "right" path, an alien force with its seductive power of (beguiling) cheer, threatening the "true" values touted by the Web site: "God, family, and republic." The article proclaims that the "American people" aren't fooled by such enthusiasm. The dominant pedagogy in the *American View* disciplines the citizen in opposition to the model minority cheerleader and her anti-Christian, anti-family, and ultimately unpatriotic adulation.

The various, contradictory messages for which the model minority cheerleader is hailed reveal the interstices along which alternative Asian American cultural formations might emerge, as argued by Lowe (1996) (also see Hesford and Kulbaga 2003). Yamaoka's cheer can be read as an exaggerated emotional display that has the potential to destabilize both dominant and model minority affects. However, with Bow, I question whether "the spectacle of the Asian body performing the public rituals of citizenship creates cultural dissonance in the form of disruptive mimicry or whether it merely works to normalizing effect" (2001, 43). Theorizing specific material situations can reveal the intricacies of resistance and the nuances of the challenges that are posed to our intended counterhegemonic strategies. Looking at something like Asian American pedagogy in the most literal sense brings us into the

---

dents to high-level university administrators of skipping over or overcomplicating "unpronounceable" names. Though not intended to be othering, such belabored discomfort projected onto someone's name can have the effect of highlighting his or her outsider status.

21. According to Lofton, Sekulow's weakness is evident in his uncritical support of Bush's decision to forward Harriet Meyer as a Supreme Court nominee—a candidate that Lofton did not see as fully advancing the Christian cause.

context of the classroom, where we can examine the local manifestations of racialized affective performance. As a primary site of cultural pedagogy, the classroom affords us an important opportunity to analyze the implications of an Asian American teacher performing the model minority for both potentially subversive and potentially hegemonic ends. I turn now to the classroom to reflect on how Asian American female teachers may be perceived by dominant students, and also how minority female teachers might negotiate relations of power and emotion in the classroom.

AFFECTIVE PEDAGOGY

In her compelling narrative about teaching a course on Asian women, Piya Chatterjee (2000) explores how "[p]edagogy becomes a medium through which . . . larger scripts are translated into the microcosm of classroom cultures" (90). As a South Asian woman, she experienced the gaze of her audience in a kind of "pedagogy of the spectacle" (89), which helped her to articulate the "vectors of unease" that students feel in their "perceptions, conflations and connections with gendered difference" (95). Her awareness that her "professorial authority . . . is often delegitimized by inscriptions of gendered otherness" contributed to her sense that "a more palpable and bodied" set of contradictions was involved in "teaching difference" (93). I contend that those palpable, bodied dynamics reflect the affective nature of how teacher authority and student power are negotiated and enacted. Such dynamics further complicate the emancipation narratives that critical pedagogy often constructs about the relationships between teachers and students.

The role of emotion has long been a concern for critical pedagogy, most often articulated as desire or in terms of repression and/or false consciousness, especially in theorizing the social construction of emotions and the attachments that the oppressed or students feel to the pleasures and rewards of subscribing to dominant ideologies. Critical teachers' obligations are to help students reinvest their desires in more liberatory ventures. This duty is often complicated by teachers' own emotional dispositions, which are both constructed and contradicted by professional and moral discourses, with critical pedagogy being key among those discourses, about what it means to teach and to be a teacher. Theorists in composition studies have taken up emotion in recent years to help explain the ties that teachers and professionals have felt to their work and to uncover the problematics of such ties from a materialist and social constructivist perspective (see Worsham 1998; Schell 1998a, 1998b; Micciche 2000, 2002; Jacobs and Micciche 2003). For Asian American women, the expectations of teachers' pedagogical labor and emotion work are intensified and complicated by gender and race, and the act of teaching comes with it particular burdens and contradictions: the expectation to function as a model minority and the injunction to perform euphoria and cheer in exchange for the privilege of belonging.

Affective stereotypes texture the ideological landscape that conditions the perceptions and the self-stylings of subjects, with women and people of color laboring against the most repressive (see hooks 1992, 1994; and Collins 1991). If the emotional norm in the classroom is represented by the figure of a middle-class white male, the emblem of reasonableness, emotional neutrality, and appropriate, middle-class politeness, what kind of emotion work is an African American woman, for example, expected to perform to overcome dominant perspectives that are primed to see her as an angry black woman? For Asian American women, the cheerful model is only one among several predominant stereotypes; others include the evil, scheming, and arguably masculinized Dragon Lady; the Martial Arts Mistress popularized by Wayne Wang's (2000) *Crouching Tiger, Hidden Dragon* and Quentin Tarantino's (2003, 2004) *Kill Bill* series; the prostitute with a "heart of gold" in *The World of Suzie Wong* (1960), or the less flattering "me-so-ho'ny" wartime prostitute from Stanley Kubrick's (1987) *Full Metal Jacket.*[22] The impassive and stoic Asian figure also comes to mind, as does Margaret Cho's rendition of the loud, shrill Asian mother;[23] and the not-so-cheery but nevertheless devoted Butterfly.[24] These iconic roles teach us about how the dominant culture is conditioned to view Asian American women, often reinforcing a fantastical image that mediates perceptions and relationships between Asian American women and dominant subjects.[25]

22. See Liu 2000 for filmic representations of the Dragon Lady. See Prasso 2006 on the relatively new filmic representations of the Martial Arts Mistress. See Feng 2000 for recent analysis of Nancy Kwan's depiction of Suzie Wong.

23. From Margaret Cho's (2000) HBO comedy special, *I'm the One That I Want.* Also see Lee's (2004) analysis of Cho's embodied performance.

24. See Marchetti 1993 on the persistence of the Butterfly figure in Hollywood depictions of interracial romance.

25. Interestingly, Asian American male bodies are more often seen playing the role of teachers in the dominant cultural imagination. While a full elaboration of this is not possible within the constraints of this chapter, it is worth noting the male-gendered Asian American teacher figure, embodied in the wise, old Shaolin monks

While Asian American women are not frequently seen in the positions of teachers per se,[26] we can analyze how their frequent representations as guides, even initiators, into the mysterious world of the Orient vis-à-vis their coy sexuality, patience, and submission, are projected into pedagogical relationships in the classroom.[27] In these particular roles, cheer is a general, preferred disposition that is expected from Asian American women: if they are not always euphoric or excessive, at the very least they are expected to be willing and pleasant. This expectation reveals the displaced identification and projection of dominant emotional standards and gender and race performances—the affective job that women of color are often expected to perform to maintain the ideological and emotionological order—reminders that, as Yamaoka succinctly asserted, we should know our job and just do our thing.

Maia Ettinger (1994) offers an apt metaphor for the female teacher of color's relationship to students, and by extension to dominant culture, in the "Pocahontas paradigm."[28] This allusion, while describing

---

in the *Kung Fu* television series of the 1970s (also see Hamamoto 1994), Mr. Miyagi in *The Karate Kid* (1984), or as recently as Ken Watanabe's role as philosopher-samurai in *The Last Samurai* (2003) with Tom Cruise. These images valorize and validate violent masculinity as a philosophically and morally grounded way of life. They also construct the role of teachers and the idea of pedagogy as mysterious, elliptical, promoting a sense of inner righteousness, courage, and resolve, by equivocal lessons in snatching the pebble from the master's hand, the "wax on and wax off" approach to fighting bullies, and the model samurai warrior who composes haikus, admires cherry blossoms, and honorably commits seppuku rather than be overtaken by western modernity. Worth further exploration is the effeminization of Asian masculinity and its role in constituting this teacher figure. See Eng 2001 for discussion of Asian masculinity.

26. There are complex cultural and ideological reasons for the relatively small number of Asian Americans in the teaching professions (see Gordon 2000; Kim 1993). See also Shu 2005 on the constructedness of "Asian values."

27. This role is not uncommon in television and film depictions wherein dominant subjects are introduced to or accompanied in their exploits into the East, the Asian woman functioning as a kind of passport and as a tour guide, translating the foreignness of Asian cultures for the western male gaze, often through sexualized initiations: see Prasso's (2006) analysis of travel narratives by early explorers like Marco Polo recounting harems of available women and the depiction of William Adams in the television miniseries *Shogun* (1980). Even in contemporary, minor Disneyesque movies like *Two Brothers* (2004), an intrepid gamesman is guided by an exotic village girl into the jungles of Thailand. Also see *Good Morning Vietnam* (1987) for a similar role played by Robin Williams's love interest. This guide/initiator role is depicted in its most complicated iteration in the character of Song, played by John Lone in Cronenberg's 1993 film adaptation of David Henry Hwang's *M. Butterfly*.

28. The story of Pocahontas, regardless of the historical reality of the fraught relationship between early explorers and Native Americans, continues to capture the popular imagination, evinced in Disney's animated *Pocahontas* (2000) and the recent

a specific relationship between early colonial and Native cultures, also provides a befitting metaphor for the raced and sexualized affective functions that many female teachers of color may be called upon to perform.[29] According to Ettinger, Pocahontas is portrayed as the idealized counterpart to the dominant subject, i.e., John Smith. To the intrepid pioneer, she represents "promise of aid and comfort from the Other." As a teacher/guide for dominant subjects, she provides a map through uncharted and unfamiliar territory. Her "spontaneous, unsolicited love" drives her to "protect" them (dominant subjects) (52). It is not her job to challenge, to contradict or problematize the roles, selves, or status of the dominant group in the New World. Instead, she is to rescue them from any guilt that they may feel in association with their place and their ways of being. Pocahontas smoothes over difference and articulates a "common ground" on which they can feel at home—their dominance reaffirmed (53). The Pocahontas narrative illustrates the ways that cultural discourses mediate and in some cases impede the work of teachers who are committed to critical pedagogy and who ask students to explore what is uncomfortable and foreign to them.

When "Pocahontas" fails to comfort or reaffirm their dominance, or does not properly perform her love and devotion to them, the resulting resistance, discomfort, and "radical disorientation" (Knoblauch 1991) can take on a whole other kind of emotional intensity. Students might expect or wish, in the case of Asian American women, for the Lotus Blossom/Geisha to tend to their interests and needs.[30] However, they may more likely perceive and resist the Dragon Lady, who compels them to the difficult work of critical thinking. Students' sense of effrontery and betrayal and their ways of coping with these feelings are further intensified by the cultural stereotype of Asians as inscrutable, villainous,

release of *The New World* (2005) with Colin Farrell and the much-exoticized new actress, then sixteen years old, Q'Orianka Kilcher.

29. Leslie Bow (2001) suggests in her reading of *Farewell to Manzanar* by Jeanne Wakatsuki Houston and James D. Houston (1973) that Asian American and native cultures have a complex relationship to each other. According to Bow, in the Houstons' narrative, playing the "native" (in this case the exotic Hawaiian native) is "a means of becoming American," one way for Asian American women to transform their foreignness through identifying with and adopting an exoticizing gaze themselves (51).

30. Sumi K. Cho (2000) points out that these expectations have material, social, and relational repercussions. Unsurprisingly, racist and sexist stereotypes about Asian women being submissive and "easy to have sex with" have come into play in a number of cases of sexual harassment of Asian American women (533).

and dissembling. The teacher's work and emotional labor are encumbered with the obligation to compensate for the dominant subject's preconceptions, and offer moral support and build team spirit and cohesion by displaying and modeling her own allegiance to the "team," the nation, often at her own cost. The current climate of consumer-driven education, where accountability in higher education is increasingly equated with customer satisfaction, has, to my mind, placed an even more intense emphasis on teacher affects and dispositions, particularly those that solicit positive feelings from students.[31] Such trends threaten to reduce the role of the teacher to that of a cheerleader—or worse, the willowy Asian hostess who quietly guides patrons to their tables at trendy Asian fusion restaurants.

MODEL TEACHER? MODEL PEDAGOGY?

Ideologies of race, gender, and sexuality, in particular, are embodied, countervailing forces to the ideas that are to be promoted in a critical classroom. A model minority female teacher, regardless of how self-empowered she may feel, may also face the nullifying effects of cultural discourses that sexualize and patronize women of color. In this context, how does a model minority female subject perform the emotion work of teaching? How is she perceived by dominant and minority students in her conflicting roles? How does she conform to and/or resist those expectations? And what are the costs of doing so? The following narrative describes one particular pedagogical encounter and tries to shed light on how culture invades the classroom and how subject formation and affective labor is an ongoing, interactive process that shapes teachers and students alike.

I taught a course called "Growing Up in America" when I was a graduate student in a public university in upstate New York. A white female student helped me glimpse how nationalistic and pedagogic discourses merge and act upon dominant as well as Asian American subjects. During a discussion of Jonathan Kozol's (1992) *Savage Inequalities*, Linda, a young woman of Jewish background who had grown up in Manhattan, announced that she finally understood what I was trying to get at with the notion of "privilege," which we had been discussing in

31. Studies of student evaluations of teachers have shown that many factors contribute to students' perceptions of teaching effectiveness, including students' dispositions and interests, teachers' perceived attractiveness and personableness, and expected grades (Felton, Mitchell, and Stinson 2004; Wright and Palmer 2006).

relation to Peggy McIntosh's (1989) article "Unpacking the Backpack" on white privilege. Linda said, with due humility, that she was privileged to have been able to attend schools in New York City that didn't have the "problems" that Kozol describes, coming to the reassuring conclusion that inequalities are local and isolated instances, for in her school, the school calendar was peppered with months and days that celebrated some minority group or another. At the end of her impassioned and sincerely intended monologue, she pronounced very graciously that her great fortune was only further verified by virtue of having someone like me as a teacher, the first Asian teacher she had ever had.[32]

Linda said it in a very flattering way: she felt truly lucky to be in a country where she had the "privilege" of learning from an Asian woman. She felt this spoke well of the opportunities this country affords to all people. In fact, I was proof to her that anyone *could* pull themselves up by their bootstraps and not be shackled by their race and gender. At the time, I was stunned by the flattery embedded in Linda's statements, and as a young teacher, I was grateful to know that I was appreciated. Yet, I also felt quite undermined by Linda's pedagogy of "the way things are." As critical pedagogy reminds us, students are not blank slates, and this was made clear to me by what I later came to understand were discourses that were being projected and read onto me. Extending Rey Chow's observation that students bring stereotyped "terms of references" to their reading of Asian American literature, Cheryl Johnson (1994, 1995) argues that this same process works in how students read the teacher's raced and gendered body as text (1995, 130–133). This was confirmed for me as I found that my body, my presence in the classroom, the histories and investments that brought me there, my identities and various performances (intentional and perceived) of femininity and model minority-ness represented knowledges, perspectives, and narratives that superseded the frightening picture of the world laid out in the texts of Kozol and McIntosh.

32. A Google search for "Asian teacher" resulted in a gendered and sexualized search list with many hits for porn sites, relatively few of them either from Asia or by and for Asian/Americans, even fewer related to education. Perhaps only slightly behind nurses and cheerleaders in the sexual imaginary, the female teacher is a highly sexualized and fetishized figure that riffs on power plays because of her institutional power and associations with authoritarianism that link her to images of ruthless schoolmarms, as much as she is linked to the soft, nurturing, usually white teacher—both images functioning to defuse and delegitimize her authority (Tischio 2004).

If we believe in the real power of students as agents rather than as victims of pedagogical situations, we must also contend with the active roles they play in constructing the discourse of the classroom and interpellating (one might say disciplining) each other and the teacher. Linda held up a mirror and reflected back an image of me that I had not wanted to see, the view from the eyes of the dominant. In that mirror I saw a figure barely legible underneath a palimpsest of terms of reference—a chimera of caricatures: a broad, sallow face; slanted eyes; bound feet; kimono; white-face; a triangle straw hat; an abacus in one hand, chopsticks in the other; bowing; scuttling; bowing; and a thought-bubble that read "Me so ho'ny." Even as I write this, the hyperbole seems a little distasteful, excessive; yet, dominant perceptions and Asian American subjectivity are often shaped by such fetishized bits and pieces of stereotypes and grand narratives, most of which are just beyond conscious grasp. Linda unknowingly interpellated me into the model minority subject position, which constrained what I was able or, in some light, "allowed" to do.

Linda's monologue produced a palpable logic that swept across the classroom: since I obviously benefited from the system, how could I criticize it? I should, instead, show my gratitude for that access, and be thrilled for being included. The discourse of the model minority, by virtue of "allowing" me to become a professor, afforded me a position from which to speak with authority about the world. However, that very authority, benevolently bestowed, compromised my right to criticize American culture and society. As an obvious "foreigner," my critiques came across as particularly anti-American, diminishing the authority of the structures and institutions that granted me my position in the first place, and made me look like an ungrateful guest, thumbing my nose at American hospitality. Amid all these contradictions, I felt as if the only "right" thing to do would've been to put my palms together and bow. After that class, I half expected to see bags of laundry slumped outside my office door, but found only a pile of papers. Soiled texts to clean. An attached note read: "I'm concerned with the ending of this paper. I don't think it flows." *Light on the starch, please.*

Linda's speech act was suffused with conditions. When people say things like, "Those Asians are so hardworking!" it is a compliment underscored with a warning—i.e., "Stay hardworking." What happens when the model minority falls, fails, not only refuses "to sing the praises of the American way," but in fact denounces it altogether? As we have seen, they can be made examples of, vilified in the public and political arenas, like Tokyo Rose and Yoko Ono, or hailed and reified as an emblem of American spirit itself like Yamaoka. In other instances, as my narrative suggests, model minority teachers are hailed in other ways, urged, sometimes benevolently, back to their "true" selves. In reflecting on my interaction with Linda, the classroom appears to me as a kind of dramatic production with the teacher in the spotlight, except I kept missing my cues. I was supposed to speak in favor of the system that had "allowed" me to "make it." In quiet embarrassment for me, Linda gently read my lines to me from offstage. Her iterations of immigrant discourse, "lucky to be in such a country" with "opportunities for all people," was for my benefit, a kind of ventriloquism, modeling for me what *should* be coming out of *my* mouth. Linda was pointing me not only toward the grateful, high-achieving model, but also the model feminine teacher who dresses "like a girl," dresses "like us," as was often noted in my teaching evaluations. She was guiding me away from the strident, critical, "thinks she knows everything" "witch," as I've been (in recent years) called on RateMyProfessor.com, and toward the kind of teacher who earns the RateMyProfessor's chili peppers, and feels duly flattered.[33] Linda was reminding me to fulfill my role, to give her what her fortunate education had bought her: someone to verify the luck and fortune of this great country and grant her the rights to the "privilege" she had just discovered. Helping me to, as Johnson (1995, 129) puts it, "disinfect" the dialogue of the classroom, to remove the "funkiness," or the dissonances of race and gender, and to recenter the happy monologue of the grateful immigrant.

As I'll illustrate in my final anecdote, the performative citation of the happy immigrant is reiterated everywhere: from immigrant shopkeepers to the images (and self-representations) of cheery and successful Asian American professionals. I was witness to one particularly ritualized public performance of Asian American gratitude at the national conference of the American Immigration Lawyers Association in 2005 in Salt Lake City, Utah. During this conference, the American Immigration Law Foundation held its seventeenth annual benefit, this year to honor Vietnamese American immigrants. From the favors of "hand-crafted"

33. Immortalized by the 1980s rock band Van Halen in their music video "Hot for Teacher" (1984), a sexy teacher performs a striptease for her students. Sites like RateMyProfessor.com reinforce the larger cultural notion that there are "hot" teachers who deserve to be noticed and marked with the racist and sexist symbol of the chili pepper—the online analogy of waving bills in a strip club or the stereotypical gauntlet of cat-calling construction workers showing their "appreciation."

bamboo chopsticks to the pressed chicken entrée, which the event organizer and many of my fellow diners insisted was quite "authentic," to the Vietnamese décor and music, the slightly dingy conference space of the Salt Palace Ballroom had all the ambience of a high school prom.

The spotlight, however, was on the honorees on the podium, all Vietnamese American immigrants, refugees, in fact, who had made something of themselves in America, among them a business owner, a computer executive, the actress Kieu Chinh from the film *The Joy Luck Club*, and writer Le Ly Hayslip. The foundation presented each honoree with an American Heritage Award plaque. In exchange, each offered an acceptance speech to the predominantly white, and largely female, audience of immigration lawyers from around the country. Each speech followed the same pleasing narrative pattern: suffering, journeying, and eventual success. Each speaker concluded his/her speech with affirmations of the American Dream and expressions of immense gratitude to the foundation and to the lawyers who filled the banquet hall for helping them and others like them to make it. The ceremony was topped off by announcing the winner of a best essay contest, an enthusiastic, white fifth-grader from Buffalo, New York, who won for his essay, "Why I am *Glad* America is a Nation of Immigrants" (emphasis added).

My telling of this story is not to diminish the narratives and the real struggles that the honorees experienced. Indeed, their lives are moving testimonies about survival, all of them having experienced extreme hardships and trauma that undeniably come from living through war: poverty, hunger, displacement, death, and separation from loved ones. It is remarkable what they have overcome. However, I could not get over the feeling that this event was not to celebrate them as much as it served a larger ideological function to reinforce the model minority stereotype. In typical model minority style, the speeches were all marked by the "bravery, perseverance, and strength which helped them succeed in the United States," as observed in the foundation's newsletter (American Immigration Law Foundation 2005).

Not unlike the classroom drama I described, the podium became the stage for a pedagogical act; the Vietnamese American immigrants, models that teach an object lesson about perseverance and whose narratives preserve the illusion of the American Dream. The interactive flows of emotion and expectation infuse the whole scene—a rhetorical setup that directs what the speakers could say to an audience eager to be touched by stories of suffering and who expect ultimately to be cheered on. Indeed, there would've been no "appropriate" occasion had someone been so ungracious as to mention America's complicity in the political and military circumstances that contributed to their suffering and their eventual flight to the United States. The solicitation of feelings and confessions of trauma (typical of Foucauldian discourse) and the pat cheerful conclusions of immigrant experience were meant to disavow the proverbial elephant in the room and to reassure and reward the white lawyers for the work they've done, as each speaker turned to acknowledge them. The largesse, the poignance, the hypersincerity of the honorees' speeches reflect an overcompensation—an excess that won't quite resolve the contradictions that rive this scene. The Vietnamese American immigrants euphorically sing the praises of the American way and make everything all right for the dominant subjects, the lawyers, who—moved, pleased, self-congratulatory—shuffle out of the ballroom, many leaving behind their chopsticks untouched.

CONCLUSION

In the context of a critical classroom, where issues of race, class, gender, sexuality are expected to be raised, educators have reported ambivalent, often discomforting results.[34] The anecdotes above are intended to flesh out the broader discourses that contribute to the potential problematics that may arise in the critical classroom. Critical pedagogy tries to address this potential problem of student resistance by hailing an affect-conscious critical teacher who, as a model and leader, would help dominant and subordinate subjects redirect their ideological and affective investments along more emancipatory lines. Often, the teachers of critical pedagogy are assumed, as part of the professional class, to be already in a position of power, who have managed successfully to disinvest their repressive affects in order to become well-meaning, conscious, liberated, and liberatory critical teachers.[35] The teacher as a dominant, enfranchised insider, marked as citizen-intellectual, is a key figure and, arguably, the central agent of the social transformation that is espoused in much of the critical pedagogy literature.[36] However, the construction

34. See Ellsworth 1989; Tassoni and Thelin 2000; Hurlbert and Blitz 1991. Also see Thelin 2005 for a rationalization for maintaining critical pedagogy's mission despite its problematics in the classroom.

35. See Yoon 2005 for elaboration of this particular thread in critical pedagogy literature.

36. For further critiques of these tendencies in critical pedagogy, see Lee 2000; Gore 1992; Orner 1992; and Ellsworth 1989.

of this would-be teacher is too often glossed over, leaving unaddressed the complications of this subject position, particularly when it is occupied by multiply constructed and contradictory subjects who do not fit the image of the dominant citizen assumed by critical pedagogy.

The model minority tells a story of conflicted liberation, citizenship, and democracy that at once contradicts and also conforms to the emancipation narrative of critical pedagogy. Like the model minority, the critical teacher is interpellated in the name of assimilating to a particular vision of the citizen, to shed "alien" status and become "naturalized," to metamorphose from the uncritical to the transformative intellectual, to gain entry into a community of mythical common good, be it of American citizenship or the rolls of critical pedagogues.[37] However, when the teacher who shows up in class is not the transformed and emancipated dominant subject, but the perpetually alien, fictionalized body of Pocahontas and Suzie Wong, the dynamics of the class and the ultimate goals that can be claimed of such a class are problematized.

In such potentially "hostile" environments, there is great pressure and desire for teachers to relieve the tension and fear which, according to bell hooks (1994), can lead to "professorial investment in bourgeois decorum as a means of maintaining . . . order" (188). hooks shines a light on what I see as the mutually constructive force of the emotions of teachers and students, which shapes the power dynamics in the class. It is not simply up to the teacher to decide rationally to dispose of or perform particular affects for herself or for her students. As hooks points out, the range of acceptable or necessary affective strategies are already to some extent overdetermined; for example, Linda's interpellation hailed me, against my own desires, to behave in a proper, model minority feminine way: not disillusioned, but cheerful; not critical, but loving. This model disposition would be the screen through which my performance would be interpreted, contributing to "misreadings" of any particular affect I may have intended to perform, either in resistance to or in compliance with dominant expectations. Furthermore, the expectation of a cheerful, nurturing, and compliant teacher serves as a benchmark against which any affective performance would be disciplined.

Therefore, it is important for teachers to critically examine their own affective constitution, not simply as individual weaknesses or insecurities, but as techniques that are informed by discourses of race, gender,

37. See feminist and Asian Americanist critiques of citizenship and democracy: Fraser 1994; Luke 1992; Lowe 1996; and Palumbo-Liu 1999.

and sexuality, in particular. In addition, such an inquiry into broader social and cultural discourses may prove useful in illuminating the roles we are called upon to play and the particular emotion work we are called upon to perform in order to maintain the affective interlaces of the ideological order. As I've suggested here, an alternative discourse of affect articulated from the conflicted position of "insider/outsider," like that of the ambivalent model minority female teacher, may promise to shed new light on the problematics of power and how and in what forms it is exercised in the classroom.

Nevertheless, it is always a difficult proposition to suggest ways out of such pedagogical quandaries. We must continue to ask questions: What does this mean for Asian American subjects and their potential (passive and active) resistance and collusion in relations of domination? How can a race-conscious emotionology potentially serve both liberatory and oppressive ends? What do we do with our increased emotional literacy? As critical teachers, how should we direct our and our students' emotional energies? How can we avoid the trap of trying to "manage" emotion even as we broaden our understanding of it? (see Boler 1999)

Most of all, asking and trying to answer these questions must be predicated on a critical and sustained skepticism of any perspective that claims to be beyond implication. Asian Americans may be called into the model minority subject position and may be rewarded with the feelings of uplift and belonging. In some instances, such lures may keep individuals complacent, despite the advances of the Asian American movement and Asian American studies. However, there are costs, and there is affective labor involved that is compensated only by the promise of inclusion, the illusion of being set apart from the least enfranchised of society, when, in fact, the model minority is kept out along with those he/she helps bar from entering. A more thorough history of political, economic, and social contexts may reveal Asian Americans' rejection and suspicion of prevailing sociopolitical structures, which have been understood conveniently as passivity by those in power. Yet, while such affective dispositions are stereotypes of the dominant culture, they have the power to shape future Asian American affects and continue to style passive or cheerful or forbearing Asian American subjects. Asian Americans may not build the master's house, yet if we also don't want to be his tools, as the blogger suggests of Yamaoka, we must be willing to examine our internalizations and the affective rewards we receive for playing our parts and reading the scripts. As much as we'd like to find potential resistance and parody, which has been a legitimate endeavor of much scholarship in Asian American studies, we must also be willing to investigate our complicities.

And lastly, we must be willing to acknowledge the contributions our students make to classroom affects and power relations; rather than patronize their disempowerment or bemoan their wrongheadedness, there may be insight and transformation to be found when we are willing to credit, and not just demonize, their affective investments as potentially useful texts that they have a hand in generating in the class.

REFERENCES

Allatt, P. 1993. Becoming Privileged: The Role of Family Processes. In *Youth and Inequality,* edited by I. Bates and G. Riseborough. Buckingham: Open University Press.

American Immigration Law Foundation. 2005. 17th Annual Benefit. *AILF Update: Newsletter of the American Immigration Law Foundation* 2 (3): 1.

Bhabha, Homi. 1984. Of Mimicry and Man: The Ambivalence of Colonial Discourse. *October* 28:125–133.

Boler, Megan. 1999. *Feeling Power: Emotions and Education.* New York: Routledge.

Bourdieu, Pierre. 1986. The Forms of Capital. In *Handbook of Theory and Research for the Sociology of Education,* edited by J. G. Richardson. New York: Greenwood.

Bow, Leslie. 2001. *Betrayal and Other Acts of Subversion: Feminism, Sexual Politics, and Asian American Women's Literature.* Princeton, NJ: Princeton University Press.

Chan, Connie S. 1987. Asian-American Women: Psychological Responses to Sexual Exploitation and Cultural Stereotypes. *Women and Therapy* 6 (4): 33–38.

Chatterjee, Piya. 2000. De/Colonizing the Exotic: Teaching "Asian Women" in a U.S. Classroom. *Frontiers: A Journal of Women's Studies* 21 (1/2): 87–110.

Cheng, Anne Anlin. 2000. *The Melancholy of Race: Psychoanalysis, Assimilation, and Hidden Grief.* Oxford: Oxford University Press.

Cho, Sumi K. 2000. Converging Stereotypes in Racialized Sexual Harassment: Where the Model Minority Meets Suzie Wong. In *Critical Race Theory: The Cutting Edge* 2nd ed., edited by Richard Delgado and Jean Stefancic. Philadelphia: Temple University Press.

Collins, Patricia Hill. 1991. *Black Feminist Thought: Knowledge, Consciousness, and the Politics of Empowerment.* New York: Routledge.

Daughter of YipYee. 2006. A Bit Too Much School Spirit? March 8. http://daughterofyipyee.blogspot.com (accessed July 21, 2006).

Dreyfus, H. L., and P. Rabinow, eds. 1983. *Michel Foucault: Beyond Structuralism and Hermeneutics.* 2nd ed. Chicago: University of Chicago Press.

Ellsworth, Elizabeth. 1989. Why Doesn't This Feel Empowering? Working through the Repressive Myths of Critical Pedagogy. *Harvard Educational Review* 39 (3): 297–324.

Eng, David L. 2001. *Racial Castration: Managing Masculinity in Asian America.* Durham, NC: Duke University Press.

Ettinger, Maia. 1994. The Pocahontas Paradigm; or, Will the Subaltern Please Shut Up? In *Tilting the Tower: Lesbians, Teaching, Queer Subject,* edited by Linda Garber. New York: Routledge.

Feher, Michel. 1987. On Bodies and Technologies. In *Discussions in Contemporary Culture,* edited by H. Foster. Seattle: Bay Press.

Felton, James, John Mitchell, and Michael Stinson. 2004. Web-based Student Evaluations of Professors: The Relations between Perceived Quality, Easiness and Sexiness. *Assessment and Evaluation in Higher Education* 29 (1): 91–108.

Feng, Peter X. 2000. Recuperating Suzie Wong: A Fan's Nancy Kwan-Dary. In Hamamoto and Liu 2000.

Ferganchick-Neufang, Julia. 1996. Women's Work and Critical Pedagogy. *Writing Instructor 16.1*: 21–33.

Ford, William. 2006. SUI Cheerleader Hospitalized After Fall: Sophomore Suffers Concussion, Chipped Vertebra. *Daily Egyptian*. March 5. http://newshound.de.siu.edu/sports/ sports05/stories (accessed July 17, 2007).

Foucault, Michel. 1977. *Discipline and Punish: The Birth of the Prison*. New York: Pantheon.

———. 1980. Truth and Power. In *Power/Knowledge: Selected Interviews and Other Writings 1972–1977*, edited by C. Gordon. New York: Pantheon.

———. 1983a. Afterword: The Subject and Power. In Dreyfus and Rabinow 1983.

———. 1983b. On the Genealogy of Ethics: An Overview of Work in Progress. In Dreyfus and Rabinow 1983.

———. 1988. The Political Technology of Individuals. In *Technologies of the Self: A Seminar with Michel Foucault*, edited by L. H. Marting, H. Gutman, and P. H. Hutton. Amherst: University of Massachusetts Press.

Fraser, Nancy. 1994. Rethinking the Public Sphere: A Contribution to the Critique of Actually Existing Democracy. In *Between Borders: Pedagogy and the Politics of Cultural Studies*, edited by Henry A. Giroux and Peter McLaren. New York: Routledge.

Friedman, Susan Stanford. 1985. Authority in the Feminist Classroom: A Contradiction in Terms. In *Gendered Subjects: The Dynamics of Feminist Teaching*, edited by Margo Culley and Catherine Portuges. New York: Routledge.

Giroux, Henry A. 1983. *Theory and Resistance in Education: A Pedagogy for the Opposition*. South Hadley, MA: Bergin and Garvey.

Gordon, June A. 2000. Asian American Resistance to Selecting Teaching as a Career: The Power of Community and Tradition. *Teachers College Record* 102 (1): 173–196.

Gore, Jennifer M. 1992. What We Can Do for You! What Can "We" Do for "You"? Struggling over Empowerment in Critical and Feminist Pedagogy. In Luke and Gore 1992. (Orig. pub. 1990.)

———. 1993. *The Struggle for Pedagogies: Critical and Feminist Discourses as Regimes of Truth*. New York: Routledge.

Greene, Ronald Walter. 2004. Rhetoric and Capitalism: Rhetorical Agency as Communicative Labor. *Philosophy and Rhetoric* 37 (3): 188–206.

Halloran, S. Michael. 2001. Text and Experience in a Historical Pageant: Toward a Rhetoric of Spectacle. *Rhetoric Society Quarterly* 31 (4): 5–17.

Hamamoto, Darrell Y. 1994. *Monitored Peril: Asian Americans and the Politics of TV Representation*. Minneapolis: University of Minnesota Press.

Hamamoto, Darrell Y., and Sandra Liu, eds. 2000. *Countervisions: Asian American Film Criticism*. Philadelphia: Temple University Press.

Hancock, Black Hawk. 2005. Steppin' out of Whiteness. *Ethnography* 6 (4): 427–461.

Hardt, Michael. 1999. Affective Labor. *boundary 2* 26 (2): 89–100.

Hesford, Wendy S., and Theresa A. Kulbaga. 2003. Labored Realisms: Geopolitical Rhetoric and Asian American and Asian (Im)migrant Women's (Auto)biography. *JAC* 23 (1): 77–107.

Ho, Pensri. 2003. Performing the "Oriental": Professionals and the Asian Model Minority Myth. *Journal of Asian American Studies* 6 (2): 149–175.

Hochschild, Arlie Russell. 1983. *The Managed Heart: The Commercialization of Human Feeling*. Berkeley: University of California Press.

hooks, bell. 1992. *Black Looks: Race and Representation*. Boston: South End.

———. 1994. *Teaching to Transgress: Education as the Practice of Freedom.* New York: Routledge.

Hu, Arthur. 1989. Asian Americans: Model Minority or Double Minority? *Amerasia Journal* 15 (1): 243–257.

Humphrey, P. A. 1998. Does Cheerleading Kill Brain Cells? *Fort Worth Weekly Wire,* July 6. http://weeklywire.com/ww/07-06-09/fw_cover.html (accessed July 21, 2006).

Hurlbert, C. Mark, and Michael Blitz, eds. 1991. *Composition and Resistance.* Portsmouth, NH: Boynton/Cook.

Jacobs, Dale, and Laura R. Micciche, eds. 2003. *A Way to Move: Rhetorics of Emotion and Composition Studies.* Portsmouth, NH: Boynton/Cook.

Jaggar, Allison. 1989. Love and Knowledge: Emotion in Feminist Epistemology. In *Women, Knowledge, and Reality: Explorations in Feminist Philosophy,* edited by Garry Pearsall and M. Pearsall. Boston: Unwin Hyman.

Jo, Ji-Yeon O. 2003–4. Educating "Good" Citizens: Imagining Citizens of the New Millennium. *High School Journal* 87.2: 34–43.

Johnson, Cheryl. 1994. Participatory Rhetoric and the Teacher as Racial/Gendered Subject. *College English* 56 (4): 409–419.

———. 1995. Disinfecting Dialogues. In *Pedagogy: The Question of Impersonation,* edited by Jane Gallop. Bloomington: Indiana University Press. 129–137

Katie Couric Moves to CBS News. 2006. *CBS News,* April 6. http://www.cbsnews.com/stories /2006/04/05/ national/main1472375.shtml (accessed July 20, 2006).

Kerr, Tom. 2003. The Feeling of What Happens in Departments of English. In Jacobs and Micciche 2003.

Kim, Eun-Young. 1993. Career Choice among Second-Generation Korean-Americans: Reflections of a Cultural Model of Success. *Anthropology and Education Quarterly* 24 (3): 224–248.

Kincheloe, Joe L. 2005. *Critical Pedagogy Primer.* New York: Peter Lang.

Knoblauch, C. H. 1991. Critical Teaching and Dominant Culture. In Hurlbert and Blitz 1991.

Kopelson, Karen. 2003. Rhetoric on the Edge of Cunning; or, The Performance of Neutrality (Re)Considered as a Composition Pedagogy for Student Resistance. *College Composition and Communication* 55:115–146.

Kotchemidova, Christina. 2005. From Good Cheer to "Drive-by Smiling": A Social History of Cheerfulness. *Journal of Social History* 39 (1). History Cooperative.

Kozol, Jonathan. 1992. *Savage Inequalities: Children in America's Schools.* New York: Harper Perennial.

Kristi Yamaoka Falls during Basketball Game. 2006. *Youtube.com,* March 8. http://www.youtube.com/watch?v=Ki4Lw7Iy09c (accessed April 21, 2008).

Lee, Amy M. 2000. *Composing Critical Pedagogies: Teaching Writing as Revision.* Urbana, IL: National Council of Teachers of English.

Lee, Rachel C. 2004. "Where's My Parade?" Margaret Cho and the Asian American Body in Space. *Drama Review* 48 (2): 108–132.

Lee, Robert G. 1999. *Orientals: Asian Americans in Popular Culture.* Philadelphia: Temple University Press.

Liu, Cynthia W. 2000. When Dragon Ladies Die, Do They Come Back as Butterflies? Re-imagining Anna May Wong. In Hamamoto and Liu 2000.

Lofton, John. 2006. A Cautionary Tale for Kristi Yamaoka and Jay Sekulow: Cheerleading Can Be Hazardous to Your Health. *American View,* January–April. http://www. theamericanview.com/index.php?id=176 (accessed July 17, 2006).

Lowe, Lisa. 1996. *Immigrant Acts: On Asian American Cultural Politics.* Durham, NC: Duke University Press.

Luke, Carmen. 1992. Feminist Politics in Radical Pedagogy. In Luke and Gore 1992.

Luke, Carmen, and Jennifer Gore, eds. 1992. *Feminisms and Critical Pedagogy.* New York: Routledge.

Marchetti, Gina. 1993. *Romance and the "Yellow Peril": Race, Sex, and Discursive Strategies in Hollywood Fiction.* Berkeley: California University Press.

Maxwell, Richard, and Toby Miller. 2005. The Cultural Labor Issue. *Social Semiotics* 15 (3): 261–266.

McIntosh, Peggy. 1989. White Privilege: Unpacking the Invisible Knapsack. *Peace and Freedom* (July–August): 10–12.

McLaren Peter. 1991. Schooling the Postmodern Body: Critical Pedagogy and the Politics of Enfleshment. In *Postmodernism, Feminism, and Cultural Politics,* edited by Henry A. Giroux. Albany: SUNY Press. (Orig. pub. 1988.)

Micciche, Laura R. 2000. When Class Equals Crass: A Working-Class Student's Ways with Anger. In Tassoni and Thelin 2000.

———. 2002. More Than a Feeling: Disappointment and WPA Work. *College English* 64 (4): 432–458.

Negri, Antonio. 1999. Value and Affect. Translated by Michael Hardt. *boundary 2* 26 (2): 77–88.

Ngai, Sianne. 2002. "A Foul Lump Started Making Promises in My Voice": Race, Affect, and the Animated Subject." *American Literature* 74 (3): 571–601.

Orner, Mimi. 1992. Interrupting the Calls for Student Voice in "Liberatory" Education: A Feminist Poststructuralist Perspective. In Luke and Gore 1992.

Palumbo-Liu, David. 1999. *Asian/American: Historical Crossings of a Racial Frontier.* Stanford, CA: Stanford University Press.

Payne, Michelle. 1994. Rend(er)ing Women's Authority in the Writing Classroom. In *Taking Stock: the Writing Process Movement in the '90s,* edited by Lad Tobin and Thomas Newkirk. Portsmouth, NH: Boynton/Cook.

Petersen, William. 1966. Success Story, Japanese American Style. *New York Times Magazine,* January 9.

Prasso, Sheridan. 2006. *The Asian Mystique: Dragon Ladies, Geisha Girls, and Our Fantasies of the Exotic Orient.* New York: Perseus.

Pyke, Karen D., and Denise L. Johnson. 2003. Asian American Women and Racialized Femininities: "Doing" Gender across Cultural Worlds. *Gender and Society* 17 (1): 33–53.

Reay, Diane. 2004. Gendering Bourdieu's Concepts of Capitals? Emotional Capital, Women, and Social Class. *Sociological Review* 51.3: 57–74.

Reyes, Robert Paul. 2006. Kristi Yamaoka, the Injured Cheerleader, an Inspiration to Us All. *Santa Barbara Chronicle,* May 22. http://www.santabarbarachronicle.com (accessed August 30, 2006).

Richmond, Vanessa. 2005. Today's "Cheer Athletes": What Does Mixing Gymnastic Discipline with Sex Appeal Teach Teen Girls? *Tyee,* November 17. <http://thetyee.ca/Lilfe/2005/11/17/Cheerathletes/ (accessed July 21, 2006).

Ross, Andrew. 2000. The Mental Labor Problem. *Social Text 63* 18 (2): 1–31.

Scarry, Elaine. 1985. *The Body in Pain: The Making and Unmaking of the World.* New York: Oxford University Press.

Schell, Eileen. 1998a. The Costs of Caring: "Feminism" and Contingent Women Workers in Composition Studies. In *Feminism and Composition Studies: In Other Words,* edited by Susan Jarratt and Lynn Worsham. New York: MLA.

———. 1998b. *Gypsy Academics and Mother-Teachers: Gender, Contingent Labor, and Writing Instruction.* Portsmouth, NH: Boynton/Cook.

Schwalbe, Michael. 2006. The Sport of Empire. *Common Dreams News Center,* January 6. http:/www.commondreams.org (accessed July 21, 2006).

Shu, Yuan. 2005. Globalization and "Asian Values": Teaching and Theorizing Asian American Literature. *College Literature* 32 (1): 86–102.

Stearns, Carol Z., and Peter N. Stearns, eds. 1988. *Emotion and Social Change: Toward a New Psychohistory*. New York: Homes.

Suhr, Jim. 2006. Conference Bans Some Cheerleader Routines. *ABC News,* March 7. http://abcnews.go.com/Sports (accessed July 17, 2006).

Suzuki, Bob H. 1977. Education and the Socialization of Asian Americans: A Revisionist Analysis of "Model Minority" Thesis. *Amerasia* 4 (2): 23–51.

Tassoni, John Paul, and William H. Thelin, eds. 2000. *Blundering for a Change: Errors and Expectations in Critical Pedagogy*. Portsmouth, NH: Boynton/Cook.

Taylor, Phil. 2006. Give Them a Cheer: They're Cute, but Cheerleaders Are Also Tough, Gutsy. *Sports Illustrated,* March 15. http://sportsillustrated.cnn.com/ /2006/writers/phil_taylor/ (accessed July 17, 2006).

Terranova, Tiziana. 2000. Free Labor: Producing Culture for the Digital Economy. *Social Text 63* 18 (2): 33–58.

Thelin, William H. 2005. Understanding Problems in Critical Classrooms. *College Composition and Communication* 57:114–141.

Tischio, Victoria. 2004. Images of Women Teachers in Film. Lecture. West Chester University, West Chester, PA, 23 March 2004.

Tuan, Mia. 2001. *Forever Foreigners or Honorary Whites? The Asian Ethnic Experience Today*. New Brunswick, NJ: Rutgers University Press.

Wang, Oliver. 2006 Inspir-Asians. *Poplicks.com,* March 6. http://poplicks.com/2006_03_01_poplicks_archive.html (accessed July 21, 2006).

Wells, Steven. 2006. Cheerleading: A Sport in Crisis. *Guardian Unlimited,* March 15. http://sport.guardian.co.uk/americansports/story/0,,1731412,00.html (accessed July 21, 2006).

Worsham, Lynn. 1998. Going Postal: Pedagogic Violence and the Schooling of Emotion. *JAC* 18 (2): 213–245.

Wright, R. E., and J. C. Palmer. 2006. Comparative Analysis of Different Models Explaining the Relationship between Instructor Ratings and Expected Student Grades. *Educational Research Quarterly* 30 (2): 3–18.

Yamaoka, Kristi. 2006. Injured Cheerleader Keeps Her Spirit. Interview by Katie Couric, *Today Show,* March 8. NBC. *MSNBC Video Archive.* http://www.msnbc.msn .com /id/ 11699607 (accessed July 7, 2006).

Yoon, K. Hyoejin. 2005. Affecting the Transformative Intellectual: Questioning Noble Sentiments in Critical Pedagogy and Composition. *JAC* 25 (4): 717–759.

AFTERWORD

Toward a Theory of Asian American Rhetoric: What Is to Be Done?

LuMing Mao and Morris Young

Now that we are about to bring an end to this project, we feel both satisfied and in want of more. Satisfied because we, together with our contributors in this volume, have now given much-needed voice to Asian Americans, to their efforts to use language and other discursive means to effect change and to write themselves into the larger American narrative. In want of more because we have been made acutely aware, by our work, of the urgent need to press on with this rhetorical project and to open up more space for Asian American rhetoric and for other minority discourses. In particular, our work has made it possible to raise some broader questions for doing Asian American rhetoric and for the representation of an Other in the twenty-first century.

We have, both in our introduction and throughout this volume, characterized Asian American rhetoric as a rhetoric of becoming. In so doing, we want to emphasize that Asian American rhetoric is always situated in particularizing situations and that it always generates new meanings and new significations at every discursive turn possible. Does it, then, mean that we can now look for any or every occasion, past and present, where Asian Americans have used language and other discursive means to have their stories told and heard, and say, "That's it! That's Asian American rhetoric!"? Are there any necessary constituents that make the discursive acts of Asian Americans sufficiently rhetorical? Further, if the emphasis now is on the specific occasions of use, can we claim a sense of history or tradition for Asian American rhetoric? Are there any family resemblances between what Asian Americans did in the past and what they are doing now? What are those rhetorical strategies that have been deployed by Asian Americans across time, space, and purpose? Are there any strategies or discursive forms that have newly emerged and that are in direct response to the rhetorical exigency of our own time? Is there, ultimately, any sense of contradiction between calling Asian American rhetoric a rhetoric of becoming and wanting to anoint it with a sense of history or continuity?

Central to what we are doing in this volume has to do with the idea of representation and the consequences, both material and symbolic, of actually doing it. We staked our position early in our introduction when we chose the singular "rhetoric" in representing Asian American rhetoric. That is, we want to use Asian American rhetoric as a singular signifier to represent a distinctive rhetorical identity *and* to "insist that others recognize that what they [we] have to say comes out of particular histories and cultures and that *everyone* speaks from positions within the global distribution of power" (Hall 1989, 133; emphasis in the original). At the same time, we are quite mindful that the tension will forever vex and challenge us between the desire to reclaim discursive agency and authority by using the singular signifier and the need to recognize and represent Asian American rhetoric realized in, or made possible by, its various and heterogeneous forms. For example, how can we most effectively negotiate such a tension without either erasing internal difficulties and conflicts or presuming unity and collective identity as the basis of our rhetorical action? More specifically, how best can we represent Asian American rhetoric when it is being performed in myriad temporal and spatial contexts? Further, what happens when such contexts begin to cross cultural and national boundaries, and when such contexts become fraught with expressions of hybridity and intertextuality? How Asian American or *un*–Asian American will our discursive practices then become? How do these kinds of engagements or entanglements in turn affect our identity as Asian American? And finally, in what ways will such experiences intrude upon and transform our discursive experiences in the Asian American community within the United States?

In the introduction to their edited collection, *The Nature and Context of Minority Discourse* (1991), Abdul R. JanMohamed and David Lloyd describe the project of minority discourse and the constituent practices that must be taken up in order to address what they identify as a history of marginalization of minority cultures at the hands of dominant western hegemony. We echo JanMohamed and Lloyd's call in the title of their introduction, "Toward a Theory of Minority Discourse: What Is to Be Done?" by offering our own challenge: "Toward a Theory of Asian American Rhetoric: What Is to Be Done?" We issue this call because as the work in this collection has argued, Asian American rhetoric has been underexamined and undertheorized.

While this project has begun the work of organizing our ideas about Asian American rhetoric and has offered illustrations of where Asian American rhetoric exists, what it does, how it does, and why it matters, much work remains to be done. Building on JanMohamed and Lloyd's articulation of a theory of minority discourse and maintaining our belief that Asian American rhetoric is a rhetoric of becoming, we suggest the following strategies for further engaging in this project.

RECOVERY AND DISCOVERY

As the essays in this collection have illustrated, there is much to recover and discover in Asian American rhetoric. To counter "institutional forgetting" and the damage done by the erasure, denial, or ignorance of a culture and its practices, archival and recuperative work has often been undertaken as an important act of countermemory. In recent years there has been much rhetorical activity by many scholars who have sought to broaden discussions about the history of rhetoric, rhetorical theory, and rhetorical action. Perhaps most substantial have been the critical studies and archival/editorial work by scholars such as Anne Ruggles Gere, Cheryl Glenn, Susan Jarratt, Nan Johnson, Andrea Lunsford, and Joy Ritchie and Kate Ronald, who have brought to light the important contributions of women to the rhetorical tradition. Work by Keith Gilyard, Shirley Wilson Logan, Elaine Richardson and Ronald Jackson, and Jacqueline Jones Royster has theorized an African American rhetorical tradition that stretches back two hundred years. And collections such as Ernest Stromberg's *American Indian Rhetorics of Survivance* (2006) or Elizabeth Hill Boone and Walter Mignolo's *Writing without Words* (1994) have helped to recover the rhetorical and literacy practices of indigenous peoples of the Americas. In the efforts of the scholars named above and many others, we have seen important archival work that broadens our understanding of the rhetorical tradition and points to the possibilities of much more work to be done in many other communities, including the Asian American community.

Perhaps a first step is to identify where those "archives" of Asian American rhetoric exist and to uncover or make visible those events and circumstances where Asian American rhetorical activity has occurred. The history of Asians in America began as far back as the eighteenth century, when Filipinos left Spanish ships and settled in Louisiana and moved forward through the nineteenth century as the United States extended its reach across the Pacific to Asia, and substantial numbers of Asians, especially the Chinese, started to flow into the United States. In the twentieth century immigrants from a variety of Asian countries entered the United States as laborers, while restrictions on immigration and conflicts with Japan, Korea, and Vietnam created tensions in Asian American communities. Since comprehensive immigration reform in 1965 and the rising tide of globalization, Asian American culture has moved beyond exotic and orientalist stereotypes and in fact has become ubiquitous, as Asian cuisines (beyond the typical Chinese) are popular, yoga studios exist in every neighborhood, and Kanji character tattoos are commonplace. But does this infusion of Asian/Asian American culture into the American imaginary mask the rhetorical work of Asian Americans? Worse still, does it create a false sense of "togetherness-in-harmony?"

In this collection, the work of recovery has begun through Haivan Hoang's examination of rhetorical memory performed by Asian American student activists, Terese Guinsatao Monberg's look at the Filipino American National Historical Society, Mira Chieko Shimabukuro's discussion of texts produced in Japanese American internment camps, and Subhasree Chakravarty's look at educational materials used in North American Hindu communities. But there is still much out there to recover and examine as rhetorical texts, from the oral histories and written accounts by the descendants of those first Filipino settlers in eighteenth-century Louisiana to the Angel Island poetry written by nineteenth-century Chinese immigrants to the many legal cases where Asians and Asian Americans have had to argue for their place in U.S. society. Other oral history archives, from the plantation era in Hawai'i or Chinatowns across the country, in public history sites/museums such as the Japanese American National Museum or the Wing Luke Asian Museum, all act as sites of countermemory that teem with rhetorical possibilities and that call for our immediate attention.

In this collection, the work of discovery has also begun through the examination of new media technology and rhetorical expressions by Jolivette Mecenas, or in looking at the rhetorical work of performers such as Margaret Cho or Jake Shimabukuro by Michaela Meyer and Jeffrey Carroll. These examinations identify new rhetorical work that is taking place and that is being transformed through technologies, genres, forms, or other means of production or forms of expression to create new knowledge and ideas. But there is still more out there to discover. For example, American vernacular work such as hip-hop has been taken up by a variety of communities within the United States to address specific cultural experiences. More recently, we have seen a rise in Asian American spoken-word and hip-hop artists, from Yellow Rage, whose members refute powerfully the gendered stereotypes of passive and exotic Asian women; to i was born with two tongues, a Chicago-based Pan-Asian Spoken Word Troupe that has developed a highly inventive, heterogeneous form to confront racism and to legitimate Asian American experiences; to Jin, a Chinese American performer who has integrated Cantonese language into his rhymes. In addition, we have witnessed the transnational movement of hip-hop into Asia, where performers from South Korea to the Philippines, Taiwan, Hong Kong, and China have transformed this distinctive American form into one marked by their local contexts and local exigencies. It is this kind of rhetorical work across and within the borders of the nation-state by Asians and Asian Americans that demands our immediate action.

REFRAMING AND REVISION

While an important part of our call for action has been to recognize and recover the cultural work in minority and emergent cultures, there is also a need to understand how dominant discourses have constructed minority cultures. For example, Mary Louise Pratt's (1991) theory of autoethnography describes how dominant and minority cultures engage each other and how such engagement can allow for minority cultures to reimagine and subvert the representations that have been constructed of them. Similarly, we take up this autoethnographic practice in considering how dominant disciplinary discourses (such as history, literary studies, and other fields of study) have often marginalized rhetoric as a discipline and mode of inquiry. What does it mean to reframe and revision a text within a rhetorical framework rather than within a literary or historical mode of inquiry? How does considering an expressive act in its rhetorical dimensions differ from considering it for its aesthetic or explicitly political value? Tomo Hattori and Stuart Ching begin the important work of finding connections between disciplinary discourses by examining shared metaphors between rhetoric and composition and Asian American studies.

An obvious but important body of work to examine with a rhetorical lens has to be Asian American texts that have been taken up in Asian American literary and cultural studies. In general, the field of Asian American literary and cultural studies acts as a critical model for Asian

American rhetorical studies as it has moved through the stages of recuperation, criticism, and development of new modes and forms. Asian American literary and cultural studies has exploded over the last twenty-five years, as a generation of students and faculty, trained and prepared to engage in research and teaching of Asian American texts, began to develop and contribute scholarship about literature produced by writers of Asian descent.[1] But in the early 1990s, there still existed only a handful of critical studies that examined Asian American literature as their central focus, including the still-important *Asian American Literature: An Introduction to the Writings and Their Social Contexts* (1982) by Elaine Kim, *And the View from the Shore: Literary Traditions of Hawai'i* (1991) by Stephen H. Sumida, and *Reading the Literatures of Asian America* (1992) edited by Shirley Geok-lin Lim and Amy Ling. *AIIIEEEEE!: An Anthology of Asian American Writers* (1974) and *The Big AIIIEEEEE!: An Anthology of Chinese American and Japanese American Writers* (1991), both edited by Jeffrey Chan, Frank Chin, Lawson Inada, and Shawn Wong, were still often turned to as important early critical expressions about the cultural work of Asian American writing. However, just as we saw an explosion in creative work by Asian American authors in the years following Maxine Hong Kingston and Amy Tan, we have also seen an explosion of critical production following the groundbreaking work of Kim, Sumida, Lim, Ling, and others. Since the early 1990s we have seen dozens of dissertations written that focus squarely on or at least in part on Asian American literature, and since 1993 in excess of thirty critical studies, edited collections of criticism, and resource guides have been published.

However, much of this critical work has not applied a rhetorical framework in the examination of texts despite the fact that themes of language, identity (or *ethos*), and political expression are often explicit or embedded in these works. As we discuss in our introduction, *AIIIEEEEE!* and *The Big AIIIEEEEE!* can be read as Asian American rhetorical texts for their arguments about language, sensibility, and the power of Asian American writing. Read as Asian American rhetoric, then, the introductions to *AIIIEEEEE!* and *The Big AIIIEEEEE!* work to reframe and revision the work collected in these anthologies as having specific rhetorical projects, whether in reading Carlos Bulosan's *America Is in the Heart* as a social protest novel or John Okada's *No-No Boy* as a narrative of ethical formation or Michi Weglyn's *Years of Infamy* as a documentary exposition

1. See Young 2006 for a discussion about the development of the field.

on the Japanese American internment. In this collection, Bo Wang and Mary Louise Buley-Meissner each reframe the texts of Asian American writers that have been read through a literary studies lens as rhetorical texts offering specific arguments that address identity formation and the Asian American experience.

But how might we reframe and revision other Asian American texts as rhetorical texts? For example, how might *The Forbidden Stitch: An Asian American Women's Anthology* (1989), edited by Shirley Geok-lin Lim, Mayumi Tsutakawa, and Margarita Donnelly, or *Making Waves: An Anthology of Writings by and about Asian American Women* (1989), compiled and edited by the collective Asian Women United of California, be reframed and revisioned as collections of Asian American rhetoric more broadly and Asian American women's rhetoric more specifically? In particular, these collections were conceived as a challenge to orientalist stereotypes of Asian and Asian American women as passive and submissive and to argue that Asian/Asian American women have always been engaged in the work of writing, which has been sometimes forbidden but is now "making waves." Especially in the context of Third Wave and women of color feminism, anthologies such as *The Forbidden Stitch* and *Making Waves* offer specific histories of women's rhetoric as informed by and expressed within and beyond the Asian American community. How do the writers included in these anthologies address the topoi of gender, race, cultural identity, and social justice, among many other topics, as shaped by their experiences as Asian American women? How do these collections imagine and deploy genre (poetry, fiction, prose) and form (textual and visual) for rhetorical purposes? And finally, how do Asian American women employ the available means to persuade, argue, and situate themselves in the history of the United States and in the history of rhetoric?

Similarly, we might want to reframe discussions about Asian American alternative discourses. For example, the *AIIIEEEEE!* editors argue for an authentic language that reflects an Asian American sensibility, while examinations of Hawai'i pidgin or similar Asian American discourses have often been characterized as authentic expressive forms or highly stylized literary languages. While this suggests on one hand the idea that there are language practices that "capture" and reflect the experiences of a community, on the other hand this reduces these practices as simply organic expressions of being. However, what does it mean to consider pidgin or other Asian American linguistic forms, as Robyn Tasaka does in her chapter on Asian American student writing, as an intentional rhetorical act that is aware of the subversive nature of form and its effect (either positive or negative) on an audience?

Finally, how might we reframe popular cultural texts that have often been consumed and interpreted for their social and political consequences but often undertheorized for the rhetorical work that they do? While American culture may have progressed to the point where we no longer see white actors performing "yellowface" in films (such as Mickey Rooney in *Breakfast at Tiffany's* or Katherine Hepburn in *Dragon Seed*), the construction and reception of Asian American actors and/or characters in media such as film and television can remain problematic. How do Asian Americans reframe and revision popular culture to intervene in the dominant discourses that have either romanticized or stigmatized Asian Americans, with serious material and symbolic consequences? In their chapters, Rory Ong and Vincent N. Pham and Kent Ono each offer alternative popular cultural texts that act in the interests of Asian Americans, to examine how these cultural texts are intentional rhetorical acts that challenge dominant representations.

DOING ASIAN AMERICAN RHETORIC

As the title of this collection suggests, representation is a central concern in the project of Asian American rhetoric. Not only does such a project involve the representation of Asian Americans in the Rhetorical Tradition and in doing rhetorical work, it is also about how Asian Americans and their cultures have been represented through the use of language and other symbolic means. We hope that this collection has begun the work of "translating" and "transforming" discourses about Asian Americans and their rhetorical work. As the essays in this collection illustrate, self-presentation or the development of ethos is an important rhetorical act for Asian Americans, who have often been subject to having ethos imposed upon them by others. However, what is also clear throughout this collection, and as Hyoejin Yoon has argued in her chapter, Asian American rhetoric is an embodied practice, where Asian Americans are in a constant process of challenging the ways they have been constructed through the available, and yet-to-be-available, means of persuasion.

We call on the field to do the work of Asian American rhetoric: to participate in the representation of self and community, to engage with representations, and to challenge those representations that produce damage for Asian Americans. Doing Asian American rhetoric is not simply the process of using language for persuasive purposes. Rather, it involves the work of recovering and discovering Asian American rhetoric, of reframing and revisioning those texts produced by Asian Americans through a rhetorical lens, and of representing this rhetorical work within and beyond our community and within and beyond our nation-state. What is to be done? Much, and these projects become more significant and consequential as the U.S. community continues to change and as globalization challenges us to engage with the Other across cultures and communities to seek better understanding and to cultivate a common sense of purpose that can bind us all.

It is perhaps befitting for us to end this volume here by returning to where it all began—that is, to the book cover image by Susan Sponsler, a Korean adoptee and an Asian American artist. The image, titled "All American Girl I," superimposes an American flag over the barely visible face of an Asian girl, whose Asian/alien identity is made visible only by her *slanted* eyes. We chose this image for the cover of this volume for two main reasons.

First, we wanted to use this image to remind us all that the world this image evokes or symbolizes may still be lurking in our lives in ways big and small. It is a world where Asian Americans can only make their presence felt, if at all, not by what they truly stand for, but by what they may look like; not by being in the foreground, but by being in the background or on the periphery; and not by an identity that is being realized through their own words and actions, but by an identity that can only be seen on the strength of and/or due to the visibility of an American flag.

Second, and more important, we wanted to juxtapose this image or the world it symbolizes with a very different world—one that this volume begins to portray and one that we very much want to use to supplant the other. We wanted to suggest that this is a world where Asians and Asian Americans have begun to re-present what has been represented of them and to reassert and perform an identity that has been denied them for so long. It is a world where the American flag is no longer their sole *cover* for identification or existence but becomes *one* of many discursive means to represent their identity. To the extent that we have done that in this volume, and to the extent that we have made Asians and Asian Americans visible with this rhetoric of becoming, we will have realized our objectives, and we will have moved a step closer toward developing a theory of Asian American rhetoric.

REFERENCES

Asian Women United of California. 1989. *Making Waves: An Anthology of Writings by and about Asian American Women.* Boston: Beacon.

Boone, Elizabeth Hill, and Walter Mignolo, eds. 1994. *Writing without Words: Alternative Literacies in Mesoamerica and the Andes.* Durham, NC: Duke University Press.

Chan, Jeffrey Paul, Frank Chin, Lawson Inada, and Shawn Wong, eds. 1991. *The Big AIIIEEEEE: An Anthology of Chinese American and Japanese American Writers.* New York: Meridian.

Chin, Frank, Jeffrey Paul Chan, Lawson Inada, and Shawn Wong, eds. 1991. *AIIIEEEEE: An Anthology of Asian American Writers.* New York: Mentor. (Orig. pub. 1974.)

Hall, Stuart. 1989. The Meaning of New Times. In *New Times,* edited by Stuart Hall and Martin Jacques. London: Lawrence and Wishart.

JanMohamed, Abdul R., and David Lloyd, eds. 1991. Introduction: Toward a Theory of Minority Discourse: What Is to Be Done? In *The Nature and Context of Minority Discourse,* edited by Abdul R. JanMohamed, and David Lloyd. New York: Oxford University Press.

Kim, Elaine. 1982. *Asian American Literature: An Introduction to the Writings and Their Social Context.* Philadelphia: Temple University Press.

Lim, Shirley Geok-lin, and Amy Ling, eds. 1992. *Reading the Literatures of Asian America.* Philadelphia: Temple University Press.

Lim, Shirley Geok-lin, Mayumi Tsutakawa, and Margarita Donnelly, eds. 1989. *The Forbidden Stitch: An Asian American Women's Anthology.* Corvallis, OR: Calyx.

Pratt, Mary Louise. 1991. Arts of the Contact Zone. *Profession* 91:33–40.

Stromberg, Ernest, ed. 2006. *American Indian Rhetorics of Survivance: Word Medicine, Word Magic.* Pittsburgh: University of Pittsburgh Press.

Sumida, Stephen H. 1991. *And the View from the Shore: Literary Traditions of Hawai'i.* Seattle: University of Washington Press.

Young, Morris. 2006. Growing Resources in Asian American Literary Studies. *College English* 69 (1): 74–83.

INDEX

CONTRIBUTORS

LuMing Mao is professor of English and director of graduate studies in the department of English at Miami University. He teaches and researches comparative rhetoric, borderland rhetorics, Chinese and European American rhetorical traditions, pragmatics, and critical discourse analysis. He is author of *Reading Chinese Fortune Cookie: The Making of Chinese American Rhetoric* and coeditor, with C. Jan Swearingen, of *Double Trouble: Seeing Chinese Rhetoric through Its Own Lens,* a special symposium to be published in the July 2009 issue of *College Composition and Communication.* He is also coediting, with Robert Hariman, Susan Jarratt, Andrea Lunsford, Thomas Miller, and Jacqueline Jones Royster, the forthcoming *Norton Anthology of Rhetoric and Writing.* His recent essay "Studying the Chinese Rhetorical Tradition in the Present: Re-presenting the Native's Point of View" won the 2007 Richard Ohmann Award for an outstanding essay published in *College English.*

Morris Young is associate professor of English and faculty affiliate in Asian American studies at the University of Wisconsin, Madison. Formerly, he taught at Miami University in Oxford, Ohio. His research and teaching focus on composition and rhetoric, literacy studies, and Asian American literature and culture. His essays and reviews have appeared in *College English, Journal of Basic Writing, Amerasia,* and *Composition Forum,* and he has contributed chapters to many edited collections, including *The Sage Handbook of Rhetoric, Women and Literacy: Local and Global Inquiries for a New Century* and *East Main Street: Asian American Popular Culture.* His book, *Minor Re/Visions: Asian American Literacy Narratives as a Rhetoric of Citizenship,* received the 2004 W. Ross Winterowd Award and the 2006 Outstanding Book Award from the Conference on College Composition and Communication.

Mary Louise Buley-Meissner, an associate professor of English, has been involved in cross-cultural education for over twenty years, including work with the Fulbright program in China and a wide range of campus-community projects with the University of Wisconsin, Milwaukee and the Hmong American community. With Vincent K. Her, she cofounded the Hmong American Studies Initiative (HASI) at UWM; their professional collaboration also includes recent articles in *Hmong Studies Journal, Future Hmong,* and *EYE.D* (an online magazine). Her teaching interests include Asian American literature (foundational, contemporary, and experimental). Her current research focuses on social change in China, as reflected in the life stories of her former students.

Jeffrey Carroll is a professor of English at the University of Hawai'i at Manoa. He is the author of four books: *The Active Reader* (coauthored with Anne Ruggles Gere), *Dialogs, Climbing to the Sun* (a novel) and, most recently, *When Your Way Gets Dark: A Rhetoric of the Blues.* He has published articles on the intersections of literary and composition theories, blues music, rhetorical theories of definition, and the uses of cultural artifacts in writing classrooms. He is currently working on an analysis of the fabled relationship of Eric Clapton and Jimi Hendrix.

Subhasree Chakravarty is currently a postdoctoral fellow in rhetorical studies at Stanford University. She received her PhD in rhetorical and cultural studies from the department of English at the Ohio State University.

STUART CHING is an associate professor of English at Loyola Marymount University. His professional interests include the politics of literacy and cross-cultural research in English education and composition and rhetoric studies. He has published articles in journals such as *Language Arts, Writing on the Edge,* and the *New Advocate* as well as chapters in volumes such as *Fractured Feminisms* and *The Subject Is Story*.

TOMO HATTORI is a visiting assistant professor of English at Loyola Marymount University. He has published articles on Asian American literature and critical theory in *differences: A Journal of Feminist Cultural Studies, Novel: A Forum on Fiction,* and in the anthology *Other Sisterhoods: Literary Theory and U.S. Women of Color.* He has taught at Vassar College, the University of Utah, and UCLA.

HAIVAN V. HOANG is assistant professor of English and director of the writing center at the University of Massachusetts, Amherst. With broad interests in college composition and literacy studies, her scholarship centers on issues of race, literacy, and ethnography. Presently, she is writing a book tentatively titled *Rewriting Injury: Asian American Rhetoric and Campus Racial Politics.* She has been co-chair of the NCTE Asian/Asian American Caucus since 2005, and has served on the CCCC Committee on Diversity. Most recently, she was invited to write a commentary for that committee's special blog on diversity.

BRUCE HORNER is Endowed Chair in Rhetoric and Composition and professor of English at the University of Louisville, where he teaches courses in composition, composition theory and pedagogy, and literacy studies. His books include *Terms of Work for Composition: A Materialist Critique,* winner of the 2001 W. Ross Winterowd Award for the Most Outstanding Book on Composition Theory, and, with Min-Zhan Lu, *Representing the "Other": Basic Writers and the Teaching of Basic Writing* and *Writing Conventions.* "English Only and U.S. College Composition," an essay he coauthored with John Trimbur, won the 2002 Richard Braddock Award.

MIN-ZHAN LU is University Scholar and professor of English at the University of Louisville, where she teaches courses in composition, composition pedagogy and theory, life writing, critical and cultural theory, and theories of languages and literacies. Her books include *Shanghai Quartet: The Crossings of Four Women of China* and *Comp Tales,* coedited with Richard Haswell, as well as *Representing the "Other": Basic Writers and the Teaching of Basic Writing* and *Writing Conventions,* both coauthored with Bruce Horner. Her "Essay on the Work of Composition" was winner of the 2005 Richard Braddock Award, and her essay "Redefining the Legacy of Mina Shaughnessy: A Critique of the Politics of Linguistic Innocence" was recipient of the 1992 Mina Shaughnessy Award.

JOLIVETTE MECENAS is completing a PhD in English at the University of Hawai'i at Mānoa. Her research and teaching interests include public sphere theory and diasporic publics, cross-cultural rhetorics, language diversity in U.S. composition, and the intersections of race, gender, and sexuality in public argumentation. She also enjoys reading and teaching satire from various cultures, and has a short humorous essay published in the anthology *Imagining Ourselves: A Global Generation of Women.* When not teaching or writing, she plugs into her various communities by volunteering with local arts organizations, such as the Kearny Street Workshop in San Francisco and GirlFest Hawai'i, an anti–violence against women arts nonprofit in Honolulu.

MICHAELA D. E. MEYER is assistant professor of communication at Christopher Newport University in Virginia. Her essay in this volume was presented at the 2007 National Communication Association Convention in Chicago. A prior version of this essay was coauthored with Dr. Mark Hopson of George Mason University and Yih-Shan Shih of Ohio University. That iteration of the work was presented at the 2004 Central States Communication Association annual convention in Cleveland, Ohio, as part of the Top Graduate Student Paper panel.

TERESE GUINSATAO MONBERG is assistant professor in the Residential College in the Arts & Humanities and a core faculty member in the graduate program in rhetoric & writing at Michigan State University. She has published essays in *Rhetorical Agendas: Political, Ethical, and Spiritual* (2006) and *Under Construction: Working at the Intersections of Composition Theory, Research, and Practice* (1998; with Ellen Cushman). She is currently working on a book-length manuscript on the emergence of the Filipino American National Historical Society (FANHS) as a public sphere against larger social and historical changes. A new project focuses on Filipina American writers and rhetors. Terese is a third-generation Filipina American mestiza/mixed-blood from the Midwest.

RORY ONG received his PhD in English (rhetoric) from Miami University of Ohio in 1992. He is currently an associate professor at Washington State University in the Department of Comparative Ethnic Studies and a member of the American studies graduate faculty. He has taught graduate and undergraduate course work in classical and Enlightenment rhetoric, race and ethnicity studies, Asian American literature, and Asian Americans and popular culture. His pedagogy and writing have endeavored to situate rhetorical analysis within the fields of ethnic studies and American studies in order to interrogate the relationship between historical processes of racialization and discourse production and practice, and their impact on trans/national identity and everyday life. His research interests cross rhetorical theory, race and ethnicity theory, and cultural and critical theory with globalization, transnationalism, and postcolonial and disapora theories.

KENT A. ONO is professor in the Asian American Studies Program and professor in the Institute of Communications Research at the University of Illinois, Urbana-Champaign. He conducts critical and theoretical analyses of print, film, and television, specifically focusing on representations of race, gender, sexuality, class, and nation. He has contributed articles to numerous journals and anthologies. In addition to coauthoring *Shifting Borders: Rhetoric, Immigration, and California's Proposition 187,* he has coedited *Enterprise Zones: Critical Positions on "Star Trek,"* and edited *Asian American Studies after Critical Mass* and *A Companion to Asian American Studies.* He is currently completing a book on films and videos about the incarceration of Japanese Americans during World War II, *Forgetting to Remember: Representations of Japanese American Incarceration on Film and Video.*

VINCENT N. PHAM is a PhD student in the department of speech communication at the University of Illinois, Urbana-Champaign. He conducts critical and theoretical analyses of media and organizations, specifically focusing on the intersections of race, rhetoric, and media organizations. Prior to graduate school, he was a member of the Asian American Artists Collective in Chicago and cowrote the closing show, *Mars, Marriage, and Mass DistrAction,* for the 2004 Chicago Asian American Showcase. He is currently coauthoring a book with Professor Kent Ono titled *Asian Americans and the Media.*

MIRA CHIEKO SHIMABUKURO is a poet and teacher as well as a PhD candidate in the composition and rhetoric program at University of Wisconsin, Madison. Her poetry has been published in such journals as *CALYX,* the *Seattle Review,* and *Raven Chronicles* as well as in the edited anthology *Intersecting Circles: Writings by Hapa Women.* As part of the CALYX Young Women's Editorial Collective, Mira also coedited the 1996 anthology *Present*

Tense: Writing and Art by Young Women. Currently she is teaching composition at Cal State Fullerton while working on two writing projects: a book-length poem titled *The Winter Drafts* and her comp/rhet dissertation, tentatively titled "Relocating Authority: Japanese Americans Writing out of Mass Incarceration."

ROBYN TASAKA is a doctoral student in rhetoric and writing at Michigan State University. Her current research interests include online representations of race, influences of social class and region on Asian American identity, and teaching in computer classrooms.

BO WANG is assistant professor of English at California State University, Fresno. She teaches and researches rhetorical theory and criticism, comparative/ethnic rhetoric, women's rhetoric, and writing in multicultural spaces. She has published in *Rhetoric Review* and in *Sizing up Rhetoric* (coedited by David Zarefsky and Elizabeth Benacka). Her two essays on the rhetoric of early twentieth-century Chinese women are forthcoming in *College Composition and Communication* and *College English*.

K. HYOEJIN YOON is associate professor of English at West Chester University of Pennsylvania. Her research and teaching interests include theory, critical pedagogy, affect, history of composition studies, Asian American feminist theory, and computers and writing. Some of her courses include first-year writing, computers and writing, literary theory, Asian American women, and women's studies, as well as graduate courses in theory, research, and pedagogy.